Persuasive Imagery

*A Consumer Response
Perspective*

ADVERTISING AND CONSUMER PSYCHOLOGY
A series sponsored by the Society for Consumer Psychology

AAKER/BIEL
(1993)
• Brand Equity & Advertising:
Advertising's Role in Building Strong Brands

CLARK/BROCK/STEWART
(1994)
• Attention, Attitude, and Affect
in Response to Advertising

ENGLIS
(1994)
• Global and Multi-National Advertising

KAHLE/CHIAGOURIS
(1997)
• Values, Lifestyles, and Psychographics

MITCHELL
(1993)
• Advertising Exposure, Memory,
and Choice

SCHUMANN/THORSON
(1999)
• Advertising and the World Wide Web

SCOTT/BATRA
(2003)
• Persuasive Imagery:
A Consumer Response Perspective

THORSON/MOORE
(1996)
• Integrated Communication:
Synergy of Persuasive Voices

WELLS
(1997)
• Measuring Advertising Effectiveness

Persuasive Imagery

A Consumer Response Perspective

Edited by

LINDA M. SCOTT
University of Illinois

RAJEEV BATRA
University of Michigan

LEA LAWRENCE ERLBAUM ASSOCIATES, PUBLISHERS
2003 Mahwah, New Jersey   London

Lawrence Erlbaum Associates, Inc., Publishers
10 Industrial Avenue
Mahwah, NJ 07430

Cover design by Kathryn Houghtaling Lacey

Library of Congress Cataloging-in-Publication Data

Persuasive imagery : a consumer response perspective / edited
by Linda M. Scott, Rajeev Batra.
  p.   cm. — (Advertising and consumer psychology)
Includes bibliographical references and index.
ISBN 0-8058-4202-0 (alk. paper)
  Imagery (Psychology) 2. Persuasion (Psychology) 3. Advertising—
Psychological aspects. I. Scott, Linda M. II. Batra, Rajeev. III. Series.
BF367 .P464 2002
153.8'52—dc21   2002021630

Books published by Lawrence Erlbaum Associates are printed on acid-free paper,
and their bindings are chosen for strength and durability.

Printed in the United States of America
10 9 8 7 6 5 4 3 2 1

Table of Contents

Acknowledgment

The editors of this book would like to thank the Yaffe Center for Persuasive Communication at the University of Michigan for its financial and logistical support in organizing the Conference on Visual Persuasion held in Ann Arbor, Michigan, in May 2000. The Yaffe Center, as part of its mission, supports multidisciplinary research into persuasive communication. It is a "joint venture" of the School of Art & Design, and the School of Business, at the University of Michigan. Details about its programs can be found at www.yaffecenter.org.

Introduction

Linda M. Scott
University of Illinois

Rajeev Batra
University of Michigan

From Bill Moyers to Marshall McLuhan to Raymond Williams, cultural observers of the late 20th century have charged the images of consumer culture with profound effects on life and consciousness. In tones of utter certainty, critics like these have warned of the deleterious effects persuasive commercial imagery has on the human mind, the collective behavior, and the society's values. Folk beliefs about the powers of advertisers to manipulate viewers from behind the screen of conscious rationality have shown remarkable steadfastness since they first appeared on the scene in the 1950s. Whether the discourse occurs in a tavern or a lecture hall, the power of persuasive imagery has become one of the given premises of post-industrial life.

It is remarkable in light of all that has been claimed to find how little, even at the dawn of the 21st century, is really known about the human response to visual images, including those of persuasive intent. Despite the almost religious tone of conviction that attends charges of "manipulation" or "subliminal seduction" through pictures, the hard evidence that such effects can be consistently produced is simply not there. Instead, researchers who have chosen actually to investigate how consumers respond to the visual aspects of advertising, packaging, and other corporate signs have discovered that the questions are much more complex, the phenomenon more subtle, the viewers sturdier, and the sense of certainty more elusive than most observers have taken the time to imagine.

We have been fortunate, as the editors of this volume, to have attracted the participation of the leading scholars in the area of consumer response to commercial imagery. Several who have investigated particular phenomena—such as the effects of visual tropes or the response to corporate logos—have offered here a reflective account of their journeys of inquiry so that a wide range of readers can share and appreciate the difficulty of studying an issue that has been so broadly oversimplified in cultural commentary. What emerges from the total of what is contained here is a sense of the enormous challenges presented by the complexity of the messages, the subtlety of the mental processing, and the contextual contingencies reflected in consumer response. The outcome of any attempt at visual persuasion seems extremely difficulty to analyze, let alone predict.

The book begins with an overview section intended to situate the reader in the discourse. The first essay, "Persuasion by Design: The State of Expertise on Visual Influence Tactics," describes the state of knowledge in both academic research and actual practice. Malkewitz, Wright, and Friestad conclude that academic research has only just begun to scratch the surface of the question of response, whereas the practical literature is so wholly focused on production issues that it offers nothing to suggest professionals have access to a secret trove of persuasive powers. The second entry, "A Review of the Visual Rhetoric Literature," by Keith Kenney and Linda Scott, is a bibliographic essay designed to provide both an overview and concrete sources for scholars to pursue. The remainder of the book is divided into four sections, "Image and Response," "Image and Word," "Image and Ad," and "Image and Object."

IMAGE AND RESPONSE

Although all of the essays are more concerned with consumer response than is traditional in academic writing on commercial imagery, we have chosen to highlight the issue of response in titling the first section. Through these four essays, the reader can discover the difficulty encountered even in investigating the basic influences, processes, and effects of "mere exposure" to imagery. In the first essay, Jane Raymond of the Centre for Experimental Consumer Psychology at the University of Wales begins by illuminating the impressive task that the brain performs in scanning the visual field, selecting items for attention, and organizing the stimuli presented in a comprehensible and usable way. The idea that visual information is merely absorbed unproblematically and without the engagement of the brain—a prejudice that so often underpins cultural criticism—falls immediately under her expert account of what actually occurs in everyday visual response. Raymond goes on to discuss the attentional limitations of this remarkable system, suggesting that the rapid-fire nature of today's advertisements may be delivering information in a way that results in message loss during "blinks" caused when the brain pauses to process. A practical inference from the evidence Raymond presents would be that advertisers who want to be sure their messages are fully comprehended should either present simple ads or repeat complex messages often enough that audiences have multiple opportunities to attend to the whole message. But these two seemingly obvious conclusions are the grist for the next few essays and the questions raised therein resurface often, sometimes in unexpected places, throughout the remainder of the book.

In the literature on response to advertising, for instance, there are two apparently contradictory phenomena that produce a conundrum for those who study the effects of frequent exposures. In the late 1960s, Robert Zajonc demonstrated experimentally that people form a positive feeling toward images to which they have been previously been exposed, a phenomenon that came to be known as the "mere exposure effect." Within a few years, however, this account was challenged by Daniel Berlyne, whose studies suggested that the positive effect produced by familiarity had limits: Eventually, the viewers would become bored and the affect toward the stimulus would turn negative. Furthermore, over the course of the next two decades, studies that investigated the response *specifically to advertisements* in repeated exposure consistently showed that although people initially responded positively to repeated ads, they eventually would respond negatively if the exposures were repeated often enough. This effect, referred to as the "inverted U curve," had the additional advantage of being intuitively consistent with our everyday experience of the cute ad that becomes annoying after excessive exposure. From a research point of view, however, the inverted U response to advertising was in contradiction to the mere exposure effect that had been demonstrated on other images. Thus, an explanation was required.

The essay by Winkielman, Schwarz, Reber, and Fazendeiro argues that the effect of an image on viewers is a function of the *experience of processing*, rather than any formal property of the ad itself. As part of this argument, they propose that the pleasant experience of "visual fluency" that can occur as an outcome of repeated exposures is what causes viewers to prefer familiar images, rather than the mere fact of repetition. Their position is that any condition that makes an image easy to process (e.g., darkness, lightness, clarity) will cause that image to be preferred, regardless of whether the picture has been previously viewed. Thus, repeated exposure would be expected to cause a positive feeling toward the image, but because of the increased visual fluency achieved through repeated exposure, not because of the exposure per se. Winkielman et al. qualify their argument in an important way, however, by proposing that the visual fluency effect will be mitigated by the *viewer's expectations* about the ease of processing. So in a case where ease of processing is expected, the positive affect of visual fluency would not occur. Instead, we might even expect boredom or irritation. One condition in which easy processing would be expected is, of course, repeated exposure.

In contrast, Nordhielm builds on the same literature to suggest that the *level of processing* produces different attitudes toward the ad in repeated exposures. She offers evidence to demonstrate that when an image is processed in a shallow manner, the positive affect from repeated exposures will increase. But, she says, if an image is processed in a deeper manner, *such that the viewer elaborates on its semantic meaning,* the U-shaped pattern of response will occur with repeated exposures. Nordhielm furthermore demonstrates her thesis by showing that a single feature of an ad may be repeated with positive effect, even though an entire ad that is repeated will eventually produce the legendary U-shaped curve. Indeed, she suggests that putting familiar elements in an ad can help to produce a positive feeling toward the ad as a whole. Such thinking is consistent with advertising practice, in which slogans, logos, and trade characters are repeated in each ad, but other elements are varied to avoid consumer boredom. However, Nordhielm's position goes against Raymond's suggestion somewhat because it suggests that the minimal processing that occurs when the brain's attentional limitations are surpassed will result in positive affect, rather than confusion. Returning to the Winkielman thesis, we might hypothesize that the acquisition of fluency over repeated exposures, but minimized processing, might have a positive effect on attitude, too. Yet both essays suggest that the very information absorption Raymond says gets lost without enough time to process is what causes viewers to eventually get bored and irritated.

The next essay adds a radically different element and produces a major departure in its conclusion. Building also on the literature on familiarity versus novelty effects, Pimentel and Heckler offer a fascinating narrative of their own research into consumer response to altered logos. The extant literature on exposure effects, they suggest, would predict that, over time, consumers would become bored with logos and characters like the Prudential Rock or Betty Crocker. Thus, it would seem that the impulse of graphic designers to update these logos periodically is well advised. The question is, how much change should be allowed? To answer this question, they bring in the discrepancy hypothesis. This hypothesis suggests that small changes to a familiar stimulus will be preferred over the original because of novelty effects, but that radical changes will be seen as negative. The support for this thesis includes Haber (1958) and Conners (1964), who used varying water temperatures and simple geometric images, respectively. After several studies that attempt to build on these works, however, Pimentel and Heckler found that they could not demonstrate the effect suggested by these earlier studies when using logos. Instead, they found that the most familiar version of the logo was always preferred, although small changes were acceptable. No boredom effects were found, even for logos that had gone unchanged for decades.

In querying the respondents, Pimentel and Heckler discovered that the cultural meaning associated with the logo was most often cited as the key factor affecting attitude. In subsequent studies, they found that meanings associated with the logo (in the case of Tony the Tiger, such meanings would include not only the cereal, but the "grrrrreat" slogan, childhood experiences, and so on) were by far more important to response than were visual properties. They concluded that the simple shapes from the Conners study, which were designed specifically to have no associated meaning, were not comparable to logos for the purpose of theorizing response. Further, Conners's own findings had not been as strong as Haber's; thus, the jump even from the psychophysical to the psychological had, perhaps, been one too far. Thus, Pimentel and Heckler propose that social judgment theory is a better explanation for the response to a logo than those offered to explain responses to stimuli that have less cultural content.

In social judgment theory, the familiar logo (or other complex image) would provide a frame of reference for incoming messages, thus serving as an anchor much as the adaptation level did in the Haber and Conners studies. However, in social judgment theory, the individual judges new messages as acceptable, as long as they are relatively close to/consistent with the original reference point. If found to be within the range of acceptance, the message will be subject to an assimilation effect that causes the new material to seem even more consistent with the original referent than it actually is. When a message diverges significantly from the frame, however, it is not only rejected, but viewed as being more divergent than it actually is.

If we return to the previous three essays with this new information about logos, the problem of commercial imagery can be seen to be gaining in complexity. (The essay by Goossens offers a model that addresses some of the complexity in these issues.) In contrast to Nordhielm, for instance, Pimentel and Heckler imply that familiar logos are preferred *because* of the complex meanings associated with them, which suggests that semantic processing *does not* necessarily lead to negative affect when repeated and elaborated over time. Furthermore, with reference to Winkielman et al., the fact that the logos in the study had been used for decades suggests that the visual fluency — probably gained through multiple exposures — did not ultimately result in boredom in spite of the high degree of familiarity that certainly would have produced an expectation of easy processing. Instead, the layering of multiple meanings on the image seems to have mitigated against the overfamiliarity that would have otherwise resulted — a phenomenon that would be hard to characterize simply as "easy processing." Rather, the phenomenon seems to be more consistent with Raymond's position in that the multiple exposures had allowed the viewer to add information to what was initially *just a simple image.* Such a complex act of cognition does not seem beyond the sophisticated mental-visual system Raymond describes, but it does bring the question of visual response to a new level of complexity. At this point, we are not just dealing with perception of a picture, but with specific, complex semantic meaning associated with that picture. Thus, we are necessarily stepping over the traditional Western conceptual boundary that separates "picture" from "word." The next section in the book, "Image and Word," explores that boundary in a response context.

IMAGE AND WORD

Although it is common to assert a clear separation between words and pictures, culture presents us with many instances in which the line is blurred. One of these is the corporate logo, which, although often pictorial in nature, communicates on an abstract level usually attributed to words. In fact, corporate logos have strong similarities to pictographic writing, in which pictorial signs are given, through social convention, meanings that cannot be inferred through mere object recognition.

A pictorial logo with complex semantic meanings that are broadly shared is an example of something widely recognized in non-Western, nonalphabetic writing systems, such as modern Chinese or ancient Egyptian. Variously called a *picto-graph, logograph, petroglyph,* or *hieroglyph,* such a sign refers *by convention* (i.e., through social agreement) to a concept that cannot be pictured through resemblance, but does not make use of an alphabetic code for translation of sounds (sometimes pictures of homonyms — a form called a *rebus* — are used, however). Logos, like pictographs, often retain traces of resemblance to some aspect of corporate symbology — the Disney ears, Merrill Lynch bull, and Prudential rock are examples — but the meanings have been expanded greatly beyond concrete picturing to include the metaphorical, fictive, and conceptual. In some instances, such as the Lucent circle, the relationship is purely conceptual. In others, a concrete picture is used, but the associations are conceptual rather than iconic — as in the Apple logo. When we engage thoughtfully with the number of images in consumer culture that have that kind of semantic power, we can begin to appreciate that the boundary between picture and word is not as clear-cut as we in the Western alphabetic cultures often presume. Obviously, among those viewers who come from nonalphabetic cultures, those boundaries would be different, perhaps even less clear.

The essay by Nader Tavassoli takes us into the issue of word–image relationships by investigating whether readers from logographic systems process writing differently from readers of alphabetic systems. In "Scripted Thought," he concludes that different forms of script can, independent of language, affect thought in important ways. Part of this is due to the different cognitive processes involved in reading logographic versus alphabetic scripts. For instance, English, as an alphabetic script, is based on the encoding of discrete sounds. Thus, writing in English is read using greater reliance on the short-term memory's phonological loop. On the other hand, Chinese relies more on visual short-term memory. Such differences, as Tavassoli shows, have an impact on what is noticed and remembered by respondents from these two cultures. As consumer culture globalizes, such findings will have important practical implications. However, from a purely theoretical point of view, the implications are potentially even greater. Tavassoli, like several others in this volume, reminds readers that pictures and language are merely two codes for representing thought. Thought itself is in neither form, but is currently believed to operate at a level "above" representation — perhaps more abstract, perhaps more basic, perhaps its own "meta" language. Thus, some of the popular theories that underpin criticism of commercial imagery — which consistently privilege the relationship of language to thought — would fall out of bed with contemporary knowledge. More to the point at hand, the example of logographic scripts — in which, as with corporate logos, the boundaries between word and image are often fluid from an alphabetic point of view — may cause us to rethink the degree of separation that actually exists between these two "codes."

Luna and Peracchio also aver that pictures and words are both codes the mind uses to represent a more abstract system of meaning. Thus, the language properties they describe in their article raise important questions about what properties the "visual code" might have and whether that varies by culture. For instance, although Western viewers see pictures as more "concrete" and less "conceptual" than words —Luna and Peracchio discuss evidence for this—we might ask whether Chinese viewers, who use a writing system having many pictographs that denote concepts, would respond in the same way. Such questions raise further issues about the overlap between these two "codes." Luna and Peracchio's work, like that of Tavassoli, is likely to become increasingly important with the globalization of consumer culture. As they point out, the population of the world is largely bilingual at this time because of the premium placed on learning English for a number of activities from business to research. Thus, their report of the use of pictures by bilinguals to aid in the processing of accompanying verbal messages in the second language can be seen as an important future issue.

The questions investigated by Mani and MacInnis contribute to our appreciation for the complexity of the interface between word and image. The objects of their inquiry are not the pictures that we see in ads or elsewhere in the environment, but the mental images we create in our minds. Their review concerns the findings of research into the effects of instructions to imagine, whether given in words or pictures—or both. The findings from this research stream are as yet inconclusive when applied to advertising, as the authors discuss. Some of the reasons thought to be contributing to the variability of results are, however, instructive for the broad topic of visual persuasion. Here we find that the quality of the instructions to imagine may themselves have an effect on the response. If, for instance, the instructions occur in an obviously persuasive context—especially an advertisement—the response demonstrated in nonpersuasive contexts often does not appear. (This effect is reminiscent of some studies cited in Winkielman et al. and Nordhielm where viewers who were informed of the "intent" of stimulus manipulation did not evidence the same response as those who were not told.) Sometimes the instructions to imagine seem "exaggerated" or "too obvious" to respondents, causing the effect to be insignificant. Finally, whether the instructions themselves are appealing in terms often important to ads (e.g., executional elements, product benefits, medium) also has an effect.

If we take into account all the issues raised thus far—the probability of boredom or irritation caused by a repeated message, the importance of cultural associations to the evaluation of a logo, the overlap between word and image observable when complex meanings are introduced, the invocation of skepticism when presented with an ad rather than a nonpersuasive message—we are stepping closer to a social, textual model of visual persuasion rather than a sensory or perceptual one. Yet many of these ideas are perfectly consistent with our shared experience of advertising *as consumers*. Most of us, after all, enjoy a clever ad at first, but soon tire of it as we are "bombarded" by its repetition. Most of us have experienced the nostalgia of familiarity for an old logo. Most of us throw up our defenses a little bit (sometimes a lot) when we see an advertisement. It's a commonplace that some ads are better than others; because of the "executional elements" (music, story, character), we actually *like* some of them. We also "know," however, from our own experience that our personal reactions to an ad are not the same as everyone else's. Our children like ads we find annoying, for instance. Beer ads sometimes insult feminists; condom ads outrage conservatives. And so on.

At this point in our analysis, we are in fact emerging into one of the oldest fields of human inquiry, rhetoric. A study of persuasion based on understanding the audience and its cultural context, adapting form to overcome boredom and skepticism, and dressing up an argument in an appealing way, dates at least to Aristotle. Many are surprised to learn that rhetoric comprised the backbone of higher education in the West through the Middle Ages and into the modern period. Indeed, in the early American university system, degrees in rhetoric were among the first, the most primary, the most popular, and the most respected. In the age of science, however, rhetoric fell into disrepute. That situation changed radically in the mid-20th century as the result of the influence of Kenneth Burke. This literary critic and philosopher broadened the scope of rhetoric to include not only political oratory (as was its traditional focus) but commercial applications and other more commonplace instances. He applied the principles of rhetoric to many examples, but, more importantly, paved the way for those who followed to apply rhetorical thinking to a broad range of forms, including images and even culture itself. The anthropology of Clifford Geertz, which so profoundly affected that field in the last quarter of the 20th century, was solidly and admittedly based on Burke. So, too, was the work of Michael Baxandall, who had a major impact on art history by applying rhetoric to architecture and painting. Others have now applied rhetoric to forms from music to dress to film. The writers whose essays form the next section draw from rhetoric to study advertisements. Like the authors in the other sections, however, they share a strong interest in investigating actual consumer response. Thus, their approaches differ slightly from those traditionally found in more humanistic fields—they are concerned with using concepts borne of rhetoric to explicate consumer response, often adopting scientific methods to do so.

IMAGE AND THE AD

As if the mental processes underpinning visual response were not complex enough, this section adds to our appreciation for the exquisite variations among advertising texts—and the resultant variability in response, not only to different ads, but among different viewers of the same ad. The first essay explicates the research of Edward McQuarrie and David Mick, who made a major contribution to the study of consumer response by focusing on the effects of complex rhetorical forms that are represented in commercial images, particularly the visual trope. In this essay, McQuarrie and Mick delineate between two orientations to research questions in the area: one focused on "the human system that processes the visual elements" and one concentrating on "the visual elements within the ad system." Their own objective is to bring text-oriented disciplines, such as rhetoric and semiotics, to the investigation of human response in such a way that the two approaches can be better integrated. They aver that text-centered approaches offer not only "guidance in differentiating text properties" but also the potential to link the different text properties with response outcomes. As we have seen from the previous sections, the stimuli used to investigate response to persuasive visuals tend to be quite simple. Indeed, when Pimentel and Heckler used logos to test response—visuals that are formally fairly simple, but culturally complex—they concluded that the difference between these stimuli and the sensory stimuli or simple geometrics used in the foundational literature had not only produced a contraindicated response, but had also raised questions about the advisability of generalizing from the results of studies using simple stimuli to predict the effects of more meaningful pictures. Thus, the direction of the McQuarrie and Mick argument seems to extend the path of the previous sections in the focal shift toward understanding and categorizing actual ads, rather than attempting to "build up" from simpler stimuli.

The Mick and McQuarrie research stream is a rich one, with many provocative issues that could be pursued in future research. However, two particular findings seem to warrant highlighting here because of their relationship to other essays contained in this book. First, the general finding of the McQuarrie and Mick work so far has been that ads with tropes are more memorable and pleasant for consumers, apparently because of the cognitive challenge involved in resolving the initial incongruity typical of tropes. This finding tends to contradict Winkielman et al., who say that the simpler a visual is to process, the better people will like it. On the other hand, the Mick/McQuarrie postulates about the response to schemes versus tropes appear to fit well with Nordhielm's findings on superficial versus depthful processing. Finally, the finding that viewers from other cultures were not able to resolve the incongruity of a trope—and thus did not "get it" or respond positively—raises questions that tend to magnify the overall issue of cultural difference in orientation to visuals, as mentioned by Tavassoli and by Luna and Peracchio. Thus, although Mick and McQuarrie travel far afield from psychology to bring literary tools to the question of visual persuasion, their findings do, in fact, seem to interface nicely with the state of the investigation.

The next chapter, by Michael Mulvey and Carmen Medina, investigates a phenomenon that presents a challenge to conventional wisdom in both literary studies and psychology. So far, the studies that have investigated the impact of spokespersons in advertisements have focused on flat constructs such as attractiveness, credibility, or likeability. Such studies presume that consumers will respond positively to those who are good-looking, believable, and amiable. Yet, clearly, there are far more subtle differences among the people who appear in ads. And a large number of ads contain characters who are not beautiful (Alice Cooper for Marriott), not credible (Joe Isuzu), and not likeable (Mr. Whipple). Further, the measurement of abstract qualities ignores the narrative context in which characters often appear. The commercial stories can themselves present the characters in either a positive or negative way, thus potentially affecting the viewer's evaluation. Mulvey and Medina, using ideas borrowed from both Aristotle and Burke, have devised a study in which the ability of viewers to identify and interpret the signs (visual and verbal) that communicate character is demonstrated. They then go further to show that viewers use these cues as the basis for forming identifications with a character—or choosing to reject the character as being dissimilar either to themselves or their values. The inclusion of visual cues (everything from gesture to clothing) in the basis for identification is, as the authors point out, completely consistent with classical rhetoric as defined by Aristotle. Yet literary critics often attempt to argue that rhetoric is not applicable to visuals, asserting that only words can constitute an argument (see the review by Kenney and Scott in this section).

Persuasion through sexual imagery also would not be included in rhetoric according to literary traditionalists—yet it is widely believed in American culture that goods can be sold with naughty pictures. The next article, "Promises, Promises" by Lambiase and Reichert, explores the viability of erotic rhetoric. It is worth highlighting that these authors have reviewed the extant empirical research on the impact of sexual appeals in advertisements—only to report that no evidence currently exists to suggest that such appeals are, in fact, broadly effective. In addition, they raise a question that dovetails well with the findings by Mulvey and Medina. As the study on character showed, some viewers will identify with a character in an ad, whereas others will reject the same character because they either don't see themselves as similar to him or her or don't share the same orientation to the product/service. Much of the (at this point speculative) literature claiming profound effectiveness for sex appeals presumes a heterosexual, male identity for the implied viewer. Yet, as these authors point out, ads are often viewed by women as well as men, and by homosexuals as well as heterosexuals. This variability in sex and sexual preference would surely lead to differences in response to sexual imagery—thus calling into question the broad-based claims often made for the power of sexual pictures based on a male heterosexual orientation. The variability in response also, however, has important implications for the broader investigation of visual response. To the degree that response among consumers is systematically variable—that is, by age or gender or other identifying segmentation scheme—then studies of visual response will have to address the social influences on response. Clearly, if different viewers have varying responses to the same image exposed under the same conditions, then explanations will have to reach beyond formal features and the conditions of exposure.

The next two essays explore the phenomenon of visual metaphor. The first, by Amy Wiggin and Christine Miller, discusses the interaction between verbal and visual content in producing an overriding metaphorical argument, particularly within the narrative context of television. The second, by Barbara Phillips, focuses on categorizing different types of visual figures and posing related research questions. In both cases, the topic itself calls traditional literary criticism into doubt. It is common among more conservative critics to argue against the existence of visual metaphor on the basis that a distinction between tenor and vehicle cannot be made in the same way that it can be in a verbal metaphor (see the review by Kenney and Scott for more on this issue). The highly figurative visuals so prevalent in advertising should cast doubt on this antiquated notion, but they should also cause psychological theorists to adjust their own reference points. Much of the theorizing and testing in the psychology of response is based on the assumption that pictures are merely referents, via resemblance, to objects in the real world. But the average consumer, who is called on many times a day to make sense of a range of highly fanciful visual metaphors and trade characters, is clearly doing something that goes well beyond identifying object analogs.

IMAGE AND OBJECT

The multiple ways that an advertisement may represent objects—particularly products—points to a key difference between commercial imagery and other kinds of picturing. Ads are placed with intentions toward purchase, which itself will involve either a concrete object in the form of a product or a concrete experience in the delivery of a service. Thus, the text of an ad reaches outward into the world of actual experience toward the concrete objects we see, use, and know in practical reality. The purpose of this last section is to try to carry the inquiry of visual response over the bridge toward object interaction.

The first essay, by Garber and Hyatt, begins with an exhaustive and fascinating analysis of the literature on color response. The authors then go on to demonstrate, using a new methodology, the complexity of the consumer interface with package colors, as it has unfolded in their own research. What emerges is an important path into the thicket of yet a third "system"—both the human system and the ad system, as identified by Mick and McQuarrie, must eventually come into contact with what Jean Baudrillard has called "the system of objects." The object world, as Garber and Hyatt make so clear, is far from a purely sensory or strictly utilitarian experience. Even such a basic component as color is shown to have differing effects depending on the product category, the brand, various features and ingredients (flavor, for instance), the environment in which the package appears, the cultural associations with a particular color, and so on. This very smart article shows in a complete and articulate way that the system of objects must be conceptualized as thoroughly and subtly as the "ad system," if the "human system" is to be successfully explained.

The chapter that follows on graphic design describes a methodology created by Howard Moskowitz and Richard Bernstein. This article describes an application of conjoint methodology to designing "optimal" product design by quantifying and evaluating the many components of a package design decision.

Jonathan Schroeder also looks at imagery in cyberspace, but does so with a long historical view, providing in the process a fascinating study in the iconography of service provision. In "Building Brands: Architectural Expression in the Electronic Age," he documents and explains the meaningful history of classical architecture and the way it has been adapted over hundreds of years to communicate desirable properties in banking, such as stability, prestige, and so on. He then goes on to show how today's financial institutions still include this architectural iconography, now thousands of years old, to communicate the desirable properties of money management in the age of the internet. As Schroeder points out, the image of an edifice in a given bank's website or brochure may not even be its own building — may not even exist in real life — but will be included as a semantically rich symbol. Here again, then, we see the influence of a picture that borders on the turf normally conceded to words — an image that is not included for the purpose of concrete reference but to articulate a complex of concepts. The viewer who "reads" these pictorial symbols must have prior knowledge that allows him or her to comprehend the message. This prior knowledge is clearly culturally, historically specific, and so raises yet again the kinds of questions that Pimentel and Heckler, as well as Tavassoli, bring to our attention, with implications for the kinds of studies being conducted by Winkielman et al., Nordhielm, and Luna and Peracchio. Thus, although the Schroeder analysis goes a long way into history and art, it returns with implications that are important for the ongoing investigation of human response to pictures.

"No One Looks That Good in Real Life!" by Wood, Solomon, and Englis addresses a controversial issue in the matter of advertising effects. For the past 30 years, the presumed negative impact of beautiful female images on women's self-esteem has been a concern of feminists and others, such as mental health professionals. This essay first reviews the studies that try to quantify and demonstrate these effects. As with the literature on sex appeals, the results are, at best, inconclusive. These authors go on to construct an exploratory study that investigates the relationship between viewers' estimates and evaluations of their own bodies and images of themselves in the context of online clothing purchases. Here the technology provides a new opportunity to investigate the interface between self, self-perception, the actual body, the body image, the commercial image, and the purchase. Online sites now include models that can be altered to reflect the viewer's own measurements, hair color, and so on. Although these models of the self are still pretty crude, they provide an important alternative condition to consumers looking at clothing as pictured on supermodels. The findings of Wood et al. are provocative, even at this early stage in the technology.

The final essay brings the question of persuasion through form to the object itself. Dora Horvath investigates the meanings attributed to a newly popular object in Hungary, the mobile telephone.

Having traveled a path that has gone from the precise working of the brain in processing visual stimuli all the way to the history of classical architecture, the reader of this volume will, we hope, have a new respect for the complexity of human visual response and the research that is trying to explain it. Few of the folk theories that find their way into academic work can accommodate the nuances we have seen here, nor could they contemplate the many difficult questions that still remain. Some of the most intractable of these ideas—such as the sex appeal belief and the fear of beautiful images of women—seem considerably less robust when looked at empirically. Perhaps the most heartening conclusion, from the viewpoint of those who believe in the damaging effects of commercial imagery, is the picture of the human viewer implicitly painted here. The respondents in these studies are skeptical, culturally situated creatures who cannot be consistently "manipulated" through mere exposure to visual tricks, but instead respond in ways so subtle and provisional as to have escaped easy analysis. The research needed to fully respect the capabilities of the human viewer when confronted with persuasive imagery is still to be done.

REFERENCES

Conners, C. K. (1964). Visual and verbal approach motives as a function of discrepancy from expectancy level. *Perceptual and Motor Skills, 18*, 457–464.

Haber, R. N. (1958). Discrepancy from adaptation level as a source of affect. *Journal of Experimental Psychology, 56*(4), 370–375.

I. PERSUASIVE IMAGERY:
WHAT DO WE REALLY KNOW?

CHAPTER ONE

Persuasion by Design: The State of Expertise on Visual Influence Tactics

Keven Malkewitz
North Carolina State University

Peter Wright
University of Oregon

Marian Friestad
University of Oregon

In this chapter we assess the accumulated expertise on visual persuasion in American society at the beginning of the 21st century. Attempts to influence and persuade others via the strategic alteration of visual stimuli occur on a grand scale in modern American society. It may seem tempting to view this deluge of human-generated visual stuff as evidence in itself that practical expertise in visual persuasion is highly advanced. If so, experts in visual persuasion would operate to craftily control our visual world's elements and thereby predictably alter our everyday thoughts and behavior in ways they intend.

However, our analysis suggests that practical expertise in applied everyday visual persuasion is not very well developed. Effective persuasion is fairly difficult to achieve in real world practice. Knowledge about influence and persuasion tactics is a societal good. It is widely shared within a society. The psychology of successful persuasion is complex. And the rate of change in the technologies for visual communication available to a prospective influence agent is very high, making technological mastery in itself quite challenging.

To gain better insight on this, we asked the following questions. As best we can tell, what is the current state of the art in applied visual persuasion? What do experts in the practice of visual influence know, as evidenced in their writings and teachings across domains of the applied visual arts and behavioral sciences? In practice, how effectively can the most knowledgeable of these experts apply what they know to engineer visual persuasion in a predictable and precise manner? How does the everyday knowledge of lay people about visual influence tactics and practices compare to that of experts?

The actual domain of attempted visual influence in society is very broad. To realistically assess the knowledge base available in society to guide a prospective agent of influence, we surveyed the literatures in many realms of potential visual manipulation. We examined what teachers, practitioners, and researchers had to say about visual manipulation and persuasion in the following diverse areas of human thought: cognitive psychology, social psychology, evolutionary psychology, architecture, urban design, landscape design, visual culture broadly defined, product design, graphic design, applied and theoretical aesthetics, still photography, television and film, computer games and virtual reality, media literacy, illusions and magic, advertising, and consumer behavior. In addition, we three augment this state-of-the-art study with what we have learned from our own professional experiences over the years. These include working closely with professional product designers and advertising agencies.

We exclude the visual reading of verbal language from our discussion. To include language reading would, we feel, trivialize the discussion and distract us from this volume's goal of separating visual persuasion from persuasion in general. Of course, visual stimuli are often used in conjunction with written language in persuasion attempts. We return to this situation later because it represents a particularly problematic one in terms of exploiting visual communication.

PERSUASION BY DESIGN

In everyday usage the term *design* often implies the manipulation of visual elements. We employ it here in that sense and in its broader meaning. Intentionality is at the heart of persuasion. Thus, successful persuasion can only occur by design, that is, via a scheme or plan conceived in the human mind to engineer an intended change in someone's mental states that is instrumental to their performing an action sought by the agent. We state this basic idea to remind readers of what persuasion *is not*. It is not simply any manipulation of stimuli that produces some (coincidental; unpredicted; unintended) psychological effect on others. Nor is it merely the production in others of an intended psychological effect that in itself is not at all or only weakly related in actuality to the ultimate production of the intended behavioral effect. For example, expertise in getting attention is not in itself necessarily an indicator of persuasion expertise (despite the well-known importance of getting attention as a stage setter).

PRACTICAL EXPERTISE IN VISUAL PERSUASION

Practical expertise would enable a person to do one or both of the two persuasion related tasks: (a) persuading others, and (b) coping with others' attempts to persuade oneself. What would someone with advanced practical expertise in visual persuasion be able to do more effectively than someone with typical everyday common sense expertise? How are the two distinguishable?

Persuading Others

The truly advanced expert at *persuading others* would be able to exploit more valid and refined knowledge about four things:

1. Mental states expertise: The basic mental states psychology of persuasion and attitude change.

2. Production technology expertise: The technical manipulations of visual elements possible with visual materials and within visual media to alter the visual content available to observers.

3. Strategic persuasion expertise: The strategic manipulations of particular visual elements and patterns of visual–verbal elements to predictably influence multiple targeted mental states of particular observers, including attention, perception, associations and beliefs, affective feelings and attitudes, emotions, intentions, and so on, in ways predictably and strongly instrumental to an intended persuasion goal, within particular contexts and situations.

4. Persuasion research expertise: The qualitative or quantitative testing of visual presentations to assess their actual persuasive effects in a given context, and the ensuing adjustment of visual presentations based on this learning to make them more situationally effective.

Coping With Others' Persuasion Attempts

The expert at coping with others' attempts at visual persuasion would have to primarily exploit mental states expertise and strategic persuasion expertise. That is, to cope effectively, a person needs basic mental states understanding and the capacity to effectively recognize and interpret the intentions behind human-produced visual manipulations. However, being advanced in persuasion coping does not seem to require advanced production technology expertise. That is, someone does not have to grasp the technology of producing, say, digital photographs or curved polycarbon steel tools to be able to recognize and cope with the intended visual manipulations of an advertiser or product designer. To cope well, someone needs only to know about the types of technical manipulations currently possible—for example, to know that photos can be digitally doctored, to know that artificial materials can be made to closely resemble rocks and stones, and so on. Nor does coping expertise require persuasion research expertise, as the coping task does not itself entail effects measurements or tactical fine-tuning.

However, practical coping expertise would include one other type of skill:

5. Persuasion coping expertise: The capability to practice effective psychological and physical self control so as to functionally manage (permit; correct and modify; thwart) intended visual persuasion, once intent is suspected.

ACQUIRING PERSUASION EXPERTISE

How might some individual or enclave acquire special expertise on using visuals to persuade others? This could presumably happen if they were somehow able to make sizable gains in insight over their lifetime in one or more of the areas just cited, which then separated them from everyday lay people's commonsense understandings. This can occur from extensive education and training by enclaves of professionals (scientists; educators), if the professionals have an advanced, communicable, coherent, and valid body of knowledge to pass along. It can also occur if individuals invest themselves in domain-specific expertise building throughout adulthood. Practical expertise continues to increase over the life span under certain conditions.

However, the emergence of expertise in visual persuasion depends on a gap developing between what individuals know (that is valid) and what the everyday commonsense beliefs are in a society. Several factors work to keep that gap from growing very large in a short time period. One is our historical evolutionary legacy of social intelligence. A second is the relative scarcity of scientific knowledge on visual persuasion and persuasion in general. A third is the pervasive exchange of ideas and information on social influence practices that occurs in everyday society. Observers have pointed out how interested people have been throughout history in persuasion knowledge, how important persuasion-related task efficacy is to everyday life, and consequently how much continual sharing of information on persuasion takes place within societies (Friestad & Wright, 1994). This social sharing mitigates against the outbreak of advanced expertise, except for brief historical moments and particular types of knowledge. A fourth is rapid change in the visual presentation production technologies and capabilities, which must continually be mastered by prospective visual persuasion agents merely to generate visual stimuli. This preoccupies practitioners with continuing education on production technology expertise.

We searched through a lot of literatures to see what is known. In this search, we basically looked for evidence of whether the people who "ought" to display special advanced expertise on these topics do indeed display it. If so, what type of expertise do they display? We also examined what evolutionary psychologists are now proposing about the evolution of the human mind and of special domains of human intelligence. We next attempt to summarize what we learned.

HUMAN SOCIAL INTELLIGENCE IS HIGHLY EVOLVED AND HIGHLY VISUAL

There has been an outpouring of research and writing on evolutionary psychology in the last decade or so. This work has been done by people originally trained in biology and anthropology as well as trained psychologists and art theorists. Examples include Aiken (1998), Baron-Cohen (1999), Byrne & Whiten (1997), Dissanayake (1992), Gigerenzer (1997), Power (1999), and Whiten (1997, 1999). Their goal is to understand the evolution of the human mind by understanding its functional rationale as an organ suited for performing essential recurring human tasks.

Several ideas are germane to us here. First, the visual system has been the underpinning to the evolution of the human mind. Second, social intelligence has driven much of the mind's evolution. Taken together, these ideas mean that from the start humans have been developing and refining their capabilities to effectively use visuals in communication and social influence activities. This refinement went on for a long, long time before the development and wide use of written communication. Third, the evolution of a mental states psychology, and with it the capacity to understand human intentionality, was a critical process in our evolutionary history. This implies that by this time in our evolution there is a well-developed, widely shared mental states intelligence that all humans are by and large equipped to exploit during their lives.

Developmental psychologists have uncovered the emergence within children of a working "theory of mind" starting at about age 6 (Astington & Jenkins, 1995; Bartsch & London, 2000; Kline & Clinton, 1998; Malle, Moses, & Baldwin, 2001; Roedder John, 1999; Wellman, 1990). That is, children all demonstrate a grasp of the essentials of a belief–intention folk psychology, which they refine and elaborate as a basis for social cooperation and competition throughout life. To the extent that this provides a fairly high "floor" under the achieved visual persuasion expertise of all people, it suppresses the emergence and sustenance of substantial expertise advantages by groups of experts.

SCIENTIFIC RESEARCH ON VISUAL PERSUASION ADDS LITTLE TO FOLK PSYCHOLOGY

By and large, scientific theories of persuasion and communication are not well developed yet. If anything, the latest efforts to summarize and make sense of the scattered disparate empirical findings dramatize this state of relative ignorance (Eagly & Chaiken, 1993; Friestad & Wright, 1994). More frustrating for our purposes, theories of persuasion have not developed in ways that deal well with visual stimulus effects or visual media effects per se. For example, in testing a theoretical proposition about a persuasion tactic (say, threat or reciprocity), researchers have relied on stimuli of all types—written, spoken, visuals of all sorts—and in all combinations, without keeping track of or theoretically pondering how specific visual manipulations per se are contributing to achieved persuasion.

Theories and research that do try to directly account for visual effects and, most commonly, effects due to visuals of various sorts in conjunction with verbal rhetoric paint a very daunting picture. This work indicates how sensitive the effects from visual–verbal combinations are to small alterations in one or another aspect of the overall message, and how difficult it is in practice to use visual elements to achieve high control over even the basic processes of attention, association and elaboration (e.g., Anand & Sternthal, 1989; Bither & Wright, 1973; Campbell, 1995; Campbell & Kirmani, 2000; Debevec & Romeo, 1992; Hodge & Tripp, 1986; Kiselius & Sternthal, 1984; MacInnis & Price, 1987; McQuarrie & Mick, 1999; Meyers-Levy & Peracchio, 1995, 1996; Miniard et al., 1991; Scott, 1994; Unnava & Burnkrant, 1991; Wright, 1979). The complexities suggested by current research are made even more daunting by the realization that in experimental studies the researchers often have to tweak and try out many different visual stimuli or visual–verbal patterns in pilot tests before choosing the stimuli they finally report on.

What about the simple psychological notion of "attention"? At the least, isn't knowledge of attention well developed? Well, yes and no. Attention has been the topic of human thought and discourse for centuries, ensuring that much of what is readily knowable about everyday attention getting and attention holding is part of everyday folk knowledge. Indeed, primates demonstrate an understanding of tactical visual distraction because signals of attentional focus by others are readily discernible and the value of distraction in simple influence situations readily learnable through observation and trial (Whiten, 1997, 1999). All of us understand how to get attention in a broad heavy-handed sense and recognize others' attention getting tactics fairly easily. But beyond the most obvious, control of visual attention is not all that well understood (Ericksen & Murphy, 1987; Farah, 1988; Gregory, 1997; Hatfield, 1998; Laberge, 1995; Mack & Rock, 1998; Posner, 1995; Ramachandran & Hirstein, 1999; Sewall, 1999; Wright & Ward, 1998). Metaphoric definitions (often evidence of a commonsense psychology at work) by researchers include a filter, a skill, a resource, a "spotlight beam" within which processing is enhanced, and a glue that binds features together, and specific paradigms have emphasized attention's supposed capacity, selectivity, control, relation to arousal, or relation to elaborative (Wright & Ward, 1998). Current researchers on the control of visual attention are outspoken in admitting how poorly developed their theories are.

PRODUCTION TECHNOLOGY EXPERTISE AND TRAINING DOMINATES ALL DOMAINS OF APPLIED VISUAL ARTS

We diligently scanned the abundant writings in various domains of applied visual arts. This included writings in:

Architecture, landscape, and environmental design (Alexander, 1979; Alexander, Ishakawa, & Silverstein, 1977; Bloch, 1979; Braudel, 1979; Choay, 1997; Dreyfus, 1951; Eco, 1986; Fisher, 2000; Hall, 1998; Heidigger, 1971; Lefebvre, 1991; Preziosi, 1979; Pye, 1978; Robinson, 2001; Sommer, 1983; Spirn, 1998; Sutton, 2001; Vanderburgh & Ellis, 2001; Willis, 1999).

Photography, film, and video (Barry, 1997; Beilin, 1991; Block, 2001; Bolter & Grusin, 1999; Cartwright, 1995; Damer, 1998; Forrester, 2000; Gibson, 1979; Messaris, 1992; Mitchell, 1994; Newton, 2001; Ninio, 2001; Poole, 2000; Silverblatt, 1995; Solomon-Godeay, 1991; Virilio, 1994; Wade, 1990; Zettl, 1990).

Graphic design, product design, and visual culture (Abram, 1996; Arnheim, 1974; Blauvelt, 1997; Bloch, 1979; Bloch, 1995; Caplan, 1982; Cutting & Vishton, 1995; Danto, 1998; Davis, 1998a; Davis, 1998b; de Certeau, 1984; Gombrich, 1973, 1984; Hollins & Pugh, 1990; Illich, 1973; Jencks, 1995; McCoy, 1998; Mirzoeff, 1998; Norman, 1988; Panati, 1987; Panofsky, 1955; Penrose, 1973; Petrofsky, 1985; Reynolds, 1998; Sanoff, 1990; Tufte, 1983, 1990, 1997, Ulrich & Eppinger, 2000; Veryzer & Hutchinson, 1998; Wild, 1997).

This review enables the following generalization: *The shared knowledge available in visual presentation domains is saturated with production technology information.* By and large, the visual persuasion expertise of those in society most directly engaged in and trained for visual communication concerns the practical details of "how to produce a particular type of visual stimulus." This is totally understandable, given the enormous complexities of mastering the use of modern technologies for making buildings, televised images, physical objects, pictorial renderings, digitized images, and so forth. These technologies of production keep changing at a very rapid pace. Just keeping up with the "how to produce it" knowledge that grows exponentially must preoccupy professionals.

As an example, someone trying to master the art of still photography or film must learn how to manipulate a multitude of variables: framing, angles, focus depth, lens width, exposure, aperture opening, shutter speed, film type, filters, color balances, contrast, image size and shape, cropping, fade-ins and fade-outs, dissolves, cuts, zooms and dollies, pans, screen splits, and so on. Even worse, their production expertise must cover the juxtapositions of visual images and audio sounds. They must establish production mastery in both traditional contexts and newer ones, such as computer games, digitized photography, photorealistic graphics, virtual reality, ubiquitous computing systems, and more.

In bridging their expertise from traditional media into the realm of supposedly new media, they must confront the issue of how much to import and how much to create anew, in their production tactics. For example, during the 20th century, the photographic image seemed to present us with a secure authentic credible representation of a reality. For over a hundred years, when we saw a photo we tended to trust in what it showed. We knew that photo images could be doctored, but for a long time the doctoring was fairly detectable. Photography was believed. That is no longer true. Photography is now almost entirely suspect, because of the new digital editing capabilities that even lay people can master. The practical uses of photographic images must therefore be rethought by visual communication professionals.

The necessity of concentrating on production technology education as a bedrock for visual persuasion practical expertise means, however, that gains in the other aspects of visual persuasion expertise must be sacrificed. An individual can only gain valid expertise in a limited domain during some time period. If technical information in that narrow domain keeps changing, its mastery requires continual attention.

Thus, the writings and teachings in the applied visual arts fields provides only basics about the mental states psychology of human communication and social influence. Budding experts in architecture, graphic design, film, TV and photography, and product design do not as a matter of standard practice also acquire expertise on social influence or the psychology of communication. The touchpoints in the visual arts literatures with advanced scientific psychology are few.

ASSESSING INDIVIDUALS' PRACTICAL EXPERTISE IN VISUAL DESIGN AND PERSUASION OVER THE LIFETIME: A RESEARCH FRONTIER

Individuals can of course get extensive practice over their lifetime in the construction and presentation of visual stimuli in particular persuasion venues (Alba & Hutchinson, 1987; Baltes & Staudinger, 1996; Berg, 2000; Chi, Glaser, & Farr, 1988; Ericsson & Smith, 1991; Friestad & Wright, 1994, 1995). This appears to be the route by which someone may acquire synthesized expertise that integrates an advanced production technology expertise with an advanced mental states psychology expertise and advanced strategic persuasion expertise. This seems like a daunting learning task, however, and the number of individuals who concentrate attention on it persistently and successfully may be fairly limited.

Little is now known about lay people's or purported experts' attainments in this form of expertise as they progress through adulthood. Children, adolescents and adults all appear to have a ready ability to note and interpret visual tactics in the context of advertising (Boush, Friestad, & Rose, 1994; Campbell, 1995; Hodge & Tripp, 1986). But evidence of this in other contexts is scarce (Malkewitz, 2000). Measurement of visual persuasion expertise is an important challenge. There are few existing measurement instruments that have been validated. Measuring practical expertise is a fairly recent undertaking (Malkewitz, 2000; Sternberg et al., 2000), but this is a vital research activity if our understanding of visual persuasion by design is to increase.

REFERENCES

Abram, D. (1996). *The spell of the sensuous.* New York: Vintage Books.

Aiken, N. E. (1998). *The biological origins of art.* Westport, CT: Praeger Press.

Alba, J. W., & Hutchinson, J. W. (1987). Dimensions of consumer expertise. *Journal of Consumer Research, 13,* 411–454.

Alexander, C. (1979). *The timeless way of building.* New York: Oxford University Press.

Alexander, C., Ishakawa, S., & Silverstein, M. (1977). *A pattern language: Towns, building, construction.* New York: Oxford University Press.

Anand, P., & Sternthal, A. (1989). Strategies for designing persuasive messages: Deductions from the resource matching hypothesis. In P. Caffera & A. Tybout (Eds.), *Cognitive and affective responses to advertising* (pp. 135–159). Lexington, MA: Lexington Books.

Arnheim, R. (1974). *Art and visual perception: A psychology of the creative eye.* Berkeley: University of California Press.

Astington, J. W., & Jenkins, J. M. (1995). Theory of mind development and social understanding. *Cognition and Emotion, 9,* 151–165.

Baltes, P. B., & Staudinger, U. M. (1996). *Interactive minds: Life-span perspectives on the social foundation of cognition.* Cambridge: Cambridge University Press.

Baron-Cohen, S. (1999). The evolution of a theory of mind. In M. C. Corballis & S. E. G. Lea (Eds.), *The descent of mind: Psychological perspectives on hominid evolution* (pp. 261–277). Oxford: Oxford University Press.

Barry, A. M. S. (1997). *Visual intelligence.* Albany, NY: State University of New York Press.

Bartsch, K., & London, K. (2000). Children's use of mental state information in selecting persuasive arguments. *Developmental Psychology, 36,* 352–365.

Beilin, H. (1991). Developmental aesthetics and the psychology of photography. In R. M. Downs, L. S. Liben, & D. S. Palermo (Eds.), *Visions of aesthetics, the environment & development* (pp. 45–86). Hillsdale, NJ: Lawrence Erlbaum Associates.

Berg, C.A. (2000). Intellectual development in adulthood. In R. J. Sternberg (Ed.), *Handbook of intelligence* (pp. 117–140). Cambridge: Cambridge University Press.

Bither, S., & Wright, P. (1973). The self-confidence-advertising response relationship: A function of situational distraction. *Journal of Marketing Research, 10,* 146–152.

Blauvelt, A. (1997). Remaking theory, rethinking practice. In S. Heller (Ed.), *The education of a graphic designer* (pp. 71–77). New York: Allport Press.

Bloch, E. (1979). Formative education, engineering form, ornament. In N. Leach (Ed.), *Rethinking architecture* (pp. 43–50). New York: Routledge.

Bloch, P. H. (1995). Seeking the ideal form: Product design and consumer response. *Journal of Marketing, 59,* 14–24.

Block, B. (2001). *The visual story: Seeing the structure of film, TV, and new media.* Boston: Focal Press.

Bolter, J. D., & Grusin, R. (1999). *Remediation: Understanding new media.* Cambridge MA: MIT Press.

Boush, D. M., Friestad, M., & Rose, G. M. (1994). Adolescent skepticism toward TV advertising and knowledge of advertiser tactics. *Journal of Consumer Research, 21,* 165–175.

Braudel, F. (1979). *The structures of everyday life.* New York: Harper & Row.

Byrne, R. W., & Whiten, A. (1997). Machiavellian intelligence. In A. Whiten & R. W. Byrne (Eds.), *Machiavellian intelligence II: Extensions and evaluations* (pp. 1–24). Cambridge: Cambridge University Press.

Campbell, M. C. (1995). When attention-getting advertising tactics elicit consumer inferences of manipulative intent: The importance of balancing benefits and investments. *Journal of Consumer Psychology, 22,* 17–27.

Campbell, M. C., & Kirmani, A. (2000). Consumers' use of persuasion knowledge: The effects of accessibility and cognitive capacity on perceptions of an influence agent. *Journal of Consumer Research, 27,* 69–83.

Caplan, R. (1982). *By design: Why there are no locks on the bathroom doors in Hotel Louis XIV and other object lessons.* New York: St. Martin's Press.

Cartwright, L. (1995). Science and the cinema. In N. Mirzoeff (Ed.), *The visual culture reader* (pp. 199–213). New York: Routledge.

Chi, M. T. H., Glaser, R., & Farr, M. J. (1988). *The nature of expertise.* Hillsdale, NJ: Lawrence Erlbaum Associates.

Choay, F. (1997). *The rule and the model: On the theory of architecture and urbanism.* Cambridge, MA: MIT Press.

Cutting, J. E., & Vishton, P. M. (1995). Perceiving layout and knowing distances. In W. Epstein & S. Rogers (Eds.), *Perception of space and motion* (pp. 71–110). San Diego: Academic Press.

Damer, B. (1998). *Avatars! Exploring and building virtual worlds on the Internet.* Berkeley: Peachpit Press.

Danto, A. C. (1998). The artworld and its outsiders. *In self-taught artists of the 20th century* (pp. 18–27). San Francisco: Chronicle Books.

Davis, M. (1998a). How high do we set the bar in design education? In S. Heller (Ed.), *The education of a graphic designer* (pp. 25–30). New York: Allworth Press.

Davis, M. (1998b). Graphic design as cognitive artifact. In S. Heller (Ed.), *The education of a graphic designer* (pp. 211–214). New York: Allworth Press.

Debevec, K., & Romeo, J. B. (1992). Self-referent processing in perceptions of verbal and visual commercial information. *Journal of Consumer Psychology, 1,* 83–102.

de Certeau, M. (1984). *The practice of everyday life.* Berkeley: University of California Press.

Dissanayake, E. (1992). *Homo aestheticus: Where art comes from and why.* New York: Free Press.

Dreyfus, H. (1951). *Designing for people.* New York: Simon & Schuster.

Eagly, A. H., & Chaiken, S. (1993). *The psychology of attitudes.* Orlando, FL: Harcourt Brace Jovanovich.

Eco, U. (1986). Functionalism and sign: The semiotics of architecture. In M. Gottdiener & A. Lagopoulos (Eds.), *The city and the sign* (pp. 56–85). New York: Columbia University Press.

Ericksen, C. A., & Murphy, T. D. (1987). Movement of attentional focus across the visual field: A critical look at the evidence. *Perception and Psychophysics, 42,* 299–305.

Ericsson, K. A., & Smith, J. A. (1991). *Toward a general theory of expertise.* New York: Cambridge University Press.

Farah, M. J. (1988). Is visual imagery really visual? Overlooked evidence from neuropsychology. *Psychological Review, 95,* 307–317.

Fisher, T. (2000). *In the scheme of things: Alternative thinking on the practice of architecture.* Minneapolis: University of Minnesota Press.

Forrester, M. (2000). *Psychology of the image.* London: Routledge.

Friestad, M., & Wright, P. (1994). The persuasion knowledge model: How people cope with persuasion attempts. *Journal of Consumer Research, 21,* 1–31.

Friestad, M., & Wright, P. (1995). Persuasion knowledge: Lay people's and researchers' beliefs about the psychology of persuasion. *Journal of Consumer Research, 22,* 62–74.

Gibson, J. J. (1979). *The ecological approach to visual perception.* Boston: Houghton Mifflin.

Gigerenzer, G. (1997). The modularity of social intelligence. In A. Whiten & R. S. Byrne (Eds.), *Machiavellian intelligence II: Extensions and adaptations* (pp. 264–288). Cambridge: Cambridge University Press.

Gombrich, E. H. (1973). Illusion and art. In R. L. Gregory & E. H. Gombrich (Eds.), *Illusion in nature and art.* New York: Charles Scribner's Sons.

Gombrich, E. H. (1984). *The sense of order: A study in the psychology of decorative art.* London: Phaidon.

Gregory, R. L. (1997). *Eye and brain: The psychology of seeing*. Princeton, NJ: Princeton University Press.

Hall, P. (1998). *Cities in civilization*. New York: Pantheon.

Hatfield, G. (1998). Attention in early scientific psychology. In R. D. Wright (Ed.), *Visual attention* (pp. 3–25). New York: Oxford University Press.

Heidigger, M. (1971). *Building, dwelling, thinking. Poetry, language, thought* (pp. 143–161). New York: Harper & Row.

Hodge, R., & Tripp, D. (1986). *Children and television: A semiotic approach*. Oxford: Basil Blackwell.

Hollins, B., & Pugh, S. (1990). *Successful product design*. London: Butterworths.

Illich, I. (1973). *Tools for conviviality*. New York: Harper & Row.

Jenks, C. (1995). *Visual culture*. London: Routledge.

Kiselius, J., & Sternthal, B. (1984). Detecting and explaining vividness effects in attitudinal judgments. *Journal of Marketing Research, 21,* 54–64.

Kline, S. L., & Clinton, B. L. (1998). Developments in children's persuasive message practices. *Communication Education, 47,* 120–135.

Laberge, D. (1995). *Attentional processing: The brain's art of mindfulness*. Cambridge, MA: Harvard University Press.

Lefebvre, H. (1991). *The production of space*. London: Blackwell.

MacInnis, D., & Price, L. L. (1987). The role of imagery in information processing: Review and extensions. *Journal of Consumer Research, 13,* 473–491.

Mack, A., & Rock, I. (1998). *Inattentional Blindness*. Cambridge MA: MIT Press.

Malkewitz, K. (2000). *The effect of representational fidelity and product design quality on attitude toward the product and product recognition*. Unpublished doctoral dissertation, University of Oregon.

Malle, B., Moses, L. J., & Baldwin, D. A. (2001). *Intentions and intentionality: Foundations of social cognition*. Cambridge, MA: MIT Press.

McCoy, K. (1998). Education in an adolescent profession. In S. Heller (Ed.), *The education of a graphic designer* (pp. 3–12). New York: Alworth Press.

McQuarrie, E. F., & Mick, D. G. (1999). Visual rhetoric in advertising: Text-interpretive, experimental, and reader-response analyses. *Journal of Consumer Research, 26,* 37–54.

Messaris, P. (1992). Visual "manipulation": Visual means of affecting responses to images. *Communication, 13,* 181–195.

Messaris, P. (1995). Visual "literacy" in cross-cultural perspective. In R. Kubey (Ed.), *Media literacy in the information age* (pp. 135–162). New Brunswick, NJ: Transaction.

Meyers-Levy, J., & Peracchio, L. A. (1995). Understanding the effects of color: How the correspondence between available and required resources affects attitudes. *Journal of Consumer Research, 22,* 121–138.

Meyers-Levy, J., & Peracchio, L. A. (1996). Moderators of the impact of self-reference on persuasion. *Journal of Consumer Research, 22,* 408–423.

Miniard, P. W., Bhatla, S., Lord, K. R., Dicksomn, P. R., & Unnava, H. R. (1991). Picture-based persuasion processes and the moderating role of involvement. *Journal of Consumer Research, 18,* 92–107.

Mirzoeff, N. (1998). What is visual culture? In N. Mirzoeff (Ed.), *The visual culture reader* (pp. 3–13). New York: Routledge.

Mitchell, W. J. T. (1994). *Picture theory*. Chicago: University of Chicago Press.

Newton, J. H. (2001). *The burden of visual truth: The role of photojournalism in mediating reality*. Mahwah, NJ: Lawrence Erlbaum Associates.

Ninio, J. (2001). *The science of illusions*. Ithaca, NY: Cornell University Press.

Norman, D. A. (1988). *The design of everyday things*. New York: Doubleday.

Panati, C. (1987). *Extraordinary origins of everyday things*. New York: Harper & Row.

Panofsky, E. (1955). *Meaning in the visual arts*. Garden City, NY: Doubleday.

Penrose, R. (1973). In praise of illusion. In R. L. Gregory & E. H. Gombrich (Eds.), *Illusion in nature and art* (pp. 245–284). New York: Charles Scribner's Sons.

Peracchio, L. A., & Meyers-Levy, J. (1997). Evaluating persuasion-enhancing techniques from a resource-matching perspective. *Journal of Consumer Research, 24,* 178–191.

Petrosky, H. (1985). *To engineer is human: The role of failure in successful design.* New York: St. Martin's Press.

Poole, S. (2000). *Trigger happy: The inner life of videogames.* London: Fourth Estate.

Posner, M. (1995). Attention in cognitive neuroscience. In M. Gazzaniga (Ed.), *The cognitive neurosciences* (pp. 615–624). Cambridge, MA: MIT Press.

Power, C. (1999). "Beauty" magic: The origins of art. In R. Dunbar et al. (Eds.), *The evolution of culture* (pp. 92–112). Edinburgh University Press.

Preziosi, D. (1979). *The semiotics of the built environment.* Bloomington: Indiana University Press.

Pye, D. (1978). *The nature and aesthetics of design.* New York: Van Nostrand.

Ramachandran, V. S., & Hirstein, W. (1999). The science of art: A neurological theory of aesthetic expereience. *Journal of Consciousness Studies, 6,* 15–51.

Reynolds, A. (1998). Visual stories. In N. Mirzoeff (Ed.), *The visual culture reader* (pp. 133–147). New York: Routledge

Robinson, J. W. (2001). The form and structure of architectural knowledge. In A. Piotrowski, & J. W. Robinson (Eds.), *The discipline of architecture* (pp. 61–82). Minneapolis: University of Minnesota Press.

Roedder John, D. (1999). Consumer socialization of children: A retrospective look at twenty-five years of research. *Journal of Consumer Research, 26,* 182–213.

Sanoff, H. (1990). Participatory design in focus. In H. Sanoff (Ed.), *Participatory design: Theory and techniques* (pp. 1–25). Raleigh: North Carolina State University Press.

Scott, L. M. (1994). Images in advertising: The need for a theory of visual rhetoric. *Journal of Consumer Research, 21,* 252–273.

Sewall, S. (1999). *Sight and sensibility: The ecopsychology of perception.* New York: Penguin Putnam.

Silverblatt, A. (1995). *Media literacy: Keys to interpreting media messages.* Westport, CT: Praeger.

Solomon-Godeay, A. (1991). *Photography at the dock.* Minneapolis: University of Minnesota Press.

Sommer, R. (1983). *Social design: Creating buildings with people in mind.* Englewood Cliffs, NJ: Prentice Hall.

Spirn, A. W. (1998). *The language of landscape.* New Haven, CT: Yale University Press.

Sternberg, R. J., Forsythe, G. B., Hedlund, J, Horvath, J. A., Wagner, R. K., Williams, W. M., Snook, S. A., & Grigorenko, E. L. (2000). *Practical intelligence in everyday life.* Cambridge: Cambridge University Press.

Sutton, S. E. (2001). Reinventing professional privilege as inclusivity: A proposal for an enriched mission in architecture. In A. Piotrowski, & J. W. Robinson (Eds.), *The disciplne of architecture* (pp. 173–207). Minneapolis: University of Minnesota Press.

Tufte, E. R. (1983). *The visual display of quantitative information.* Cheshire, CT: Graphics Press.

Tufte, E. R. (1990). *Envisioning information.* Cheshire, CT: Graphics Press.

Tufte, E. R. (1997). *Visual explanations.* Cheshire, CT: Graphics Press.

Ulrich, K. T., & Eppinger, S. D. (2000). *Product design and development.* New York: McGraw-Hill.

Unnava, H. R., & Burnkrant, R. E. (1991). An imagery processing view of the role of pictures in print advertising. *Journal of Marketing Research, 28,* 226–231.

Vanderburgh, D. J. T., & Ellis, W. R. (2001). A dialectics of determination: Social truth-claims in architectural writing, 1970–1995. In A. Piotrowski & J. W. Robinson (Eds.), *The discipline of architecture* (pp. 103–126). Minneapolis: University of Minnesota Press.

Veryzer, R. W., & Hutchinson, J. W. (1998). The influence of unity and prototypicality on aesthetic responses to new product designs. *Journal of Consumer Research, 24,* 374–394.

Virilio, P. (1994). *The vision machine.* Bloomington: Indiana University Press.

Wade, N. (1990). *Visual allusions.* Hillsdale, NJ: Lawrence Erlbaum Associates.

Wellman, H. A. (1990). *The child's theory of mind.* Cambridge, MA: MIT Press.

Whiten, A. (1997). The Machiavellian mindreader. In A. Whiten & R. W. Byrne (Eds.), *Machiavellian intelligence II: Extensions and evaluations* (pp. 144–173). Cambridge: Cambridge University Press.

Whiten, A. (1999). The evolution of deep social mind in humans. In M. C. Corballis & S. E. G. Lea (Eds.), *The descent of mind: Psychological perspectives on hominid evolution* (pp. 173–193). Oxford: Oxford University Press.

Wild, L. (1997). That was then: Corrections and amplifications. In S. Heller (Ed.), *The education of a graphic designer* (pp. 39–52). New York: Allworth Press.

Willis, D. (1999). *The emerald city, and other essays on the architectural imagination.* New York: Princeton Architectural Press.

Wright, P. (1979). Concrete action plans in TV messages to increase the reading of drug warnings. *Journal of Consumer Research, 6,* 429–443.

Wright, R. D., & Ward, L.M. (1998). The control of visual attention. In R. D. Wright (Ed.), *Visual attention* (pp. 132–186). New York: Oxford University Press.

Zettl, H. (1990). *Sight sound motion: Applied media aesthetics.* Belmont, CA: Wadsworth.

CHAPTER TWO

A Review of the
Visual Rhetoric Literature

Keith Kenney
University of South Carolina

Linda M. Scott
University of Illinois

For the first half of the 20th century in America, rhetoric was primarily the domain of speech teachers, who gave practical advice about influencing audiences through public oratory, radio announcing, drama, debate, and town meetings. The writings of classical rhetoricians like Plato, Aristotle, Cicero, and Quintilian were used to teach students how to choose and speak their words. Although visual elements like facial expression, posture, dress, and gesture were then, as always, encompassed by rhetorical principles, the emphasis was so squarely on verbal aspects of communication that many came to identify rhetoric with language.

In the second half of the 20th century, much about both the expression and conceptualization of persuasion changed. Although graphical rhetoric had become finely tuned in the posters and magazines of the early century, the explosion of television in the postwar period foregrounded the visual conduits for persuasion with greater impact and urgency. Not only were political movements increasingly orchestrated around "photo opportunities" like marches and sit-ins, but the "image management" of politicians became central to campaigns from the 1960 Kennedy–Nixon debate through the saxophone-playing "sound bites" of Bill Clinton. Throughout these five decades, the growing importance of a new conceptualization of rhetoric, advanced by philosopher and literary critic Kenneth Burke, was felt in academic disciplines from literature to art. In this new approach to persuasion, nonverbal forms were more prominently included. And, in turn, other areas of study—anthropology and even economics—were recast and reanalyzed in rhetorical terms. Thus, by the end of the century, a major shift had occurred on two fronts: Not only was the idea of "persuasion" being expanded to cover the enormous proliferation in nonverbal forms of communication, but rhetoric itself broadened to become a major theory informing not only the study of literature and speech, but of culture, art, and even science.

This book takes as its subject the response of consumers to commercial forms of visual persuasion. Several of the essays contained here include specific references to rhetoric, both classical and contemporary. Others, although not drawing from rhetoric per se, are fundamentally rhetorical in their focus on the impact of persuasive materials upon human attitudes, cognition, or memory. Thus, this volume shows the imprint of the rhetorical turn in late 20th-century thought. This bibliographical essay is intended to provide an orientation to the theoretical issues of visual rhetoric, as well as a comprehensive list of references dealing with visual communication in a rhetorical framework. Importantly, one thing that became quite clear from reviewing the existing literature on visual rhetoric is that most of this work speculates broadly about the effects of particular messages or forms on audiences, but very little has actually investigated response empirically, whether through experiments, surveys, interviews, or any other method. So it is our hope that this bibliography will prove useful for scholars who, after reading this book, wish to pursue a rhetorical line of inquiry in empirical research.

To this end, we offer the following outline. First, we discuss the broad theoretical issues that confront an application of rhetoric either to visual messages or to material artifacts. Obviously, pictorial texts (ads), concrete objects (products), and combined forms (packages) must be addressed in the study of *consumer* response. After glossing the theoretical issues, we demonstrate the application of rhetoric to a broad range of ads and products, using the literature included in the bibliography, as well as advertisements as exemplars. Three different approaches to rhetorical analysis are included: classical, Burkeian, and "critical." Finally, we briefly discuss the path of inquiry into consumer response. And, of course, the list of references at the end of this chapter is a key part of its value.

The search for relevant literature was conducted from a *communications* perspective. First, *Communication Abstracts* was searched for the years 1978 to 2000 using the descriptors "rhetoric," "rhetorical analysis," "rhetorical strategy," "rhetorical theory," "visual advertising," "visual arts," "visual communication," "visual elements," "political rhetoric," and "presidential rhetoric." Next, the following electronic databases were searched: *Art Index* (1984–2000), *Dissertation Abstracts* (1861–2000), *ERIC* (1966–2000), *Philosopher's Index* (1940–2000), *Psych INFO* (1887–2000), and *Sociology Abstracts* (1963–2000). For these databases, the following descriptors were used: "visual rhetoric," "visual persuasion," "visual argument," "visual propaganda," "visual ideology," and "visual politics." In addition, descriptors restricted to title only were searched as follows: "rhetoric" and "pictures," "rhetoric" and "design," "rhetoric" and "painting," "rhetoric" and "images," "rhetoric" and "video," "rhetoric" and "photography," "rhetoric" and "architecture," "rhetoric" and "memorials," "rhetoric" and "cartoons," "rhetoric" and "comics," and "rhetoric" and "film." Of course, articles also were identified via the ancestry approach (tracking research cited in already obtained relevant studies). The review was restricted to published sources. Conference papers, dissertations, and Internet sources were sometimes read but were not included. In the end, 172 sources were obtained, all of which are included here.

THE RHETORIC OF THE VISUAL

Aristotle defined rhetoric as "the faculty wherein one discovers the available means of persuasion in any case whatsoever" (1991, p. 36). Although the phrase "available means" clearly gives permission to go beyond speech, many academics vested in the power of the word (e.g., professors of English or speech) have insisted on defining rhetoric as the exclusive province of verbal language. Furthermore, such factions often try to constrain the practice of rhetoric to particular venues—debates, editorials, and so on—despite the long-standing claim that rhetoric can be used "in any case whatsoever." Therefore, much of this introduction addresses questions about and objections to the notion of "visual rhetoric," as well as its applicability in the "discourse" of advertising, packaging, and trade.

Kenneth Burke opened out the scope by declaring rhetoric to be use of symbols to persuade creatures who *by their nature* respond to symbols (1945, 1950, 1966, 1967). Just as others have defined humans by their use of tools, Burke defined *Homo sapiens* as the symbol-using animal. Thus, accepting the notion of "visual rhetoric" swings largely on being able to include pictures (and other cultural signs, such as numbers and objects) as a type of symbol. Although semiotics has defined pictures as symbols since the lectures of Ferdinand de Saussure and the writings of Charles Peirce, there has been a tendency to classify pictures as "iconic" or "indexical" signs, thus implying a kind of "natural sign" (Mitchell, 1986, and see also Barthes, 1971). Typically, a rhetorical framework is based the assumption that the symbols of discourse are "conventional." That is to say, the symbols are based on social agreement, not resemblance or cause, and therefore are *arbitrary* in nature. Thus, if we assert that pictures are merely signs of resemblance, then they cannot be arbitrary or conventional—and thus are not the stuff of rhetoric. Such a classification unfortunately dovetails with a long-standing Western prejudice—known as "copy theory"—that assumes pictures signify merely by resembling objects in the real world (see Scott, 1994a). This prejudice, in turn, stands on two historical peculiarities about Western culture: the techniques of representation in its art, and its use of alphabetic writing systems.

The conventions of "realistic" representation in Western art date only from the 15th century, although picturing has been common among humans for millions of years. Other cultures and other times have used different geometries of representation to "reflect reality" *when they chose to do so* (Hagen, 1980). However, the assumption that the *purpose* of picturing is to reflect reality is also peculiar to Western culture—it is equally valid (and more common) in other cultures to use pictures to evoke or depict other realms, such as the spiritual and the fictive (see Scott, 1994a). Ironically, it is not difficult to see that art in the Western world frequently pictures the "nonreal"—religious painting and advertising trade characters being just two prominent examples—but the notion that pictures signify through resemblance to actual objects is nevertheless intransigent in both theory and research.

Equally problematic are the blinders created by alphabetic script. Again, irony emerges if we consider that when Aristotle was first setting forth the principles of rhetoric and poetics, the technology he was using—alphabetic writing—was new. The Greek alphabet, invented around 750 B.C.E., was the first to encode speech using symbols for sounds. For at least three thousand years prior to that breakthrough, humanity had been writing with some adaptation of picturing, in the form of pictographies and syllabaries. The earliest of these was the Mesopotamian cuneiform (3500 B.C.E.), but Egyptian hieroglyphs and Chinese ideographs are now better known. In each case, however, these rich and sophisticated civilizations used picture-based symbols to create extensive literatures, write elaborate philosophies, and account for extensive trade, as well as for many other purposes from grand to mundane. The contention that pictures cannot argue or "be discursive," therefore, is clearly rooted in ethnocentricity: The full scope of human history shows pictures, not alphabetic words, as the primary mode of discourse (Goody, 1968; also Scott, 1993).

A little understanding of the way world pictographies work will help us to address another issue that is commonly controversial in the debate about visual rhetoric. All known pictographies are initially based on a principle of resemblance; however, the immediate limitations of such a system have caused *all* of them to make adaptations in order to accommodate concepts, actions, nonvisible qualities, and proper names. In each case, the solution is formed through a convention whereby the juxtaposition of other symbols, the addition of some abstract shape, the use of a particular color, or stylization is used to reach beyond the principle of resemblance. Thus, although the system remains pictorial, it is no longer based on resemblance but on shared cultural understanding (or convention) (Goody, 1968). Again, in Western culture, we have many such conventional symbols: the American flag, the Lucent logo, and the peace sign are a few.

The capability to interpret such symbols clearly depends on shared cultural experience. Indeed, many important scholars have argued that even the most realistic photograph depends on a shared symbolic system of picturing, present in the culture for hundreds of years and enculturated in each viewer from birth (here the pioneering work is Gombrich, 1960). Thus, a truly rhetorical approach to visual communications includes the firm premise that the making and viewing of pictures is fundamentally a culture-based practice, just as is writing and reading. That means, in turn, that culture is "present" in all pictures, not just some of them.

As important as the concept of "convention" is the principle of "selection." Classical criticism is based on consideration of all the possible choices available to a communicator, followed by identification and evaluation of the communicator's choices, given a particular audience at a particular moment:

> A rhetorical critic is interested in why an artist chose to deal with certain topics (and not others); why the artistic elements chosen were structured as they were (and not some other way); why certain characteristics of the medium are emphasized and others are not; what purpose, among all those possible, seems to be governing these choices; and to what audience the work addresses itself with what potential effect. (Medhurst & Benson, 1984, p. x)

In pictures, the principle of selectivity is always at work, despite the common assertion that images simply show things "as they are." Art theorist Nelson Goodman wrote:

> "To make a faithful picture, come as close as possible to copying the object just as it is." This simple-minded injunction baffles me; for the object before me is a man, a swarm of atoms, a complex of cells, a fiddler, a friend, a fool, and much more. If none of these constitute the object as it is, what else might? If all are ways the object is, then none is *the* way the object is. I cannot copy all these at once; and the more nearly I succeeded, the less would the result be a realistic picture. (Goodman, 1976, pp. 6–7)

Kenneth Burke (1966) defined each individual instance of rhetoric as a "symbolic action" in *which someone is trying to get someone else to do something* (or to think or feel something). To that end, the one producing any rhetorical text will select *from among a range of options* the word, tone, color, view, or tune that he or she feels is most likely to have the desired effect among the intended audience. Obviously, that "effect" depends on the accurate communication of the intended meaning, as well as other rhetorical possibilities such as being pleasing to the eye. Because each visual view of an object necessarily excludes some or all of the other views (if we see the front, we don't see the back; if we see it in sunlight, we don't see it in moonlight), then all pictures are unavoidably selective and, therefore, irretrievably rhetorical. The rhetorical intention is articulated by the selection of one view *instead of* another. Thus, in pictorial rhetoric, the persuasive intent is as manifest in what is *not* shown as in what *is* shown. Further, it is axiomatic that *how* something is shown is as important as *what* is shown.

Here an example may be helpful. Consider, for instance, that there is only one way to spell "cat," but there are many ways to *say* "cat": feline, calico, kitten, *une chatte,* and so on. Further, the tone in which each of these words is articulated, as well as the accompanying words, would affect exactly what was being said by a given statement (and therefore what symbolic action was being accomplished). Similarly, there are many ways to *show* even one particular cat (sleeping, running, from the front, head only, tail only, and so on), in addition to many kinds of cats that can be shown (Siamese cats, toy cats, fat cats, Halloween cats, the Cat in the Hat). Further, there are many manners for showing a cat (a photograph, a sketch, an abstraction, a cartoon, an Impressionist style, a Surrealist style). Finally, there are any number of visual contexts in which to place the cat (angry on a fence at night, sleeping on a sofa, walking on two legs while wearing a tall hat). Thus, the selection of the view of the cat, the type of cat, the visual context, *and* the manner for picturing will affect what is being said in a particular image (and therefore what symbolic action is being accomplished). In each case—verbal or imagistic—the basic operation is rhetoric and the underpinning machinery includes both convention and selectivity.

Implicit in such a model of communication is the provisional nature of the signs. If there is no one image of "cat," but always many potential images, all of which are strictly dependent for their communicative power on the viewer's prior experience with pictures of cats (and not some deeper structure of language), then the statement's persuasive impact (or failure) is utterly situated in a particular moment and audience. This "situatedness" or "provisional" approach to language is completely consistent with the classical roots of rhetoric, as well as being profoundly in tune with its late 20th-century incarnation.

In classical rhetoric, the *public* and *contextual* characteristics of speaking were emphasized, as was the *contingency* of situations. Rhetoric was public in that it affected the entire community and was typically performed before law courts, legislative assemblies, and celebratory gatherings of citizens. The relationship between language and meaning was contextual because the meaning of a particular figure of speech, narrative, or example derived from the particular experiences of a particular audience addressed by a particular speaker at a particular moment. Situations were contingent because their decisions could not be based upon any necessary or certain knowledge. Unlike philosophers who use logic, or scientists who use systematic, empirical and objective investigation, or artists who wish to create works with timeless quality, rhetors rely on probability and they seek timely and fitting action (Lucaites, Condit, & Caudill, 1999).

Contingency is one of the elements that separates rhetoric from other prevailing language theories, including semiotics. With semiotics, messages are made of signs and conveyed through sign systems called codes; meaning is derived to the degree that the receiver of the message understands the (generally arbitrary) code. In rhetoric, on the other hand, meanings are flexible; they depend on the interaction of audience and communicator. Thus, in late 20th-century terms, rhetoric is more clearly aligned with reader response theory and poststructuralism rather than with New Criticism or structuralism or any other essentialist (or formalist) view.

What this "antifoundationalist" theory of communication means for consumer response is extremely important. First, the provisional view of signs (or text) means that no one word or image will be consistently more "effective" than any other—it would depend entirely on the audience and the situation. So research that tries to find the one color or one typeface that is "better" for advertisers to use in all cases and circumstances is, from a rhetorical perspective, doomed to failure. Similarly, cultural criticism that posits either some unseen "system" through which advertisers "manipulate" consumers or that argues for the consistent power of a particular type of appeal (like sex in advertising) is equally misguided. The effectiveness of any appeal would depend *entirely* on the confluence of speaker, audience, product, and history. (For this reason, historical analysis becomes one of the main *methods* of rhetorical inquiry.) Most essential, perhaps, is that the rhetorical view empowers the audience in the conceptualization of communication. A viewer who understands a provisional code that she or he invokes as needed and responds to selectively, according to the situation, is a far more intelligent, active, and resistant viewer than any traditional writing on consumer response allows, particularly where pictures are concerned.

The whole concept of visual rhetoric is grounded in an expanded notion of both pictures and language. This view further relies on a much longer and broader look at the nature and means of human communication. In a rhetorical approach to picturing, the full range and power of visual statements are included, even fiction and quantification (see especially the works of Edward Tufte on quantification and pictures, 1983, 1990, 1997). Nevertheless, a large number of articles cited here are concerned primarily with either declaring that pictures cannot be rhetoric because they are missing some specific property of words or arguing against someone making such a proposition. The issues may be broadly broken into two groups, one in which some presumed inability of pictures is compared to an ability of words and a second group in which some presumed property of mental processing is used to discredit visuals as a mode for rhetoric. The first group of arguments can be itemized as follows:

1. That pictures cannot make arguments, particularly those in which there are both a premise and a conclusion (see Birdsell & Groarke, 1996; Fleming, 1996).

2. That pictures cannot point out the weaknesses in another argument (see Lake & Pickering, 1998).

3. That pictures are not discursive, cannot engage in debate.

The idea that pictures cannot make arguments relies heavily on a standard that is not applied equally to speech or writing. Those taking this position insist that an argument must have two steps, for instance, a premise and a conclusion as in a syllogism. However, there are many examples of arguments and argument types in which one part of the argument is unspoken but understood (especially the "enthymeme"). It seems only reasonable to allow that some parts of an argument might be *unseen* but understood (see Bostdorf, 1987; DeSousa, 1984; DeSousa & Medhurst, 1982; Edwards, 1997; Edwards & Winkler, 1997; Jameison, 1992; Medhurst & DeSousa, 1981; Morris, 1993; Sewell, 1987).

It also seems clear that pictures can, indeed, point out weaknesses in an opposing argument. For instance, in Fig. 2.1, pictures of the residue left after cleaning a stain with Clorox Clean-Up's competitors are used to demonstrate their poorer performance. Here we can see that the pictorial evidence makes a case for the "hero" brand, specifically by showing the weaknesses of the "opponents." This

FIG. 2.1.   Image shows opponent's weakness.

"argument" obviously occurs within a larger discourse about products, benefits, and effectiveness. This direct attack by Clorox may very well elicit a response from Fantastic or Lysol. Either of them might, for instance, play on common consumer fears by showing a picture implying Clorox Clean-Up took not only the stain but also the color out of a household surface. When we consider all the messages among these competitors, a competitive and contentious discourse emerges. The debate does not take place face to face or even all in one place, as in ancient Greece. In a mass communications society, however, few debates of any kind take place at one time and in one location. Even face-to-face debates between political candidates are rare—instead, individual candidates make a series of speeches at various locations that address issues and attack the stances of the absent opponent or produce commercials that do the same thing. No one would argue that a single political speech was not part of a discourse if the opponent were not actually present to answer, nor if the speaker did not explicitly outline a competitor's platform along with his or her own. Indeed, much of contemporary analysis centers upon written and recorded political speech—editorials, political advertising—in which there is no dialogue, strictly speaking. Instead, the discourse is understood to be more pervasive, to occur across time and media (linguistic and visual), and often to be implicit rather than explicit. The same is true for visual, commercial rhetoric—both pictures and words are being used as discursive elements in an ongoing commercial debate.

The second group of objections can be listed as follows:

1. Words are processed sequentially, whereas visuals are processed "all at once" (see Hart, 1997, for discussion).

2. Visuals must be translated into words before they can be understood (Bonsieppe, 1963; Condit, 1990; Meltzoff, 1970; but see also Rosteck, 1994, and Blair, 1996).

Both of these premises are contradicted by what is currently believed in psychology and neuroscience about the mental processing of pictures. As several writers in this book discuss, the nature of thought is not currently believed to be either verbal or visual, but to operate at a more abstract level. And, as Jane Raymond discusses in her chapter of this book, the processing of visual perception, comprehension, and reaction is very much one that occurs "in time" or "sequentially." Further, many ads, the one in Fig. 2.1, for example, are constructed for a viewer who will likely look at the elements in a particular sequence (see also Scott, 1994a, 1994b). Finally, it is unclear why sequential processing should be a necessary element of rhetoric. It has been axiomatic in rhetoric since classical times that the communicated character of the speaker (which is not a linear sequence of signs, but an overall impression constructed of appearance, expression, and posture, as well as word choice and voice tone) is of key importance. Dating to the late 18th century, elaborate elocutionary manuals show all possible hand movements, postures, and facial expressions that might accompany and embellish the delivery of a speech (Kostelnick, 1996). Today the visual rhetoric of face-to-face communication is treated under headings such as *kinesics* (body language) and *proxemics* (study of how speaker distance, posture and touch affect interpersonal communication). Mulvey and Medina in this volume make excellent use of both classical and contemporary rhetoric in their investigation of the way consumers interpret *all these cues* in inferring character from an advertisement. American Sign Language (as well as pictographic writing and other nonalphabetic forms) is expressed (and presumably "processed") sequentially, yet is also a visual medium that includes whole visual words and tonalities communicated through facial expression in addition to "letters." Indeed, it is helpful to remember that alphabetic writing is, after all, *speech made visible* and thus can itself be considered a visual form. With these examples in mind, the very idea that persuasion can only occur through sequentially decoded signs seems like a case of grasping at straws—and thus throws the alphabetic bias of the writers into high relief.

The first articles about visual rhetoric that turned up in this search were written by Bonsieppe in 1963 and 1965. Since then, arguments for a visual rhetoric have been advanced by Allen (1996), Barton and Barton (1985), Bernhardt (1986, 1996), Kostelnick (1989, 1990, 1994, 1996), Robinson and Schraw (1994), Tebeaux (1988, 1991), Tovey (1996), Twigg (1992), and Varga (1989). Other critics have applied rhetoric as an interpretive strategy to various visual artifacts, such as book illustrations (Brizuela, 1998), logotypes (deCosio, 1998), theater posters (Ehses, 1989), Mexican currency (Salazar, 1998), and stamps (Tapia, 1998). Like many studies that draw on semiotic and rhetorical theories, these articles provide a systematic and nuanced analysis of messages, but they *assume* that various visual and verbal elements convey meanings and they *assume* the effects of the messages.

THE RHETORIC OF THE OBJECT

Objects themselves participate in rhetoric through their design and the circumstances of their use. Design reflects the intended application and, sometimes, the objects that will be used in connection with the same practice, as well as cultural aesthetics. Circumstances of use affect the associations members of the culture connect with the object—whether it is appropriate for a holiday occasion, whether it is a "status symbol," and so on. In every case, the overriding influence of culture and history are crucial in giving the object rhetorical power.

Let's begin by considering the rhetorical implications of a simple object's appearance. Buchanan (1989), for instance, wrote about spoons in the common building block terms of rhetoric: "logos" or logic, "pathos" or emotion," and "ethos" or ethics/character. All spoons, he argued, have the same mechanical logic (logos) although they may be made of different materials and have different shapes. Some spoons are "traditional" in design and material, whereas others are "unconventional" or "contemporary." Buchanan presumed that the design of the spoon is the basis for an emotional response (pathos) to the object. Spoons, which also have a decoration value and can match the elegance or plainness of the social occasion, can even communicate subtle moral values (ethos).

Remember, however, that spoons are a relatively recent invention in Western culture; the typical American family owned few until after the Industrial Age made mass-produced eating utensils affordable, and spoons still are not used by most people in the world today (more of the global population uses either fingers or chopsticks). So the very existence of a spoon is not only culture bound, but carries associations with certain types of food, dishes, circumstances, and even economics and power. The styles of spoon—traditional, contemporary, or whatever—point directly to other formal styles in the culture from architecture to music (there are spoons in "classical" styles and "baroque" styles, for instance). The rhetoric of a spoon is fully intelligible only to the citizens of the culture (or knowledgeable others) in which it appears and is used. To one who had no past connection to Western culture whatsoever (and therefore no spoon experience), the meaningful subtleties would be absent—even the "mechanical logic" might not be readily apparent to the uninitiated. (We are reminded here of the amusing scene in Disney's "The Little Mermaid," in which the heroine and her friend speculate on the uses of objects retrieved from the land culture, including a fork, which they surmise is used to comb hair.) Therefore, to argue that the rhetoric of a spoon inheres solely in the object itself would be naive. If, however, we take the total of all these factors into account when explaining the appearance of a particular spoon in a table setting or advertisement, we would be performing a rhetorical analysis of a material object (for other examples, see Blair, 1999; Blair, Jeppeson, & Pucci, 1991; Blair & Michel, 1999; Ehrenhaus, 1988; Foss, 1986; Gallagher, 1995; Haines, 1986).

The symbolic anthropology of Clifford Geertz, which is based squarely on Burkeian rhetoric and which dramatically affected the study of culture in the late 20th century (Geertz, 1973), offers an important foundation for this kind of research. Geertz expanded the notion of rhetoric to include the objects and practices of culture. In his approach, the entire material world, its objects and its practices, is a vast web of symbolic meaning in which humans are inextricably enmeshed. Understanding the meaning behind any cultural setting or habit thus requires a deep, rich analysis and a thick form of description that may include elements from religion to economics to art to genealogy. The web of meaning is collectively spun and shared. Thus, understanding the meaning of an object (or image) created by a particular designer (or artist) is a function of shared cultural experience:

> The artist works with his audience's capacities—capacities to see, or hear, or touch, sometimes even to taste and smell, with understanding. And though elements of these capacites are indeed innate—it usually helps not to be color-blind—they are brought into actual existence by the experience of living in the midst of certain sorts of things to looks at, listen to, handle, think about, cope with, and react to; particular varieties of cabbages, particular sorts of kings. Art and the equipment to grasp it are made in the same shop. (Geertz, 1983, p. 118)

The advertisement in Fig. 2.2 provides a good point of entry to see how complex these meanings are. Here the picture of a spoon with precious gems in its bowl is paired with a headline that alludes to jewelry as well as table decoration, "The perfect setting." Traditionally in American culture, spoons are made of silver, although many, including this one, are made of other materials (plastic, wood, stainless steel). The allusion to jewelry can be fully assembled only by someone who knows that spoons are often made with a material that is also commonly used to set gems. The connection is further underpinned by the fact that many jewelers, such as Tiffany's, also sell silverware (there is a note about Stern Jewellers in the lower

The perfect setting.

ONEIDA

Shown: Cityscape pattern in stainless.

Emeralds courtesy of H. Stern Jewelers

FIG. 2.2.   The rhetoric of a simple object.

right-hand corner). The background here, a classic drape of silk or satin, alludes further to jewelry display cases—although it is also a common background for silverware ads, particularly Oneida. So the allusion this ad makes to jewelry, although its rhetorical intent is obviously to glorify the spoon through the comparison, is also likely to be seen as "appropriate" by viewers because of the common cultural links between jewelry and table settings in material experience. Silverware is often acquired as a wedding gift, and therefore ads for spoons appear frequently in bridal magazines, alongside numerous ads for diamond rings. The rhetoric associated with ads for both products oscillates between positioning the purchase as a personal expression and as a symptom of once-in-a-lifetime commitment (spoons, like diamonds, are "forever" in this discourse). Towle, for instance, uses the slogan "Enjoy it for life," and offers patterns with names like "Chippendale," "French Provincial," "Old Master," and "Queen Elizabeth I"—which obviously can only be "decoded" with cultural knowledge including history, art, or furniture. The body copy encourages the couple to pick a pattern that is "truly yours," but also promises never to discontinue a pattern because all Towle patterns are "virtually timeless." Couples choose "their" pattern of silver and list it, along with many other choices of household goods, in a registry that publicly communicates to wedding guests what "their" style, color, and expected budget for housekeeping will be like. Guests, in turn, will select from the list gifts that implicitly represent the nature and closeness of their relationship to the couple, as well as their own status (wealthy guests might be expected to give larger gifts, but so will close family members and friends). There are ads aimed at the guests, too. For instance, Lenox uses a headline, "Gifts that reflect more," and exhorts the buyer that this brand of tableware is "an enduring wish for their happiness that feels as good to give as it does to receive." Ultimately, the collection of household items given will equip the couple not just to feed themselves, but to participate in a lifelong discourse of food, in which the importance of a dinner guest or occasion is often shown by "getting out the good silver." In sum, we can see that one representation of a spoon is embedded in an elaborate web of practices from eating to jewelry-making to selling to marriage— and then some. The advertising discourse alone would include a broad range of products and services, including not only jewelry, but china and bridal registry services.

Many of the commercial practices discussed in this book are directly involved in spinning the webs of meaning that situate concrete objects and the practices of their use. Thus, there is no way to analyze the "effects" of, for instance, an advertisement, without including the product's "situatedness" in the work of material culture. In this way, the discourse about objects—which, in the case of spoons, would range from private dinner parties to state dinners, from advertisements to department store displays and so on—can be seen clearly (and the objections of purists about the venues of rhetoric refuted).

Spoons and jewels, particularly in attractive ads, could be said to be making an argument based on "beauty." Some say beauty in objects is itself a nonpropositional argument. For example, if the beauty of a painting serves to challenge the viewer's perceptions and experiences, it presents an alternative perspective on some fact of the viewer's existence. The argumentative function of beauty thus lies in its offer to reconceptualize the viewer's everyday existence (Chase, 1990). This concept of beauty differs from that of Bouse (1990), who argues that very beautiful images are enough in themselves to engender sympathy for an endangered species or wilderness and to mobilize the public in support of its preservation. In this case, we might argue that beauty is not an argument itself but is subordinate to other arguments being made on behalf of the environment. Although it is difficult to see the beauty in Fig. 2.3 because of the lack of color, each creature's eye is presented close up and in striking hues, creating a series of beautiful images (note the effect of selectivity here). Yet the final image, the child's eye, is not only beautiful, but presents an argument, too. By ending the string of pictures with the child, the ad emphasizes the elements of sameness among these creatures, as well as their interconnectedness in terms of ecology (and clearly assumes a sequential viewing strategy). So, again, we would argue that the rhetorical value of "beauty" is a matter of situation—of what appears, how it appears, why it appears—just as in any other matter of persuasion.

The art director planned the layout for this environmental ad just like a designer who must create a product for a particular functional or aesthetic purpose. We can be sure that he or she did so as a strategy for dealing with a specific situation. Burke proposed that we view all texts as strategies for dealing with situations, and thus argues that the element of *motive* is the crucial element to determine (1950, pp. 296–297). (That's why Burke's two most famous works are called *The Grammar of Motives* and *The Rhetoric of Motives*.) Following Burke, Michael Baxandall (1985) revolutionized art criticism by insisting on treating painting (and other artworks) as solutions to particular, concrete problems. The "problems" involve everything from building a bridge in a particular location to creating a object for prayerful contemplation to painting a canvas that will meet the market for art. He emphasizes that the artist acts intentionally as a social being in certain cultural circumstances, and that the final outcome would be a function of many factors including "reassurance, irritation, ideas, roles, heredities, skills and coin" (p. 73). Further, Baxandall demonstrates the interaction that creates broader conventions of representation. For instance, he shows how patronage on the one hand, and viewer expectations on the other, combined to make of painting a socially shared system of conventions in the 15th century. The use of contractually prescribed amounts of aquamarine or gold leaf contributed to the color composition or religious iconography of a painting, but it also sent clear social messages concerning the identity and position of the patron commissioning the work. Because the paintings essentially served as social announcements or advertisements for the success and power of benefactors, the selection of materials and imagery must be interpreted with that social context in mind. The same is no less true for today's advertisements and material objects. To the extent that material symbols are *sermonic*—meaning

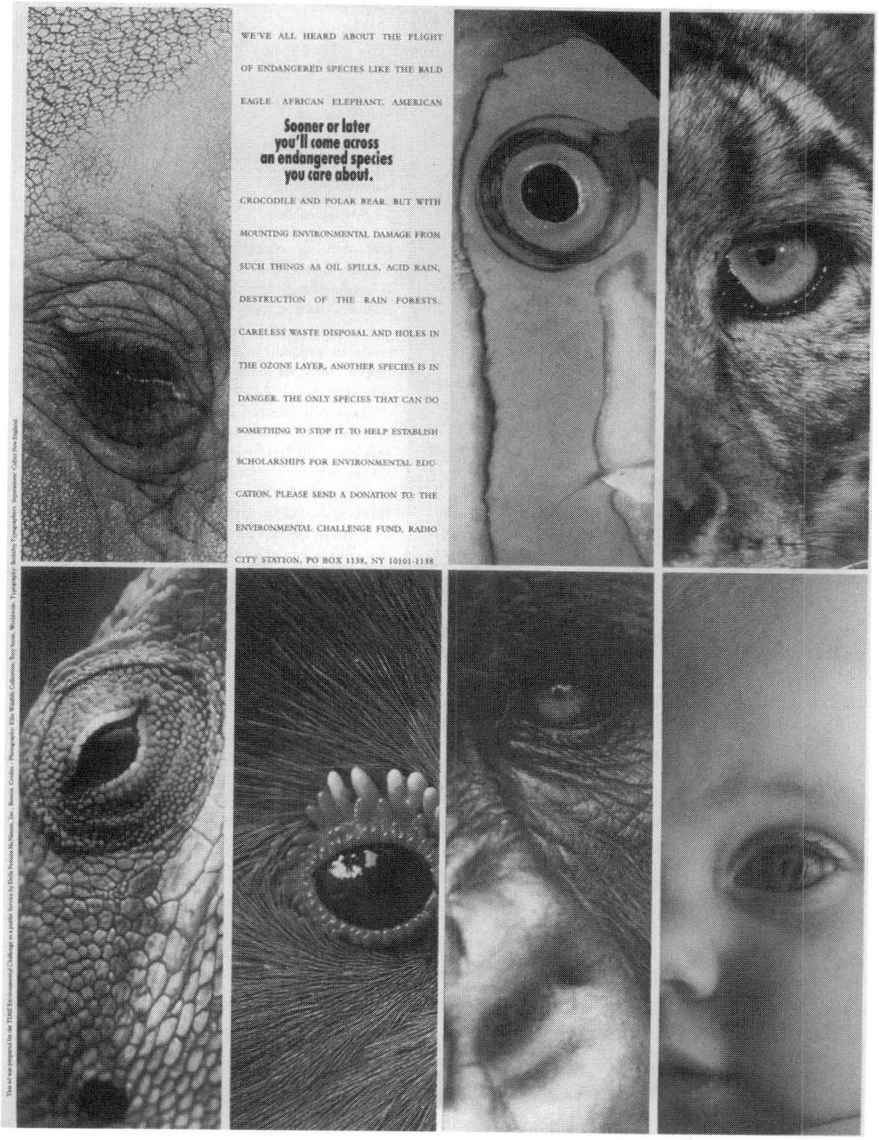
WE'VE ALL HEARD ABOUT THE PLIGHT OF ENDANGERED SPECIES LIKE THE BALD EAGLE, AFRICAN ELEPHANT, AMERICAN
Sooner or later you'll come across an endangered species you care about.
CROCODILE AND POLAR BEAR. BUT WITH MOUNTING ENVIRONMENTAL DAMAGE FROM SUCH THINGS AS OIL SPILLS, ACID RAIN, DESTRUCTION OF THE RAIN FORESTS, CARELESS WASTE DISPOSAL AND HOLES IN THE OZONE LAYER, ANOTHER SPECIES IS IN DANGER. THE ONLY SPECIES THAT CAN DO SOMETHING TO STOP IT. TO HELP ESTABLISH SCHOLARSHIPS FOR ENVIRONMENTAL EDUCATION, PLEASE SEND A DONATION TO: THE ENVIRONMENTAL CHALLENGE FUND, RADIO CITY STATION, PO BOX 1138, NY 10101-1138.

FIG. 2.3. Sequential argumentation with "beauty" as a vehicle.

they exhibit an attitude and encourage certain acts—the construction of a build-ing or design of a product also becomes an act of rhetoric (Weaver, 1970; see also Foss, 1982).

In the next section, we outline briefly three different schools of rhetorical thought as they would be applied to a particular subject of interpretation. We first begin, however, with some basic issues of formal analysis, because all rhetorical criticism (like any other type of criticism) depends in the first moment on formal competence.

RHETORICAL ANALYSIS

Basic Principles

A full-blown exercise in rhetorical criticism involves formal description, analysis of historical context, interpretation from a particular critical perspective, and evalu-ation from that perspective (see Campbell & Burkholder, 1997). Often, however, critics concentrate on describing a particular example in formal terms, either by discussing some stylistic aspect (such as metaphor) or attempting to categorize according to form (as in genre criticism). Several have focused on formal interpre-tation of ads (see Scott, 1994b), and some have worked on rhetorical criticism of films and other visual artifacts in formal terms (Benson, 1974a, 1974b, 1980, 1985; Benson & Anderson, 1984; Medhurst, 1993; Medhurst & Benson, 1981; Rosteck, 1994). The basic distinction between a rhetorical approach and a traditional for-malist one is probably the attention given to intent and effect. For instance, in Fig. 2.4, Italian shoes are shown situated among various tools and products of Ital-ian architecture. The verbal statement in itself, "Shoes From Italy," provides little clue as to the intent. However, the visual juxtaposition of a shoe with the accou-trements of a craft at which Italians have excelled for centuries presents a pictorial statement saying something like "Italian shoes are like Italian architecture." Identi-fying the image as a *trope* (which is simply rhetorical terminology for "metaphor," often defined as "a figure of thought") and perhaps going further to categorize the trope as a *metonymy* (in which juxtaposition alone points to similarities) would be typical formalist techniques. We might even break down the trope into a meta-phor's traditional parts by saying that the "tenor" is a shoe, whereas the "vehicle" is Italian architecture (and its accoutrements) (Richards, 1936, 1938). If we were to stop here, our analysis would be rhetorical only in terminology—it is essentially a formalist exercise. If, however, we go on only far enough to say that the intent appears to be to persuade the viewer to think of Italian shoes as another instance of Italian excellence, then we have stepped over into rhetoric. And if we were to look at other ads in the same campaign—in which the shoe appears with props and scores for opera, for instance—to further document the intent, then we would be well out of the territory of formalism and into the realm of rhetoric.

FIG. 2.4.   Use of metonymy; demonstration of tenor and vehicle.

The next step in a rhetorical analysis would be to document the situation that led to the design and placement of the ad. Finally, the effect might be demonstrated by looking for some evidence of outcome. The evaluation would depend on the perspective of the critic. If what is at stake is shoe sales, then the ad might be evaluated based on how many were sold. If, however, the critic is interested in a more political objective, he or she might concentrate on the way that the ad foregrounds Western cultural imperialism. Importantly, a complete rhetorical analysis would include some attempt to gauge an actual effect of some sort—yet most of the work reviewed here does not go that distance, being content merely to speculate about the actual response. Important exceptions include the work of Edward McQuarrie and David Mick, as well as Barbara Phillips (see their essays in this book), who have demonstrated that tropes are forceful additions when included in visual advertisements. The essays by Phillips and by Wiggins and Miller in this book discuss the question of visual metaphors further, including the tenor/vehicle and verbal/visual issues.

Even in rhetoric, however, formal analysis is important. It is attention to form that teaches us to search out systems of cues or structures for guiding meaningfulness. Further, because form itself is socially learned and hence represents conventionalized patterns for thought, formal analysis helps us to infer what is considered persuasive by a particular culture at a particular time (Gronbeck, 1976, 1978).

Classical rhetors catalogued various figures of speech to be used in formal analysis. Examples include rhyme, alliteration, antithesis, hyperbole, metonym, metaphor, pun, irony, and paradox. Bonsieppe (1963) believed that verbal figures have visual equivalents, and he identified many visual equivalents in various advertisements. Similar work was conducted by Jacques Durand (1987), who first classified verbal figures according to two criteria: "rhetorical operations" (addition, suppression, substitution and exchange) and "relation between the variable elements" (identity, similarity, difference and opposition). The resulting two-dimensional grid was used to categorize 30 different figures of speech. Durand then collected various magazine advertisements and succeeded in finding visual equivalents for all 30 figures. Metaphorical analysis of films occurs in Mechling and Mechling (1995) and Medhurst (1982, 1993). Similar work on political ads appears in Larson (1972, 1982) (see also Hart, Jerome, & McComb, 1984; Jamieson, 1984; Larson, 1972; Price & Lattin, 1988, as well as Kaplan, 1990, and Kennedy, 1982). Bostdorf (1987) analyzed political cartoons.

Historical–contextual analysis of the relationship between a visual and its context is conducted in order to identify the forces that contribute to, or work against, a visual's purpose. One consults external sources in search of information about the rhetor, the audiences exposed to the visual, and the persuasive forces, including other rhetorical messages, operating on the visual. Only then can critics begin to determine why the rhetor made particular artistic and strategic choices when creating the visual. The following articles include particularly good examples of the descriptive and historical stages of criticism: Thomas Benson's analysis of films (1974b, 1978, 1980, 1985); Carole Blair's analysis of memorials (1999; Blair et al., 1991; Blair & Michel, 1999); and Olson's studies of commemorative medals (1983, 1990). Dickson (1999) also provided an excellent historical–contextual analysis of the photograph of a nude, pregnant Demi Moore for *Vanity Fair*.

For commercial texts, Linda Scott's interpretation of Apple's "1984" commercial (1991) provides an example of historical–contextual analysis employed for rhetorical purpose. Here the "situation" of computer technology in 1984 is covered, along with the role played by IBM, the public persona of Steve Jobs, the media power of the Superbowl, and other issues. We might also note that the physical design of the original Macintosh, including the look of its revolutionary desktop interface, was itself an important rhetorical statement whose force would be evident only in the context of other cabinets, other screens seen at the time. Clearly, this rhetorical attitude has continued past the adoption of the Mac interface by IBM clones with the design of the candy-colored iMac.

Even architecture has become a fertile area for rhetorical analysis (Altman, 1980; Hattenhauer, 1984; Parker & Hildebrandt, 1986; Stuart, 1973). Jonathan Schroeder in this book discusses the rhetorical power of classical architecture in bank marketing.

The fourth stage of criticism is to evaluate the persuasive appeals. According to Campbell and Burkholder (1997), four basic standards of criteria are available for evaluation of rhetorical action. The *effects* criterion evaluates a message's success in achieving a goal. The *truth* criterion evaluates a message's success in accurately and fully presenting problems and carefully assessing the probably effects of proposed solutions. The *ethical* criterion weighs the impact of the values espoused by a message. The *artistic* criterion assesses the role of aesthetic form on a message's symbolic force. Most of the visual rhetoric articles used a combination of several criteria to evaluate particular films, paintings, cartoons and memorials.

These basic steps would be important to any particular rhetorical analysis. Beyond these basic principles, however, there are specific theoretical orientations that affect the techniques, language, and purpose of study. The next section explains the classical approach to rhetorical criticism, followed by some brief examples of Burkeian work, and then the "critical" perspective.

Classical

Relatively unchanged for thousands of years, classical criticism is strongly formal in its approach, working often with its numerous categories and arcane terminology. When neo-classical critics study visual forms of communication, they often adapt the five canons of rhetoric: invention, arrangement, style, delivery, and memory. The first four standards for measuring the quality of a speaker come from Aristotle's *Rhetoric*. They include the construction of an argument (invention), ordering of material (arrangement), selection of language (style), and techniques of delivery. Later, the standard of "memory" was added to the list of skills needed by great speakers.

Sometimes contemporary analysts eliminate or combine some of the canons, particularly when working with pictures. For instance, the importance of memory is considerably less relevant in a mass communications context where it is not necessary for the "speaker" to remember the argument. Instead, the "speech" is merely reproduced, sometimes repeatedly. In a visual context, the elements of style and delivery are largely redundant and are, therefore, often combined (see Scott, 1994a, and Medhurst & DeSousa, 1981).

In addition to the canons, neo-classical critics also use classical modes of proof mentioned above: *logos* or rational argument, *pathos* or audience adaptation and/or creating a state of mind or feeling, and *ethos* or the means by which rhetors make themselves seem worthy of belief. The stain removal demonstration in Fig. 2.1 is an example of *logos*. The 1984 Macintosh commercial is an example of *pathos*. Figure 2.5 is an example of *ethos*. By comparing the use of Teflon in a frying pan to its use on the Statue of Liberty—done visually *and* verbally—DuPont can position itself as worthy of trust, a supporter of freedom. Note, however, that this ad appeared in October 2001, but would have been produced several months earlier in order to make that publication date. The probable impact of this ad *after* the September 11 attacks, however, was probably different than what one would have predicted *before* the attacks, when the ad was made. After 9/11,

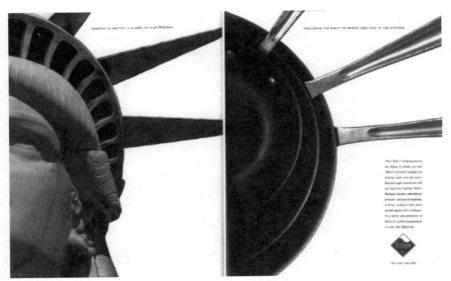

FIG. 2.5.   Demonstration of ethos, formal scheme, and historical effects.

patriotic appeals were everywhere and even images that would have seemed shrilly
nationalistic only days before were suddenly seen as inspiring. Thus, we have here
a very clear example of how much the *actual effectiveness* of a persuasive appeal
depends on *historical circumstances.* Here, too, is an example of the function of
form, as defined by Burke, and of scheme, as studied by McQuarrie and Mick.
Burke described form as "an arousing and fulfillment of desires. A work has form
insofar as one part of it leads a reader to anticipate another part, to be gratified by
the sequence" (1931, p. 124). Here the selective framing of the Statue of Liberty,
followed by an analogous frame for the pans, not only points to the argument, but
provides a formal scheme in which the first part anticipates the second (see also
Lancioni, 1996).

Critics also categorize rhetorical acts into the classical genres explained by Aristotle: deliberative, forensic, and epideictic. *Deliberative* rhetoric was political
speech, and rhetors urged their audiences to accept or reject a proposed policy or
course of action. *Forensic* rhetoric was delivered in law courts and consisted of
debates or arguments. *Epideictic* rhetoric took place on ceremonial occasions, such
as birthday dinners, funerals, or wedding ceremonies, and it served to celebrate
values, to glorify and promote.

Two examples of deliberative rhetoric in this literature search concern how
videos argue for and against the policy of abortion. Stormer's (1997) basic point is
that by showing a video of reproduction via the naturalistic and objective perspectives of biology and medicine, and without any social context, *The Miracle of Life*

is a pro-life film that rhetorically argues against abortion. Condit (1990, 1991) believed that visual images have been translated into public arguments via visual figures of speech. An example concerns synecdoche, where a part is used to stand for the whole. Pro-Life rhetors show a photograph of the tiny feet of a 10-week-old fetus held between two adult fingers, essentially a synecdoche for the entire fetus. Condit explains that an accurate, full picture of a young fetus includes features not associated with adult humans, as well as several unsightly features that could be considered "negatives." Fetal feet, however, closely resemble baby feet and we synecdochally expand the image to see a full baby. Other examples of deliberative rhetoric of visuals include Farnsworth and Crismore (1991), Kessler (1993), Moser (1992, 1996), Netzhammer (1999), and Shelley (1996).

The Benetton ad in Fig. 2.6 is a commercial example. Here the use of hearts, all the same, but labeled "black," "yellow," and "white," argues for the arbitrariness of racial labels when humans are the same "inside." For more on the Benetton campaign, see Blair (1996).

Forensic rhetoric consists of the kinds of evidence and argumentation typical of a courtroom. In the case of visuals, of course, the photograph or video is often taken as evidence of the truth of actual events. Few evidentiary tools surpass the testimony of an eyewitness. In advertising, we have many similar forms. For instance, the Clorox stain removal ad described earlier is a recent example in a long line of product "demos" in both print and television. Another staple is the "real person" testimonial, in which an ordinary citizen tells (and preferably shows) the superior results achieved by using the product. We might see wash done with Clorox bleach shown snowy white, for instance, while the unbleached load "looks dingy and dirty." Or we might see "before and after" shots of a person who successfully used a weight reduction scheme. Both of these are similar to forensic tactics.

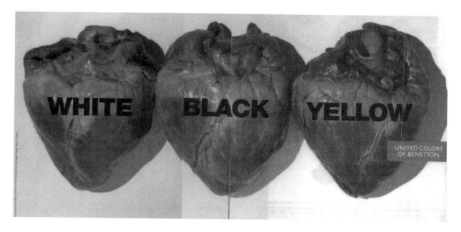

FIG. 2.6. Synecdoche used to demonstrate human "sameness" despite racial difference.

Epideictic rhetoric tries to move audiences by unifying them around a common set of values that everyone is presumed to share. These myths, clichés, and commonplaces are perceived to represent truths rather than to be facts or propositions in a linear argument. When epideictic rhetoric has been successful, strategic pictures linger in the collective memory of audiences as representative of their subjects (Osborn, 1986). An example is Fig. 2.7, in which a photograph evoking the jubilation at the end of World War II is used again in the late 1990s to sell Mumm's champagne (see also Olsen, 1983, for an interpretation of another image from the same period). We can see in this example that the epideictic rhetor, instead of trying to persuade listeners with the power of cold logic, tried instead to charm the audience.

The goal in epideictic rhetoric is to create goodwill, jubilation, and generosity of spirit. In elation, classical rhetors were seized with a desire to bear witness and to share with their community their own wonder-at-what-is (Rosenfield, 1989; see also Cook on "rapture," 1989). Although we don't normally think of advertisements as dealing with that level of community spirit, the campaign produced by the Ad Council in the aftermath of September 11 provides a perfect example. In this spot, a sequence of shots shows various people saying the same phrase, "I am an American," one after another. Importantly, however, the appearance of the people themselves, their accents, and their surroundings evoke a multicultural notion of what an American is: These are people who clearly represent a broad range of ethnic descent, as well as people of different ages and folks from different geographic areas, including recent immigrants. Thus, a statement ("I am an American") that, by itself, could have been interpreted as aggressive nationalism—and therefore rather chauvinistic and exclusionary in spirit—is instead turned into an anthem of inclusion. Note that this happens primarily by virtue of the visual accompaniment.

Burkean Rhetoric

The basic building blocks of Burke's rhetoric have already been covered. Essentially, we are talking about a view of all symbolic communication as propelled by some strategic imperative, or "motive." Thus, all messages—of whatever kind or medium or form—become "symbolic actions" in which someone tries to accomplish something. In the work of Burke, the reading of literature (or any message) is also reinterpreted in an active way. Burke argued that we use the stories we read as "equipment for living," and that therefore literature should be analyzed and evaluated in sociological terms. To the extent that viewers look at ads as a basis for acting (to buy something, wear something, give something, display something), then commercial messages, too, are "equipment for living" (Burke, 1967). Mick and Buhl (1992) and Scott (1994b) both looked at the reader's response to advertisements from this more active point of view.

In order to discover a speaker's motives, and to determine the view of reality being advocated, Burke (1945) recommended using the pentad of "act," "scene,"

FIG. 2.7.   Epideictic strategy recaptures a moment of communal jubilation.

"agent," "agency" and "purpose." These concepts, which come from drama, appear often in the literature we searched (for instance, Hendrix & Wood, 1973) and also in this book (see the chapter by Lambiase and Reichert). Rutledge (1994) provided an extended example of dramatistic criticism in her analysis of three advertisements.

Both the insight that we are symbol-using animals and the importance of the drama in Burke's thought point to the fact that humans are also storytelling animals. Some have argued (such as Fisher, 1984) that all forms of communication are fundamentally narrative (but see Scott, 1995). A few have attempted to apply the paradigm of the narrative to visual images. Condit (1987), for example, wrote that both visual images and narratives are ways to put a face on abstract values; they help a community to structure symbolic experience meaningfully. Images may either replace narratives, she wrote, or summarize narratives visually (p. 81). Ehrenhaus (1988) used narrative theory to explain how people respond to memorials such as the Vietnam Veterans Memorial. Jamieson (1988) used narrative to explain how Ronald Reagan created an identity for an audience, to involve the audience, and to bind that audience to him (p. 4). Sewell (1987), Edwards (1997), and Turner (1977) all used narratives to explain the persuasive power of editorial cartoons. Gronbeck (1992) examined presidential campaign advertisements as stories.

There are clearly narrative television commercials, with the time-worn "slice of life" being the most salient genre. There are also many print ads with narrative properties. The ad might have a "key frame" that implies a story or, in some cases, the copy block will tell the story. It is also common for the image to call to mind a well-known story, such as the image evoking "The Ugly Duckling" in Fig. 2.8.

Other streams of criticism with different names, such as "fantasy theme criticism," are essentially narrative criticism and often make similar claims for the sense-making, community-invoking, values-reinforcing power of stories (Bormann, 1972, 1982, 1985; Hattenhauer, 1984; Turner, 1977). Osborn (1990) believed that myths are a special kind of narrative. "In myth there is a story, the story must seem the answer to some compelling question, the dramatis personae must seem larger-than-life, and the story must convey the sense of the sacred in time, place, and symbol" (p. 21). Osborn believed two epideictic qualities are especially necessary for myths to function: "identification," which establishes a vital, serious contact between audience and story, and "magnification," which enlarges all narrative elements so that the story seems on scale with the large question it addresses. Myths have long been used by rhetorical analysts to explicate the persuasive power of cinematic and televisual narratives, but an especially good example—in this case the Adamic myth—appears in Medhurst's (1993) analysis of Oliver Stone's movie *JFK*. Myths may be "triggered" by archetypal symbols or visual clichés. In her study of political campaign films, Morreale (1991a, 1991b) showed how visual clichés can evoke myths, and those myths not only help us make sense of a film, but they also have a cumulative impact on our construction of reality.

Another popular concept from Burke is the idea of "identification," in which a speaker invites the audience to identify with him or her as a means of persuasion.

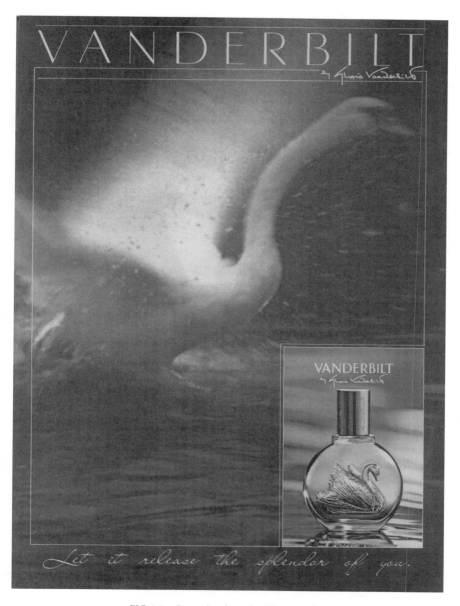

FIG. 2.8. Image invokes a familiar narrative.

This concept is particularly important for consumer culture because of the corollary idea of the "identifying nature of property." It is commonplace in advertising practice to use spokespersons, musical styles, clothing, characters, and other cues selected that the target audience will "identify with." In turn, consumers, using ads as "equipment for living," may come to use a certain product as a way of identifying themselves with a particular group or worldview. The strong identity of Mac users, often commented on by people from cultural critics to stock analysts, is a good example of this phenomenon. The ad in Fig. 2.9 is another instance—the shoes are "identified" here with liberal, unorthodox views. Presumably the woman pictured bought the shoes to express a shift in worldview (or, improbably, the shoes changed her opinions).

As a means of analyzing texts sociologically, Burke recommended the procedure of gathering recurring metaphors, symbols, motifs, and so on, in search of a clustering pattern. To conduct a cluster analysis, first one selects the important elements used in the visual message. Then one identifies what clusters around each key term each time it appears in the visual. The clusters are interpreted to reveal what potential messages are being presented by the communicator. Finally the interpretations are examined as a whole to determine an overall interpretation of the visual and a possible explanation of the communicator's motive (Reid, 1990). "By isolating a rhetor's range of metaphors and comparing them with other habitual rhetorical behaviors, critics can minimize the likelihood that they are generalizing from aberrant rhetorical cues" (Jameson, 1992, p. 70). Reid (1993) and Medhurst (1978) used cluster analysis to learn about a communicator's motive for creating the work. Because products are so strongly embedded in culture and history, there are often clusters of images that consistently revolve around them. For instance, we often see flowers, exotic places, birds, and fans in perfume ads, the vestiges of thousand of years of expressing not only the sources for ingredients, but the "airborne" nature of scent.

A rhetorical genre, Hart (1976) wrote, is that which delimits similar rhetorical responses made by similar speakers to similar audiences bound by similar relational constraints in similar speech settings. By studying genres, we can make generalizations that will lead to theory building, which Hart advocates over the case study approach of most rhetorical criticism. Benson (1980) agreed that genre criticism can help to combat the fallacious notion of the work of art as singular and independent (p. 246). Instead, we respond to works of art depending, in part, on what sort of a work we take it to be. Benson wrote: "A rhetorical approach to genre is interested not only in the formal requirements of the genre considered as a historical or stylistic matter, and not only in the constraints that generic situations impose upon authors, but also in the experience of an audience, and the way in which genre constitutes the context within which a work can be apprehended" (p. 247). The possibility for studying genres of visual media seems worthwhile, and similar studies have been conducted from other traditions, but only a few examples appear in the visual rhetoric literature. Doughty (1993), for example, commented

FIG. 2.9.   Identification and property.

upon the social documentary genre, in which pictures are presented to viewers as if they were mirrors of reality or purely mechanical recordings of what appeared before the camera's lens. The genre implies messages are not constructed but rather are unmediated artifacts that "presented themselves" (p. 7).

Some visual communicators, however, may intentionally avoid the conventions of a genre. Foss (1993), for example, believed visual images have appeal because they don't fit a genre. She explained that when a novel technical aspect of an image violates viewers' expectations, then this violation functions both to sustain interest in the image and to decontextualize it. Connotations commonly associated with the technical aspect then provide an unexpected but familiar context in which to interpret the image. The result is an arousal of interest in the image and an assignment of a new, perhaps more positive, evaluation to the image.

Although Aristotle's concept of rhetoric as persuasion seems to rely on an early basic model of communication as a linear, one-way process from source to destination for purposes of control, Burke's rhetoric seems closer to a ritual model of communication. According to James Carey, "Communication is linked to such terms as sharing, participation, association, fellowship and the possession of a common faith. . . . A ritual view is not directed towards the extension of messages in space, but the maintenance of society in time; not the act of importing information but the representation of shared beliefs" (1975, p. 18). As we saw in our brief excursion into the discourse of spoons, ritual often plays heavily in the communication of objects. Otnes and Scott (1994) discussed the ritual nature of advertising.

"CRITICAL" ANALYSIS

We employ the convention of quotation marks when we mention the "critical" rhetorical approach to call attention to a misnomer. All schools of literary analysis—formalist, structuralist, poststructuralist, rhetorical, mythic, and so on—are "critical" in that they involve close, rigorous, skeptical analysis for the purpose of producing "criticism." In the last half of the 20th century, the term *critical* was coopted in literary and cultural studies to denote a type of analysis with a particular political perspective. Variously dubbed "Marxist," "Marxian," "neomarxist," "feminist," and so on, this type of criticism borrows heavily from the theories of Karl Marx and the "Critical Theory" developed by the Frankfurt School and later followers such as the Birmingham School. This political perspective has become de rigueur in media studies, effectively undermining the use of the term *critical* as it had more commonly been used. Rather than continue to use quotation marks or merely to use the generic term, we specify this politically oriented approach with a capital letter, *Critical*.

In the Critical perspective, the analysis is undertaken for the purpose of exposing something about the power structure of the society. Thus, it is closely reliant on the concept of "ideology." In the tradition of Marx, "ideology" is a representation of a false belief that supports the power structure, but has become so pervasive and naturalized that it is no longer visible to the populace for what it is. Definition of the term *ideology* and, especially, its relationship to images has been quite problematic (Mitchell, 1986). Nevertheless, it is an important concept, particularly for artifacts related to capitalism, most notably advertising.

McGee (1980), for instance, defined ideology as a political language with the capacity to dictate decisions and control public belief and actions. He argued that "ideographs" are the building blocks of political language, specific to cultures that have evolved gradually. Examples of ideographs are concepts such as liberty, equality, property, and religion. In examining political discourse, wrote McGee, critics can identify ideographs, trace their development over time, and analyze the ways in which they clash with each other. Ideographs, in his view, exist at the juncture between the objective reality of the human environment and the social reality projected in rhetorical discourse. Williams, on the other hand, wrote that ideology is "a structure of inter-related arguments which, if taken as a 'screen' through which to view the world, not only makes the world coherent, but also tends to place the individual in relation to the world" (1987, p. 300). Ideographs, as one-term summations of an ideology, cannot serve as ideologies, but can "re-present" ideologies. Called "ideological analogons," such visual images stand in a synecdochic relationship with a formal ideology. For example, in the propaganda film *The Wandering Jew*, the visuals are the "part" that stood for the "whole" racist ideology that Jews are not human beings.

In Fig. 2.10, we can see an advertising example that may help illustrate. We might infer that the turnovers attached to the thighs and the phrase "respect yourself in the morning" are both ideographs grounded in the ideology that renders women second-class citizens. Two components of that ideology, the one that demands physical beauty (in this case, slenderness) and the one that demands chastity, are fused into a single message and used to motivate purchase of a breakfast food.

Osborn's (1986) concept of "depictive rhetoric" seems quite similar to ideological analogons or visual ideographs. He defines "depiction" as verbal or nonverbal visualizations that have been compressed and that linger in the collective memory of audiences. Depiction, wrote Osborn, is "a key to synchronic, multiple, simultaneous meanings in rhetoric, just as enthymeme is the elemental model for diachronic or linear demonstrations" (p. 80). Osborn (1986) outlined five functions for depiction. The first, "presentation," is broken down into repetitive and innovative symbols. Repetitive symbols grounded in a particular culture are called "culturetypes," whereas repetitive symbols with timeless and cross-cultural power are called archetypal symbols. The second function of depiction is "intensification of feeling." Metaphors, synecdoches, and juxtaposition in montages, for example, can provoke and arouse an audience by allowing us to transfer feelings to a subject.

FIG. 2.10.   Two ideographs fused in a single message.

The third function is to facilitate "identification," or a sense of closeness of feeling in a community. Identification occurs via culturetypes and archetypes transmitted quickly by mass media and understood easily by a mass audience. When culture-types and archetypes work in harmonious combination, Osborn wrote (1990, p. 123), they generate successful myths. The fourth function is "implementation," which he defined as applied identification. Implementation includes the classical idea of deliberative rhetoric discussed earlier. The fifth function is to *reaffirm identity,* "often in ceremonies during which heroes, martyrs, villains, and the role of the people are recalled and renewed in common appreciation" (p. 95). In other words, the fifth function is the same as epideictic rhetoric. (For an in-depth application of depiction, see Rosteck, 1994.)

Edwards and Winkler (1997) introduced the concept of "representative form," building on Osborn and McGee. They contended that the 1945 photograph of the flag raising at Iwo Jima has been used and parodied in editorial cartoons and has become a special type of symbolic form; it is an instance of depictive rhetoric that functions as a visual ideograph (p. 303). Edwards and Winkler (1997) defined representative form as an image that "transcends the specifics of its immediate visual references and, through a cumulative process of visual and symbolic meaning, rhetorically identifies and delineates the ideals of the body politic" (p. 295). A representative form originates in actuality and specificity, but is abstracted into a symbol or concentrated image, and provides an explanatory model for human motive (p. 296).

In Fig. 2.11, the word and image of "mother," arguably an archetype, is used to sell toasters. However, the particular rendering of the mother here (the style/delivery) is evocative of the early postwar period, as are the appliances featured (and their style of design). The design styles here evoke a culturetype or, perhaps, an instance of representative form, that recalls a whole constellation of ideologies from that period—belief in the power of science, faith in consumer culture, articulation of the Feminine Mystique, the competitiveness of the Cold War, and so on.

An excellent example of ideological criticism is the work of DeLuca (1999; DeLuca & Demo, 2000), who studied how environmental activists influenced the way they were verbally and visually presented to the general public and how they shifted the parameters of discussion about the environment. Drawing on McGee, he wrote that social movements are changes in the meanings of the world, and such redefinitions of reality are always constructed through rhetoric. It is public discourse that changes human consciousness. Environmental groups are attempting not merely to move the meanings of key ideographs but also to disarticulate and rearticulate the links between ideographs. In Fig. 2.3, we can, perhaps, see an example of this, in which the separation between humans and animals is being *disarticulated* and, importantly, the linkage between a healthy world for children and the health of the environment is being *rearticulated.*

FIG. 2.11. Culturetype, archetype, representative form.

CONCLUSION

Although the bibliography contains more than 150 references, and most are directly concerned with visual rhetoric, it seems that what is "missing" from the literature is greater than what is "present." At a glance, it appears that the theoretical side of the literature is in better shape because so many articles are about theory building. The problem, however, is that few of the essays test the same theories, and if they do, then they test the theories in different ways. Only one or two references focus on methodological concerns, and in many of the essays there is no mention of how the author(s) conducted their analysis.

Replication is uncommon. Few critics even study the same phenomenon. The type of (useful) repetition that is most likely, therefore, is either the conscious development of more genre studies or the work of an individual over the course of a career. Benson and Medhurst, for example, both critique a number of movies, and readers of their articles can clearly see how these two developed a critical perspective. Blair seems to be doing the same with memorials, Edwards with cartoons, Jamieson with political television advertisements, and Olson with historical images. The work of Mick and McQuarrie also showed a coherent point of view, as did Scott's. Book-length treatments, such as DeLuca's study of environmental activism, also are useful.

There are great differences in how rhetoric is defined and, when visual rhetoric is defined, there also is great variability. Scholars approach the field of visual rhetoric with such different ontological assumptions and such different conceptual bases that progress towards theory building is slow. Things can become even more confusing as scholars merge rhetorical ideas with ideas in semiology, cultural studies, postmodernism, feminist studies, and cognitive and behavioral psychology.

Too much of the literature remains fixated on the way pictures, especially photographs, seem to resemble their subjects. Too many scholars seem to believe that visual images are "comprehended at a glance" and have "universal meaning." To move forward, visual rhetoricians must investigate the way pictures and films operate as symbols and must better understand the nature of seeing and responding. Humans make conscious choices about which paint to apply where, which camera angle to use, and which film structure to adopt, but human action also is required for the process of interpretation. Rather than learn how a critic *interprets* a visual image or material item, we must learn how people at the time *identified* with the image/item and how they were *persuaded*. Rather than *infer* conscious and unconscious intentions and interpretations, we need scholars like Geertz and Baxandall, who conduct ethnographies of symbolic action. Or more like Mick and McQuarrie, who test rhetorical operations empirically. Importantly, we need to learn and document the functions of visual images for their audiences, the employment of images as equipment for living.

REFERENCES

Allen, N. (1996, Winter). Ethics and visual rhetorics: Seeing's not believing anymore. *Technical Communication Quarterly, 5,* 87–105.

Altman, C. (1980). The medieval marquee: Church portal sculpture as publicity. *Journal of Popular Culture, 14,* 37–46.

Aristotle. (1991). *On rhetoric: A theory of civil discourse,* George A. Kennedy (Ed. and Trans.). New York: Oxford University Press.

Barthes, R. (1971, Spring). Rhetoric of the image. *Working Papers in Cultural Studies, 1,* 37–51.

Barton, B. F., & Barton, M. S. (1985, Fall). Toward a rhetoric of visuals for the computer era. *Technical Writing Teacher, 12,* 126–145.

Baxandall, M. (1985). *Patterns of intention: On the historical explanation of pictures.* New Haven, CT: Yale University Press.

Benson, T. W. (1974a). Joe: An essay in the rhetorical criticism of film. *Journal of Popular Culture, 8*(4), 610–618.

Benson, T. W. (1974b, February). Rhetoric and autobiography: The case of Malcolm X. *Quarterly Journal of Speech, 60,* 1–13.

Benson, T. W. (1978, Winter). The senses of rhetoric: A topical system for critics. *Central States Speech Journal, 29,* 237–250.

Benson, T. W. (1980, November). The rhetorical structure of Frederick Wiseman's *High School. Communication Monographs, 47,* 233–261.

Benson, T. W. (1985). The rhetorical structure of Frederick Wiseman's *Primate. Quarterly Journal of Speech, 71*(2), 204–217.

Benson, T. W., & Anderson, C. (1984, Fall). The rhetorical structure of Frederick Wiseman's *Model. Journal of Film and Video, 36,* 30–40.

Bernhardt, S. A. (1986, February). Seeing the text. *College composition and communication, 37,* 66–78.

Bernhardt, S. A. (1996). Visual rhetoric. In T. Enos (Ed.), *Encyclopedia of rhetoric and composition* (pp. 746–748). New York: Garland.

Birdsell, D. S., & Groarke, L. (1996, Summer). Toward a theory of visual argument. *Argumentation and Advocacy, 33,* 1–10.

Blair, C. (1999). Contemporary U.S. memorial sites as exemplars of rhetoric's materiality. In J. Selzer & S. Crowley (Eds.), *Rhetorical bodies* (pp. 16–57). Madison: University of Wisconsin Press.

Blair, C., Jeppeson, M. S., & Pucci, E., Jr. (1991). Public memorializing in Postmodernity: The Vietnam Veterans Memorial as prototype. *Quarterly Journal of Speech, 77,* 263–288.

Blair, C. & Michel, N. (1999). Commemorating in the theme park zone: Reading the Astronauts Memorial. In T. Rosteck (Ed.), *At the intersection: Cultural studies and rhetorical studies* (pp. 29–83). New York: Guilford Press.

Blair, J. A. (1996, Summer). The possibility and actuality of visual argument. *Argumentation and Advocacy, 33,* 23–39.

Bonsiepe, G. (1963). Persuasive communication: Towards a visual rhetoric. In T. Crosby (Ed.), *Uppercase 5* (pp. 19–34). London: Whitefriars Press.

Bonsiepe, G. (1965). Visual/verbal rhetoric. *Ulm, 14/15/16,* 23–40.

Bormann, E. G. (1972, December). Fantasy and rhetorical vision: The rhetorical criticism of social reality. *Quarterly Journal of Speech, 58,* 396–407.

Bormann, E. G. (1982, February). A fantasy theme analysis of the television coverage of the hostage release and the Reagan inaugural. *Quarterly Journal of Speech, 68,* 133–145.

Bormann, E. G. (1985). *The Force of fantasy: Restoring the American dream* (pp. 1–25). Carbondale: Southern Illinois University Press.

Bostdorf, D. M. (1987). Making light of James Watt: A Burkean approach to the form and attitude of political cartoons. *Quarterly Journal of Speech, 73,* 43–59.

Bouse, D. (1990). The visual rhetoric of wilderness: contemporary environmentalism and the depiction of nature. In D. G. Beauchamp, J. C. Baca, & R. A. Braden (Eds.), *Investigating visual literacy* (pp. 163–172). Blacksburg, VA: International Visual Literacy Association.

Brizuela, A. (1998). Tale of the origin: A rhetorical visual analysis of a Mexican mythical tale. *Visible Language, 32*(3), 234–255.

Buchanan, R. (1989). Declaration by design: Rhetoric, argument and demonstration in design practice. In V. Margolin (Ed.), *Design discourse: History theory criticism* (pp. 91–110). Chicago: University of Chicago Press.

Burke, K. (1931). *Counter-statement.* New York: Harcourt, Brace.

Burke, K. (1945). *Grammar of motives.* New York: Prentice Hall.

Burke, K. (1950). *A Rhetoric of motives.* Englewood Cliffs, NJ: Prentice Hall.

Burke, K. (1966). *Language as symbolic action.* Berkeley: University of California Press.

Burke, K. (1967). *The philosophy of literary form: Studies in symbolic action* (2nd. rev. ed.). Baton Rouge: Louisiana State University Press.

Campbell, K. K., & Burkholder, T. R. (1997). *Critiques of contemporary rhetoric* (2nd ed.). Belmont: Wadsworth.

Carey, J. (1975). A cultural approach to communication. *Communication, 2,* 1–22.

Chase, K. (1990). Argument and beauty: A review and exploration of connections. In R. Trapp & J. Schuetz (Eds.), *Perspectives on argumentation: Essays in honor of Wayne Brockriede* (pp. 258–271). Prospect Heights, IL: Waveland Press.

Condit, C. M. (1987). Crafting virtue: The rhetorical construction of public morality. *Quarterly Journal of Speech, 73,* 79–87.

Condit, C. M. (1990). Constructing visions of the fetus and freedom: Rhetoric and image. *Decoding abortion rhetoric: Communicating social change* (pp. 78–95). Urbana: University of Illinois Press.

Condit, C. M. (1991). *Decoding abortion rhetoric: Communicating social change.* Urbana: University of Illinois Press.

Cook, A. (1989). Rhetoric and rapture: The interdependence of signification and depth-communication in the arts. In *Dimensions of the sign in art* (pp. 3–23). Hanover, NH: University Press of New England.

de Cosio, M. G. (1998). Rhetoric in logotypes. *Visible Language, 32,* 264–279.

DeLuca, K. M. (1999). *Image politics: The new rhetoric of environmental activism.* New York: Guilford Press.

DeLuca, K. M., & Demo, A. T. (2000, September). Imaging nature: Watkins, Yosemite, and the birth of environmentalism. *Critical Studies in Media Communication, 17,* 241–260.

DeSousa, M. A., & Medhurst, M. J. (1982). The editorial cartoon as visual rhetoric: Rethinking Boss Tweed. *Journal of Visual Verbal Languaging, 2*(2), 52–61.

Dickson, B. (1999). Reading maternity materially: The case of Demi Moore. In J. Selzer & S. Crowley (Eds.), *Rhetorical bodies* (pp. 297–313). Madison: University of Wisconsin Press.

Doughty, D. (1993). Constructing Palestinians: Visual rhetoric and work organization in a news magazine documentary. *Visual Sociology, 8,* 4–20.

Durand, J. (1987). Rhetorical figures in the advertising image. In J. Umiker-Sebeok (Ed.), *Marketing and semiotics: New directions in the study of signs for sale* (pp. 295–318). Berlin: Mouton de Gruyter.

Edwards, J. L. (1997). *Political cartoons in the 1988 presidential campaign: Image, metaphor, and narrative.* New York: Garland Press.

Edwards, J. L., & Winkler, C. K. (1997). Representative form and the visual ideograph: The Iwo Jima image in editorial cartoons. *Quarterly Journal of Speech, 83*(3), 289–310.

Ehrenhaus, P. (1988, Fall). The Vietnam Veterans Memorial: An invitation to argument. *Journal of the American Forensic Association, 25,* 54–64.

Ehses, H. H. J. (1989). Representing *Macbeth:* A case study in visual rhetoric. In V. Margolin (Ed.), *Design discourse: History theory criticism* (pp. 187–198). Chicago: University of Chicago Press.

Farnsworth, R., & Crismore, A. (1991, Spring). On the reefs: The verbal and visual rhetoric of Darwin's other big theory. *Rhetoric Society Quarterly, 21,* 11–25.

Fisher, W. R. (1984). Narration as a human communication paradigm: The case of public moral argument. *Communication Monographs, 51,* 1–22.

Fleming, D. (1996, Summer). Can pictures be arguments? *Argumentation and Advocacy, 33,* 11–22.

Foss, S. K. (1982, January). Rhetoric and the visual image: A resource unit. *Communication Education, 31,* 55–66.

Foss, S. K. (1986, Summer). Ambiguity as persuasion: The Vietnam Veterans Memorial. *Communication Quarterly, 34,* 326–340.

Foss, S. K. (1993). The construction of appeal in visual images: A hypothesis. In D. Zarefsky (Ed.), *Rhetorical movement: Essays in honor of Leland M. Griffin* (pp. 210–224). Evanston, IL: Northwestern University Press.

Gallagher, V. J. (1995, Winter). Remembering together: Rhetorical integration and the case of the Martin Luther King, Jr. Memorial. *Southern Communication Journal, 60,* 109–119.

Geertz, C. (1973). *The interpretation of cultures.* New York: Basic Books, 1973.

Geertz, C. (1983). *Local knowledge: Further essays in interpretive anthropology.* New York: Basic Books.

Gombrich, E. H. (1960). *Art and illusion: A study in the psychology of pictorial representation.* Princeton, NJ: Princeton University Press.

Goodman, N. (1976). *Languages of art: An approach to a theory of symbols.* Indianapolis, IN: Hackett.

Goody, J. (1968). *Literacy in traditional societies.* New York: Cambridge University Press.

Grolnick, B. E. (1978). Cellulid rhetoric: On genres of documentary. In K. K. Campbell and K. H. Jamieson (Eds.), *Form and genre: Shaping rhetorical action* (pp. 139–161). Falls Church, VA: Speech Communication Association.

Gronbeck, B. E. (1976). Celluloid rhetoric: On genres of documentary. In K. Campbell & K. H. Jamieson (Eds.), *Form and genre: Shaping rhetorical action* (pp. 139–161). Falls Church, VA: Speech Communication Association.

Gronbeck, B. E. (1992). Negative narrative in 1988 presidential campaign ads. *Quarterly Journal of Speech, 78,* 333–346.

Hagen, M. A. (1986). *Varieties of realism: Geometries of representational art.* New York: Cambridge University Press.

Haines, H. W. (1986, March). "What kind of war?": An analysis of the Vietnam Veterans Memorial. *Critical Studies in Mass Communication, 3,* 1–20.

Hart, R. P. (1976, Spring). Theory-building and rhetorical criticism: An informal statement of opinion. *Central States Speech Journal, 27,* 70–77.

Hart, R. P., Jerome, P., & McComb, K. (1984, September). Rhetorical features of newscasts about the President. *Critical Studies in Mass Communication, 1,* 260–286.

Hattenhauer, D. (1984). The rhetoric of architecture: A semiotic approach. *Communication Quarterly, 32*(1), 71–77.

Hendrix, J., & Wood, J. A. (1973, Winter). The rhetoric of film: Toward a critical methodology. *Southern Speech Communication Journal, 39,* 105–122.

Jamieson, K. H. (1984). *Packaging the presidency: A history and criticism of presidential campaign advertising* (pp. 449–450). New York: Oxford University Press.

Jamieson, K. H. (1988). *Eloquence in an electronic age: The transformation of political speechmaking.* New York: Oxford University Press.

Jamieson, K. H. (1992). *Dirty politics: Deception, distraction, and democracy* (pp. 15–42, 43–63, 64–120, 281–288). New York: Oxford University Press.

Kaplan, S. J. (1990, March). Visual metaphors in the representation of communication technology. *Critical Studies in Mass Communication, 7,* 37–47.

Kennedy, J. M. (1982). Metaphor in pictures. *Perception, 11,* 589–602.

Kessler, H. L. (1993). Medieval art as argument. In B. Cassidy (Ed.), *Iconography at the crossroads* (pp. 59–73). Princeton, NJ: Index of Christian Art, Deptartment of Art and Archaeology.

Kostelnick, C. (1989, Winter). Visual rhetoric: A reader-oriented approach to graphics and designs. *Technical Writing Teacher, 16*, 77–88.

Kostelnick, C. (1990, Fall). The rhetoric of text design in professional communication. *Technical Writing Teacher, 17*, 189–202.

Kostelnick, C. (1994, January). Pen to print: The new visual landscape of professional communication. *Journal of Business and Technical Communication, 8*, 91–117.

Kostelnick, C. (1996, Winter). Supra-textual design: The visual rhetoric of whole documents. *Technical Communication Quarterly, 5*, 9–33.

Lake, R. A., & Pickering, B. A. (1998). Argumentation, the visual, and the possibility of refutation: An exploration. *Argumentation, 12*, 79–93.

Lancioni, J. (1996, Fall). The rhetoric of the frame revisioning archival photographs in *The Civil War. Western Journal of Communication*, pp. 397–414.

Larson, B. A. (1972, Summer). The election eve address of Edmund Muskie: A case study of the televised public address. *Central States Speech Journal, 23*, 78–85.

Larson, C. U. (1982, Winter). Media metaphors: Two models for rhetorically criticizing the political television spot advertisement. *Central States Speech Journal, 33*, 533–546.

Lucaites, J. L., Condit, C. M., & Caudill, S. (1999). *Contemporary rhetorical theory: A reader.* New York: Guilford Press.

McGee, M. C. (1980, February). The ideograph: A link between rhetoric and ideology. *Quarterly Journal of Speech, 66*, 1–16.

Mechling, E. W., & Mechling, J. (1995). The atom according to Disney. *Quarterly Journal of Speech, 81*, 436–453.

Medhurst, M. J. (1978, Fall). Image and ambiguity: A rhetorical approach to *The Exorcist. Southern Speech Communication Journal, 44*, 73–92.

Medhurst, M. J. (1982, November). *Hiroshima, Mon Amour:* From iconography to rhetoric. *Quarterly Journal of Speech, 68*, 345–370.

Medhurst, M. J. (1993). The rhetorical structure of Oliver Stone's *JFK. Critical Studies in Mass Communication, 10*, 128–143.

Medhurst, M. J., & Benson, T. W. (1981, March). *The City:* The rhetoric of rhythm. *Communication Monographs, 48*, 54–72.

Medhurst, M. J., & Benson, T. W. (1984). Rhetorical studies in a media age. In their *Rhetorical dimensions in media* (pp. ix–xxiii). Dubuque, IA: Kendall/Hunt.

Medhurst, M. J., & DeSousa, M. A. (1981, September). Political cartoons as rhetorical form: A taxonomy of graphic discourse. *Communication Monographs, 48*, 197–237.

Meltzoff, S. (1970, January). On the rhetoric of vision. *Leonardo, 3*, 27–38.

Mick, D. G., & Buhl, C. (1992, December). A meaning-based model of advertising experiences. *Journal of Consumer Research, 19*, 317–338.

Mitchell, W. J. T. (1986). *Iconology: Image, text, ideology.* Chicago: University of Chicago Press.

Morreale, J. (1991a). The political campaign film: Epideictic rhetoric in a documentary frame. In F. Biocca (Ed.), *Television and political advertising* (vol. 2, pp. 187–210). Hillsdale, NJ: Lawrence Erlbaum Associates.

Morreale, J. (1991b). *A new beginning: A textual frame analysis of the political campaign film.* Albany, NY: SUNY Press.

Morris, R. (1993). Visual rhetoric in political cartoons: A structuralist approach. *Metaphor and Symbolic Activity, 8*(3), 195–210.

Moser, S. (1992). The visual language of Archaeology: A case study of the Neanderthals. *Antiquity, 66*, 831–844.

Moser, S. (1996). Visual representation in archaeology: Depicting the missing-link in human origins. In Brian S. Baigrie (Ed.), *Picturing knowledge: Historical and philosophical problems concerning the use of art in science* (pp. 184–214). Toronto: University of Toronto Press.

Netzhammer, E. C. (1999). Competing rhetorical strategies in the gay and lesbian video wars: *Marching for freedom* and *gay rights, special rights.* In M. G. Carstarphen & S. C. Zavoina (Eds.), *Sexual rhet-oric: Media perspectives on sexuality, gender and identity* (pp. 211–224). Westport, CT: Greenwood Press.

Olson, L. C. (1983, February). Portraits in praise of a people: A rhetorical analysis of Norman Rock-well's icons in Franklin D. Roosevelt's "Four Freedoms" campaign. *Quarterly Journal of Speech, 69,* 15–24.

Olson, L. C. (1990, February). Benjamin Franklin's commemorative medal, *Libertas Americana: A study in rhetorical iconology. Quarterly Journal of Speech, 76,* 23–45.

Osborn, M. (1986). Rhetorical depiction. In H. W. Simons & A. A. Aghazarian (Eds.), *Form, genre, and the study of political discourse* (pp. 79–107). Columbia: University of South Carolina Press.

Osborn, M. (1990). In defense of broad mythic criticism—A reply to Rowland. *Communication Stud-ies, 41*(2), 121–127.

Otnes, C., & Scott, L. M. (1996, Spring). Something old, something new: Exploring the interaction between ritual and advertising. *Journal of Advertising, 25,* 33–50.

Parker, R. D., & Hildebrandt, H. W. (1996, November). Business communication and architecture: Is there a parallel? *Management Communication Quarterly, 10,* 226–242.

Price, D. C., & Lattin, B. (1988, Fall). The death of partisanship in Idaho? A rhetorical analysis of the 1986 Idaho gubernatorial election. *Rendezvous, 24,* 44–52.

Reid, K. (1990, Summer). The Hay-Wain: Cluster analysis in visual communication. *Journal of Com-munication Inquiry, 14,* 40–54.

Reid, K. (1993). A rhetorical approach to non-discursive messages in information campaigns. In N. Metallinos (Ed.), *Verbo-visual literacy* (pp. 170–182). Blacksburg, VA: International Visual Lit-eracy Association.

Richards, I. A. (1936). *Philosophy of rhetoric.* New York: Oxford University Press.

Richards, I. A. (1938). *Interpretation in teaching.* New York: Harcourt, Brace.

Robinson, D. H., & Schraw, G. (1994). Computational efficiency through visual argument: Do graphic organizers communicate relations in text too effectively. *Contemporary Educational Psychology, 19,* 399–415.

Rosenfield, L. W. (1989). Central Park and the celebration of civic virtue. In T. W. Benson (Ed.), *Ameri-can rhetoric: Context and criticism* (pp. 221–265). Carbondale: Southern Illinois University Press.

Rosteck, T. (1994). *"See It Now" confronts McCarthyism.* Tuscaloosa: University of Alabama Press.

Rutledge, K. E. (1994). Analyzing visual persuasion: The art of duck hunting. In R. F. Fox (Ed.), *Images in language, media, and mind* (pp. 204–217). Urbana, IL: NCTE.

Salazar, M. (1998). National currency as rhetoric: The peso. *Visible Language, 32,* 280–293.

Scott, L. M. (1991, Summer). "For the rest of us:" A reader-oriented interpretation of Apple's "1984" commercial. *Journal of Popular Culture, 25,* 67–82.

Scott, L. M. (1993, June). Spectacular vernacular: Literacy and commercial culture in the postmodern age. *International Journal of Research in Marketing, 10,* 251–275.

Scott, L. M. (1994a, September). Images in advertising: The need for a theory of visual rhetoric. *Jour-nal of Consumer Research, 21,* 252–273.

Scott, L. M. (1994b, December). The bridge from text to mind: Adapting reader-response theory for consumer research. *Journal of Consumer Research,* pp. 461–490.

Scott, L. M. (1995). Representation and narrative. In Robert Wyer (Ed.), *Advances in social cognition.* Hillsdale, NJ: Lawrence Erlbaum Associates.

Scott, R. L. (1977, Spring). Diego Rivera at Rockefeller Center: Fresco painting and rhetoric. *Western Journal of Speech Communication, 41,* 70–82.

Sewell, E. H. (1987). Narrative communication in editorial cartoons. In *On narratives: proceedings of the 10th International Colloquium on Speech Communication* (pp. 260–268). Frankfurt am Main: Script.

Shelley, C. (1996, Fall). Rhetorical and demonstrative modes of visual argument: Looking at images of human evolution. *Argumentation and Advocacy, 33,* 53–68.

Stormer, N. (1997, May). Embodying normal miracles. *Quarterly Journal of Speech, 83,* 172–191.

Stuart, C. L. (1973, Fall). Architecture in Nazi Germany: A rhetorical perspective. *Western Journal of Speech Communication, 37,* 253–263.

Tapia, C. N. (1998). Pre-Columbian stamps. *Visible Language, 32,* 256–263.

Tebeaux, E. (1988, Fall/Winter). Writing in academe; Writing at work: Using visual rhetoric to bridge the gap. *Journal of Teaching Writing, 7,* 215–236.

Tebeaux, E. (1991, October). Ramus, visual rhetoric, and the emergence of page design in medical writing of the English Renaissance. *Written Communication, 8,* 411–445.

Tovey, J. (1996, Winter). Computer interfaces and visual rhetoric: Looking at the technology. *Technical Communication Quarterly, 5,* 61–76.

Tufte, E. (1983). *The visual display of quantitative information,* Cheshire, CT: Graphics Press.

Tufte, E. (1990). *Envisioning information,* Cheshire, CT: Graphics Press.

Tufte, E. (1997). *Visual explanations: Images and quantities, evidence and narrative,* Cheshire, CT: Graphics Press.

Turner, K. J. (1977, Spring). Comic strips: A rhetorical perspective. *Central States Speech Journal, 28,* 24–35.

Twigg, R. (1992). Aestheticizing the home: Textual strategies of taste, self-identity, and bourgeois hegemony in America's "Gilded Age." *Text and Performance Quarterly, 12,* 1–20.

Varga, A. K. (1989, Spring). Criteria for describing word-and-image relations. *Poetics Today, 10,* 31–53.

Weaver, R. M. (1970). *Language is sermonic* (R. L. Johannesen et al., Eds.). Baton Rouge: Louisiana State University Press.

Williams, D. C. (1987). Representations of ideology: Analogons, images and ideographs. In F. H. van Emeren (Ed.), *Argumentation: Analysis and practices* (pp. 298–307). Providence, RI: Foris.

FURTHER READING

Abel, E. (1999, Spring). Bathroom doors and drinking fountains: Jim Crow's racial symbolic. *Critical Inquiry, 25,* 435–481.

Autrey, K. (1984). Toward a visual/verbal rhetoric. *Journal of Visual/Verbal Languaging, 4*(1), 5–8.

Baxandall, M. (1972). *Painting and experience in fifteenth century Italy.* New York: Oxford University Press.

Bevilacqua, V. M. (1976). Classical rhetorical influences in the development of eighteenth century British aesthetic criticism. *Transactions of the American Philological Association, 106,* 11–28.

Brueggemann, B. J. (1995, Spring). The coming out of deaf culture and American sign language: An exploration into visual rhetoric and literacy. *Rhetoric Review, 13,* 409–420.

Brummett, B. (1985). Electric literature as equipment for living: Haunted house films. *Critical Studies in Mass Communication, 2,* 247–261.

Campbell, K. (1988, Fall/Winter). Enactment as a rhetorical strategy in the year of living dangerously. *Central States Speech Journal, 39,* 258–268.

DeSousa, M. A. (1984). Symbolic action and pretended insight: The Ayatollah Khomeini in U.S. editorial cartoons. In M. J. Medhurst & T. W. Benson (Eds.), *Rhetorical dimensions in media: A critical casebook* (pp. 204–230). Dubuque, IA: Kendall/Hunt.

Douard, J. W. (1995). E.-J. Marey's visual rhetoric and the graphic decomposition of the body. *Studies in History, Philosophy and Science, 26*(2), 175–204.

Ehninger, D., et al. (1971). Report of the committee on the scope of rhetoric and the place of rhetorical studies in higher education. In L. F. Bitzer & E. Black (Eds.), *The prospect of rhetoric* (pp. 208–219). Englewood Cliffs, NJ: Prentice Hall.

Foss, S. K. (1987, Summer). Body art: Insanity as communication. *Central States Speech Journal, 38,* 122–131.

Foss, S. K. (1988). Judy Chicago's *The Dinner Party:* Empowering of women's voice in visual art. In B. Bate & A. Taylor (Eds.), *Women communicating: Studies of women's talk* (pp. 9–26). Norwood, NJ: Ablex.

Foss, S. K. (1994, Fall–Winter). A rhetorical schema for the evaluation of visual imagery. *Communication Studies, 45*, 213–224.

Foss, S. K. (in press). *Visual rhetoric: Visual communication theory and research.*

Foss, S. K., & Radich, A. J. (1980). The aesthetic response to nonrepresentational art: A suggested model. *Review of Research in Visual Arts Education, 12*, 40–49.

Frentz, T. S., & Rushing, J. H. (1993). Integrating ideology and archetype in rhetorical criticism, part II: A case study of *Jaws. Quarterly Journal of Speech, 79*, 61–81.

Graves, O. F., Flesher, D. L., & Jordan, R. E. (1996). Pictures and the bottom line: The television epistemology of U.S. Annual Reports. *Accounting, Organizations and Society, 21*(1), 57–88.

Gronbeck, B. E. (1995). Rhetoric, ethics, and telespectacles in the post-everything age. In R. H. Brown (Ed.), *Postmodern representations* (pp. 216–238). Urbana: University of Illinois Press.

Hart, R. P. (1997). Analyzing media. *Modern rhetorical criticism* (2nd ed., pp. 177–208). Boston: Allyn and Bacon.

Joly, M. (1993). Information and argument in press photographs. *Visual Sociology, 8*(1), 16–22.

Kinross, R. (1989). The rhetoric of neutrality. In V. Margolin (Ed.), *Design discourse: History, theory, criticism* (pp. 131–143). Chicago: University of Chicago Press.

Lucaites, J. L. (1997, August). Visualizing "The People": Individualism vs. collectivism in *Let Us Now Praise Famous Men. Quarterly Journal of Speech, 83*, 269–288.

Margolin, V. (1979). The visual rhetoric of propaganda. *Information Design Journal, 1*, 107–122.

McQuarrie, E. F., & Mick, D. G. (1996, March). Figures of rhetoric in advertising language. *Journal of Consumer Research, 22*, 424–437.

McQuarrie, E. F., & Mick, D. G. (1999, June). Visual rhetoric in advertising: Text-interpretive, experimental, and reader-response analyses. *Journal of Consumer Research, 26*, 37–54.

Messaris, P. (1992). Visual "manipulation": Visual means of affecting responses to images. *Communication, 13*(3), 181–195.

Messaris, P. (1996). *Visual persuasion: The role of images in advertising.* Newbury Park, CA: Sage.

Olson, L. C. (1987, February). Benjamin Franklin's pictorial representations of the British colonies in America: A study in rhetorical iconography. *Quarterly Journal of Speech, 73*, 18–42.

Phillips, B. J. (1997, Summer). Thinking into it: Consumer interpretations of complex advertising images. *Journal of Advertising, 26*, 77–87.

Poggenpohl, S. H. (1998). Doubly damned: Rhetorical and visual. *Visible Language, 32*, 200–233.

Postman, N. (1985). *Amusing ourselves to death: Public discourse in the age of show business.* New York: Viking.

Roberts, W. (1997, December). The visual rhetoric of Jean-Louis Prieur. *Canadian Journal of History, 32*, 415–436.

Rogers, T. B. (1998). The look of depersonalization: Visual rhetoric in personality textbook covers. In W. E. Smythe (Ed.), *Toward a psychology of persons* (pp. 145–176). Mahwah, NJ: Lawrence Erlbaum Associates.

Rowland, R. C. (1989, March). On limiting the narrative paradigm: Three case studies. *Communication Monographs, 56*, 39–54.

Rushing, J. H. (1985, May). *E.T.* as rhetorical transcendence. *Quarterly Journal of Speech, 71*, 188–203.

Rushing, J. H. (1986, September). Mythic evolution of "The New Frontier" in mass mediated rhetoric. *Critical Studies in Mass Communication, 3*, 265–296.

Sherr, S. A. (1999). Scenes from the political playground: An analysis of the symbolic use of children in presidential campaign advertising. *Political Communication, 16*, 45–59.

Staiti, P. (1992, Spring). Ideology and rhetoric in Erastus Salisbury Field's *The Historical monument of the American Republic. Winterthur Portfolio, 27*, 29–43.

Tremonte, C. (1995). Film, classical rhetoric, and visual literacy. *Journal of Teaching Writing, 14*(1&2), 3–19.

Tyler, A. C. (1992, Fall). Shaping belief: The role of audience in visual communication. *Design Issues, 9*, 21–29.

II. IMAGE AND RESPONSE

When the Mind Blinks: Attentional Limitations to the Perception of Sequential Visual Images

Jane E. Raymond
Centre for Experimental Consumer Psychology,
University of Wales-Bangor

The primary purpose of this chapter is to bring recent knowledge about human visual perception garnered from research in neuroscience and experimental psychology to the attention of people working in advertising and visual persuasion. In the last decade, scientists have made significant advances in understanding the limitations the brain imposes on perceptual awareness and the processing of visual images by people in busy dynamic environments. This work suggest that fast-paced, complex visual messages frequently used in modern advertising may exceed the cognitive capacity of most people. In this chapter, I briefly review a general model of how visual information, especially briefly presented complex information, may be perceptually processed and how it reaches our awareness and memory. I also describe recent research using different but related procedures that asks questions about the special cognitive and perceptual loads produced when different complex images are presented rapidly and successively.

I begin with a short reminder that the brain performs an extraordinarily difficult set of tasks and that it is, of course, a filter between the real world and the one that we perceive to exist. I then describe how and why humans have to be so selective about what they attend and how this is particularly important when images change with time. Lastly I describe how recent laboratory-based research provides insights into why some persuasive visual communications may fail to persuade.

OUR AMAZING BRAIN

We take it for granted when it works properly and, as a source of information, we trust it completely. Our brain, like the CPU in a computer, works steadily in the background, day and night, extracting information from the physical world and translating it into a semidigital neural code. The code is processed in multiple ways, circulated rapidly to many different systems within the brain, and then ultimately controls our muscles and thus our behavior. Thankfully, we are unaware of most of the many frenetic neural conversations that occur within our heads every minute, being privy only to the most interesting commentaries that provoke the need for thinking.

We call this small subset of the brain's activity "awareness" and live under the pleasant illusion that the world of which we are *aware* is the world in which we live. This, of course, is not the case. Our rich and meaningful mental representations are the product of the brain's synthesis of incoming sensory information and internal stored memorial representations. They are the result of much editing, some biophysical censorship (e.g., we cannot see infared light), and a significant amount of cognitive and emotional spin doctoring. Although these persuasive mental inventions sensibly guide our actions in response to physical objects most of the time, they can also misinform, leading to inappropriate actions (e.g., accidents) and simple failures to perceive that which may be obvious to others.

VISUAL PERCEPTION

Let's now consider this discrepancy between the "real" physical world and mental representations in the domain of visual processing and its implications for visual advertising. To understand this we must review the main tasks the brain confronts in making vision function effectively in our busy, dynamic environment. First, the brain must distil a huge quantity of visual information into a concise "sketch" of the visual scene. Second, it must decide which objects in the scene deserve greater consideration and access to awareness. Third, it must link current visual information with other information stored in durable memory (including semantic and emotional information) to enable learning.

The only part of the human body that is sensitive to light are two small patches in the back of the eyes that together make up a surface just slightly larger than a business card. The 210 million neural cells on these two-dimensional receptor surfaces provide point-by-point information regarding light patterns that comprise the visual stimulus. The two retinae receive slightly different images, and a comparison between them adds a third dimension (depth) to each point. Because the eyes, head, and world move frequently, the retinal images also change and computations needed to render a functionally useful description of the physical world must incorporate yet a fourth dimension, time. Taken together, a vast quantity of information is captured by the retinae and allowed to flow centrally to the brain.

A problem arises when we consider that our thinking, decision making, and volitional action systems (e.g., looking, reaching) are limited in how much information they can handle at a time. For example, we cannot look to the left while simultaneously looking to the right. Information that informs us to make one action must be selected from information indicating a competing action. If our behavior is to be coordinated into appropriate sequences, we need to limit and prioritize information capable of controlling responses so that we are not caught in the conflict of behavioral indecision and disorganization. What is true for motor behavior is also true for mental activities. We cannot absorb information from a video while thinking about an unrelated topic, nor discuss one subject while listening to someone talk about an unrelated one. These things, like many of our motor behaviors, must be done serially. So on the input side we a have vast flow of complex, dynamic visual information, and on the output side we have a limited number of behavioral options at any point in time. How does the brain achieve the necessary degree of information distillation to allow the smooth, coordinated, and rapid mental and behavioral responses so characteristic of humans?

The Visual Sketch

The first step in the distillation of visual information is to derive a simple visual "sketch" from the retinal image (Marr, 1982). This sketch seems to be comprised of multiple visual surfaces: of both objects and backgrounds. Information from each surface is collapsed into a small set of perceptual "tags" descriptive of each surfaces' features. Because different brain areas and networks analyze different visual features (e.g., color, depth, motion, etc.), a neural binding process must be undertaken to create a coherent representation of each surface (Kanwisher & Driver, 1992; Prinzmetal, 1995; Triesman, 1996). Surface representations are then connected into object representations, so that in a split second, the main objects in a scene can be recognized.

Consider the image in Fig. 3.1. To make sense of this complex scene, the surface of the mug must be segregated from that of the similarly patterned tablecloth. The diverse visual elements within each surface boundary must be "grouped" so that two different coherent surfaces are perceived and only two different objects are seen. This type of analysis makes sense if your task is to pick up the mug. However, if your task is changed and for some reason you must find the triangle on the centre of the mug, distilling the scene into two simple objects would be disadvantageous. For this task, the triangle and other elements on the cup's surface must assume the status of "objects" in the scene and all other parts of the scene will be grouped as "background." As in many scenes, sometimes the whole object is of interest and at other times a detail on the object is critical. Construction of the

FIG. 3.1.   A complex image with two objects. See text for details.

visual sketch depends on what we need to see in a scene and is created differently, on the fly, as needed.

Selective Attention

The ability to incorporate current task requirements into the perceptual process of distilling information from a complex input array is critical for functional vision. To do this, humans have evolved a complex set of neural mechanisms, collectively called *attention*. Attention performs two basic functions: *selecting* and *ignoring*. Selecting is when neural mechanisms actively facilitate processing of certain chunks of information (objects in the visual sketch) that are relevant for appropriate action (including thinking) in an ongoing situation. Representations of the various features of selected visual objects enter awareness, are capable of controlling volitional behavior (e.g., naming of the object), and may be processed in a way that promotes long-lasting storage in memory. Visual representations available to awareness are sometimes termed *explicit* because it is relatively easy for a person to use language to refer to them. According to some views, representations of objects in awareness are complete in that all their features are bound together (Kahneman & Treisman, 1984; Wolfe & Bennett, 1997). Our awareness of a visual scene at any given point in time is thus constructed of those objects and events that are appropriate to ongoing action. Note that the content of awareness is fluid, changing rapidly as the situation demands.

Ignoring occurs when the processing of objects in the visual sketch, especially those that may provoke inappropriate actions, are *actively* inhibited. In this sense of the word, ignored information is actively excluded from awareness and will not result in explicit volition behavior. However, because ignoring involves active inhibition, it should not be confused with a lack of processing. An object's representation can only be ignored if it has been processed enough to allow a determination that it may potentially direct an action (or thought pattern) that would compete with actions (or thought patterns) dictated by selected objects. This type of "processing-without-awareness" is sometimes called *implicit* processing. Evidence that ignored information is implicitly processed to a reasonably high level of analysis is that such information can control behavior at a later time (DeSchepper & Treisman, 1996; Tipper, 1985). This is especially true when the previously selected object is no longer present or appropriate to guide behavior.

Links With Memory

Humans are particularly good at learning how things are related to one another. We are also endowed with a long-lasting memory for many things and for the various relationships among them. Our memory stores include visual (and other sensory), semantic, emotional, action-oriented, and strategic information. Whenever we view a visual stimulus, we draw on this vast store, probably in an interactive manner. Modern views on visual processing no longer espouse a simple feedforward system wherein information flows from retina to awareness in one direction only. Rather, numerous recent neuroscience and behavioral studies show that visual information is modulated shortly after entering the brain's web of connections by numerous internal states including attention (Motter, 1993; Raymond, O'Donnell, & Tipper, 1998; Treue & Maunsell, 1996) and memory (e.g., Petersen, Fox, Posner, Mintun, & Raichle, 1988).

Thus construction of the visual sketch, selection for awareness, and coding of information into memory appear to be interactive processes that determine how we construct our moment-to-moment mental representations of the visual information available to us. Many of the contributing factors are idiosyncratic resulting from an individual's personal experience and current internal state. Thus, representation and interpretation of complex visual stimuli, such as visual advertisement, will vary among viewers. Although there are many unanswered questions about the links between perception, attention, and memory, there is clear evidence that our conscious awareness of the visual world is neither a complete nor fully faithful reflection of the current visual array.

The goal in visual advertising is to provide a robust visual memory that, combined with information from other sources, including point-of-purchase stimuli, will support a favorable purchase decision. It is not enough to gain the visual orientation of a consumer to an ad (e.g., looking, noticing). Rather, a combination of selective attention to critical components of the visual information and active ignoring of other components may be essential for influencing memory successfully in ways that are capable of directing later purchase behavior. Although these possibilities are general to all aspects of visual advertising, they may be particularly important in advertising that involves successive, relatively brief presentations of complex stimuli.

COPING WITH CHANGING VISUAL INFORMATION

A key characteristic of modern visual advertisement is rapidly changing stimuli. In video, scene cuts are frequent; on web sites, banners are flashed and changed; and with print media, consumers quickly glance over and flick through the pages. Because they often do not choose to be exposed to advertisement, consumers frequently terminate looking by changing their eye position, thus compounding the temporal complexity in the input stimulus.

Evidence that rapid and frequent changes to the visual stimulus impair recall of information presented in advertisements comes from MacLachlan and Logan (1993). They reported that the average scene length in commercials had shortened from 3.8 s in 1987 to 2.3 s by 1993. For many 30-s advertisements, this rate produced over 20 different scenes. (This can be compared to the average scene length in movies of 11 s.) Importantly, they noted that ads with scene lengths averaging 6 s or more had significantly better recall and persuasion scores than ads with scenes lengths of 1.5 s on average.

How does the brain cope with visual change and is there a way to estimate the minimal scene length that would not compromise normal cognition? One way to probe this issue is to consider how humans deal with natural sources of visual change. When we scan a scene, read text, or watch a movie, we use a series of short rapid eye movements called saccades, alternated with brief periods during which the eye is held as still as possible. This creates a successive set of "scene cuts" that the brain must process, integrate and then react to. Each "scene," or fixation, is typically between 200 and 500 ms, long depending on the complexity of information viewed. Fixations are normally terminated when the visual information is "acquired" or processed. During the eye movement, the visual image is an uninterpretable blur. Our visual awareness, however, does not include these blurred saccadic episodes; instead, we experience continuously clear vision. It seems we build up our perception of the scene by knitting together the information obtained from each successive and discrete fixation (Irwin, 1992; Rayner, McConkie, & Erlich, 1978).

A question that vision researchers have asked is, how long does a fixation (or scene exposure) need to be for a person to acquire the information? To address this experimentally, a simple test image is presented for a variable amount of time followed by a visual mask (see Fig. 3.2). A mask is a patterned "nonsense" image usually consisting of meaningless lines and shapes designed to terminate perceptual processing of the test image. In some ways it mimics the blurred retinal image produced by a saccade. The observer is asked to name the object in the test image. The duration of the test image is varied and the minimum amount of time needed to achieve just accurate picture naming is taken as the time needed by the brain to perceptually process the information in the test image. Such studies have shown that for complex scenes 100–200 ms is all that is needed for high levels of accuracy

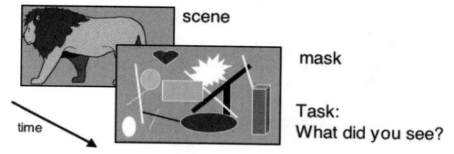

FIG. 3.2.   An illustration of sample stimuli used in a simple masked exposure duration study. The stimulus of interest (target) is immediately followed by a meaningless visual pattern. Typically the task is to name or judge the target object in some way. On different trials, the exposure duration of the stimulus is varied. (See Color Panel A)

in simple naming or judgement tasks (e.g., Turvey, 1973). These data match reasonably well with studies of fixation duration.

At first glance, such observations seem to suggest that we can acquire information successfully when presented briefly and successively as in even the most rapid cut video advertisements. However, fixation studies fail to tell us what or how much information is being acquired, and masked exposure studies fail to mimic the additional perceptual load produced when the visual scene is changing frequently. Indeed, recent research suggests that although we are able to perceptually process an image presented by itself in 200 ms or less, substantially more time is required if the image is part of a series of successive images.

Rapid Serial Visual Presentation

In the laboratory, perception of successive, different scenes can be studied using a technique called rapid serial visual presentation (RSVP), illustrated in Fig. 3.3. Images (letters, words, objects, faces, or scenes) are presented briefly one after the other at the same location in space. Potter and Levy (1969) used this presentation technique for a series of 16 objects and asked observers to recognise the objects after the series was over. When the presentation rate was slow so that each image was available for between 1.5 and 2 s, performance was extremely good, with nearly all the objects being recognized. However, with faster rates of presentation performance dropped dramatically even though the presentation rate for each object was slow enough to give observers the necessary 100–200 ms needed for single image perceptual processing. Why? One explanation is that considerably more time is needed for a perceptual representation to be encoded in some sort of durable memory store so that it can then be reported (Potter, 1999).

We do not normally view our dynamic visual environment with the expectation of coding and remember everything we see. Rather, we select things that interest us

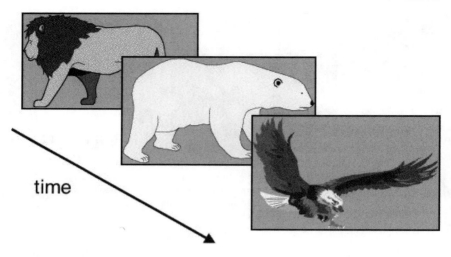

FIG. 3.3.   An illustration of stimuli used in an RSVP experiment. Images are presented serially at the same location, usually at fixation. The task is either to report all the objects seen or to select a particular target item for later report. (See Color Panel B)

or things that are necessary to support a current task. We use our attention mechanisms to speed and support the processing of "target" items. This suggests that, in an RSVP lab situation, selective attention may be deployed to enhance the likelihood that the perceptual processing of a particular object will result in a durable memory trace. If this could be demonstrated, then it would indicate that low-level perceptual processes do not impose the limitations responsible for the poor performance in the fast presentation conditions of the Potter and Levy (1969) study. Indeed, a number of single-task RSVP studies have shown that selective attention can be effectively deployed to aid recall of a specific item in a fast RSVP series (Lawrence, 1971). In these studies the observer is asked to select an item based on an identifying feature (e.g., name the red object in a series of black and white objects). Performance is very high with even extremely rapid rates of presentation (single exposures as short as 80–100 ms). These findings suggest that postperceptual processes limit the speed of information uptake when stimuli are rapidly changed. A probable source of this bottleneck is attention.

The Attentional Blink

In the visual environment outside the laboratory, we select visual stimuli from the dynamic visual array one after the other (as in the multiple fixations used in reading). Targets are selected, processed, encoded in (at least visual short-term or conceptual) memory, and enter awareness before the next target is selected. If these attentional processes are slow and impose a temporal limit on the speed of processing successive images, then this should be observable using an RSVP task requiring observers to select two targets in succession.

My colleagues and I tested this possibility with an RSVP stream of black letters, with one white letter appearing near the middle of the series (Raymond, Shapiro, & Arnell, 1992). Fig. 3.4 provides an illustration of the experimental stimuli. The observer's task was to name the white letter (target 1; T1) and then to report whether the letter "X" (target 2; T2) appeared later in the series. The interval between the onset of the two targets was varied and T2 was only presented on half the trials. Letters were presented at a rate of 11/s (yielding 90 ms between the onset of successive stimuli). Without doing the T1 task, observers were accurate on the T2 task on about 90% percent of trials. However, if they were required also to perform the T1 task and were correct on it, their performance on the T2 task dropped dramatically (to about 50%) if the interval between T1 and T2 is less than about 500 ms. Figure 3.5 shows typical data. We termed this temporary large loss in perception the "attentional blink" because it reflects a transient attentional state, not a sensory one. This effect is robust and has been replicated in many different laboratories using numbers, words, scenes, and objects using both highly specified and loosely defined targets for T1 and T2. The attentional blink demonstrates that there is a significant temporal bottleneck in processing interesting or attended images. This limits the speed of information uptake to about two "chunks" per second when scenes are brief and changing.

The attentional blink does not occur if the RSVP stream pauses briefly just after T1 or T2 is presented (Raymond et al., 1992). This suggests that the transient loss

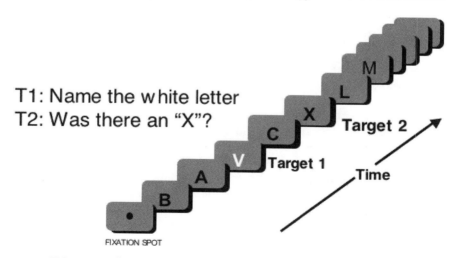

FIG. 3.4.   An illustration of stimuli used in the Raymond et al. (1992) attentional blink experiment. The first task was to identify the white letter and the second task was to report whether an X was present in the RSVP series. The serial position of the X was varied relative to the white letter.

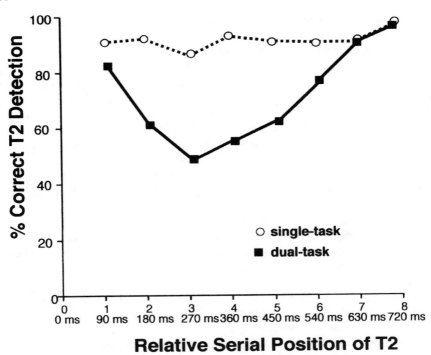

FIG. 3.5. Typical mean group data from an attentional blink study. The vertical axis is the proportion correct on the second target conditionalized on T1 correct performance. The horizontal axis is the time T2 was presented after T1.

in perception results when target processing is not given sufficient time for completion before the next item in the series is presented. Other studies have shown that information that is presented during the blink (and fails to be reported) is nevertheless processed at a relatively high semantic level in the brain (Luck, Vogel, & Shapiro, 1996) and is capable of priming subsequently presented stimuli (Shapiro, Driver, Ward, & Sorensen, 1996). Familiarity with stimuli (Shapiro, Caldwell, & Sorensen, 1997), distinctiveness (Raymond, Shapiro, & Arnell, 1995) and semantic links with other items in the series (Maki, Frigen, & Paulson, 1997) have been shown to reduce the vulnerability of images to attentional blinks.

These findings have led to two different hypotheses for the effect. One is that the attentional blink effects reflects a two-stage processing system with an initial stage for perceptual processing that is unlimited in capacity (every item is analyzed) and a second stage that is slow and severely limited, processing one target item at a time (Chun & Potter, 1995). Representation reaches awareness only after the second stage is completed. The other hypothesis is that information that matches a predetermined template (or is otherwise interesting) is selected and placed in a visual short-term memory (VSTM) store. Frequently, information that is presented in close temporal proximity to a target is also placed in the temporary VSTM store. The attentional blink reflects interference from other object representations in the store when retrieving information for report (Raymond et al., 1995; Shapiro, Raymond, & Arnell, 1996). Both hypotheses suggest that the attentional blink reflects a limitation in accessing awareness that occurs when stimuli are presented in a rapid sequence. The attentional blink demonstrates that although we experience the world as a continuous event, in fact we process it in discrete episodes. The episodic nature of this processing becomes obvious when information is presented at a rate faster than the system can process.

How might attentional blinks affect the perceptual processing of a rapid-cut video advertisement? Although this will depend on the video itself, one might start to answer the question by determining what the most interesting objects or scenes in the ad are. These would likely act as targets, grabbing attention. If these were particularly brief, then one would expect an attentional blink to ensue for the next half second. Information in this period would not be recalled, although it might act to prime subsequent presentations of the same stimuli. Slowing down scenes with particularly interesting information should avoid creating attentional blinks.

Repetition Blindness

The use of rapidly presented stimuli has also revealed other limitations in processing information. Using RSVP, Kanwisher (1987) showed that when two identical words are presented, the second presentation is frequently unreported. She asked participants to read grammatically correct sentences with each word presented in RSVP. For example, she used the sentence "It was work time so work had to get done." Even though the second instance of "work" was necessary for the sentence to read properly, participants failed to read the second "work." This phenomena was termed *repetition blindness* and was found for repetitions of visually similar stimuli including letters, words, word fragments, and objects (Kanwisher, Yin, & Wojciulik, 1999). The explanation is that the brain initially processes all stimuli but either inhibits high-level processing of something it has already processed, or ignores duplicates at the level of awareness. This effect further supports the idea that awareness of the perceptual world is selective and is often lacking in fidelity. Although repetition of brand names and images is frequently seen as advantageous in advertising, repetition blindness effects indicate that such efforts are probably pointless if the repetition occurs within short intervals.

Change Blindness

Attentional blink effects and repetition blindness effects inform us that there are temporal limitations to the uptake of serially presented visual information. Are there also limitations on the amount of information we can process from a single presentation of a complex scene, even when the presentation is not brief? Many studies have shown that when people are searching for a complex object imbedded in a complex scene, they behave as if they are serially examining each object in turn. For example, consider the pair of images in Fig. 3.6. They seem the same and careful serial search is needed to spot the difference between them.

Serial search of complex scenes suggests that when scenes are only available for a brief period of time, many aspects of the image are probably not encoded. A method to test this possibility experimentally, and one that may be useful in revealing those aspects of a scene that are encoded first, is called *change detection* (Rensink, O'Regan, & Clark, 1996). Two nearly identical scenes are presented briefly in alteration, with each scene followed by an empty field or mask. The only difference between the two scenes is that one object is absent or changed (in location, color, etc.) in one version. The task is to locate the disappearing or changing item. The measure is the time taken to perform this simple task. When an item of central interest in a scene is removed or changed, detection times are very brief (one or two alternations), but when other items are changed, detection times can be several seconds long (many alternations) and often observers seem unable to locate the changing item at all. If the images in Fig. 3.6 were viewed in an alternating change detection sequence, noticing the disappearing earring would require several sec-

FIG. 3.6.   Spot the difference in the two images. These nearly identical images are typical of the stimuli used in a change blindness experiment. See text for an explanation.

onds for many people. Once shown the location of the changing image, detecting it is easy and rapid, indicating that sensory factors do not underlie this effect. This apparent insensitivity to significant scene changes as been called *change blindness*. Such effects have been shown to be robust in video sequences, where, between scene cuts, an actor or scene object is changed in some way (Levin & Simons, 1997).

An explanation for change blindness is that at any moment in time only one or two objects in a scene are processed to the level of awareness. Information in a succeeding scene overwrites poorly analyzed information in the preceding scene but not information that has entered awareness. If the change involves objects whose representations are outside awareness, then the change goes undetected. Attention is used to select the object representations that may gain access to awareness and normally these are items of central interest in the scene. With more opportunities to view the scene, attention may be allocated to a different part and through a serial search, the location of the changing item is eventually found.

The importance of the change blindness effect lies in its clear demonstration that only a very small amount of information is encoded in any long-term sense from a briefly viewed complex scene. In advertisements, whether they are video or print, viewers are highly likely to encode the main image in a scene but to fail frequently to encode any secondary images, a role often given to brand or pack images. These are frequently tucked into the lower corner of the page or fleetingly shown at the end of a video clip. Although some small gains may be made from mere exposure (Zajonc, 1968), placing brand images secondary to other compelling images should lessen awareness of the brand and minimize links between the brand and the advertisement itself.

CONCLUDING REMARKS

Understanding the mental processes involved in visual perception is an essential component of understanding the effectiveness of visual advertisement. Although our naive experience is a sense of a continuous, coherent, rich and diverse visual environment, the fact is that the brain fabricates this pleasant illusion for us. Our awareness is limited in how much it can store and the brain is relatively slow at processing information to this high level. The brains edits out the visual images we cannot easily makes sense of (e.g., the blur during a saccadic eye movement), deletes object representations that clutter the limited store for awareness (e.g., repetitions of a object), and excludes from high-level analysis objects that are secondary in importance. Current understanding of these processes predicts that much of very briefly presented and rapidly changing visual information presented in advertisements is simply not processed to any significant extent.

However, advertisements are repeated often and many consumers are exposed to the same advertisement repeatedly. Certainly, repeated exposure will lessen information loss due to attention-based limitations to awareness. More information can be gained with each successive viewing, and the subtleties inserted by advertising creatives can eventually be uncovered. An important question for each and every advertisement is, how much repetition is needed to "get" the whole message? Another pertinent question is, how much repetition do modern consumers actually receive and tolerate? With far greater choice in their sources of entertainment (more magazines, more channels, video games, the Internet, books), it may be less likely that consumers will be exposed repeatedly to the same ad in the same form. By being aware of the sources of visual processing limitations, designers of advertisements may be skilled at enabling consumers to acquire the advertising message, at least in broad strokes, with a single viewing.

Another issue that needs exploring is whether exposing consumers to information without awareness might be advantageous. Studies of the mere exposure effect indeed suggest an increase in liking for otherwise affectively neutral objects that are viewed subliminally (Kunst-Wilson & Zajonc, 1980). However, such studies show relatively small effects and are typically conducted without reference to the visual context or attentional load given to competing objects in a scene or with very rapid successive stimuli. Certainly more research is needed to evaluate the possible gains in presenting information during, for example an attentional blink, or as secondary items in a change blindness experiment. These are exciting questions for further research and underscore the need for better understanding of human visual processing and attention and how these brain system interact in complex dynamic environments like those present in modern advertisements.

REFERENCES

Chun, M. M., & Potter, M. C. (1995). A two-stage model for multiple taaarget detection in rapid serial visual presentation. *Journal of Experimental Psychology: Human Perception and Performance, 21,* 109–127.

DeSchepper, B., & Treisman, A., (1996). Visual memory for novel shapes: Implicit coding without attention. *Journal of Experimental Psychology: Learning Memory and Cognition, 22,* 27–47.

Irwin, D. (1992). Memory for position and identity across eye movements. *Journal of Experimental Psychology: Learning Memory and Cognition, 18,* 307–317.

Kahneman, D., & Treisman, A. (1984). Changing views of attention and automaticity. In R. Parasuraman & D. R. Davies (Eds.), *Varieties of attention* (pp. 29–61). New York: Academic Press.

Kanwisher, N. G. (1987). Repetition blindness: Type recognition without token individuation. *Cognition, 27,* 117–143.

Kanwisher, N., & Driver, J. (1992). Objects, attributes, and visual attention: Which, what, and where. *Current Directions in Psychological Science, 1,* 26–31.

Kanwisher, N. G., Yin, C., & Wojciulik, E. (1999). Repetition blindness for pictures: Evidence for the rapid computation of abstract visual descriptions. In V. Coltheart (Ed.), *Fleeting memories: Cognition of brief visual stimuli* (pp. 119–150.) Cambridge, MA: MIT Press/Bradford Books.

Kunst-Wilson, W. R., & Zajonc, R. B. (1980). Affective discrimination of stimuli that cannot be recognised. *Science, 207,* 557–558.

Lawrence, D. H. (1971). Two studies of visual search for word targets with controlled rates of presentation. *Perception and Psychophysics, 10,* 85–89.

Levin, D. T., & Simons, D. J. (1997). Failure to detect changes to attended objects in motion pictures. *Psychonomic Bulletin and Review, 4,* 501–506.

Luck, S. J., Vogel, E. K., & Shapiro, K. L. (1996). Word meanings can be accessed but not recognised during the attentional blink. *Nature, 383,* 616–618.

MacLachlan, J., & Logan, M. (1993). Camera-shot length in TV commericals and their memorability and persuasiveness. *Journal of Advertising Research, 33,* 57–61.

Maki, W. S., Frigen, K., & Paulson, K. (1997). Associative priming by targets and distractors during rapid serial visual presentation: Does word meaning survive the attentional blink? *Journal of Experimental Psychology: Human Perception and Performance, 23,* 1014–1034.

Marr, D. (1982). *Vision.* San Francisco: W. H. Freeman.

Motter, B. C. (1993). Focal attention produces spatially selective processing in visual cortical areas V1, V2, and V4 in the presence of competing stimuli. *Journal of Neurophysiology, 70,* 909–919.

Petersen, S. E., Fox, P. T., Posner, M. I., Mintun, M., & Raichle, M. E. (1988). Positron emission studies of the cortical anatomy off single word processing. *Nature, 331,* 585–589.

Potter, M. C. (1999). Understanding sentences and scenes: The role of conceptual short-tem memory. In V. Coltheart (Ed.), *Fleeting memories: Cognition of brief visual stimuli* (pp. 13–46). Cambridge, MA: MIT Press/Bradford Books.

Potter, M. C., & Levy, E. I. (1969). Recognition memory for a rapid series of pictures. *Journal of Experimental Psychology, 81,* 10–15.

Prinzmetal, W. (1995). Visual feature integration inn a world of objects. *Current Directions in Psychological Science, 4,* 90–94.

Raymond, J. E., O'Donnell, H., & Tipper, S. (1998). Priming reveals attentional modulation of human motion sensitivity. *Vision Research, 38,* 2863–2867.

Raymond, J. E., Shapiro, K. L., & Arnell, K. M. (1992). Temporary suppression of visual processing in an RSVP task: An attentional blink? *Journal of Experimental Psychology: Human Perception and Performance, 18,* 849–860.

Raymond, J. E., Shapiro, K. L., & Arnell, K. M. (1995). Similarity determines the attentional blink. *Journal of Experimental Psychology: Human Perception and Performance, 21,* 653–662.

Rayner, K., McConkie, G., & Erlich, S. (1978). Eye movements and intergation of information across fixations. *Journal of Experimental Psychology: Human Perception and Performance, 4,* 529–544.

Rensink, R. A., O'Regan, J. K., & Clark, J. J. (1997). To see or not to see: The need for attention to perceive changes in scenes. *Psychological Science, 8,* 368–373.

Shapiro, K. L., Caldwell, J. I., & Sorensen, R. E. (1997). Personal names and the attentional blink: The "cocktail party" effect revisited. *Journal of Experimental Psychology: Human Perception and Performance, 23,* 504–514.

Shapiro, K. L., Driver, J., Ward, R., & Sorensen, R. (1996). Priming from the attentional blink: A failure to extract visual tokens but not visual types. *Psychological Science, 8,* 95–100.

Shapiro, K. L., Raymond, J. E., & Arnell, K. A. (1996). Attention to visual pattern information produces the attentional blink in RSVP. *Journal of Experimental Psychology: Human Perception and Performance, 20,* 357–371.

Tipper, S. P. (1985). The negative priming effect: Inhibitory effects of ignored primes. *Quarterly Journal of Experimental Psychology, 37A,* 591–511.

Treisman, A. (1996). The binding problem. *Current Opinion in Neurobiology, 6,* 171–178.

Treue, S., & Maunsell, J.H.R. (1996). Attentional modulation of visual motion processing in cortical areas MT and MST. *Nature, 382,* 539–541.

Turvey, M. T. (1973). On peripheral and central processes in vision: Inferences from an information-processing analysis of masking with patterned stimuli. *Psychological Review, 80,* 1–52.

Wolfe, J. M., & Bennett, S. C. (1997). Preattentive object files: Shapeless bundles of basic features. *Vision Research, 37,* 25–43.

Zajonc, R. B. (1968). Attitudinal effects of mere exposure. *Journal of Personality and Social Monographs, 9,* 1–27.

CHAPTER FOUR

Cognitive and Affective Consequences of Visual Fluency: When Seeing Is Easy on the Mind

Piotr Winkielman
University of Denver

Norbert Schwarz
University of Michigan

Rolf Reber
University of Berne

Tedra A. Fazendeiro
University of Denver

What makes images persuasive? This question has a long tradition in theories of aesthetics. At least since Plato and Aristotle, theoreticians have pondered what makes for a compelling picture, appealing design, pleasing scenery, evocative sculpture, or impressive building. As the Greek philosophers noted, some images influence perceivers via their symbolic meaning, such as themes of transcendence, intimacy, or heroism. Other images affect perceivers via their formal aspects, such as harmony, balance, symmetry, dynamics, proportion, and simplicity. The Greek philosophers also suggested that some images speak through the head whereas others speak through the heart, or to use more current psychological terms, convey a message or create a feeling (Gombrich, 1984, 1995; Tatarkiewicz, 1970).

This chapter addresses some of these classic questions from the perspective of recent psychological research that explored the interplay between the "message" (declarative information) and "feeling" (subjective experience) in human judgment. Traditionally, psychological models have assumed that our judgments of a given object are based primarily on the declarative information (thoughts, beliefs, memories) that come to mind at the time of judgment. Challenging this assumption, a growing body of research demonstrated that one's subjective experiences at the time of judgment serve as an important source of input into our judgments. Specifically, when evaluating some stimulus, perceivers often ask themselves, "How do I feel about this?" When choosing this route, perceivers draw on their momentary experience as a source of information, unless they perceive their current feelings as irrelevant to the judgment at (for a comprehensive review see Schwarz & Clore, 1996).

So far, this "experiential" approach to human judgment has been mostly applied to understand the impact of affective and bodily states, such as mood or physical arousal. This research showed, for example, that we evaluate many things more positively when we are in a happy rather than sad mood. Asking ourselves, "How do I feel about this?" we may misread our mood as our affective reaction to the object of judgment, resulting in mood-congruent judgments. This is not the case when we are aware that our mood is due to some irrelevant source, such as the weather, in which case our feelings do not seem informative for the judgment at hand (e.g., Schwarz & Clore, 1983). This experiential approach to human judgment can also help us understand the judgmental impact of *cognitive experiences,* that is, subjective feelings generated in the course of information processing. Here, we specifically address subjective experiences that derive from the ease or difficulty with which image information can be processed, or *visual fluency.*

The chapter is organized as follows. The first section introduces the concept of visual fluency. Next, we review research that explores the role of processing fluency in judgments of visual characteristics of stimuli. After that, we show that similar processes may underlie complex cognitive assessments, such as judgments of previous occurrence ("Have I seen this before?") and judgments of the truth value ("Is the assertion true?"). Subsequently, we address the influence of fluency experiences on preferences ("Do I like the object?") and highlight the affective consequences of visual fluency. After reviewing these findings, we contrast objectivist models of visual appeal with our "experiential" account of aesthetic judgment. This account traces the appealing nature of certain characteristics of visual stimuli (like symmetry, brightness contrast and related variables) to their facilitative effect on processing. Our theory has several implications for thinking about visual persuasion. One is that visual appeal is "in the processing experience of the perceiver" rather than "in the features of the object." Further, our theory groups different objective variables that influence visual appeal under that same theoretical umbrella as factors that influence perceiver's processing experience. Specifically, we contend that any variable that makes a stimulus easy to process will also increase the stimulus's appeal. We conclude with some caveats and a discussion of the limitations of the available evidence.

VISUAL FLUENCY

Any stimulus may be processed with differing degrees of speed, effort, and accuracy. To capture these differences, psychologists have introduced the term *processing fluency* (e.g., Jacoby, Kelley, & Dywan, 1989). Empirically, fluency can be manipulated by a large number of variables. Some of these variables affect the speed and accuracy of low-level processes concerned with the identification of a stimulus' physical identity and form; these variables influence *perceptual fluency* (e.g., Jacoby et al., 1989). Such variables include the contrast between the figure and ground, stimulus clarity, presentation duration, or the amount of previous perceptual exposure to the stimulus. Other variables affect the speed and accuracy of high-level processes concerned with the identification of stimulus meaning and its relation to semantic knowledge structures; these variables influence *conceptual fluency* (e.g., Whittlesea, 1993). Such variables include semantic predictability, consistency between the stimulus and its context, and the availability of appropriate mental concepts for stimulus classification.

The distinction between perceptual and conceptual fluency is important for thinking about the underlying mechanisms and the specific variables that may influence fluency. However, empirically both types of fluency tend to show parallel influences on judgments. Thus, we use the summary term *fluency* to refer to both perceptual and conceptual operations, and use the term *visual fluency* to specifically refer to the processing of image information. Another useful distinction is between *objective* fluency ("ease" assessed by actual processing speed and accuracy), and *subjective* fluency ("ease" assessed by the subjective feeling of low effort, high speed, and accuracy). The subjective experience of fluency usually corresponds to objective fluency, although there are important exceptions to this generalization, which we address at the end of the chapter.

A growing body of research indicates that changes in processing fluency in general, and visual fluency in particular, have consequences for a variety of cognitive and affective judgments. On the cognitive side, fluency influences judgments of perceptual characteristics, judgments of previous occurrence, and judgments of truth. On the affective side, fluency influences judgments of liking for everyday objects and abstract shapes as well as physiological affective reactions to pictures. Next, we review this research and emphasize its implication for visual persuasion.

COGNITIVE CONSEQUENCES OF VISUAL FLUENCY

It is usually easier to perceive stimuli that are presented for a long rather than a short duration or with high rather than low clarity. It is also easier to perceive stimuli that are familiar or preceded by related material, rather than stimuli that are novel or preceded by unrelated material. All of these variables (long duration, high clarity, familiarity, relatedness) have a similar facilitatory effect on processing and may lead to similar fluency experiences. Because we have only one window on our subjective experiences, however, we may misread the fluency resulting from one of these sources as being due to a different source. This process is similar to the demonstrations that people have difficulty distinguishing between different sources of physical arousal (e.g., caffeine, exercise, attractive picture) because these different sources result in a similar experience.

Judgments of Perceptual Characteristics

Consistent with this idea, several studies have demonstrated that perceptual fluency resulting from previous exposure to a stimulus can be misattributed to the duration or clarity of the stimulus presentation (e.g., Whittlesea, Jacoby, & Girard, 1990; Witherspoon & Allan, 1985). For example, people who have seen a given stimulus before, and hence find it easier to process, infer that the current presentation lasted longer, or had higher clarity, than people who have not previously seen this stimulus. The same effect can be obtained with manipulations of conceptual fluency under conditions that do not require a previous visual experience with the stimulus. For example, Masson and Caldwell (1998) asked participants to rate the visual clarity and duration with which a target word (e.g., "arrow") was presented to them on a computer screen. As expected, participants inferred longer presentation durations and higher visual clarity when a preceding semantic task (e.g., complete the sentence, "An archer shoots a bow and ____") had rendered the target word highly accessible. Again, the processing fluency resulting from a preceding task was misattributed to characteristics of the visual stimulus itself.

Memory Illusions

Conversely, the fluency resulting from visual characteristics of a stimulus may be misattributed to effects of previous exposure to the stimulus, thus leading to "memory illusions" (Jacoby & Whitehouse, 1989). For example, Whittlesea et al. (1990) exposed participants to a study list of rapidly presented words. Following this exposure, participants were shown a test list of words and asked whether or not these words had appeared on the previous list. The perceptual fluency of the test words was unobtrusively manipulated by overlaying them with visual masks consisting of dot patterns varying in density, manipulated by the number of dots. As expected, the words shown with more clarity (i.e., with a lower density mask) were more likely to be "recognized" as having appeared on the previous list. Participants presumably misattributed the higher perceptual fluency resulting from visual clarity to previous exposure. Consistent with this interpretation, this "memory illusion" disappeared when participants were aware that the clarity of the visual presentation was being manipulated.

Recently, we have demonstrated that such "memory illusions" extend to manipulations of conceptual fluency and to judgments of pictures (Fazendeiro, Winkielman, & Luo, 2002). First participants saw a study list that included pictures and words. Next the participants saw a test list and indicated which items had appeared previously. Some items on this list were presented on the study list ("old" items), whereas others were not ("new" items). Moreover, some of the new items were unrelated to anything on the study list ("new-unrelated"), whereas other new items were associatively related to stimuli from the study list ("new-related"). Further, all "new-related" items were presented in a different modality than their associates. For example, if the word "bottle" appeared on the study list, a "new-related" test stimulus might be a picture of a wineglass, whereas a "new-unrelated" stimulus might be a picture of a chair. We expected "new-related" pictures (e.g., wineglass) would be falsely recognized as having been presented earlier because the associatively related word (e.g., bottle) would result in enhanced processing fluency. Indeed, participants were more likely to claim that they had previously seen the "new-related" items than the "new-unrelated" items, presumably because they misattributed the fluency with which they could process these pictures to previous exposure. Consistent with this interpretation, the observed memory illusion was eliminated when participants were told that their feeling of familiarity could be influenced by music playing in the background, thus undermining the informational value of the fluency experience for making the memory judgment (Winkielman & Fazendeiro, 2000).

In sum, variables that increase perceptual fluency (like previous exposure, presentation duration or clarity) as well as variables that increase conceptual fluency (like thinking about associatively related concepts) can influence the subjective fluency experience that accompanies the processing of a stimulus. Because people are typically unaware of the specific source of this experience, they may misattribute it to any plausible factor that is brought to their attention. Hence, fluency due to high presentation clarity may lead one to infer that one has seen the stimulus before, much as fluency due to previous exposure may lead one to infer that the stimulus is currently shown with high clarity.

Judgments of Truth

When the objective truth of a statement is difficult to evaluate, people often draw on social consensus information to arrive at a judgment—what many believe is probably true (Festinger, 1954). Thus, we may distrust some information when we hear it for the first time, but when we hear it repeatedly from different sources, we may eventually accept it. In fact, Allport and Lepkin (1945) observed in a classic study of rumor transmission that the strongest predictor of belief in wartime rumors was simple repetition. Consistent with this logic, numerous studies demonstrated that a given statement is more likely to be judged "true" the more often it is repeated. This *illusion of truth* effect (Begg, Anas, & Farinacci, 1992) has been obtained with trivia statements or words from a foreign language (e.g., Arkes, Hackett, & Boehm, 1989; Gilbert, Krull, & Malone, 1990; Hasher, Goldstein, & Toppino, 1977) as well as advertising materials (e.g., Hawkins & Hoch, 1992).

Relating the preceding discussion of perceptual fluency to the judgments of truth, we may conjecture that statements that are easy to process should be more likely to be judged "true" than statements that are difficult to process. As reviewed earlier, people are more likely to infer that they have seen a stimulus before if the stimulus is easier to process—for example, because it is presented with high clarity or for a long duration. If so, the clarity of presentation may result in a memory illusion, which in turn may influence the likelihood that a statement is accepted as true. In an empirical test of this conjecture, Reber and Schwarz (1999) presented participants with statements like "Osorno is a city in Chile" and asked them to decide, as rapidly as possible, whether each statement is true or false. To manipulate perceptual fluency, the statements were shown in colors that made them easy (e.g., dark blue) or difficult (e.g., light blue) to read against the background color. As expected, a given statement was more likely to be judged "true" when it was easy rather than difficult to read. Thus, the ease of visual processing resulted in an illusion of truth, presumably because perceptual fluency led to a feeling of familiarity.

Fluency may also influence truth judgments by routes other than the feeling of familiarity. For example, in a clever study by McGlone and Tofighbakhsh (2000), participants judged novel aphorisms presented in a rhyming form (e.g., "woes unite foes") as more true than the same aphorisms presented in a nonrhyming form (e.g., "woes unite enemies"). The authors suggest that this phenomenon is due to people's implicit reliance on the "beauty (rhyme) equals truth" heuristic, also known as Keats's rule—a reference to the poet's famous assertion in "Ode on a Grecian Urn" that "beauty is truth, truth beauty, that is all ye need know." In either case, a given statement is more likely to be accepted as true when it is easy to process.

In combination with the findings reviewed in the preceding section, these results highlight that people are typically unaware *why* a given stimulus is easy to process. Accordingly, the experience of processing fluency can be attributed to a wide range of different variables, with different implications for subsequent judgments. Quite obviously, nobody would infer that a given statement is likely to be true because it is easy to read, for example. Yet when the subjective experience of fluency is misread as an indication of the apparent familiarity of the statement, the statement is accepted as true. Future research may fruitfully explore if variables that facilitate the fluent processing of more complex persuasive communications enhance their persuasive appeal in similar ways.

AFFECTIVE CONSEQUENCES OF VISUAL FLUENCY: JUDGMENTS OF LIKING AND PREFERENCE

The fluency effect that is probably of most interest to readers studying persuasive imagery is the observation that the ease with which a stimulus can be processed influences people's liking of the stimulus. The best known example of this phenomenon is the *mere-exposure effect* identified by Zajonc (1968). As numerous studies demonstrated, repeated exposure to a stimulus without any reinforcement leads to a gradual increase in liking (see Bornstein, 1989, for a review and limiting conditions). One interpretation of these findings traces the phenomenon to the increased fluency resulting from previous exposures (for other interpretations see Zajonc, 1998). Fluency, in turn, may influence liking in one of two ways. On the one hand, fluency itself may be experienced as affectively positive, and this experience may be misread as resulting from pleasing features of the stimulus. On the other hand, fluency may suggest that the stimulus is familiar (consistent with the findings just reviewed), and familiar stimuli may be preferred over novel ones, as initially suggested by Zajonc (1968). In either case, the assumption that fluency is at the heart of the mere-exposure effect entails that the frequency of exposure per se is not the crucial variable. Instead, any variable that increases the fluency with which a stimulus can be processed should be sufficient to increase perceivers' liking of the stimulus.

The Influence of Perceptual Fluency

Several of our own studies are consistent with this conjecture (Reber, Winkielman & Schwarz, 1998; Winkielman & Cacioppo, 2001; Winkielman & Fazendeiro, 2000). The logic of these studies is rather straightforward. Participants are asked to indicate their liking for a variety of pictures. In most of our studies, these pictures are simple line drawings with similar name agreement, image agreement, familiarity, and visual complexity. The pictures range from everyday objects, such as a wineglass, car, or lamp, to common animals, such as a horse, dog, or bird (Snodgrass & Vanderwart, 1980). In some studies, we have also used abstract objects such as patterns of dots, circles, or geometrical shapes. While participants view the pictures, the fluency with which the pictures can be processed is unobtrusively manipulated through various methods. In some studies, a target picture is preceded by a subliminally presented visual contour that either matches or mismatches the target picture, thus facilitating or impeding its perceptual processing. In other experiments, fluency is manipulated by subtle variations of the presentation duration, figure–ground contrast, or symmetry. Independent of the specific stimuli and manipulations used, the results of all studies converge on a simple conclusion: *Participants like the easy-to-process stimuli more.* From this perspective, the classic mere exposure effect is just one instantiation of a more general class of phenomena. In the case of the mere exposure effect, perceptual fluency is the result of repeated exposure, yet any other variable that increases perceptual fluency has the same positive influence on perceivers' preferences.

Moreover, this positive influence of perceptual fluency is not limited to perceivers' explicit judgments but can also be observed with physiological measures. In a recent study, we monitored perceivers' immediate affective responses to pictures using facial electromyography (Winkielman & Cacioppo, 2001). This technique relies on the observation that positive reactions to stimuli manifest themselves in small, invisible "smiles" (more electrical activity over the zygomaticus "cheek" muscle), whereas negative reactions to stimuli manifest themselves in small, invisible "frowns" (more electrical activity over the corrugator "brow" muscle). As expected, we observed that easy-to-process pictures generated stronger responses over the cheek region than hard-to-process ones. These findings are paralleled by a recent study by Harmon-Jones and Allen (2001), who observed that enhancement of fluency via repeated exposure also leads to stronger electromyographic responses over the cheek region. In combination, these findings demonstrate that increased fluency of processing elicits positive affective responses.

Finally, our findings on the influence of visual priming, figure–ground contrast, presentation duration, and symmetry dovetail with other research showing that liking for pictures can be enhanced by manipulations of image prototypicality, symmetry, and complexity (Cox & Cox, 1988; Langlois & Roggman, 1990; Martindale & Moore, 1988). From our perspective, all of these manipulations represent different ways of increasing the ease of perceptual processing, which in turn increases liking of the perceived stimulus (see also Shapiro, 1999).

The Influence of Conceptual Fluency

In our discussion of judgments of perceptual characteristics and "memory illusions," we highlighted the functional equivalence of visual and semantic priming. This equivalence holds as well for judgments of liking. In the memory illusions section of this chapter, we reviewed an experiment by Winkielman and Fazendeiro (2000) that manipulated the fluency with which a picture (e.g., of a wineglass) could be perceived by exposing participants to an associatively related word (e.g., "bottle"). This experiment also included a condition in which participants made liking judgments. As expected, participants preferred pictures that were associatively related to words presented earlier. The wineglass, for example, was rated as more appealing when preceded by "bottle" than when preceded by an unrelated word. This finding demonstrates that perceivers' preferences for visual stimuli are not only influenced by the facilitation of perceptual processing but also by the facilitation of semantic processing.

This experiment also addressed the mechanisms underlying the fluency–liking connection. One account suggests that this connection is due to the fact that fluency increases the feeling of familiarity (e.g., Klinger & Greenwald, 1994; Smith, 1998). Familiar stimuli, in turn, are preferred over less familiar ones, presumably because of the biological predisposition toward "fear of the unknown" (Zajonc, 1968). Recently, we proposed an alternative account, the *hedonic fluency model*, which proposes that processing fluency may directly trigger positive affect, without the mediation of familiarity (Winkielman, Schwarz, Fazendeiro, & Reber, 2002). Our hedonic fluency account is based on the idea that fluency indicates good progress toward stimulus recognition, coherent cognitive organization, and the availability of knowledge structures to deal with the current situations. As proposed by several researchers, such qualities tend to be associated with positive affect (e.g., Carver & Scheier, 1981; Garcia-Marques & Mackie, 2000; Ramachandran & Hirnstein, 1999; Schwarz, 1990; Simon, 1967; Vallacher & Nowak, 1999).[1] We tested the "familiarity" account against the "hedonic fluency" account by informing participants that some of the feelings they may experience when watching the stimuli may be biased by external sources and thus be uninformative for their judgments. Specifically, participants were told that an external source (music playing in a background) either may bias their feelings of familiarity or may bias their affective response. Interestingly, attributing familiarity to the background music did not eliminate the effect of fluency on liking, contrary to the predictions of the familiarity account. In contrast, attributing one's affective response to the music did eliminate the positive influence of fluency on liking. In combination with the electromyographic findings reviewed earlier, this pattern of results suggests that fluency is immediately experienced as positive and that its influence on liking is not mediated by feelings of familiarity.

These findings are especially important because they highlight differences in the mechanisms underlying the influence of fluency on cognitive and affective judgments. Recall that attributing one's feelings of familiarity (but not one's affective feelings) to background music eliminated the "memory illusion" discussed earlier. In contrast, attributing one's affective response (but not one's feelings of familiarity) to background music eliminated the influence of fluency on liking.

VISUAL APPEAL RESIDES IN THE PROCESSING EXPERIENCE OF THE PERCEIVER

Most theories of aesthetics assume that beauty resides in the object of appreciation. This perspective gave rise to numerous attempts to identify objective features responsible for visual appeal (Arnheim, 1974; Birkhoff, 1933; Fechner, 1876; Gombrich, 1984; Maritain, 1966; Solso, 1994). Among the more prominent of these features are simplicity, symmetry, balance, certain proportions such as the golden section, clarity, and contrast. Recent research has proposed additional candidates such as prototypicality or averageness of the form (e.g., Halberstadt & Rhodes, 2000; Langlois & Roggman, 1990; Martindale, 1984). Note that all of these characteristics share one important feature—they are likely to facilitate processing of the stimulus. If so, we may conjecture that these well-known characteristics render an object appealing because they enable the perceiver to experience visual fluency, either on the perceptual or conceptual level (see Reber, Schwarz, &

---

[1] These ideas are related to observations that cognitive disorganization, as in dissonance, tends to be experienced as unpleasant, as reflected in self-reports and in psychophysiological measures (Harmon-Jones, 2000; Losch & Cacioppo, 1990).

Winkielman, 2002, for a more fully developed argument). From this perspective, visual appeal does not reside in the object of appreciation but in the processing experience of the perceiver.

Such an experiential approach to aesthetic judgment provides a unified and parsimonious account for the influence of numerous, otherwise unrelated, variables. On the one hand, it plausibly accounts for the known influence of objective characteristics of visually appealing objects, as the preceding list illustrates. On the other hand, it accounts for the reviewed visual and conceptual priming effects, such as the otherwise counterintuitive observation that thinking about the concept of "bottle" increases one's appreciation of the image of a wineglass. Findings of this type fall outside the range of objectivist approaches to aesthetic judgment.

In addition, an experiential approach to aesthetic judgment can accommodate individual, situational, and cultural differences without requiring differential assumptions about the underlying processes. As illustrated by the influence of previous exposure and conceptual priming, what can be fluently processed depends on an individual's previous experience and knowledge, which are culturally contextualized. Moreover, temporary influences like the availability of cognitive and motivational resources or the presence of attributional cues may influence the generation and use of fluency experiences, resulting in systematic variation within individuals. As illustrated in studies showing that fluency manipulations result in qualitatively different experiences, such as the experience of pleasantness and the experience of familiarity, our approach allows for the richness of subjective experiences that characterize aesthetic appreciation. Finally, "fluency-like" experiences may be generated by a variety of context-specific operations within the visual and semantic system, such as component extraction, image segmentation, grouping, meaning analysis, and integration with previous knowledge structures (see Ramachandran & Hirnstein, 1999). As a result, aesthetic judgments are likely to be influenced by numerous variables that are unrelated to the object of appreciation. Yet the influence of these variables may be fruitfully traced to the perceiver's experience of visual fluency, potentially providing a unifying framework for the psychological analysis of aesthetic experience.[2]

CAVEATS AND LIMITATIONS

As already mentioned, there are important individual, cultural, and situational factors that modify the generation and use of fluency experiences. In addition, it is also worthwhile to consider the following factors. In the studies presented earlier,

---

[2]Of course, some stimulus features can elicit affective reactions independently of processing experiences. For example, the affect system is evolutionarily prepared to respond to frowning faces, snakes, spiders, erotic signals, and so on, even when these stimuli are presented subliminally (Oehman, 1997; Winkielman, Zajonc, & Schwarz, 1997).

objective fluency (actual processing speed) was closely related to subjective fluency (the feeling of processing ease). However, under some circumstances these processes may become dissociated. For example, under the influence of alcohol, the subjective feeling of fluency may greatly exceed the objective speed of processing—perhaps another reason why alcohol promotes generosity in aesthetic judgments? On the other hand, some automatic, reflex-like mental processes characterized by high objective fluency (e.g., low-level visual processes) may not be accompanied by a subjective experience of ease, and may have little effect on the type of cognitive and affective judgments just discussed. Other factors worth considering are the perceiver's expectations with regard to processing experiences. Theoretically, the fluent processing may have the most impact when fluency is unexpected. For example, we do not seem to experience a distinct feeling of familiarity when we encounter people we know well, even though objective processing is very fluent in such encounters. Consistent with this possibility, Whittlesea and Williams (1998, 2000) found that when people are surprised by being able to interpret a stimulus that initially appears uninterpretable, they are particularly likely to attribute processing ease to prior experience. This possibility may explain why a cultural cliché, such as an overplayed jingle, will not generate a pleasantness experience, even though it is cognitively processed with very high fluency. To produce a meaningful subjective experience, processing fluency may need to deviate from the person's internal norm as to how fluently a particular stimulus should be processed. Further, as pointed out by Whittlesea (personal communication, 2001), predictably fluent processing may actually reduce the experienced interest in the item, and thus reduce its overall evaluation. These speculations are consistent with earlier research by Berlyne (1974) that demonstrated a decrease in evaluation for stimuli that were very simple and very familiar (although Berlyne's explanation was different from the one proposed here).

Finally, when are perceivers most likely to draw on their subjective experiences in forming a judgment? Several authors suggested that conditions such as low involvement, low processing capacity, time pressure, and so on, tend to promote heuristic processing such as the use of the "How-do-I-feel-about-it" strategy (e.g., Chaiken & Trope, 1999; Petty & Cacioppo, 1986; Schwarz, 1990). The available evidence is consistent with these predictions (see Schwarz & Clore, 1996, for a review). Note, however, that reliance on one's feelings is only a "heuristic" strategy when the judgment pertains to non-affective dimensions. When the judgment pertains to a feeling (e.g., judgment of liking), reliance on one's feelings reflects the use of the most diagnostic substantive information available (Schwarz & Clore, 1996).

CONCLUSIONS

The reviewed research highlights the crucial role of subjective experiences in human judgment. One of these experiences is the ease with which a stimulus can be processed. The experienced processing fluency is a function of formal features of the stimulus, like figure–ground contrast or presentation duration, as well as the perceiver's previous experiences, like earlier exposures or thoughts about associatively related material. Because perceivers are typically unaware of the specific source of visual fluency, they may attribute the experience to any plausible candidate that comes to mind. Thus, they may erroneously infer from fluency that is due to previous exposure that the stimulus is presented for a long duration, or may infer from fluency due to duration that they have seen the stimulus before. This "free floating" nature of the fluency experience explains the broad range of substantive judgments—most notably judgments of truth, familiarity, and liking—for which this experience can serve as a source of information. As is the case for other types of experiential information, people only draw on their fluency experiences when the informational value of the experience for the judgment at hand is not called into question. When people are aware that their experience may be due to a source that is unrelated to the object of judgment, the otherwise observed influence is attenuated or eliminated.

On the theoretical side, our findings illustrate that analyses of visual persuasion need to consider the interplay of objective features of the stimulus, the context in which the stimulus is presented, and the perceivers' subjective experiences. On the applied side, our findings indicate that easy-to-process messages are more appealing and persuasive. Many of the variables that facilitate processing are well known to practitioners, like figure–ground contrast, clarity, symmetry, and proportion. Other variables, like priming procedures or the match between stimulus and context, have received limited attention in the applied domain. Their systematic exploration promises a fruitful avenue for future research at the interface of psychology and visual design.

REFERENCES

Allport, F. H., & Lepkin, M. (1945). Wartime rumors of waste and special privilege: Why some people believe them. *Journal of Abnormal and Social Psychology, 40,* 3–36.

Arkes, H. R., Hackett, C., & Boehm, L. (1989). The generality of the relation between familiarity and judged validity. *Journal of Behavioral Decision Making, 2,* 81–94.

Arnheim, R. (1974). *Art and visual perception: A psychology of the creative eye.* Berkeley: University of California Press.

Begg, I. M., Anas, A., & Farinacci, S. (1992). Dissociation of processes in belief: Source recollection, statement familiarity, and the illusion of truth. *Journal of Experimental Psychology: General, 121,* 446–458.

Berlyne, D. E. (1974). *Studies in the new experimental aesthetics: Steps toward an objective psychology of aesthetic appreciation.* Washington, DC: Hemisphere.

Birkhoff, G. D. (1933). *Aesthetic measure.* Cambridge, MA: Harvard University Press.

Bornstein, R. F. (1989). Exposure and affect: Overview and meta-analysis of research, 1968–1987. *Psychological Bulletin, 106,* 265–289.

Carver, C. S., & Scheier, M. F. (1981). *Attention and self-regulation: A control-theory approach to human behavior.* New York: Springer-Verlag.

Chaiken, S., & Trope, Y. (1999). *Dual-process theories in social psychology.* New York: Guilford Press.

Cox, D. S., & Cox, A. D. (1988). What does familiarity breed? Complexity as a moderator of repetition effects in advertisement evaluation. *Journal of Consumer Research, 15,* 111–116.

Fazendeiro, T. A., Winkielman, P., & Luo, C. R. (2002). *False memory for paired-associates: Evidence for the implicit activation-fluency misattribution hypothesis.* Manuscript in preparation.

Fechner, G. T. (1876). *Vorschule der Ästhetik.* Leipzig: Breitkopf & Härtel.

Festinger, L. (1954). A theory of social comparison processes. *Human Relations, 7,* 123–146.

Garcia-Marques, T., & Mackie, D. M. (2000). The positive feeling of familiarity: Mood as an information processing regulation mechanism. In H. Bless & J. Forgas (Eds.), *The message within: The role of subjective experience in social cognition and behavior* (pp. 240–261). Philadelphia: Psychology Press.

Gilbert, D. T., Krull, D. S., & Malone, P. S. (1990). Unbelieving the unbelievable: Some problems in the rejection of false information. *Journal of Personality and Social Psychology, 59,* 601–613.

Gombrich, E. H. (1984). *A sense of order* (2nd ed.). London: Phaidon.

Gombrich, E. H. (1995). *The story of art* (16th ed.). London: Phaidon.

Halberstadt, J., & Rhodes, G. (2000). The attractiveness of nonface averages: Implications for an evolutionary explanation of the attractiveness of average faces. *Psychological Science, 4,* 285–289.

Harmon-Jones, E. (2000). A cognitive dissonance theory perspective on the role of emotion in the maintenance and change of beliefs and attitudes. In N. H. Frijda, A. R. S. Manstead, & S. Bem (Eds.), *Emotion and beliefs* (pp. 185–211). Cambridge, UK: Cambridge University Press.

Harmon-Jones, E., & Allen, J. J. B. (2001). The role of affect in the mere exposure effect: Evidence from psychophysiological and individual differences approaches. *Personality and Social Psychology Bulletin, 27,* 889–898.

Hasher, L., Goldstein, D., & Toppino, T. (1977). Frequency and the conference of referential validity. *Journal of Verbal Learning and Verbal Behavior, 16,* 107–112.

Hawkins, S. A., & Hoch, S. J. (1992). Low-involvement learning: Memory without evaluation. *Journal of Consumer Research, 19,* 212–225.

Jacoby, L. L., Kelley, C. M., & Dywan J. (1989). Memory attributions. In H. L. Roediger & F. I. M. Craik (Eds.), *Varieties of memory and consciousness: Essays in honour of Endel Tulving.* (pp. 391–422). Hillsdale, NJ: Lawrence Erlbaum Associates.

Jacoby, L. L., & Whitehouse, K. (1989). An illusion of memory: False recognition influenced by unconscious perception. *Journal of Experimental Psychology: General, 118,* 126–135.

Klinger, M. R., & Greenwald A. G. (1994). Preferences need no inferences?: The cognitive basis of unconscious mere exposure effects. In P. M. Niedenthal & S. Kitayama (Eds.), *The heart's eye* (pp. 67–85). San Diego: Academic Press.

Langlois, J. H., & Roggman, L. A. (1990). Attractive faces are only average. *Psychological Science, 1,* 115–121.

Losch, M. E., & Cacioppo, J. T. (1990). Cognitive dissonance may enhance sympathetic tonus, but attitudes are changed to reduce negative affect rather than arousal. *Journal of Experimental Social Psychology, 26,* 289–304.

Maritain, J. (1966). Beauty and imitation. In M. Rader (Ed.), *A modern book of esthetics* (pp. 27–34). New York: Holt, Rinehart, and Winston.

Martindale, C. (1984). The pleasures of thought: A theory of cognitive hedonics. *Journal of Mind and Behavior, 5,* 49–80.

Martindale, C., & Moore, K. (1988). Priming, prototypicality, and preference. *Journal of Experimental Psychology: Human Perception and Performance, 14,* 661–670.

Masson, M. E. J., & Caldwell, J. I. (1998). Conceptually driven encoding episodes create perceptual misattributions. *Acta Psychologica, 98,* 183–210.

McGlone, M. S., & Tofighbakhsh, J. (2000). Birds of a feather flock conjointly(?): Rhyme as reason in aphorisms. *Psychological Science, 11,* 424–428.

Oehman, A. (1997). As fast as the blink of an eye: Evolutionary preparedness. In P. J. Lang, R. F.

Simons, & M. Balaban (Eds.), *Attention and orienting: Sensory and motivational processes* (pp. 165–184). Mahwah, NJ: Lawrence Erlbaum Associates.

Petty, R. E., & Cacioppo, J. T. (1986). *Communication and Persuasion: Central and Peripheral Routes to Attitude Change.* New York: Springer Verlag.

Ramachandran, V. S., & Hirstein, W. (1999). The science of art: A neurological theory of aesthetic experience. *Journal of Consciousness Studies, 6,* 15–51.

Reber, R., & Schwarz, N. (1999). Effects of perceptual fluency on judgments of truth. *Consciousness and Cognition, 8,* 338–342.

Reber, R., Schwarz, N., & Winkielman, P. (2002). *Processing fluency and aesthetic pleasure: Is beauty in the perceiver's processing experience?* Manuscript under review.

Reber, R., Winkielman P., & Schwarz N. (1998). Effects of perceptual fluency on affective judgments. *Psychological Science, 9,* 45–48.

Schwarz, N. (1990). Feeling as information: Informational and motivational functions of affective states. In E. T. Higgins & R. M. Sorrentino (Eds.), *Handbook of motivation and cognition* (pp. 527–561). New York: Guilford Press.

Schwarz, N., & Clore, G. L. (1983). Mood, misattribution, and judgments of well-being: Informative and directive functions of affective states. *Journal of Personality and Social Psychology, 45,* 513–523.

Schwarz, N., & Clore, G. L. (1996). Feelings and phenomenal experiences. In E. T. Higgins & A. W. Kruglanski (Eds.), *Social psychology: Handbook of basic principles* (pp. 433–465). New York: Guilford Press.

Simon, H. A. (1967). Motivational and emotional controls of cognition. *Psychological Review, 74,* 29–39.

Smith, E. R. (1998). Mental representation and memory. In D. T. Gilbert, S. T. Fiske, & G. Lindzey (Eds.), *The handbook of social psychology* (pp. 269–322). Boston: McGraw-Hill.

Snodgrass, J. G., & Vanderwart M. (1980). A standardized set of 260 pictures: Norms for name agreement, image agreement, familiarity, and visual complexity. *Journal of Experimental Psychology: Human Learning and Memory, 6,* 174–215.

Solso, R. L. (1994). *Mind and brain sciences in the 21st century.* Cambridge, MA: MIT Press.

Tatarkiewicz, W. (1970). *History of aesthetics.* The Hague: Mouton.

Vallacher, R. R., & Nowak, A. (1999). The dynamics of self-regulation. In R. S. Wyer, Jr. (Ed.), *Perspectives on behavioral self-regulation* (pp. 241–259). Mahwah, NJ: Lawrence Erlbaum Associates.

Whittlesea, B. W. A. (1993). Illusions of familiarity. *Journal of Experimental Psychology: Learning, Memory, and Cognition, 19,* 1235–1253.

Whittlesea, B. W. A., Jacoby L. L., & Girard K. (1990). Illusions of immediate memory: Evidence of an attributional basis for feelings of familiarity and perceptual quality. *Journal of Memory and Language, 29,* 716–732.

Whittlesea, B. W. A., & Williams, L. D. (1998). Why do strangers feel familiar, but friends don't? A discrepancy-attribution account of feelings of familiarity. *Acta Psychologica, 98,* 141–165.

Whittlesea, B. W. A., & Williams, L. D. (2000). The source of feelings of familiarity: The discrepancy-attribution hypothesis. *Journal of Experimental Psychology: Learning, Memory, and Cognition, 26,* 547–565.

Winkielman, P., & Cacioppo, J. T. (2001). Mind at ease puts a smile on the face: Psychophysiological evidence that processing facilitation increases positive affect. *Journal of Personality and Social Psychology, 81,* 989–1000.

Winkielman, P., & Fazendeiro, T. (2000). *The role of conceptual fluency in preference and memory.* Manuscript in preparation.

Winkielman, P., Schwarz, N., Fazendeiro, T., & Reber, R. (2002). The hedonic marking of processing fluency: Implications for evaluative judgment. In J. Musch & K. C. Klauer (Eds.), *The psychology of evaluation: Affective processes in cognition and emotion* (pp. 189–217). Mahwah, NJ: Lawrence Erlbaum Associates.

Winkielman, P., Zajonc, R. B., & Schwarz, N. (1997). Subliminal affective priming resists attributional interventions. *Cognition and Emotion, 11,* 433–465.

Witherspoon, D., & Allan, L. G. (1985). The effects of a prior presentation on temporal judgments in a perceptual identification task. *Memory and Cognition, 13,* 103–111.

Zajonc, R. B. (1968). Attitudinal effects of mere exposure. *Journal of Personality and Social Psychology: Monograph Supplement, 9,* 1–27.

Zajonc, R. B. (1998). Emotions. In D. T. Gilbert, S. T. Fiske, & G. Lindzey (Eds.), *The handbook of social psychology* (pp. 591–632). Boston: McGraw-Hill.

CHAPTER FIVE

A Levels-of-Processing Model of Advertising Repetition Effects

Christie L. Nordhielm
Northwestern University

Visual images, particularly those utilized in persuasive contexts, are rarely presented just once. In fact, a presumption of advertisers and others seeking to persuade is that one exposure will not suffice: repetition is a crucial aspect of visual persuasion. It is therefore interesting to consider how much (or little) repetition of a particular visual image is necessary to generate the hoped-for consumer response. Both popular wisdom and academic research suggest that, beyond some level, additional exposures to a particular persuasive image may have a deleterious impact on effectiveness. This issue has generated substantial research seeking to identify the optimal level of exposure under a variety of conditions. For example, advertisers have spent considerable resources attempting to determine how long and how frequently they should employ a particular advertising execution, package design, or corporate logo. Researchers who have explored this issue have termed the outcome typically produced by overexposure to an advertisement or other stimulus *wearout,* meaning that at some level of repetition, people's affective response to a visual stimulus either is no longer positive or shows a significant decline (Pechman & Stewart, 1988, p. 286). Several experimental studies found that wearout of specific advertisements occurred after 3 to 10 exposures (e.g., Batra & Ray, 1986; Belch, 1982), although the precise point at which wearout occurs presumably depends on a variety of advertising-specific (e.g., advertising complexity) and/or context-related factors. Nonetheless, the typical relationship between exposure and affective response is believed to display an inverted U-shaped pattern, where initial exposures generate increasing familiarity and positive affect, but subsequent exposures eventually lead to wearout and a decrease in positive affect.

To stave off such wearout, advertisers frequently develop a pool of ads that employ different executions but convey the same basic material and claims.

These executions typically share a number of common features, such as the brand name, logo, tag line, and advertising border or background, whereas other features such as the storyline, headline, ad copy, and setting are varied. The logic is that by introducing variation in such advertising executions, the onset of wearout will be greatly delayed. Consistent with this logic, several experimental studies have found that varying ad executions can effectively delay the onset of wearout (e.g., Calder & Sternthal, 1980; Grass, Wallace, & Winters, 1969), and this appears to hold true for print advertisements (McCullough & Ostrom, 1974), for children's television ads (Gorn & Goldberg, 1980), and for ads embodying variations of both form and content (Schumann, Petty, & Clemons, 1990). For example, work by Calder and Sternthal (1980) found that increasing the number of different executions presented in a pool of repeated ads from one to three had a significant positive impact on product evaluations. Moreover, Unnava and Burnkrant (1991) found that repetition of different versus identical print ads significantly heightened brand recall.

To date, however, research that has investigated the wearout phenomenon has consistently examined people's affective response to repeated exposures of a stimulus as a whole, where an advertisement or a product package was the repeated item. That is, repetition effects generally have been studied by varying levels of repetition of a single advertisement (Batra & Ray, 1986; Belch, 1982) or series of ads (Cacioppo & Petty, 1979; Calder & Sternthal, 1980), as opposed to examining the effects of repetition of the specific elements or features of the ad. Hence, we know very little about how repetition of a particular feature within a visual image might influence peoples' affective response to that image. This latter issue would seem to be important because if repetition of a particular feature of a persuasive image leads to wearout of that feature, this may have a negative impact on affect toward the image as a whole. If this is indeed the case, it is possible that a new image that contains a previously viewed feature may wear out more quickly than an image that does not contain such a feature.

The preceding discussion suggests that an important question is whether the relationship between repetition of a particular feature and affective response exhibits the same inverted U-shaped pattern as has been observed between repetition of an entire ad and affective response. The purpose of this chapter is to examine this question of how repeated exposure to specific features in a communication may influence people's affective response to the communication as a whole, why this occurs, and what factors may moderate such outcomes. Based on a series of studies, I develop the thesis that the impact of repeated exposure to particular ad features on people's affective response is determined by how those features are processed. Specifically, I hypothesize that when a feature is processed in a relatively shallow manner, the exposure–affect relationship is monotonically increasing, but when a feature is processed in a deeper manner where people elaborate on its semantic meaning, the relationship between frequency of feature exposure and affective response will exhibit an inverted U-shaped pattern.

THE IMPACT OF FEATURE REPETITION

A key assumption in this line of reasoning is that the repetition of a particular feature of an advertisement can have a unique, separable impact on people's affective response to the advertisement as a whole. That is, if we consider people's past exposure to a particular feature, we can better predict their affective response to a new image that contains this feature. This *feature-based* model of repetition effects proposes that affective response to a stimulus is a function of people's response to the individual features of that stimulus. This model may be compared to the more commonly accepted *holistic* model, one that does not consider past exposure to features, but only frequency of exposure to the stimulus as a whole. By manipulating people's frequency of exposure to a particular feature in an advertisement, I was able explore the possibility that, under certain conditions, repeated exposure to a particular feature of a persuasive image may not result in the wearout normally observed when the stimulus as a whole is repeated. In other words, while an ad as a whole might be subject to wearout, it might be possible to repeatedly expose a particular feature of an ad and observe an increase in affective response to the ad containing that feature with no wearout.

To explore this possibility, I conducted two studies that generated promising results (Nordhielm, 1996). In one study, I presented participants with a series of geometric patterns and asked them to assess liking on a 7-point scale. These patterns were constructed using four features: shape (square or circle), color (red or blue), border (black or colored), and pattern (open or filled). In total, 16 unique patterns were thus generated, presented in Fig. 5.1, with each pattern assuming one of two possible values associated with each feature (e.g., a red square with a black border and open pattern, a blue circle with a colored border and closed pattern, etc.). Using a 17-inch computer monitor, I presented three participants with up to 180 of these patterns in random order, asking them to assess their liking after each presentation. These presentations were random; hence the number and order of repetitions of each pattern, as well as each feature, varied from participant to participant. I then tested two different regression models to assess whether it was more accurate to predict liking based on past exposure to features or the whole pattern. For all three participants, I was better able to predict their liking for a particular pattern by considering how frequently the participant had seen the particular features of the pattern, as opposed to considering how many times the participant had seen that specific pattern.

These results were encouraging; they suggested that I might be able to influence liking for a persuasive image simply by manipulating past exposure to a particular feature of that image. In a second study I did just that. Using 88 pictures of different earrings from the same designer, I "constructed" a series of ads consisting of a headline with the designer's name, a background, and a picture of one earring. I created two simple backgrounds from either a vertical pattern or a diagonal pattern. Examples of these ads are presented in Fig. 5.2. I then asked participants to review a series of these ads on a computer screen, under the guise that they were evaluating a new web site. Half the participants saw 80 ads presented with a vertical background and 8 with a diagonal background, and half saw 80 of diagonal and 8 vertical backgrounds. Following these exposures, respondents viewed one more ad featuring a new earring displayed against either the high (80) exposure or the low (8) exposure background. For this ad, they were asked to indicated liking and purchase intent on a 9-point scale. Consistent with my predictions, liking and intent to purchase the piece of jewelry were significantly higher when it was presented against the high-exposure background, regardless of whether it was vertical or diagonal (see Table 5.1).

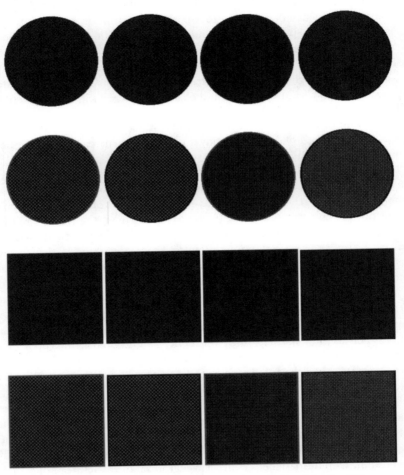

FIG. 5.1.   Sixteen unique patterns using four features. (See Color Panel C)

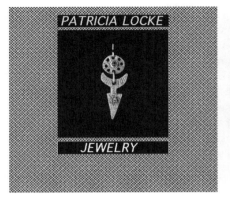 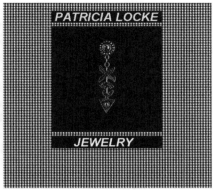

FIG. 5.2. (A) Sample jewelry ad, diagonal background. (B) Sample jewelry ad, horizontal background.

TABLE 5.1
The Effect of Feature Exposure Frequency on Affective Response
and Purchase Intentions for the Target Ad Product

Frequency of Exposure to Target Ad Background	Dependent Measure		
	Affective Response	Purchase Intention	Interestingness
High	6.40^a	4.92^a	6.24
Low	5.30^b	3.20^b	6.20

$^{a, b}$Means with different letters are different from one another at $p < .05$.

It is particularly interesting that the relationship between feature repetition and affective response remained positive as repetition of the background ad feature increased from 8 to 80 exposures. This observation is ostensibly noteworthy as it contrasts with the results of many previous advertising repetition studies, which have reported a downturn in affective response after advertisement repetition levels of as few as five exposures (e.g., Calder & Sternthal, 1980). In other words, it appears that wearout occurs for ads, but not necessarily features of those ads.

These experiments offer several interesting observations, but also leave unanswered questions. First, the studies suggest that repeated exposure to a particular feature of a stimulus heightens familiarity and liking for that stimulus as a whole. This finding is in contrast to the inverted U-shaped relationship commonly observed when the repeated element is the ad as a whole. Indeed, this apparent inconsistency echoes the more general one observed in the repetition literature as a whole (e.g., Crandall, Montgomery, & Rees, 1973, Experiment 1; Kail & Freeman, 1973; Zajonc, Crandall, Kail, & Swap, 1974, Experiment 2). Interestingly, although most repetition studies performed using advertising stimuli report an initial increase followed by a downturn in affective response as the number of exposures increases, studies that examine repetition of nonpersuasive stimuli—particularly studies involving relatively short exposure durations—generally report monotonically increasing affect with repeated exposure, which is the same outcome observed in the present study, although here the stimuli were presumably persuasive, if only because they were advertisements. These different patterns of outcomes have given rise to two alternative theories about the relationship between repeated exposure and affective response. In the sections that follow I briefly describe these two theories and then discuss further research that examines issues raised by these theories.

THEORIES OF REPETITION EFFECTS

The dominant explanation for the commonly observed inverted U-shaped relationship between exposure and affect is offered by modified two-factor theory (Cacioppo & Petty, 1979). Modified two-factor theory is derived from Berlyne's (1970) two-factor theory, which proposes that two factors, positive habituation and tedium, mediate the relationship between repetition and affective response. This is the familiar experience that we feel when subjected to multiple exposures to the same persuasive image: We tend to like it a bit more with repetition while we become accustomed to it, but at some point there is nothing more to get used to, and we become increasing bored with further exposures. Eventually our feelings of boredom outweigh our feelings of familiarity, and the net effect of additional exposures is negative instead of positive.

Modified two-factor theory builds on Berlyne's two-factor model by associating positive habituation and tedium with positively and negatively-valenced thoughts. That is, affective response to the repeated presentation of a message is mediated by the number of positive and negative thoughts that are generated in response to that message, and the valence of these thoughts depends on the relative magnitude of the positive habituation and tedium the respondent experiences (Cacioppo & Petty, 1979). Because initial repetitions generate mostly positive habituation, the number of positive thoughts is presumed to increase over these initial presentations, whereas later repetitions are presumed to generate increasing tedium and therefore more negative thoughts. Affective judgments are presumed to be the net of both positive and negative thoughts, and will therefore increase initially as the number of positive thoughts increases with increasing exposure, then decline as the influence of negative thoughts exceeds that of positive thoughts.

Although the inverted U-shaped relationship between exposure and affective response is prevalent, this relationship appears not to hold under certain conditions. Using both black-and-white photographs and simple line drawings, Bornstein and D'Agostino (1992) reported that when respondents view the stimuli repeatedly, their affective response increases and then decreases after some number of repetitions, resulting in the expected inverted U-shaped relationship between repeated exposure and affect. However, when exposure durations are extremely short (i.e., less than 1 s) so that processing of the stimuli remains a constant challenge despite relatively high exposure frequency, a monotonically increasing relationship between repeated exposure and affect emerges.

This finding suggests that when respondents engage in minimal processing of a stimulus no downturn in affective response is likely to occur even at relatively high levels of repetition. The modified two-factor model doesn't really consider the mechanism that presumably underlies this type of increase in affective response, namely, an increase in the ease with which the stimulus is processed perceptually, or perceptual fluency (Mandler, Nakamura, & Van Zandt, 1987). This is because modified two-factor theory is predicated on the assumption that conscious semantic processing mediates affective response, whereas this type of conscious processing is presumed not to occur in the case of extremely short or subliminal exposure durations. In fact, it has been argued that this lack of conscious processing on the part of the viewer, or ability to "defend" oneself against a persuasive message, may contribute to how easily persuaded the viewer may be (Bargh, 1992). Thus, when ability to process the stimulus is limited, a model that considers the influence of increased perceptual fluency may provide a better account of the mechanism that is responsible for the increasingly monotonic relationship observed between exposure and affect.

A model of this type has been suggested by Bornstein and D'Agostino (1994), and it is commonly called the perceptual fluency/misattribution model (see also Jacoby, Toth, Lindsay, & Debner, 1992; Mandler et al., 1987). According to this model, the perceptual fluency of a stimulus, which refers to the ease with which people perceive, encode, and process it, can be heightened by factors such as prior stimulus exposure, or it can be impeded by other factors such as the degraded visibility of a stimulus. Yet although people often experience fluctuations in their perceptual fluency of stimuli, they generally lack insight into the true cause of such experiences. Thus, if after experiencing such variations in perceptual fluency they are asked to assess a stimulus on a dimension that is difficult to judge (e.g., they are asked whether they like the stimulus), they often misattribute the cause of the perceptual fluency to the stimulus's status on the dimension in question. Hence, if as a result of past exposure a person is relatively perceptually fluent with a stimulus, but doesn't recall the past exposure, the person may think he or she is experiencing this feeling of fluency because he or she likes it. This perceptual fluency/misattribution phenomenon has been demonstrated by Mandler et al. (1987), who found that people misattributed enhanced perceptual fluency, which actually was caused by prior exposure to a stimulus, to their heightened liking of the stimulus, the lightness of the stimulus, or the darkness of the stimulus, depending on which of these potential causes was queried. Thus, it appears that people's misattribution of perceptual fluency is not limited to the affective dimension of a stimulus. Rather, it extends to nonaffective descriptive dimensions as well.

Bornstein and D'Agostino (1994) examined the implications of the perceptual fluency/misattribution model when applied to a repeated stimulus exposure situation where participants were given an opportunity to adjust for possible misattribution. The authors hypothesized that when participants were told that they were evaluating stimuli they had seen before, they would correct for their tendency to misattribute heightened perceptual fluency to stimulus liking. Participants in the Bornstein and D'Agostino study first took part in a familiarization task where they received brief (100-ms) exposures to 15 simple line drawings repeated randomly 10 times each. Then they were presented with 18 target stimuli to evaluate, 3 of which had been presented in the familiarization stage. However, prior to indicating their liking of the target stimuli, participants were informed either that none of the drawings they were about to see had been presented before (new condition) or that all of them had been presented previously in the familiarization phase (old condition).

As expected, liking for familiar drawings (i.e., drawings that truly had been viewed in the familiarization phase) was greater than liking for unfamiliar drawings condition. However, if respondents had been told that they had previously seen the drawings, this difference disappeared. Hence, the authors concluded that when participants are given an opportunity to adjust for misattribution by receiving explicit information about previous stimulus exposure, such "mere exposure effects" disappear. Similar results were also reported in the same study for subliminal stimulus presentations. These results open up an interesting area of repetition effects that has not previously been considered. The model I present next attempts to integrate this perceptual fluency/misattribution model with the two-factor model of repetition effects.

THE LEVELS-OF-PROCESSING MODEL

The preceding discussion suggests that although modified two-factor theory accounts for a considerable portion of the mere and repeated exposure effect findings, perceptual fluency/misattribution theory may provide a more appealing model when deeper processing of stimuli is impeded. Bargh (1992) proposed that this perceptual fluency/misattribution model applies when two conditions prevail: (a) people experience a variation in their perceptual fluency (e.g., possibly due to repeated exposure of a stimulus), and (b) they are unable to accurately identify the source of that fluency. In the aforementioned study by Bornstein and D'Agostino (1994), this inability to identify the source of perceptual fluency was caused by lack of opportunity; that is, the exposure durations were so short that respondents presumably could not determine whether or not they had been exposed to a particular stimulus previously. In essence, they were only able to engage in shallow, as opposed to deep, processing of the stimuli.

As discussed earlier, two-factor theory and perceptual fluency/misattribution theory represent the dominant explanations for why and how repeated exposure to an object or feature influences people's affective responses. At the same time, neither theory alone seems to provide the best explanation for the findings of all studies that have examined the effects of repeated stimulus/feature exposure on affective judgments. Given the inherent viability of both theories and the observation that each appears to account for some but not all findings, an important question that emerges is, what determines when the mechanisms proposed by each of these theories operate?

Examination of the extant literature provides some support for the notion that the level of processing people employ during stimulus or feature exposure might determine when repeated exposure produces effects that are more consistent with those suggested by either modified two-factor or perceptual fluency/misattribution theory. Specifically, the mechanism described by perceptual fluency/misattribution theory would seem to operate when stimuli or features are processed in a shallow manner and result in a monotonically increasing repeated exposure–affective response function. However, the modified two-factor theory may operate when stimuli/features are processed more deeply and thereby receive more elaborative analysis. Thus, in the latter case, the repeated exposure–affective response relationship would exhibit an inverted U-shaped pattern.

Some research seems to support this view that level of processing can moderate repetition effects. For example, Hawkins and Hoch (1992) found that repeated exposure to trivia statements heightened the perceived truth of these statements—a phenomenon called the "truth effect"—and that this relationship between repetition and assessed truth was moderated by the type of processing participants employed during statement exposure. Specifically, the truth effect was strongest for participants who processed the information in a shallow, nonelaborative manner (e.g., rote rehearsal) as opposed to a more elaborative manner (e.g., evaluating meaning and veracity) or extremely minimal manner (e.g., completing an orthographic task). The stronger truth effect in the shallow versus deep processing condition may have resulted from the statements' heightened perceptual fluency with increased exposures, which was then misattributed as being due to the enhanced truth of the repeated statement. In contrast, a different process is implicated in the deep processing condition. In this condition, elaborative processing likely produced an increase in the number of positive thoughts generated. As predicted by modified two-factor theory, however, at higher exposure levels continued elaboration on the same stimulus may result in tedium and the generation of fewer positive thoughts and more idiosyncratic thoughts. This in turn may have contributed to the observed weakening of the truth effect at higher exposure levels when the stimuli were processed elaboratively.

The thesis proposed here is that level of processing determines whether repetition produces a monotonically increasing or an inverted U-shaped pattern of affective response. This is based on the hypothesis that the level of processing people engage in determines whether perceptual fluency/misattribution theory or

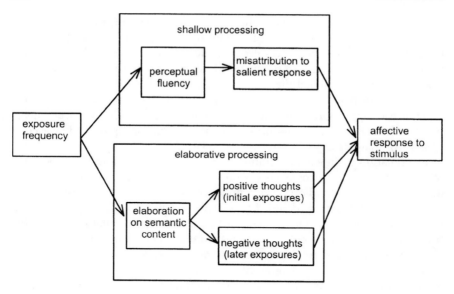

FIG. 5.3   Processing framework.

modified two-factor theory best represents the mechanism which underlies the relationship between exposure and affect. Figure 5.3 delineates these relationships graphically. When stimuli and/or features are processed in a shallow manner, repeated exposure to such items is likely to enhance perceptual fluency of these stimuli/features. In turn, the mechanism described by the perceptual fluency model should apply. That is, individuals are likely to misattribute the enhanced perceptual fluency of the items to any aspect (e.g., liking) of the items that is salient and appears to be a plausible cause of the enhanced fluency. On the other hand, when stimuli are processed in a deeper manner, more elaborative processing is implicated, and the mechanism outlined by the modified two-factor model should apply. As such, initial exposures should increase familiarity with and comprehension of the stimulus, prompting predominately positive thoughts. But as exposure increases further and message processing reaches a satiation point, the number of positive thoughts that are generated should decline as relatively negative idiosyncratic thoughts grow, resulting in net negative affect.

I have found support for this general hypothesis that the level of processing respondents engage in mediates the relationship between repeated exposure and affective response in three studies (Nordhielm, 1996, 2000). In these studies, participants engaged in a training session in which they viewed a series of advertisements at varying levels of repetition. In the deep processing condition, participants were encouraged to elaborate on the advertisement by clicking on any elements of the ad that they felt made the brand unique or preferable. In the shallow processing condition, participants were asked to click on a small red X anytime it appeared on the screen. Individual advertisements were exposed either 0, 3, 10, or 25 times. In a subsequent test session, participants evaluated these advertisements on several 9-point scales. Converging evidence from these studies supports the thesis that when participants' processing is deep, the exposure–affect relationship follows an inverted U-shaped pattern, whereas when processing is shallow, the pattern of response is generally increasing, with no downturn observed.

These findings are consistent with the view that during shallow processing, repeated exposure to a feature of a stimulus is likely to elevate how fluently respondents perceive or process that stimulus. In turn, processors may be prone to misattribute this enhanced fluency to any plausible cause that happens to be reasonably salient or accessible, which in this case was their affect toward the stimulus. To further explore the possibility that misattribution of fluency prompted by repetition might occur when shallow processing takes place and that such misattribution could affect any salient and plausible product dimension, respondents were asked to render judgments about both affective and nonaffective aspects of the product.

These judgments were collected as part of a forced-choice task where participants were presented with two products and asked which of the two possessed a descriptive characteristic (e.g., light or dark, broad or narrow distribution). Consistent with the view that misattribution of perceptual fluency is likely to mediate people's judgments when they engage in perceptual processing, ad respondents who had engaged in perceptual processing of the stimuli at encoding and who were exposed to a focal product an increasing number of times more frequently judged that the previously viewed focal product possessed a descriptive characteristic about which they were queried, regardless of the specific characteristic. For example, participants were more likely to judge a previously viewed product as either light *or* dark. This effect was not observed for respondents in the deep processing condition, where descriptive nonaffective judgments were insensitive to how frequently they had previously viewed the products, presumably because their judgments were not based on an attribution of any enhanced perceptual fluency of the stimuli.

Further support for the levels of processing model was obtained in a thought-listing task in one study (Nordhielm, 2000). For this task, respondents were simply asked to list any thoughts they had about each stimulus as it was presented. This task was included to attempt to examine the types of thoughts that participants generated in the deep versus shallow processing condition. Results from this task suggest that when respondents processed the ad stimuli deeply versus in a more shallow manner, the pattern of participants' thoughts differed significantly. Specifically, under deep processing, when respondents' frequency of exposure to the focal product content varied, the favorableness of their affective judgments of the product and the ad exhibited an inverted U-shaped pattern as frequency of exposure to the focal product mounted. This observation is compatible with the premise that when individuals are prompted to process stimuli deeply, their understanding and appreciation tend to grow as exposure frequency and thus opportunity to process this stimulus elevate to some moderate level. Thereafter, however, further exposure to the stimulus tends to stimulate considerable idiosyncratic, tedium-related, or other less favorable thoughts that generally prompt a downturn in affective judgments. Under the shallow processing condition, no such pattern was observed.

In summary, despite the significant amount of research conducted on mere exposure and repetition effects to date, no published work has provided a theoretical model that accounts for all of the results observed in this area. The two leading models that dominate this literature each provide only a partial explanation for the observed results. Specifically, although modified two-factor theory predicts a downturn in affective response after some number of exposures, it does not predict that when stimuli are viewed at an extremely short or subliminal duration, the positive effect of repeated viewing is even stronger than when such stimuli are exposed at longer durations. Further, modified two-factor theory does not adequately explain why no downturn in affective response occurs for these extremely short or subliminal exposures. The PF/M model accounts for these characteristics of repeatedly presented stimuli for short exposure durations, but does not predict a downturn in affective response for frequently exposed stimuli of longer durations.

The theorizing presented in this chapter has been offered to provide a more complete explanation of findings in the repetition effects literatures. It is not intended to discount either modified two-factor theory nor the perceptual fluency/misattribution model. Instead, this chapter integrates these two models in a way that provides a reasonable explanation for all results observed to date. Further, the research presented here begins to test this integrative model, and empirical results demonstrate its support.

IMPLICATIONS

Upon considering the practical implications of this research, a number of important questions emerge that remain to be answered. One key issue is how time influences the relationship between feature repetition and affective response. Research that has investigated perceptual and conceptual priming suggests that the effects of prior exposure on affective response can actually last as long as 1 year when the stimuli are processed perceptually, whereas when these stimuli are processed conceptually, these positive effects can diminish within as little as a few minutes (Roediger & McDermott, 1993). Hence, repeated exposure to a feature that lends itself to deeper, more elaborative processing may result in wearout and hence negative affect, but this negative response may dissipate within a relatively short period of time. In contrast, the influence of prior exposure to features that have been processed perceptually may persist for much longer.

Another important issue is the question of what factors induce individuals to process particular features in either a shallow or a deeper fashion. In both experiments 1 and 2, it appeared that the amount of semantic content possessed by a particular feature tended to determine which type of processing was employed. Hence, it may be reasonable to assess features based on their semantic content and classify them as either likely to be processed in a shallow or deeper fashion. At the same time, particular conditions under which an individual processes a specific feature are also likely to influence the type of processing he or she employs. In particular, if an individual's motivation or ability to process a particular feature is limited, he or she may process it consistently in a perceptual manner, regardless of that feature's semantic content. On the other hand, with sufficient repetition and consistent associations, any feature can become invested with semantic content over time. Therefore, from a managerial perspective, knowledge about the amount of semantic content a specific feature possesses, as well as the particular conditions under which this feature has been processed, will presumably enhance marketers' ability to anticipate the onset of wearout of repeatedly viewed stimuli.

Finally, although these results as well as those of other studies involving extremely short exposure durations (e.g., Bornstein & D'Agostino, 1992) suggest that when features are processed in a shallow fashion, no downturn in affective response occurs even at high exposure levels, this question merits further consideration. Whether or not a downturn in affective response will eventually occur under perceptual processing conditions when the exposure level is extremely high remains an empirical question.

REFERENCES

Bargh, J. A. (1992). Does subliminality matter to social psychology? In R. F. Bornstein & T. S. Pittman (Eds.), *Perception without awareness: Cognitive, clinical and social perspectives* (pp. 236–255). New York: Guilford Press.

Batra, R., & Ray, M. L. (1986). Situational effects of advertising repetition: The moderating influence of motivation, ability, and opportunity to respond. *Journal of Consumer Research, 12*, 432–445.

Berlyne, D. E. (1970). Novelty, complexity, and hedonic value. *Perception and Psychophysics, 8*, 279–286.

Bornstein, R. F., & D'Agostino, P. R. (1992). Stimulus recognition and the mere exposure effect. *Journal of Personality and Social Psychology, 63*, 545–552.

Bornstein, R. F., & D'Agostino, P. R. (1994). The attribution and discounting of perceptual fluency: Preliminary tests of a perceptual fluency/attributional model of the mere exposure effect. *Social Cognition, 12*, 103–128.

Cacioppo, J. T., & Petty, R. E. (1979). Effect of message repetition and position on cognition response, recall, and persuasion. *Journal of Personality and Social Psychology, 37*, 97–109.

Calder, B., & Sternthal, B. (1980). Television commercial wearout: An information processing view. *Journal of Marketing Research, 17*, 173–186.

Crandall, J. E., Montgomery, V. E., & Rees, W. W. (1973). "Mere" exposure versus familiarity, with implications for response competition and expectancy arousal hypotheses. *Journal of General Psychology, 88*, 105–120.

Gorn, G. J., & Goldberg, M. E. (1980). Children's responses to repetitive television commercials. *Journal of Consumer Research, 6*, 421–424.

Grass, R., & Wallace, W. H. (1969). Satiation effects of television commercials. *Journal of Advertising Research, 9*, 3–8.

Hawkins, S. A., & Hoch, S. J. (1992). Low-involvement learning: memory without evaluation. *Journal of Consumer Research, 19*, 212–225.

Jacoby, L. L., & Dallas, M. (1981). On the relationship between autobiographical memory and perceptual learning. *Journal of Experimental Psychology: General, 110*, 306–340.

Jacoby, L. L., Toth, J. P., Lindsay, D. S., & Debner, J. A. (1992). Lectures for a layperson: methods for revealing unconscious processes. In R. F. Bornstein & T. S. Pittman (Eds.), *Perception without awareness: Cognitive, clinical and social perspectives* (pp. 81–120). New York: Guilford Press.

Kail, R. V., & Freeman, H. R. (1973). Sequence redundancy, rating dimensions, and the exposure effect. *Memory and Cognition, 1*, 454–458.

Mandler, G., Nakamura, Y., & Van Zandt, B. J. S. (1987). Nonspecific effects of exposure on stimuli that cannot be recognized. *Journal of Experimental Psychology: Learning Memory and Cognition, 13*, 646–648.

McCullough, J. L., & Ostrom, T. M. (1974). Repetition of highly similar messages and attitude change. *Journal of Applied Psychology, 59*, 395–397.

Nordhielm, C. L. (1996). *A dual process model of advertising repetition effects.* Doctoral dissertation, University of Chicago.

Nordhielm, C. L. (2000). *The influence of type of processing on advertising repetition effects.* Working paper.

Pechman, C., & Stewart, D. W. (1988). Advertising repetition: A critical review of wearin and wearout. In J. Leigh & C. R. Martin, Jr. (Eds.), *Current issues and research in advertising* (pp. 285–331). Ann Arbor: University of Michigan.

Roediger, H. L., & McDermott, K. B. (1993). Implicit memory in normal human subjects. In F. Boller (Ed.), *Handbook of neuropsychology* (vol. 8, pp. 63–131). Amsterdam: Elsevier.

Schumann, D., Petty, R., & Clemons, D. S. (1990). Predicting the effectiveness of different strategies of advertising variation: a test of the repetition-variation hypotheses. *Journal of Consumer Research, 17*, 192–202.

Unnava, H. R., & Burnkrant, R. E. (1991). Effects of repeating varied ad executions on brand name memory. *Journal of Marketing Research, 28*, 406–416.

Zajonc, R., Crandall, R., Kail, R. V., & Swap, W. (1974). Effect of extreme exposure frequencies on different affective ratings of stimuli. *Perceptual and Motor Skills, 38*, 667–678.

CHAPTER SIX

Changes in Logo Designs:
Chasing the Elusive Butterfly Curve

Ronald W. Pimentel
California State University, Bakersfield

Susan E. Heckler
Georgetown University

It is human nature to take delight in exciting admiration. . . . Think, then, what a passion it becomes with a [tour] guide, whose privilege it is, every day, to show to strangers wonders that throw them into perfect ecstasies of admiration! He gets so that he could not by any possibility live in a soberer atmosphere. After we discovered this, we never went into ecstasies any more—we never admired anything—we never showed any but impassible faces and stupid indifference in the presence of the sublimest wonders a guide had to display. . . .

. . . The guides in Genoa are delighted to secure an American party, because Americans so much wonder, and deal so much in sentiment and emotion before any relic of Columbus. Our guide there fidgeted about as if he had swallowed a spring mattress. He was full of animation—full of impatience. He said:

"Come wis me, genteelmen!—come! I show you ze letter—writing by Christopher Colombo!—write it himself!—write it wis his own hand!—come!"

He took us to the municipal palace. After much impressive fumbling of keys and opening of locks, the stained and aged document was spread before us. The guide's eyes sparkled. He danced about us and tapped the parchment with his finger:

"What I tell you, genteelmen! Is it not so? See! Handwriting Christopher Colombo!—write it himself!"

We looked indifferent—unconcerned. . . . Then [we] said, without any show of interest:

"Ah—Ferguson—what—what did you say was the name of the party who wrote this?"

"Christopher Colombo! ze great Christopher Colombo!"

Another deliberate examination.

"Ah—did he write it himself, or—or how?"

"He write it himself!—Christopher Colombo! he's own handwriting, write by himself!"

[We] laid the document down and said:

"Why, I have seen boys in America only fourteen years old that could write better than that."

"But zis is ze great Christo-"

"I don't care who it is! It's the worst writing I ever saw. Now you musn't think you can impose on us because we are strangers. We are not fools, by a good deal. If you have got any specimens of penmanship of real merit, trot them out!—and if you haven't, drive on!"

We drove on. (Twain, 1869, pp. 214–216)

In the preceding excerpt from *Innocents Abroad,* Samuel Clemens and his traveling companions frustrated the tour guide by evaluating the artifact on the basis of its esthetics rather than its historical significance—or associated meaning. Similarly, it may be a mistake to focus too narrowly on the esthetic quality of a logo design, if preference for the logo is based on different factors, such as associated meaning.

Well-known trademarks, logos, and other corporate identity designs (all of which are referred to as "logos" in this study for the sake of simplicity) are valuable assets of the companies that own them and an integral part of the persuasion efforts. Many companies concern themselves with maintaining the value of these visual assets.

Logo designs appear on advertisements, packaging, annual reports, letterhead, business cards, and signs, and are incorporated into the designs of the products themselves. Identifying the brand of a product by recognizing the logo is a major aspect of the purchase process and is a particularly important function in this age when so many brands and promotional messages compete for consumer attention (Wilson, 1994).

The logo serves as a visual cue for the recall of information previously received. An old advertising campaign for Freedent gum concentrated on three benefits of the product: that it did not stick to dental work, that it freshened breath, and that it moistened mouths. A package of the gum, displaying the logo, was shown prominently in the advertisements. The hope was that when consumers saw the logo and packaging again, in product displays in stores, they would remember the benefits of the product.

In addition to the cognitive responses of identifying the brand and remembering information, the logo can also elicit affective responses. It may activate emotionally charged memories of experiences with the brand or with promotional activities of the brand, such as appealing advertising. The Kool-Aid smiley-faced pitcher is a symbol that has emotional meaning attached to it. The image was originally created in 1954, and consequently, spans generations (Pollack, 1999). In the

1970s, Grey Advertising transformed the image into "Pitcher Man" and later, "Kool-Aid Man," making him an "active" figure. When Ogilvy and Mather took over the advertising in 1998, it was a $25 million account of a brand that boasted 100% awareness among mothers and children (Thompson, 1999). Ogilvy and Mather initially considered tinkering with the image. Through research, however, they learned that Kool-Aid Man is strongly entrenched. Children are emotionally attached to the image because he is familiar to them from television advertising and is associated with product use, which often occurs at parties, picnics, and other recreational events. A separate Kool-Aid campaign is targeted at mothers, who are emotionally connected through childhood memories of the product and the smiley-faced logo. It also features the trademark symbol. A recent campaign featured depictions of multigenerational groups enjoying Kool-Aid together at family gatherings.

The logo may also represent the image of the brand. The familiar Mercedes Benz logo is an example. The encircled three-pointed star is recognized worldwide as a symbol of superior engineering, quality workmanship, and prestige.

If a logo is particularly effective in its design, it may not only represent the image of the brand, but also help to formulate that image. For example, Lucent Technologies adopted an "innovation circle" logo in hopes that it would help to create the desired image of a "bold and innovative" company (Barboza, 1996, p. D3). Less effective logos, on the other hand, may actually detract from the image of the brand. Before they became part of Interbrand, the Schechter Group conducted surveys of "logo value." The 1994 survey tested 27 logos and found that 17 of them actually had a detrimental effect on the consumers' image of the company or brand. For example, the FedEx logo had recently been redesigned and got negative reactions from survey participants (Elliott, 1994). More recently, in an effort to change their perceived image, Lipton Tea removed the image of Sir Thomas J. Lipton from their packaging. The trademark image dated back to 1890 and did not suit the brand's objective of getting people to think more of tea as an alternative to Coke or Pepsi (O'Connell, 2001).

In some cases, the logo may represent not only the image of the brand, but also the image of the consumer. Logos provide a means for consumers to display their personal identification with a brand, beyond consumption of the brand or service (Holman, 1980). An example is when a consumer wears a t-shirt or baseball cap bearing a logo design to publicly show an association with the represented brand. Some brands have a specific image that appeals to the consumer, such as an image of prestige or exclusivity. Some consumers may enjoy wearing a shirt with the Ferrari logo on it—whether they own a Ferrari or aspire to own one. In some cases, consumers seek to display a logo to fit in with a group. This is common with teenagers who display the appropriate logos in hopes of being identified with the "preps" or the "surfers." Adults may display the Harley Davidson logo to express involvement with a biker subculture. Sometimes logos are displayed to express dis-

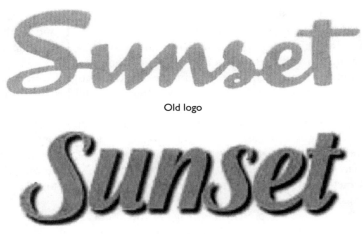

Old logo

New logo

FIG. 6.1.

tinctiveness. A few courageous individuals will wear a Honda jacket to a Harley-dominated event, such as Bike Week in Daytona Beach.

Sunset magazine discovered just how attached customers can become to a logo when they changed theirs and received letters of complaint (Fig. 6.1). One reader stated, "The old logo was an especially valued symbol to us baby boomers" ("Thumbs Go Up," 1996, p. 10). Another compared changing the logo to changing "Half Dome, the Grand Canyon, and Mount Rushmore" ("New Logo," 1996a, p. 10). At the same time, however, *Sunset* also received letters supporting the logo change. There are theoretical models to support various approaches to changing or retaining logo designs.

Commonly, companies try to take advantage of familiarity effects in order to develop greater preference for the logo and the brand, through repeated exposures of the logo (Zajonc, 1968). Some logos, such as the Arm and Hammer trademark, have remained the same for decades. Many companies, however, also wish to take advantage of novelty effects or to avoid boredom effects (Berlyne, 1971). Consequently, many logos, such as Mr. Peanut, Betty Crocker, and the Prudential rock, have evolved over the years through successive changes.

LITERATURE REVIEW

Theoretical concepts that can be applied to changing logo designs include familiarity effects, novelty effects, boredom effects, the two-factor model of exposure effects, the discrepancy hypothesis, and social judgment theory.

Familiarity Effects

The concept of familiarity effects comes from research such as that published by Zajonc in 1968. Zajonc found that preference for a stimulus could increase through "mere exposure"—that it becomes more preferred simply by being seen more. This response is thought to have evolved from defensive mechanisms that make individuals wary of the unfamiliar. According to the concept of familiarity (or mere exposure) effects, a process called "stimulus habituation" will occur such that logos that have been seen more often or for longer periods of time will be preferred more. This is consistent with the practice of leaving logos unchanged, such as the Arm and Hammer logo, which has been the same for decades.

Novelty Effects

In contrast to Zajonc's findings, in 1971 Berlyne reported observing novelty effects. Subjects of his experiments reported that pictures of animals that they had not seen before were more "pleasing" and "interesting" than pictures that they had seen repeatedly. These results might encourage brands to come up with new, novel logo designs.

Boredom Effects

The seeming conflict between familiarity effects and novelty effects is resolved by Bornstein's finding in 1989 that boredom effects can create a limit for familiarity effects. In addition to repeated or prolonged exposures making the individual more comfortable with the stimulus, too much exposure can make the stimulus boring.

Two-Factor Model of Exposure Effects

Berlyne (1970) and Bornstein, Kale, and Cornell (1990) recognized that exposure effects can include both familiarity effects and boredom effects. They are the two factors of the two-factor model of exposure effects. According to this model, preference grows with additional exposure to the stimulus up to a certain point. After that point, the stimulus becomes more boring and preference decreases with additional exposure. Accordingly, consumers would be expected to become bored with logo designs to which they were exposed too much.

Discrepancy Hypothesis

The discrepancy hypothesis lends itself well to discussions of changes in logo designs because it addresses the concept of change more directly. It also accommodates familiarity effects, boredom effects, and novelty effects simultaneously. According to this hypothesis, once an individual has become adapted to a stimulus, slightly altered versions of the stimulus (e.g., logo) would allow for novelty effects and would be preferred over the current version. If the stimulus is changed too much, however, it is perceived as a new image and is preferred less than the previous version. Haber (1958) demonstrated results consistent with the discrepancy hypothesis, using water of different temperatures as stimuli. These results are described by the distinctive *butterfly curve* (Fig. 6.2).

Haber had subjects place their hands in buckets of water at skin temperature. After a time, the subjects would become adapted to that temperature. This adaptation level is represented as the center point on the curve ("AL" in Fig. 6.2). Once the adaptation level was established, one of the hands would be moved to a bucket of water at a different temperature. If the temperature of the water in the new bucket was slightly warmer (1–3°C) or slightly cooler (1°C), the subjects preferred the new temperature. This effect is illustrated on the butterfly curve (Fig. 6.2)— the curve rises on both sides of the adaptation level point. If the temperature was changed too drastically (+7°C or −3°C), however, subjects preferred the new temperature less than the original temperature. This is represented on the portions of the curve (Fig. 6.2) that slope down enough to be lower than the preference for the adaptation level.

We interpret the discrepancy hypothesis and butterfly curve in terms of the other theoretical concepts. The adaptation level is established through exposure to the stimulus. This exposure allows for familiarity affects, so the preference for the adaptation level is elevated. Because the adaptation level is not the highest level of

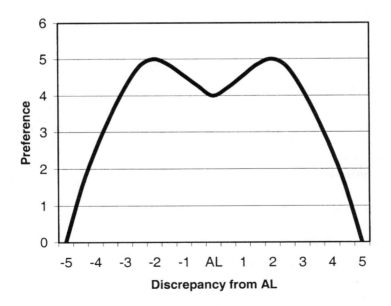

FIG. 6.2. Butterfly curve.

FIG. 6.3. Stimuli from Conners (1964) experiment.

preference, however, boredom effects may have moderated preference for the stimulus at that level. Novelty effects are shown by increased preference for slight changes in the stimulus. When the stimulus is changed too much, though, it is perceived as a new stimulus and the preference level drops due to the loss of the familiarity effects.

It would be a giant leap to make inferences about preferences for logo designs from Haber's study with its psychophysical stimuli. A study by Conners in 1964 used geometric shapes as stimuli. It bridged the gap partially by applying the discrepancy hypothesis to preference for visual images (Pimentel & Heckler, 1999).

Conners' stimuli consisted of seven eight-sided polygons (Fig. 6.3) that represent a series of progressive changes. In his experiment, subjects were instructed to concentrate on the first stimulus for a given length of time. They were then shown two stimuli from the set and asked to state their preference between the two. He reported support for the applicability of the discrepancy hypothesis to geometric shapes. His results, however, did not exhibit the hypothesis as clearly as did those of Haber.

The geometric shapes from Conners were simple designs and were designed to have no associated meaning. Even if his results had been as elegant and convincing as Haber's, it would still be another giant leap to make inferences from them about preference for changes in logo designs that are more complex and may have strong associated meaning. Consequently, we allowed for the idea that different theoretical models may be more applicable for our particular research focus, such as social judgment theory.

Social Judgment Theory

Another theoretical model that addresses difference or change is social judgment theory (Sherif & Hovland, 1961). This theory was developed concerning attitude expression. According to it, individuals have an initial attitude that serves as a frame of reference for comparison with incoming messages. This frame of reference serves as an anchor, similar to the adaptation level in the discrepancy hypothesis.

Along with the frame of reference, the individual develops a *latitude of acceptance* surrounding it. When new statements are presented to the individual, they are judged in relation to the frame of reference. Statements that are similar enough to the frame of reference attitude will fall within the latitude of acceptance and be acceptable to the individual. Statements that are sufficiently different from the frame of reference will fall into a *latitude of rejection*.

Statements that fall within the latitude of acceptance are subject to *assimilation effects,* meaning that the statements will be interpreted as being even more similar to the frame of reference attitude than they actually are. Statements that fall into a latitude of rejection will seem even more extreme and different from the frame of reference due to *contrast effects.*

Although the theory was formulated with very different sorts of stimuli in mind, it can be applied to preference for changes in logo designs. The existing, familiar version of the logo becomes the frame of reference. Actually, because this frame of reference is established through exposure, it could be appropriately termed the "adaptation level." New versions of the logo design would serve as the "new statements" of the common formulation of social judgment theory.

Although the discrepancy hypothesis predicts increased preference for slightly changed stimuli, according to social judgment theory, such stimuli would fall within the latitude of acceptance and be subject to assimilation effects. Conse-

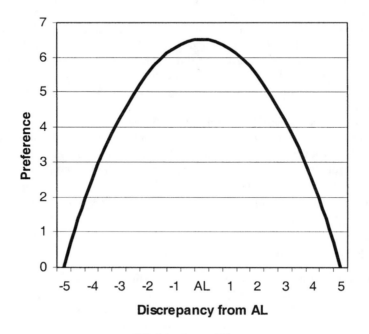

FIG. 6.4.   Inverted-U.

quently, logo designs that are changed only slightly from the current version would be considered acceptable, but would not be preferred. Stimuli that represent a drastic change from the adaptation level would fall into a latitude of rejection and would be judged as being an even more extreme change.

These results are represented graphically by an inverted-U (Fig. 6.4), in contrast to the bimodal butterfly curve of the discrepancy hypothesis. The adaptation level (or frame of reference) at the center of the curve is the most preferred version, and consequently the peak of the curve. Moving away from the center point, initially the curve is fairly flat. This is the portion of the curve that represents the latitude of acceptance—slight changes are acceptable. Moving farther away from the center point, the curve slopes more steeply. These portions of the curve represent the latitudes of rejection—the more drastic changes in the stimulus result in the sharp drops in preference.

Having identified both the discrepancy hypothesis and social judgment theory as possible models for preference for changes in logo designs, we designed a series of studies to determine which, if either, is appropriate. We also investigated whether different models were appropriate under different circumstances.

STUDY I—EXPLORATORY EXAMINATION OF CONSUMER PREFERENCE FOR VISUAL IMAGES

Although our research specifically addresses preferences for changes in logo designs, we started by setting logos aside and doing an exploratory examination of preferences for representational images that are not connected to specific brands. In Study 1, we used qualitative methods in order to gain a broad view of how consumers view visual designs, allowing for emergent findings. In this study we investigated the basic question of whether individuals form preferences for visual images (Pimentel, 1996). We also sought a basic understanding of the relative importance of the form versus the content for preference for visual images. We use the term *form* to mean basically how the logo "looks." It could include the design style, elements of design execution (balance, composition, contrast, etc.), color, quality of execution (how well was it rendered and reproduced), and so on. *Content* refers to the subject matter (if the image is representational) and associated meanings. Previous research has made similar distinctions, although often using different terminology (e.g., Bell, Holbrook, & Solomon, 1991; Winston & Cupchik, 1992). We also sought to examine whether preferences for visual images involve cognitive processes, affective (emotional) responses, or both. Gaining a broad view of preference for visual designs provided a basis for comparison with the results from the following studies that involve logos more specifically.

Respondents for Study 1 were taken from marketing principles classes at a major southwestern university. They included 24 business students and 2 architecture students.

Stimuli consisted of 11 color photographs. They were selected to represent various possible criteria for preference. Some were selected for strong visual effects (form), such as the photograph of an oil derrick appearing as a silhouette against a striking sunset. Other photographs were selected for potential meaning (content), such as the closeup of a bald eagle or the photograph of the university mascots.

An individual interview was conducted with each participant and recorded on audiotape. Participants were asked to examine the set of 11 randomly ordered color photographs, indicate liking or disliking for each, and explain their preference criteria.

Participant comments were coded as being either positive or negative and as regarding either form or content. The comments indicated that the respondents did have preferences that they were willing to discuss, sometimes reflecting affective responses and stated in strong terms such as "love," "means a lot to me," "hate with a passion," or "pitiful." The preferences were different from individual to individual, as were the criteria for the preferences.

Respondents cited subject matter of the image more often than visual attributes as a criterion for preference (167 times vs. 69 times). The emphasis on content was great enough that some of the respondents persisted in speaking in terms of the content or meaning of the image even when being asked specifically about its visual quality, that is, its appearance "as a picture."

Content was acknowledged at various levels. Many of the comments reflected conditioned responses to the stimuli. Examples include "I love chocolate ice cream," "I like to play golf," and "I like beer." Some included an emotional aspect in the response, using terms such as "serene," "happy," and "proud." A few of the comments reflected antecedent states. Some of the respondents reported liking the image of chocolate ice cream, because they were hungry. Another expressed dislike for the image of a mug of beer, because of a recent overindulgence in alcohol at a wedding. Other comments reflected deeper meaning and/or autobiographical memories, such as "my mother and grandmother made quilts," "makes me think of my boyfriend because he's a roper," and "reminds me of growing up in Nebraska."

Although most comments were in regard to content and personal meaning, there were some comments regarding the form of the images, such as "pretty picture with the sun coming up," "kind of cool looking," and "very colorful." An important exceptional case to the emphasis on content was the approach of one of the two architecture students. He described preferences exclusively in terms of form, using expert terms such as "composition," "balance," and "unity." There are a number of possible explanations for the contrast between his comments and those of the other respondents. It could be that he was taking advantage of an opportunity to display his expertise. It is possible that other respondents would have spoken more about form if they had the vocabulary to better verbalize this basis for preference. Finally, it could be that due to his expertise and orientation, this respondent really was distinctive from other respondents and really did consider form more than content when viewing visual images. The influence of an individual's background in design was examined further in Studies 5 and 6.

Previous research has indicated that consumers can be influenced by both form and content at the same time (Bell, Holbrook, & Solomon, 1991). The results of Study 1 support this idea, with form and content (especially the latter) both affecting preferences for visual images. There are important implications of this finding for logo designs. If the results of Study 1 can be generalized to include logo designs, they would indicate that the meaning associated with the logo is of primary importance. For example, it might mean that for Allstate's logo, it is more important that it clearly portrays "good hands" than that it is esthetically pleasing. The results also suggest that consumers will be generally satisfied with the esthetics of the logo as long as it is attractive at a basic level. As exploratory research, Study 1 did more to raise questions than it did to give conclusive evidence. We pursued answers in the studies that followed.

STUDY 2—CHANGES IN LOGO DESIGNS, PREFERRED OR TOLERATED?

The second study tested to discover if our inferences from the findings of Study 1 can be supported and applied to logo designs, and more specifically, to changes in logo designs. The influence of form of the image on preference may allow for some increased preference for an image that is changed in a way that makes it more esthetically pleasing. We inferred from the stronger emphasis on content in Study 1, however, that individuals would not like changes in meaningful visual images that change or obscure the meaning of the image. The combination of these influences might suggest a further inference that changes, if any, should be small. Such a recommendation could be consistent with either the discrepancy hypothesis or social judgment theory. The second study tested between the two concepts, to determine if consumers prefer changes in familiar logo designs, or no changes. We also tested to see how much change is preferred, if changes are preferred, or how many changes are tolerated if they are not preferred.

Familiar logo designs served as the stimuli in the second study (Pimentel, 1997). Incrementally altered versions of well-known logos were tested for consumer preference. A series of involved pretests were needed for the development of the stimuli for the study.

Logos were selected that were familiar enough so that the respondents had become adapted to them. Logos were also selected with respect to two additional variables. One of these variables was the level of meaning associated with the design. For example, respondents were able to name many associations for Tony the Tiger, such as tigers in general, the brand (Kellogg's Frosted Flakes), childhood memories of breakfast, Saturday morning cartoons, and "they're grrreat!" Other logos brought very little to the minds of the respondents. The other variable was the level

TABLE 6.1
Logos as Stimuli for Consumer Preference

	Low Meaning	High Meaning
High Preference for AL	Toys 'R' Us *Geoffrey the Giraffe* John Deere *Leaping deer*	Kellogg's Frosted Flakes *Tony the Tiger* Kellogg's Froot Loops *Toucan Sam*
Low Preference for AL	Arizona Cardinals *Cardinal head profile* Chuck E. Cheese *Chuck E. Cheese (mouse)*	Camel Cigarettes *"Old Joe," Joe Camel* Bic Pens *Spherical-headed humanoid*

of preference for the design at the adaptation level (the current version, to which consumers had become adapted through exposure in the marketplace). Different levels of these variables were represented in the stimuli that were selected—two logos for each of four cells: high meaning/high preference, high meaning/low preference, low meaning/high preference, and low meaning/low preference (Table 6.1).

The selected stimuli are identified only by name—because the represented companies did not give permission for their logos to appear in a publication. Each of the logo designs in the study is based on an animal or human form. As examples of the logos in the various cells, John Deere, a manufacturer of agricultural and landscaping equipment, was rated high by respondents in terms of preference for the design of the logo in its current (adaptation level) form, but relatively low for levels of meaning associated with it. Tony the Tiger, the cartoon character symbol of a breakfast cereal that has been popular for decades, scored high on both preference and meaning. The Bic Pen humanoid figure had a high level of meaning for respondents, but the design of the logo was not well preferred. Chuck E. Cheese, low in both meaning and preference, is a cartoon character that is the symbol for a chain of restaurant/amusement facilities that is targeted at families with young children, and not so much at the college student demographics of our sample.

Stimuli were created as pen-and-ink renderings. First the actual logo was rendered in pen and ink (traced) so that its quality of execution was the same as the other stimuli. The other stimuli were created as progressive changes from the adaptation level, becoming progressively more abstract or more naturalistic. This process is illustrated in Fig. 6.5, for a fictional logo (for the fictional brand: Sophie Dog Treats), which was created to illustrate the process. Testing, alterations, and retesting assured that differences between versions were discernable in at least 75% of trials, but not in 100% of trials (see Pimentel, 1997, for a detailed description of the process).

Abstraction was chosen as the variable to manipulate to create change because it represents a trend in changes to logo designs over the past century (Morgan, 1986). The experiment required to test between theories was of mixed design.

Interval data were collected between subjects. Each participant rated seven different stimuli on a semantic differential ("liking") scale, each at a different level of abstraction, and each from a different logo. So, for example, one respondent might have been asked to rate Toucan Sam in the adaptation level version, the John Deere logo at one step more abstract than the adaptation level, Joe Camel two steps more abstract, Chuck E. Cheese three steps more abstract, the Bic Pen logo one step more

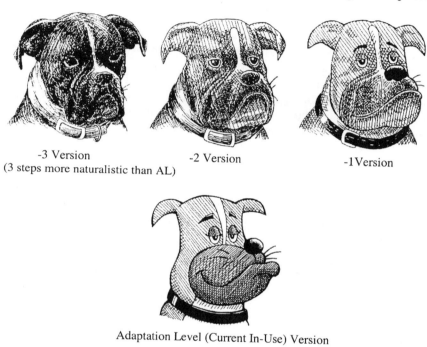

-3 Version
(3 steps more naturalistic than AL)

-2 Version

-1 Version

Adaptation Level (Current In-Use) Version

-1 Version
(1 step more abstract than AL)

-2 Version

-3 Version

FIG. 6.5. Stimulus creation—Sophie Dog Treats brand.

naturalistic than the adaptation level version, Tony the Tiger two steps more naturalistic, and Geoffrey the Giraffe three steps more naturalistic. The stimuli were
placed in random order, so the respondents did not see them ordered systematically. Each unique stimulus was rated by 16 to 21 respondents.

Ordinal data were collected within subjects. This was accomplished by supplying each subject with a pile of cards on which were printed the various stimuli
from a single brand. For, example, some of the respondents saw all the versions of
the Arizona Cardinal. They were asked to place them in order of preference. The
sample size for each brand was 32 to 42.

If the discrepancy hypothesis applied in this case, it could be predicted that
those versions of the logo that represented slight changes from the version currently in use (the adaptation-level version) would be most preferred. Ordinal data
showed, consistently through the brands, however, that it was the current version
that was most preferred (Fig. 6.6 gives data for Toucan Sam as an example). Interval data showed that the difference between the preference for the current version
and the preference for those most closely resembling it was generally small, and
in many cases, not statistically significant (Fig. 6.7). This indicates that, although
small changes were not *preferred,* they were considered *acceptable.* These results
support the applicability of social judgment theory over the discrepancy hypothesis for preference for changes in familiar logo designs. They also indicate that the
two-factor model of exposure effects is not appropriate in this case, as there were
no boredom effects found.

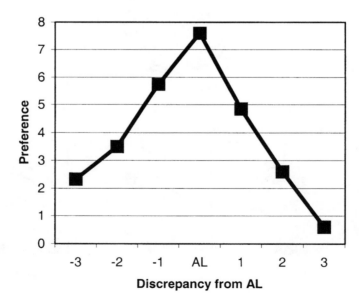

FIG. 6.6.   Kellogg's Froot Loops (Toucan Sam) ordinal data—within subjects.

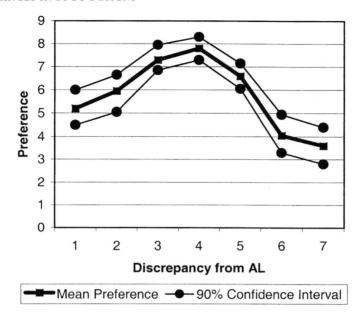

FIG. 6.7.   Kellogg's Froot Loops (Toucan Sam) interval data—between subjects.

The results of Study 2 are in contrast to the findings of Conners (1964), which found boredom effects and supported the discrepancy hypothesis for preference for changes in visual images. There were a number of differences, however, between the studies. These differences were explored in Study 3.

STUDY 3 — AN ATTEMPT TO RECONCILE RESULTS

Some of the differences between Study 2 and Conners's (1964) study are important in terms of potential exposure effects. Bornstein (1989) conducted a meta-analysis of 20 years of exposure effects research. This study began with Zajonc's 1968 study, which showed increased preference for a stimulus merely through exposure to it, that is, familiarity effects. More recently, Harmon-Jones (1995) developed a succinct listing of the seven factors that have shown the most robust familiarity effects. Three of these factors represent differences between Study 2 and the Conners study; they are the first three on the list of differences given next. In contrast to Conners' study, Study 2 featured the following:

- There was a heterogeneous rather than a homogeneous exposure sequence of stimuli (the various stimuli are mixed together in the sequence rather than doing all the exposures of the first stimulus before moving to the next).

- There was a delay between the exposures and ratings of the stimuli.
- Stimuli were complex rather than simple.
- Stimuli were clearly representational and had meaning attached, instead of being intentionally nonrepresentational and not meaningful.

These differences suggest that the conditions of Study 2 allowed for greater familiarity effects—more improved liking for stimulus with repeated exposures. This raises the possibility that boredom effects were found by Conners but not in Study 2 because the familiarity effects in Study 2 were stronger due to the conditions of exposure or because of the meaning associated with the stimuli. If the differences between the studies can be explained thus, it would mean that boredom effects could possibly be averted by providing for exceptionally strong familiarity effects or by attaching sufficient meaning to the stimulus. Study 3 tested to see if these differences between the two studies would account for the difference in results. In order to do so, the third study used Conners's stimuli, but manipulated their meaningfulness and the manner of exposure.

Conners created stimuli that were intended to have no associated meaning. In fact, he made alterations to some of the designs when subjects referred to them as looking like familiar objects. Study 2 utilized familiar logo designs that pretests showed to be recognizable and meaningful. Although Conners's (1964) stimuli were used in Study 3, "associated meaning" was manipulated by reciting a narrative about the one of the stimuli that associated meaning with it. The narrative identified one of the experimental stimuli as being a representation of a small dog who is courageous, creative, and tenacious, and consequently a good marketer (see Fig. 6.8).

Study 3 followed a 2 × 2 between-subjects design. The two dimensions were associated meaning (or no associated meaning), and exposure conditions (homogeneous exposure with no delay, or heterogeneous exposure with delay). "Homo-

FIG. 6.8.   Meaning assigned.

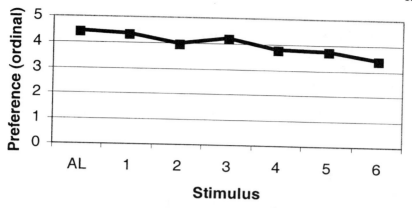

FIG. 6.9.   Group 3, homogeneous presentation, no meaning.

geneous exposure with no delay" means that the subjects viewed only the stimulus presented, then went directly to the preference evaluation task without interruption or display of other stimuli. This is the type of exposure utilized in the Conners (1964) experiment. Study 2 utilized the subjects' experiences in the marketplace as exposure to the stimuli. This would be classified as "heterogeneous exposure with delay." In such cases, the experimental stimulus is viewed at various times, with subjects viewing other stimuli between times and between the final viewing of the stimulus and the preference evaluation task.

None of the four experimental conditions reproduced Conners's (1964) results, not even Group 3 (Fig. 6.9), which had conditions most similar (no associated meaning, homogeneous exposure with no delay). For Group 3, the adaptation level stimulus was projected on a screen and subjects were instructed to concentrate on it so that they could draw it from memory. The exposure lasted one minute. Immediately after viewing the stimulus, the subjects were instructed to arrange a set of cards in order of preference. Each card displayed one of the stimuli.

Although Conners reported support for the discrepancy hypothesis, it was not represented by a butterfly curve. Unlike Haber, who altered his water temperature stimuli in two directions (warmer and cooler), Conners started with one stimulus and altered it in seven progressive steps in one direction. His results were depicted more as half a butterfly curve—just one wing. Consequently, because it is also representing only half a curve, Fig. 6.9 slopes in one direction instead of being an inverted-U.

Conners (1964) found the greatest preference for stimuli that were altered slightly from the adaptation-level version. In Study 3, however, as found in Study 2, respondents most preferred the stimulus to which they had become adapted. They did not display the boredom effects. One explanation might be that Conners's results were an artifact of his specific lab and his small sample size. Study 4 explored that possibility.

STUDY 4—AN EFFORT TO REPLICATE RESULTS

The fourth study replicated Conners's 1964 experiment to see if the same results would occur, or if Conners's results are an anomaly facilitated by a small sample size or extreme experimental conditions. The conditions of this final experiment were the same as for Group 3 in Study 3, but were accomplished in a different manner. Instead of viewing the experimental stimulus for one extended period and then ranking all the stimuli at once, Conners (1964) had subjects view the experimental stimulus for 40 s and then express preference between just two of the stimuli from the set. This process was repeated 20 times with the same experimental stimulus and different pairs of stimuli for the preference task. Study 4 tested to see if these activities were oppressive to subjects and if the results were reactions to extreme experimental conditions.

While duplicating Conners's (1964) experiment, a few adjustments were made to allow for efficiencies due to technological advances. For example, subjects viewed the stimuli on a computer screen, instead of in a plywood box with mechanically operated slide viewers.

The experiment was conducted in 16 sessions that ran through the summer and fall of 1999. Subjects were students in the introductory marketing course at a large southeastern university. They used computers in the business school computer lab. A total of 528 subjects participated. This was enough to allow for an assumption of normal distribution for each of the 18 versions of the experiment, for conducting nonparametric signs tests on the data. In contrast, Conners (1964) had a total sample size of 18, one for each version. The different versions allowed for a control group and for different subjects to have different stimuli for the adaptation-level stimulus and different random orderings of preference tasks.

Conners's (1964) results were not replicated. Once again there were no boredom effects and no support for the discrepancy hypothesis (Fig. 6.10). Thus,

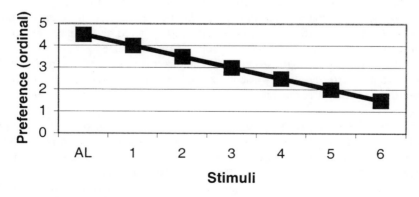

FIG. 6.10.   Replication of Conners (1964) methods, but not the results.

neither conceptual nor exact replication of Conners's (1964) experiment produced results consistent with those he reported.

STUDY 5—EXPERTISE

There was only one occasion in the course of our series of studies when we obtained results that appeared to approximate a butterfly curve. This occurred when we used advanced graphic design students as respondents for a pilot study. The sample size, however, was too small for the results to be conclusive. The fifth study followed up on this pilot study. It also followed up on an emergent finding from the first study, that a student with more visual design background evaluated visual images differently from those with less background in visual design. This is consistent with the research of Winston and Cupchik (1992), who used paintings as stimuli and found differences in the way naive and trained viewers process artworks, at both perceptual and experiential levels. Responses of naive viewers tend to be subjective with a strong preference for familiar subject matter. They prefer "popular art" that has broad appeal and induces pleasant feelings. Subject matter also has a strong effect on experienced viewers. These viewers, however, also objectively consider the visual attributes of the work. They prefer "high art" that is challenging to the viewer and involves a deep expression of the artist.

To investigate the relationship between expertise and preference for visual images, Study 1 was repeated with a new set of 26 respondents, from the next semester of the marketing principles classes. They participated in interviews using the same visual stimuli (the 11 color photographs). These respondents, however, were also asked to report on their background in visual design. Based on their self-reports, they were ranked in terms of visual design expertise. Those who were ranked above the median were compared with those ranked below the median.

Many of Winston and Cupchik's findings concerning preference for paintings were supported for preference for photographic images, by the results of this study. The set of comments for each respondent was rated on a scale of 1 to 18. A rating of 1 indicates that the respondent gave only comments regarding visual aspects, and a rating of 18 indicates that there were only comments about subject matter. Those respondents with a level of visual design expertise above the median had a mean rating on the comment scale of 10.5, which means that they were much more likely to use visual aspect criteria for preference than those below the median level of expertise, who had a mean score of 15.2. These scores also indicate that some of those with lower levels of expertise also mentioned visual aspects, but consistent with Winston and Cupchik (1992), the criterion in most cases was color, not other design principles that are acknowledged by experts. Comments included, "more colorful" and "the blue water is very pretty." Color was also an important criterion for the more expert viewers, but other factors such as composition, contrast, and lighting were also cited.

The visual/subject matter scores also indicate that both those with high levels of experience and those with low levels gave much importance to subject matter criteria for preference determination. Those with more experience were more likely to add cognitive, objective, visual evaluations to the criteria, while the naive viewers tended to rely more exclusively on affective, subjective responses to subject matter.

The fifth study added to our understanding of expert versus nonexpert preferences for visual images. The sixth study applies these findings to our focus—preference for changes in familiar logo designs.

STUDY 6—EXPERTISE CONTINUED

In order to determine the effect of expertise on preference for changes in visual images, specifically, familiar logo designs, Study 2 (using versions of familiar logos as stimuli) was repeated, but with professional graphic designers and advanced graphic design students as respondents, instead of business students. Also, only ordinal, within-subjects data were collected. Professional graphic designers were recruited by phone and by e-mail. Leads were obtained from referrals, a website search, and directories. The questionnaires were sent and returned by mail. A total of 55 usable questionnaires were completed from the 127 that were sent

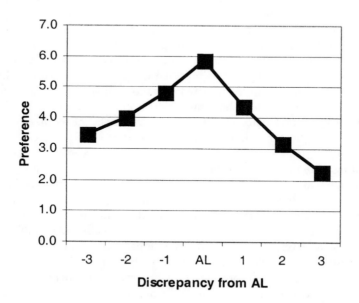

FIG. 6.11.   Kellogg's Froot Loops (Toucan Sam), expert respondents, ordinal data—within subjects.

(43.3%). In addition to the professionals, 40 students from advanced graphic design classes at a large southeastern university also participated. In total, 95 respondents participated. This allowed for a sample size of 68 to 74 for each brand represented by stimuli in the study. Including or removing the students from the sample did not alter the results in any significant way.

As with the business student respondents in Study 2, the experts of this experiment also failed to show boredom effects—no butterfly curve, no support for the discrepancy hypothesis. Figure 6.11 shows the results for Toucan Sam (Kellogg's Froot Loops). A comparison with the results for Toucan Sam in Study 2 (Fig. 6.6) shows that the pattern is the same. Once again, the current (adaptation level) version of the logo was the most preferred.

The expert respondents of the fifth study were asked for their opinions regarding when a logo design should be changed. The results of our studies are important because experts cannot agree in this matter. Although the majority of respondents (54%) disagreed with the notion that logos and other trademarks need to be updated on a fairly regular basis, 29% felt that logos should be changed for the sake of change alone. This latter group expressed an opinion that is not supported by the results of our studies.

DISCUSSION

Our interpretation of the results is that the discrepancy hypothesis is not a correct representation of consumer preference for changes in familiar logo designs, nor does it represent the preferences of graphic design experts. Discrepancy theory is more applicable to the realm of psychophysical stimuli, such as Haber's (1958) water temperatures, than to psychological phenomena such as investigated by Conners (1964), or to content-laden icons such as the familiar logos in our studies. One of the important findings of this series of six studies is the importance of associated meaning for preference for visual images. This concept is aptly illustrated by the excerpt from Mark Twain's (1869) *Innocents Abroad* quoted at the beginning of this chapter. Twain and his traveling companions deliberately ignored the attached meaning of an artifact and instead proceeded to evaluate the document on the basis of the quality of the handwriting, which they found wanting.

Clearly, as with a manuscript penned by Columbus, the meaning attached to a logo design must be considered of greater importance than the esthetic value of the logo. We expected to find that associated meaning would enhance familiarity effects and delay boredom effects. The findings indicate that there are familiarity effects, but not boredom effects, for familiar logo designs, regardless of the level of meaning. Consequently, if a logo is to be changed, it should be changed for a specific compelling reason and not for a concern that consumers are becoming tired of it.

In addition to identifying the primary importance of content over form for preference for changes in logo designs, our results also have implications for the generalizability of the theoretical constructs. There is a tendency in the field to try to generalize effects between radically different stimuli. Indeed, Conners (1964) tried to show that the discrepancy hypothesis was generalizable from water temperature to geometric shapes. We then tested to see whether it can be further generalized to logo designs. We found that it does not. We also found empirical evidence to seriously question the generalization that Conners made.

Despite our findings to refute the generalizability of the discrepancy hypothesis, our results were not without theoretical basis. Only specific aspects of exposure effects seem to apply to familiar logo designs—familiarity effects, but not boredom effects or novelty effects. Our results have led us to suggest that preference for changes in logo designs is subject to effects similar to those of social judgment theory. Once again, it is a great leap to generalize from statements of opinion to visual designs. Because we have determined that the meaning of the logo is of primary importance, the gap between the two kinds of stimuli is narrowed to some degree. In both cases, individuals tend to resist drastic changes to meaningful stimuli, but are accepting of small changes.

A natural extension of this study would be to test the generalizability of the findings to other sorts of changes. For some brands, the design of the packaging is also strongly symbolic of the brand. Consumers who do not know how to pronounce Toblerone, or cannot remember the name, refer to the triangular box. Identification with the shape of the glass Coca-Cola bottle is strong enough that the company has fashioned plastic bottles that approximate the shape and has included a picture of the bottle on cans of the product.

Another possible extension would be to contrast these findings of consumers resisting change with marketing situations for which change is the norm—such as clothing fashions and automobile design. Although fashions change with each season and automobile models change every few years, the logo often remains unchanged through many fashion cycles. Future studies could determine whether a consistent logo aids loyalty for brands with frequently changing designs.

At a more basic level, it may be instructive to determine the importance of the visual design of logos and other aspects of the brand to consumers (Henderson & Cote, 1998). Although specific researchers tend to be vitally interested in these issues, it does not necessarily follow that consumers are also. The results of the present study indicate that content is of primary importance, but we do not know how much less importance is given to form. It could be that when respondents are asked for their preference among the visual stimuli, they actually have no preference in regard to the esthetics. Consequently, they look for another criterion with which to make a selection. Consciously or not, they may select familiarity to use as this criterion. It could be that they experience nonspecific activation, or that the experience of recognition is interpreted as liking. It would add strength to the inference that is drawn from the present study, that it is more important to make a symbol familiar than to make it esthetically pleasing.

REFERENCES

Barboza, D. (1996, June 3). Now that is is a separate company, Lucent is spending $50 million to create an image. *New York Times*, p. D9.

Bell, S. S., Holbrook, M. B., & Solomon, M. R. (1991). Combining esthetic and social value to explain preferences for product styles with the incorporation of personality and ensemble effects. *Journal of Social Behavior and Personality, 6*(6), 243–274.

Berlyne, D. E. (1970). Novelty, complexity, and hedonic value. *Perception and Psychophysics, 8*(5A), 279–286.

Berlyne, D. E. (1971). *Aesthetics and psychobiology*. New York: Appleton-Century-Crofts.

Bornstein, R. F. (1989). Exposure and affect: Overview and meta-analysis of research, 1968–1987. *Psychological Bulletin, 106*(2), 265–289.

Bornstein, R. F., Kale, R., & Cornell, A. K. R. (1990). Boredom as a limiting condition on the mere exposure effect. *Journal of Personality and Social Psychology, 58,* 791–800.

Conners, C. K. (1964). Visual and verbal approach motives as a function of discrepancy from expectancy level. *Perceptual and Motor Skills, 18,* 457–464.

Elliott, S. (1994, November 1). A new survey finds that for some brands and companies, logos can be image breakers. *New York Times*, p. D6.

Haber, R. N. (1958). Discrepancy from adaptation level as a source of affect. *Journal of Experimental Psychology 56*(4), 370–375.

Harmon-Jones, E. (1995). *The mere exposure effect and emotion: A psychophysiological investigation.* Tucson: University of Arizona Press.

Henderson, P. W., & Cote, J. A. (1998). Guidelines for selecting or modifying logos. *Journal of Marketing, 62,* 14–30.

Holman, R. H. (1980). Apparel as communication. In E. Hirschman & M. Holbrook (Eds.), *Proceedings of the conference on consumer esthetics and symbolic consumption. Symbolic consumption behavior* (pp. 7–12). Ann Arbor, MI: Association for Consumer Research.

Morgan, H. (1986). *Symbols of America*. New York: Viking Penguin.

New logo: More mixed reviews. (1996, September). *Sunset*, p. 10.

Pimentel, R. W. (1997). *Consumer preference for logo designs: Visual design and meaning.* Unpublished doctoral dissertation, University of Arizona, Tucson.

Pimentel, R. W., & Heckler, S. E. (1999). *Logo design change: A test of competing theories.* Working paper.

Pollack. J. (1999). Kool-Aid Pitcherman stays, but Ogilvy puts him to work. *Advertising Age, 70,* 57.

Sherif, M., & Hovland, C. I. (1961). *Social judgment: Assimilation and contrast effects in communication and attitude change.* New Haven, CT: Yale University Press.

Thompson, S. (1999). Kool-Aid hits road, fueled with smiles. *Brandweek, 40,* 6.

Thumbs go up—and down—for the new Sunset logo. (1996, August). *Sunset*, p. 10.

Twain, M. (1869). *The innocents abroad.* Hartford, CT: American Publishing Company.

Wilson, L. (1994). Clearance for design trademarks—Keeping your client out of court. *Communication Arts–Design Annual, 36,* 261–264.

Winston, A. S., & Cupchik, A. G. C. (1992). The evaluation of high art and popular art by naive and experienced viewers. *Visual Arts Research, 18,* 1–14.

Zajonc, R. B. (1968). Attitudinal effects of mere exposure. *Journal of Personality and Social Psychology, 9*(2, Pt. 2).

CHAPTER SEVEN

Visual Persuasion: Mental Imagery Processing and Emotional Experiences

Cees Goossens
Tilburg University, The Netherlands

Recently, Meyers-Levy and Malaviya (1999) provided an integrative framework of judgment formation and persuasion. The framework assumes that, when exposed to an advertisement, people use either a fairly effortful and deliberative "systematic" approach to judgment formation or a far less demanding and less rigorous "heuristic" approach. Furthermore, there is an "experiential processing strategy." When this third strategy operates, judgments are not based on thoughts prompted by a message content per se but rather on sensations or feelings prompted by the very act of processing (Strack, 1992). Judgments that are based on these sensations may require only the most meager level of cognitive resources, as suggested by experiential processing having been demonstrated most frequently in conditions in which cognitive capacity is severely constrained. Other research, however, indicates that the effect of process-generated experiential responses on judgments need not be limited to severely resource-constrained conditions (Meyers-Levy & Malaviya, 1999). Regarding this, this chapter considers an experiential processing strategy that requires elaborated cognitions.

According to Aylwin (1990), adults can use three different, although interconnected forms of mental representation: verbal representation, or inner speech; visual imagery, or "pictures in the mind's eye"; and enactive imagery, a kind of imagined action or role play. Enactive imagery is specialized for representing the temporal and affective aspects of a stimulus. This is consistent with Lang's (1984, 1994) work, which shows that representations involving active participation are accompanied by more affective arousal than purely visual representations. In general, emotion research indicates that dimensions of affective valence (i.e., pleasantness or quality), arousal (i.e., intensity or impact), and, to a lesser extent, dominance are consistently found to organize judgments for stimuli as diverse as words, pictures, mood states, advertisements, and more (Bradley, 1994). In this context more research is needed to explain how process-generated experience influences judgment. This chapter regards the relation between information processing, emotional experience and appraisal. In particular, a mental imagery processing (MIP) model is discussed (see Goossens, 1994).

RESEARCH ISSUE

MacInnis and Price (1987) distinguished two different modes of information processing, namely, discursive (symbolic, linguistic or verbal) information processing, which means proceeding by reasoning and argument, and imagery processing, which includes perceptual or sensory representations in working memory that are used in much the same way as perceptions of external stimuli. Basically, imagery processes are evoked as sensory experiences in working memory. It is important to note that elaborated imagery and discursive processing are in actual fact not mutually exclusive processes (Bugelski, 1983). This means that when consumers in "real" contexts engage in imagery, it is quite likely that discursive and imagery processing and the contents of each become elaborately interwined. Apart from that, the information-processing system is mainly verbal, and language is the standard medium for the elicitation of imagery (Staats & Lohr, 1979). Because of this knowledge, the MIP model tries to meet realistic situations, in which pure discursive (verbal) and pure imagery (visual) processes do not exist. To simplify matters, two empirical situations of information processing are distinguished:

1. Nonenactive imagery—that is, situations in which subjects process verbal and visual information, but rather detached. In fact, these subjects just read, or listen to, and look at the presented stimuli.
2. Enactive imagery—that is, situations in which subjects process verbal and visual information, but personally involved.

The primary research question is: What is the interrelation between information processing, enactive imagery, appraisal and emotional experience? In the next sections the MIP model describes these interrelations theoretically.

A MENTAL IMAGERY PROCESSING MODEL

In the MIP model, imagery is conceptualized as a mode of processing, which includes perceptual or sensory (in particular visual) representations in working memory. In accordance with Staats and Lohr (1979), mental images are defined here as conditioned sensory responses. However, the model starts from a principle that in an empirical context it is not realistic to distinguish pure imagery processes. Mental imagery is namely generated by an individual's word–image repertoire.

Therefore the model states that elaborated imagery processes are made up of a continious interaction between a person's image system and verbal system.

The MIP model is based on Paivio's (1986) dual coding theory and the cognitive framework provided by Yuille and Catchpole (1977). In accordance with Paivio's dual code model, the MIP model contains a verbal and an image system. Analogous to Yuille and Catchpole's (1977) framework of cognition, the model consists of two fundamental levels of cognitive operation, namely the abstract plane and the representational plane. The MIP model is schematically presented in Fig. 7.1. In fact the model describes the relation between cognitive processes and an emotional system.

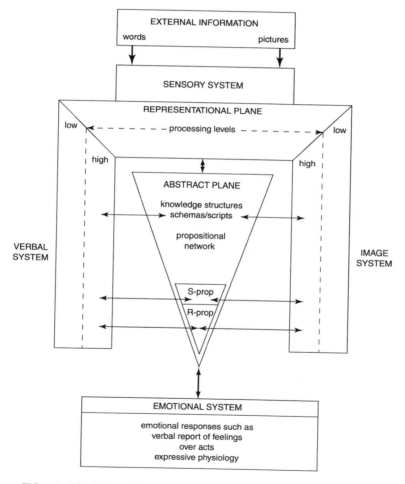

FIG. 7.1. The MIP-model. Source: Adapted from Goossens, Enactive Imagery: Information Processing. Emotional Responses and Behavioral Intentions, Journal of Mental Imagery, 1994.

The core concepts of the MIP model are knowledge structures, and propositions. In accordance with Bower (1981), and Lang (1984, 1994), I assume that there
is an *emotion generator* with emotion connected to specific cognitions. In this context a propositional network is connected with an emotional system.

THE ABSTRACT PLANE

The abstract plane is the storehouse of an individual's basic knowledge structures,
such as schemas and scripts. Schemas are organized meaning structures that
encapsulate knowledge about the self or the world; they provide selection criteria
for regulating attention and lend a focus to the encoding, storage, and retrieval
of information in a domain. More specifically, they allow the receiver to identify
stimuli quickly, to cluster them into manageable units, and to select a strategy for
obtaining further information in order to solve a problem or reach a goal (Singer
& Kolligian, 1987). A self-schema, for instance, is an organized body of knowledge
about one's intentions. The major function of such a self-schema is anticipatory,
that is, it incorporates hypotheses about incoming stimuli, as well as plans for
interpreting relevant information about the self. Information-processing differences may result from individual differences in schemas influencing people's an-
ticipation, perception, and memory of situations (Dworkin & Goldfinger, 1985).
Scripts are schemas about the appropriate sequence of events in well-known situations. The script concept demonstrates its efficacy as an organizing principle and
exploratory mechanism in both the short term, such as planning a trip, and the
long term, such as planning one's life. In the MIP model, schemas and scripts are
functional, because individuals can evoke images or recall words through the
instantiation of these knowledge structures (see Fig. 7.1; double-headed arrows
between the abstract and the representational plane). With regard to remembered
experiences the MIP model contains a propositional network of emotion information—for instance, schemas about feelings like pleasure and relaxation.

THE REPRESENTATIONAL PLANE

The representational plane is the servant of the abstract plane, and permits representations that support the operative activities like thinking, remembering, and
appraisal. Consistent with Paivio's (1986) dual code theory, the MIP model consists of two representational systems: (a) an image system and (b) a verbal system.
In essence, dual coding theory postulates verbal and imaginal representations that
encode word and object information, respectively, as well as connections that exist
between (a) sensory events and symbolic representations, (b) verbal and imaginal
representations, and (c) representations within the two symbolic systems.

From this point of view the MIP model is a blend of Paivio's (1986) dual coding
theory and Yuille and Catchpole's (1977) theoretical framework. Analogous to

Paivio's dual code model, I assume that information can be represented concretely in two types of cognitive codes. Analogous to Yuille and Cathpole (1977), I suppose that there must be a more abstract representation of information that is located in the so called abstract plane. The latter premise is based on Pylyshyn's (1973) statement that "as long as we recognize that people can go from mental pictures to mental words and vice versa, we are forced to conclude that there must be a representation (which is more abstract and not available to conscious experience) which encompasses both" (p. 5).

From this point of view images and words are figurative, and are constructed under the control of the abstract plane. Consequently, the abstract plane is the location where associations between words and images are made. According to the network theory, such associations are made via "nodes" (see Bower, 1981). Actually, the representational plane reflects that people have word–image repertoires. Once the individual has learned an extensive repertoire of word-image units (through conditioning principles), he or she can have an extensive and varied imagery experience based on (external) presentation of words. Moreover, the individual is capable of voluntarily constructing language sequences that can call forth imagery (Staats & Lohr, 1979). Information processed in the abstract plane is not available to conscious experience, whereas the information represented in the image- and verbal system is available to conscious experience.

THE PROCESSING SYSTEM

The representational plane is divided into a number of subsystems proposed by Gibson (1966). Three functions of these subsystems are relevant: The first function of these subsystems is to construct representations of the environment on the basis of information transmitted from appropriate sense organs (see Fig. 7.1, sensory system). The level to which stimuli information is processed or represented depends on such restrictions as the nature of the information, attentional demands, the content of self-schemas, competing information, the level of personal involvement, and so on. The MIP model does not describe a direct connection between the sensory system and the emotional system because this connection is not available to conscious experience (it is largely controlled by the autonomic nervous system; see Izard, 1993).

Information can be processed at different levels of cognitive elaboration (e.g., Chaiken, 1980; Petty & Cacioppo, 1983). According to the MIP model, the level of elaboration reflects the extent to which information in the representational plane is integrated with prior knowledge structures. The external information in Fig. 7.1 is, for example, a visual ad with the slogan "Experience Puerto Rico, enjoy it!". This persuasive information can be processed at a low or high level of elaboration (see Fig. 7.1, processing levels). The major question is: What is the relation between processing levels and emotional responses?

Low Processing Levels

Processes at a low level of cognitive elaboration evoke simple responses in the representational plane, such as the retrieval of a verbal label, or an image of a perceptual object. In this case, the second function of the representational modes is to establish a kind of raw memory, which permits direct recovery of past experience. At this low level of cognitive elaboration, images and words are just concrete representations, which are not involved with dynamic operations of thought. For instance, a person reads the word "beach" and evokes an image of it, but without any special thoughts and feelings. In fact, these are relatively autonomic processes emanating from the word–image repertoire. In this particular situation we may speak of a situation of low involvement with the presented object. That is, the individual is not motivated (or in the mood) to process detailed information. In this particular case people can process images or words but without physiological feelings.

High Processing Levels

Further, the MIP model distinguishes processes at a high level of elaboration. Information processing at a high level of elaboration establishes connections between encoded information and the knowledge structures (schemas and scripts) in the abstract plane. Thus, if processes are at a high level of elaboration, the third principal function of the representational plane is to permit the reconstruction of concrete representations of emotional experiences that have been incorporated into the abstract plane (see Fig. 7.1, the propositional network). From this point of view, elaborated imagery and discursive (verbal) processing are dynamic tools of thought. In this case there is a high involvement state with the presented object. The main reason for developing the MIP model is to provide a theoretical framework to understand and to investigate the effect of enactive imagery on the consumer's affective responses. In respect of the visual persuasion and experiential processing, enactive imagery is defined as "experience-it-yourself thoughts, which integrate images and words in corresponding knowledge structures." Thus far, this pertains to the MIP model's structure and processing system. Next the relation between information processing and emotional responses is discussed.

STIMULUS AND RESPONSE INFORMATION

In accordance with Staats and Lohr (1979), the MIP model states that both words and images can serve to elicit an emotional response. However, words and images by themselves are not sufficient to produce emotional states. In this context we need a theory that offers a description of the cognitive processes involved in emotions. Peter Lang formulated such a theory.

According to Lang (1984), there exists a cognitive mechanism that is responsible for the activation of affective or emotional responses: Emotion is conceived to be an action set, defined by a specific information structure in memory. Analogous to Lang's emotion theory, the MIP model assumes that emotional responses are generated by an associative network of propositions. It is suggested that emotion information is coded in memory in the form of propositions. Propositions are logical relationships between concepts, which are organized into an associative network (see Fig. 7.1). The MIP model assumes that this type of information is in essence amodal. The emotion-information network is a sort of prototype or schema, which is processed as a unit when a critical number of propositions are accessed. The conceptual network that organizes an emotional response includes two primary information categories: (a) stimulus propositions, and (b) response propositions.

The network is activated when a person attends to information that matches these propositions in the network. Lang's basic assumption is that activation of response propositions starts an associated motor program, which in turn occasions the emotional response (see Fig. 7.1, emotional system). Activation of stimulus propositions only has an indirect influence on the emotional response via association with response propositions.

According to the MIP model, stimulus and/or response information, processed at a high cognitive elaboration level, can activate the propositional network. If the stimulus and response propositions have been activated, its information is available to conscious experience through the representational plane. That is, stimulus propositions describe external stimuli and the context in which an emotional response occurs. An example is, "I see people sunbathing on a restful beach" (see Fig. 7.1, the double-headed arrows between the representational plane and the stimulus propositions [S-prop.]). Response propositions describe the emotional response, including verbal behavior, visceral and somatic changes, and overt behavior. Examples are, "I feel relaxed," "I feel the hot sun on my skin," and "I am sweating" (see Fig. 7.1, the double-headed arrows between the representational plane and the response propositions [R-prop.]). In fact, there is empirical evidence that processing of response (i.e., experiential) information occasions more emotional responses than processing of stimulus information. In several experiments it was shown that subjects encouraged to imagine stimulus as well as response information had a stronger physiological response than subjects encouraged to imagine stimulus information only; see, for example, Dekker and Everaerd (1988) and Lang (1984, 1994).

MEANINGS AND APPRAISALS

In addition to stimulus and response propositions, Lang's theory also incorporates meaning propositions addressing how stimulus and response propositions are

interpreted. The MIP model does not explicitly consider these meaning propositions, because their function is already incorporated in the individual knowledge
structures (e.g., sunbathing can mean "health" to one and "pleasure" to another).
According to Lazarus (1990, p. 145), knowledge is the cold cognitive stuff of which
personal meaning is made. As such, mere knowledge does not result directly in
emotion. Knowledge has to do with beliefs about how things work in general
and in specific contexts. Appraisal is a personal evaluation of the significance of
this knowledge in a particular encounter or existentially. The cognitive activity
"appraisal" consists of a continuing evaluation of the significance of what is hap-
pening for one's personal well-being. In fact, there is general agreement that
appraisal is the process by which knowledge-by-acquaintance (i.e., the immediate
experience of events in the external or internal environment) is transformed into
knowledge-by-description, which is the appraisal and labeling of these events
(Buck, 1988). Emotions are formed as a result of a process of appraisals of what an
event/stimulus can do for one's well-being. Further, the pattern of evaluations
made by an individual on a small set of appraisals determines what emotions are
felt by the person (Kumar & Oliver, 1997). Appraisals, and feelings such as "It's
OK" and "I feel good," can be represented in the MIP model's verbal system, with
"I feel good about it" as a final judgment.

CONCLUSION: ELABORATED COGNITIONS AND EMOTIONAL EXPERIENCES

Lang (1984) assumed that information on stimuli and responses is always represented in the cognitive system as an associative network of propositions. The MIP
model suggests that both stimuli and response information can be represented
in the cognitive system without sensations or feelings. In this particular case the
information is cognitively represented in the periphery of the representational
plane, that is, the information is processed at a low level of cognitive elaboration
(see Fig. 7.1, low processing level). Consequently, the propositional network and
the motor programs of the emotional system can not be activated. Activation is
only possible through an intensive instantiation of word–image repertoires, as well
as the corresponding knowledge and meaning structures within the abstract plane.
Subsequently, the MIP model states that nonelaborated cognitions just occasion
primary affective responses. For example, a person who is just looking at a picture
of a sunny beach, without special thoughts, only judges this picture as good or
bad, attractive or not attractive, and so on. On the other hand, if a person inten-
sively activates the word–image repertoire regarding "sunny beaches," an intensive
connection with the abstract plane is made. In this case the instantation of "beach
schemas" may generate both elaborated imagery and discursive processes about
this object. According to the MIP model, these highly elaborated processes (e.g.,
enactive imagery) have the potency to match response propositions efficiently,

which occasions an emotional response. Based on the empirical results of Lang's emotion theory, we may conclude that response information elicits a stronger emotional response than stimulus information. Therefore the first hypothesis is: H1: *Stimulus and response information elicits a stronger appraisal and emotional experience than mere stimulus information.* Regarding visual pursuasion the model suggests that enactive imagery is an experiential processing strategy with elaborated cognitions. H2: *Enactive imagery has a stronger potency to elicit appraisal and emotional experience than nonenactive imagery.* This can be explained because subjects who imagine themselves interacting with a situation have to activate relevant experience schemas. On the contrary, nonenactive imagery is more detached— that is, the self-experience schemas are not involved, so that it is less likely that the emotion network and corresponding knowledge structures will be activated. The MIP model takes imagery processing, memories, and emotional experiences (e.g., feelings) as interrelated concepts. A person can, for example, renew feelings (as opposed to simply recalling them) by mentally reliving an event that has already happened. The more vivid is the reliving, the stronger is the affect experienced. In such a case, the affect would not simply be retrieved from memory, it would be regenerated (Frijda, 1988). In a marketing context, the vividness of message information is assumed to influence consumers' evaluations or judgments. Information may be described as vivid, that is, as likely to attract and hold attention and to excite the imagination to the extent that it is: (a) emotionally interesting, (b) concrete ande imagery provoking, and (c) proximate in a sensory, temporal, or spatial way (McGill & Anand, 1989, p. 188). Marketers can use these ingredients in visual advertising, in order to stimulate enactive imagery. Finally, the model can be considered as a framework for future research on visual persuasion and experiential processing.

REFERENCES

Aylwin, S. (1990). Imagery and affect: Big questions, little answers. In P. J.Hampson, D. F. Marks, & J. T. E. Richardson (Eds.), *Imagery: Current developments* (pp. 247–267). New York: Routledge, International Library of Psychology.

Bower, G. H. (1981). Mood and memory. *American Psychologist, 36,* 129–148.

Bradley, M. M. (1994). Emotional memory: A dimensional analysis. In S. Van Goozen, N. E. Van de Poll, & J. A. Sergeant (Eds.), *Emotions: Essays on current issues in the field of emotion theory* (pp. 97–134). Hillsdale, NJ: Lawrence Erlbaum Associates.

Buck, R. (1988). *Human motivation and emotion* (2nd ed.). New York: John Wiley.

Bugelski, B. R. (1983). Imagery and the thought processes. In A. Sheikh (Ed.), *Imagery: Current theory, research and application* (pp. 72–95). New York: John Wiley.

Chaiken, S. (1980). Heuristic vs systematic information processing and the use of source vs message cues in persuasion. *Journal of Personality and Social Psychology, 39*(5), 752.

Dekker, J., & Everaerd, W. (1988). Attentional effects on sexual arousal. *Psychophysiology, 25,* 45–54.

Dworkin, R. H., & Goldfinger, S. H. (1985). Processing bias: Individual differences in the cognition of situations. *Journal of Personality, 53,* 480–501.

Frijda, N. (1988). The laws of emotions. *American Psychologist, 43*(5), 349–358.

Gibson, J. J. (1966). *The senses considered as perceptual system.* Boston: Houghton-Mifflin.

Goossens, C. F. (1994). Enactive imagery: Information processing, emotional responses, and behavioral intentions. *Journal of Mental Imagery, 18*(3&4), 119–150.

Izard, C. E. (1993). Four systems for emotion activation: Cognitive and noncognitive processes. *Psychological Review, 100*(1), 68–90.

Kumar, A., & Oliver, R. L. (1997). Cognitive appraisals, consumer emotions, and consumer response. *Advances in Consumer Research, 24,* 17–18.

Lang, P. J. (1984). Cognition in emotion: Concept and action. In C. E. Izard, J. Kagan, & R. B. Zajonc (Eds.), *Emotions, cognitions and behavior.* New York: Cambridge University Press.

Lang, P. J. (1994). The motivational organization of emotion: Affect–reflex connections. In S. Van Goozen, N. E. Van de Poll, & J. A. Sergeant (Eds.), *Emotions: Essays on current issues in the field of emotion theory* (pp. 61–93). Hillsdale, NJ: Lawrence Erlbaum Associates.

Lazarus, R. S. (1990). *Emotion and Adaptation.* New York: Oxford University Press.

MacInnis, D. J., and Price, L. L. (1987). The role of imagery in information processing: Review and extensions. *Journal of Consumer Research, 13,* 473–491.

McGill, A. L., & Anand, P. (1989). The effect of vivid attributes on the evaluation of alternatives: The role of differential attention and cognitive elaboration. *Journal of Consumer Research, 16,* 188–196.

Meyers-Levy, J., & Malaviya, P. (1999). Consumers' processing of persuasive advertisements: An integrative framework of persuasion theories. *Journal of Marketing, 63,* 45–60.

Paivio, A. (1986). *Mental representations: A dual coding approach.* Oxford, England: Oxford University Press.

Petty, R. E., and Cacioppo, J. (1983). *Attitudes and persuasion: Classic and contemporary approaches.* Dubuque, IA: William C. Brown.

Pylyshyn, Z. W. (1973). What the mind's eye tells the mind's brain: A critique of mental imagery. *Psychological Bulletin, 80,* 1–24.

Singer, J. L., & Kolligian, J. (1987). Personality: Developments in the study of private experience. *Annual Review of Psychology, 38,* 533–574.

Staats, A. W., & Lohr, J. M. (1979). Images, language, emotions, and personality: Social behaviorism's theory. *Journal of Mental Imagery, 3,* 85–106.

Strack, F. (1992). The different routes to social judgments: Experiential versus informational strategies." In L. L. Martin & A. Tesser (Eds.), *The construction of social judgments* (pp. 249–76). Hillsdale, NJ: Lawrence Erlbaum Associates.

Yuille. J. C., & Catchpole, M. J. (1977). The role of imagery in models of cognition. *Journal of Mental Imagery, 1,* 171–180.

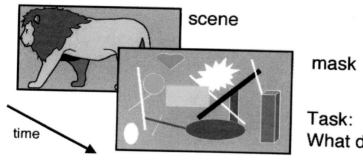

scene

mask

Task:
What did you see?

Fig. 3.2

Color Panel A

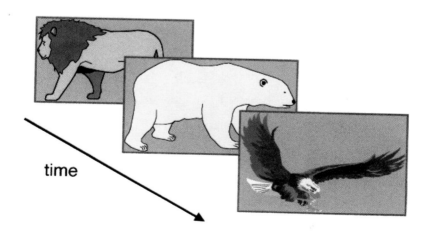

time

Fig. 3.3

Color Panel B

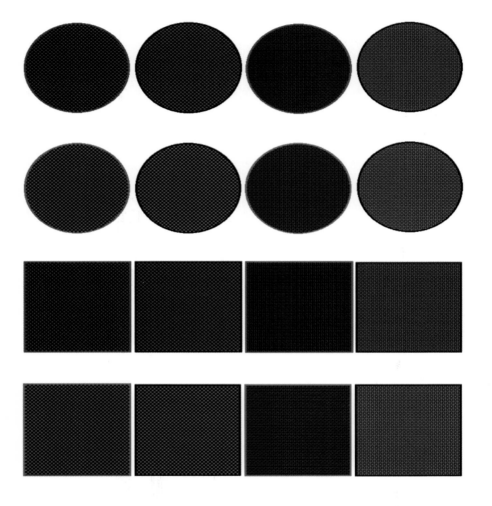

Fig. 5.1   Color Panel C

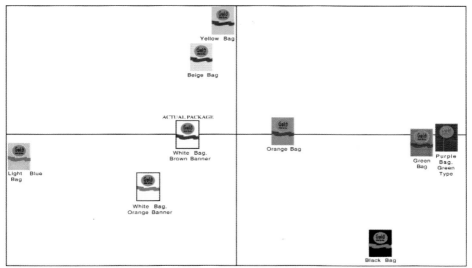

from Garber, Burke, and Jones (2000), with permission.

Fig. 16.2   Color Panel D

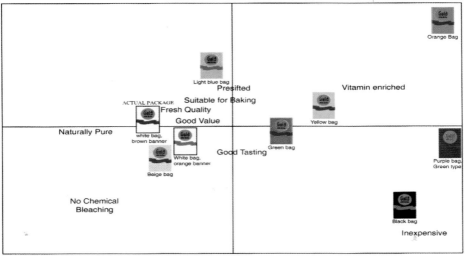

from Garber, Burke, and Jones (2000), with permission.

Fig. 16.3   Color Panel E

Beige Bag: Very Similar
Visual Type

Light Blue Bag: Moderately
Dissimilar

Green bag: Very Dissimilar
and Consistent

Black Bag: Very Dissimilar and
Inconsistent

Fig. 16.4   Color Panel F

III. IMAGE AND WORD

CHAPTER EIGHT

Scripted Thought

Nader T. Tavassoli

London Business School

Writing pervades modern life as a principle vehicle of communication. Writing is also the vehicle in which cognitive and social psychologists present experimental stimuli and collect responses, as evidence of mental activity. Written language is, therefore, a central aspect of everyday life and is at the core of research on memory, attitude formation, persuasion, inference making, problem solving, and so on. However, most psychological knowledge is derived from and tested in research conducted with participants processing and reporting words written in alphabetic scripts.

Most languages rely on alphabetic writing systems that consist of symbols representing sounds. Alphabetic scripts include the Latin alphabet (e.g., English and Spanish) and Arabic, Hebrew, and Cyrillic scripts (e.g., Russian). However, approximately one-quarter of the world population reads Chinese logographs, which are morphemes: symbols that represent meaning. Japanese and Korean use both types of script. For example, Korean uses Hancha, which is based on Chinese logographs, and Hangul, which is an alphabet. The premise of this review is that the basic processing of alphabetic and logographic scripts differs in fundamental ways.

I begin by highlighting relative differences in reading alphabetic and logographic scripts. I then review a growing body of research that shows how these relative differences can affect higher order processes involved in memory and evaluative judgments. This includes findings on memory for a word's font style and print color, associations in memory between words and nonverbal images and sounds, and auditory and visual interference in the processing of words. I also review findings on spatial and temporal processing differences that provide the basis for memory-based judgments, complex thought, and decision making. I conclude by summarizing how scripts, independent of language, can affect thought in profound ways.

READING ALPHABETIC AND LOGOGRAPHIC SCRIPTS

The notion that short-term memory is involved in language comprehension dates back to Huey (1908). Important for present purposes is the processing of language in short-term memory's phonological loop and in visual short-term memory in terms of their storage and rehearsal components. The phonological loop stores information in a phonological code and rehearses that information by recirculating it in a serial manner (Baddeley, 1986). Visual short-term memory stores information in an imaginal code and rehearses it perceptlike (Kosslyn, 1980) in a holistic manner (Paivio, 1986). Reading any script relies on each of these components. However, reading alphabetic and reading logographic scripts appear to do so to differing degrees.

Phonological aspects pervade in reading alphabetic scripts. Readers of English, for example, tend to phonologically recode (subvocalize) written words (e.g., Mc-Cusker, Hillinger, & Bias, 1981). English words are primarily rehearsed phonologically in short-term memory's phonological loop (Baddeley, 1986; Paivio, 1986; Van Orden, 1987).

The process of reading Chinese differs considerably. A reader has to visually distinguish upward of 7,000 logographs. Even when logographs represent sound, the association with pronunciation is largely arbitrary and acquired via rote associative learning. Moreover, because there are only about 400 syllables in Mandarin (1300 including tones), compared to about 4,000 in English, there are a large number of homophones in Chinese, such as *so, sow, sew* in English. This makes sound an ambiguous mental code, a problem that is eliminated in writing, where there are 10 times more logographic components available than spoken utterances (Cheng, 1981). Finally, because logographs are symbols that represent meaning, a Chinese reader is able to mentally access meaning unmediated by phonology, or subvocalization (Perfetti & Zhang, 1991). Not surprisingly, reading logographs is thus not dominated by phonological processes and relies more on visual processes than does reading alphabetic words (Hung & Tzeng, 1981; Zhou & Marslen-Wilson, 1999).

To summarize, there are some basic differences in the cognitive processes involved in reading alphabetic and logographic scripts. English relies to a greater degree on short-term memory's phonological loop, whereas Chinese relies more on visual short-term memory. It is important to note, however, that this does not suggest that a Chinese reader views a logograph as a pictorial representation of a concept and that both Chinese and English involve phonological *and* visual codes (cf. Zhang & Simon, 1985). Differences must therefore be considered a matter of degree (cf. Hung & Tzeng, 1981).

Finally, these differential processes are not restricted to monolinguals compared across different languages. For example, Koreans rely more on phonological processes in the processing of alphabetic Hangul words, and more on visual processes in processing logographic Hancha words (Cho & Chen, 1999; Tavassoli & Han, 2001). These differences also appear to extend to proficient bilinguals (Tavassoli & Han, 2002; Tavassoli & Lee, 2001a, 2001b), who rely on different scripts to access a single conceptual system (Francis, 1999; for Chinese, see Chen & Leung, 1989). Bilinguals have also been found to be flexible in the way in which they process words in a mixed-language context, depending on the emphasis given to alphabetic English words and to logographic Chinese words (Zhang & Schmitt, 2001). Differences in processing alphabetic and logographic scripts may therefore have far-reaching implications.

PHONOLOGICAL AND VISUAL ASPECTS OF PROCESSING WRITTEN LANGUAGE

Visual Attention

Relative processing differences have been found to affect a variety of behaviors. The psycholinguistic literature has predominantly examined the role of phonology in gaining lexical access for different scripts. For example, sound-related nonsense words (e.g., rait) facilitated the identification of very briefly presented target words in English (e.g., rate) more than visually related nonsense words (e.g., ralt; Perfetti, Bell, & Delaney, 1988). It is important to note, however, that both types of nonsense words facilitated word identification—by activating properties of the target word—compared to a control condition (e.g., busk). In contrast to English, visually related nonsense words facilitated Chinese target word identification more than did sound-related ones, whereas both were more effective than controls (Perfetti & Zhang, 1991).

These low-level processing differences can extend to higher order processes involved in memory and judgment. Pan and Schmitt (1996) examined the impact of a script's visual features on evaluation. Heightened visual attention in reading logographs should raise the perceptual significance of visual features, such as the font used. They found that attitude ratings provided by Chinese consumers were more sensitive than those of American consumers to the match between the femininity or masculinity of fonts for brand names of feminine (e.g., lipstick) and masculine (e.g., motorcycles) products. Although the font of alphabetic brand names did not affect evaluations, Chinese consumers more favorably evaluated feminine (masculine) products written in fonts that had been rated as more feminine (masculine).

Differences in visual attention should also affect memory for words' visual features, such as their print colors. Studies of attention suggest that color and form are perceived as separate features of a letter and that focal attention is required for the conjoining of color and form in memory (Treisman & Gelade, 1980) as represented in visual short-term memory (Smith & Jonides, 1994). Compared to the processing of alphabetic words, heightened visual attention and a greater involvement of visual short-term memory should therefore facilitate the binding of logographs with their print colors in long-term memory.

Although incidental memory of a word's print color is rare during the normal reading of alphabetic English words (Light, Berger, & Bardales, 1975), I found that color memory for otherwise equally memorable words (but not of pictures) was better for Chinese logographs than for alphabetic English words (Tavassoli, 2001). This processing difference also had evaluative implications. Consider Apple's former rainbow-colored logo, which acquired connotations of freedom and fun, compared to IBM's blue, which signals solidity, or worse, stodginess. Would a new brand that copied Apple's or IBM's colors be influenced by their connotations? I found that Chinese readers, but not English readers, evaluated an unknown brand more positively if it shared the color of highly rated brands than if it shared the color of poorly rated brands (Tavassoli, 2001). This type of process has been receiving growing legal attention, and several countries have recently passed laws against "brand piracy" through copying another brand's color if this has acquired secondary meaning.

Associative Memory

Script differences affect not only the way in which single words are encoded, but also how words are integrated with nonverbal stimuli. Research on cross-modal associative memory (Penney, 1989; Tavassoli, 1998) and cross-modal coordination (Yee, Hunt, & Pellegrino, 1991) suggests that associative memory between two stimuli should be stronger the greater the overlap in short-term memory processes active during encoding and rehearsal. A relatively greater reliance on visual short-term memory for logographic scripts should therefore facilitate the integration of words with images, whereas a relatively greater reliance on phonological short-term memory for alphabetic scripts should facilitate the integration of words with sounds.

Consider the goal of enhancing brand memory and brand meaning by associating the "fizz" sound associated with opening a bottle of Coke, or the power of Nike's "swoosh" logo. It has long been one of the most important advertising strategies to associate words in memory with visual information (e.g., Lutz & Lutz, 1977; Schmitt, Tavassoli, & Millard, 1993). More recently, companies also began registering auditory brand identifiers as intellectual property, such as NBC's familiar three-tone chime and the MGM lion's roar. My coauthors and I tested word–sound and word–logo memory in a pair-recognition task, where half of the pairs were in the same pairing as at learning and half were cross-matched. Associative memory was stronger between images and logographic words, whereas it was stronger between sounds and alphabetic words. We found this relative effect for the same Korean words written in the alphabetic Hangul compared to the logographic Hancha (Tavassoli & Han, 2001), for Chinese and English words with native Mandarin speakers compared to native English speakers, and for bilingual speakers of Cantonese and English (Tavassoli & Han, 2002).

To summarize, there is a difference between alphabetic and logographic scripts in the potency with which mnemonic associations are formed with auditory and visual information. These types of associations have broad application. Using visual symbols or a color code is common in signage and complex information displays. Colors and shapes are used to highlight category membership and signify thematic relations among items of verbal information. This is helpful in environments such as museums and theme parks, as well as for static and dynamic textual information. The navigation of web sites, for example, is more efficient when verbal information adheres to a visual scheme because print colors and shapes can help orient the user towards goal-relevant information. These results suggest that it should be easier for readers of Chinese logographs to learn visual–verbal associations that could aid them in navigating complex environments. Conversely, it should also be more confusing when visual codes are changed in information displays that contain logographic compared to alphabetic words.

Auditory and Visual Interference

The reciprocal effect of the association of two items of information is often interference (Penney, 1989; Tavassoli, 1998). In the preceding examples, the goal was to integrate information, and this was facilitated by an overlap in processing requirements. When stimuli compete for attention, such as in a dual-task setting, interference is also greater the greater the overlap in processing requirements (Duncan, 1980). As a result, auditory distractors should interfere more with reading alphabetic words, whereas visual distractors should interfere more with reading logographic words. For example, listening to music while studying should be more detrimental to memory and comprehension in English than in Chinese. Similarly, the use of unrelated background music in a television advertisement should interfere more with the processing of reading English, whereas the use of unrelated visual graphics should interfere more with reading Chinese.

My coauthors and I have begun to explore these possibilities. For example, we found that bilinguals were better at recalling English words after a visual filler task than after an auditory filler task, and vice versa for the recall of Chinese words (Tavassoli & Lee, 2001a). Similarly, Koreans were better at recalling a list of alphabetic Hangul words when each word was followed by a visual distractor than if each word was followed by an auditory distractor, and vice versa for logographic Hancha words (Tavassoli & Han, 2001). There may even be interesting within-language implications for languages that use a combination of logographic and syllabic or alphabetic scripts. We found that recognition memory in Japanese was better when words were presented such that they alternated between the syllabic Hiragana and the logographic Kanji scripts than if they were all presented only in Hiragana or only in Kanji (Schmitt & Tavassoli, 1994). These findings are consistent with the notion that more resources for processing item-specific information are available in short-term memory when words use different scripts rather than the same script.

Distraction can also affect inference making, including evaluative judgments. Festinger and Maccoby (1964) showed that counterattitudinal messages can be more persuasive when accompanied by some form of distractor by reducing counter-arguing. Petty, Wells, and Brock (1976) showed that the effect of distraction is not limited to counterattitudinal messages but also that it inhibits the dominant cognitive response. Although distraction can enhance message reception for counterattitudinal or weak messages, for which unfavorable thoughts are the dominant response, distraction reduces message reception for strong messages, for which favorable thoughts dominate (see also Chattopadhyay & Alba, 1988).

In line with this reasoning, my coauthor and I found that for products described by strong attributes, as in advertisements, memory-based product judgments and online person evaluations were better in Chinese when the logographic information was learned among distracting sounds. In contrast, judgments based on strong attributes were better in English when the alphabetic information was learned among distracting images (Tavassoli & Lee, 2001a). The opposite effect was observed for weak attribute information, such as provided by a critic. In the case of weak product or person attributes, judgments were better in Chinese when the logographic information was learned among distracting images, but judgments were better in English when the alphabetic information was learned among distracting sounds (Tavassoli & Lee, 2001a). Finally, we found the same pattern of results for nonevaluative inference making, such as correctly inferring health benefits of certain foods (Tavassoli & Lee, 2001a).

In the preceding examples, distraction had a quantitative effect on memory and thought such that auditory distractors interfere more with the amount of information remembered and the degree of elaboration for alphabetic words, whereas visual distractors interfere more with the processing of logographic words. As the ability to process information decreases, attitude formation and change are affected less by the careful scrutiny of arguments and more by a less careful examination of the same information, or the effortful examination of less information (e.g., examining just the first argument in a message; Petty & Wegener, 1998). Distraction can also have a *qualitative* effect on judgments. One example is the shift in the degree of influence from central to peripheral mechanisms which do not involve thought about the substantive merits of the arguments (for a review, see Petty and Wegener 1998).

Memory Structure and Retrieval

The previous sections examined quantitative differences in encoding and elaboration. Scripts may also affect processing in qualitative ways, through the structure of memory and memory accessibility during retrieval. For example, my coauthors and I found that, regardless of whether words were learned auditorily or visually, Chinese speakers were able to recall words better by writing them down during free recall, whereas English speakers were better at recalling words by speaking them (Schmitt, Pan, & Tavassoli, 1994). We suggested that the attempt to write primed a word's visual representation in memory, which should be more pronounced for Chinese logographs, and that the attempt to speak primed a word's phonological representation in memory, which should be more pronounced for alphabetic words. This sets up the intriguing possibility that there is a shift in the information remembered based on response mode; word-of-mouth may be based on different information when memory retrieval is oral than when it is written, or typed as in Internet chat rooms, for example.

Relative differences in the reliance on the phonological loop can also affect the qualitative nature of processing, because the phonological loop rehearses information in a serial manner. My coauthors and I examined the ability to reconstruct a word list's order of presentation in a card sort task. We found that the encoding of the presentation order of words was more pronounced in English than in Chinese (Tavassoli, 1999) and for alphabetic Hangul words than for logographic Hancha words (Tavassoli & Han, 2001). We also found that bilinguals were more likely to retrieve words from memory based on the order in which they learned them in English than in Chinese (Tavassoli & Lee, 2001b). This resulted in a greater primacy effect in the recall of English words, such that words learned early in a list were also more likely to be recalled and to be recalled early.

The order in which information is recalled has an important effect on memory-based consumer and social judgments (Hastie & Park, 1986; Lichtenstein & Srull, 1987; Reyes, Thomson, & Bower, 1980; Unnava, Burnkrant, & Erevelles, 1994). We found that product and person judgments were more sensitive to the order of presentation and that "putting one's best foot forward" was more important for alphabetic English information than for logographic Chinese information (Tavassoli & Lee, 2001b). We also found that the first few words recalled mediated the effect of presentation order on memory-based judgments.

In contrast to temporal order, visual short-term memory organizes items of information based on spatial configuration, specifying the location of an item as well as its relationship to other items in a display (Jiang, Olson, & Chun, 2000). If reading logographs involves to a greater degree visual short-term memory, then spatial memory should be better for logographic words than for alphabetic words. This is what my coauthors and I found. Readers of Chinese logographs remembered better the spatial location of real and of nonsense words scattered on a single page (but not of pictures and symbols) than readers of alphabetic English words (Tavassoli, 2002). Spatial memory was also better for logographic Hancha words than for the same words written in the alphabetic Hangul (Tavassoli & Han, 2001).

The implications of these findings may be broad because spatial memory underlies many everyday behaviors, including not only orientation and navigation but also processes such as discourse comprehension (van Dijk & Kintsch, 1983), information search (Biederman, Glass, & Webb, 1973), spatial thinking (Shah & Miyake, 1996), and competition for visual attention among stimuli in advertising displays (Janiszewski, 1998). Basic short-term memory processes such as the encoding of spatial and serial information are also fundamental to pragmatic processes in reasoning and decision making (Johnson-Laird, 1983; Jonides, 1995). Written language may therefore prove to be an important contextual factor moderating complex thought processes. Through inherent biases in short-term memory processing—temporal versus spatial—scripts may affect the shape of a decision outcome.

CONCLUSIONS

Language and Thought

The argument that language affects thought is most commonly associated with Whorf's linguistic relativity principle (Sapir, 1929; Whorf, 1940/1956). Whorf argued that there is no constant or universal way of arranging data but that linguistic factors influence the way in which "we cut nature up, organize it into concepts, and ascribe significance" (Whorf, 1940/1956). Earlier tests of the hypothesis primarily focused on the idea that differences in language map onto differences in perception, such that, for example, people with different color terminologies might perceive hues differently (Brown & Lenneberg, 1954; Heider & Oliver, 1972).

Whorf's ideas have drawn sharp criticism, however. The possibility that perception of fundamental physical elements necessary for survival such as space and time would differ has been dismissed on a priori grounds (Feuer, 1953). And it has been argued that natural languages may be too ambiguous and schematic to be functional as a mental code (Pinker, 1994). Instead, we may share a universal "mentalese" (Pinker, 1994), and the deep structure of grammar may not only be universal (Chomsky, 1986) but even innate (Pinker, 1994). This position implies that language does not affect thought—that we learn and evaluate verbal information using similar mental processes across languages.

More recently, the Whorfian hypothesis has been reconceptualized in terms of how linguistic forms are represented, how they operate in the mind and how they affect the concepts and categories which denote objects and relations in the world (Hunt & Agnoli, 1991). The idea that language affects *conception* has been tested using the grammatical construct of classifier that some languages contain (Schmitt & Zhang, 1998; Zhang & Schmitt, 1998). Classifiers often depict perceptual properties of objects such as shape, size, thickness, and length, and conceptual properties such as bendable, elastic, graspable. They are special types of measures that are used in conjunction with numerals (one, two, three, etc.) or determiners (a, the, that, this) to form noun phrases. For example, the counterparts in Chinese for the

English noun phrases "a table" is *yi* (numeral) *zhang* (classifier used for flat, extended objects such as table or paper) *zhuo-zi* (table) (Schmitt & Zhang, 1998; Zhang & Schmitt, 1998).

Classifiers have been found to affect consumer choice if the conceptual knowledge triggered by syntactic and semantic components provides relevant information (Schmitt & Zhang, 1998; Zhang & Schmitt, 1998). For example, speakers of classifier languages were more likely to place objects with common classifiers into classifier-related schematic clusters such as into categories of "flat objects," "long objects," or "graspable objects" (Schmitt & Zhang, 1998).

Scripts and Thought

The research reviewed here does not concern languages per se, but the writing systems used to represent language. In that regard, the research reviewed differs critically from the reconceptualized Whorfian hypothesis by Hunt and Agnoli (1991), who "assume that when language stimuli are received they are converted from a visual or auditory code to an abstract lexical code" (p. 379). Although I do not disagree with this assumption, the results presented here suggest that there are relative differences in visual and phonological processes involved in the everyday reading of alphabetic and logographic script, in the encoding, rehearsal, and retrieval of words. This offers a new way of thinking about how languages may affect thought independent of grammar or symbolic content: through their writing systems.

Relative differences in the reliance on visual short-term memory and the phonological loop can have quantitative as well as qualitative effects on the processing of words written in alphabetic and logographic scripts. Short-term memory's limited-capacity storage components affect memory and elaboration in quantitative ways. Scripts quantitatively affect memory for words' visual features, associative memory of words with images and sounds, and the degree to which auditory and visual information interferes with inference making and the scrutiny of message arguments.

Short-term memory's rehearsal components affect information processing in qualitative ways. Auditory and visual distractors differentially affect the ability to process alphabetic and logographic information. This can cause a qualitative shift in attitude formation and change from the careful scrutiny of arguments to the reliance on peripheral cues. Scripts can also qualitatively affect judgments through differences in the spatial versus temporal organization of words in memory. Memory structure affects the order in which information is retrieved from memory, for example, thereby affecting the weight attributes receive in memory-based judgments.

These information-processing differences are not only relevant to educators and practitioners designing information formats, but also to how researchers design stimuli, filler activities, and response formats. Consider, for example, a hypothetical experiment comparing the relative effects of central and peripheral processes on persons' opinions in China and the United States. If the researchers arbitrarily choose a filler task such as solving a visual puzzle, they might conclude that Chinese respondents, whose verbal processing should be relatively more distracted by a visual task, are more influenced by peripheral cues and less by central arguments than are American respondents. They might reach exactly the opposite conclusion if they choose an auditory filler task instead, which should be relatively more distracting for the processing of alphabetic English words.

To summarize, scripts have quantitative and qualitative effects on memory, evaluative judgments, and inference making. These differences not only have cross-cultural implications for the comparison of information processing involving alphabetic and logographic scripts, but also highlight everyday effects the writing system has within a single language. In other words, thought appears to be scripted by the writing system adopted by a culture.

ACKNOWLEDGMENTS

The author thanks Bernd Schmitt and Shi Zhang for their insightful comments on an earlier draft of this chapter.

REFERENCES

Baddeley, A. D. (1986). *Working memory.* Oxford: Clarendon Press.

Biederman, I., Glass, A. L., & Webb, S. E., Jr. (1973). Searching for objects in real-world scenes. *Journal of Experimental Psychology, 921,* 22–27.

Brown, R., & Lenneberg, E. (1954). A study in language and cognition. *Journal of Abnormal and Social Psychology, 49,* 454–462.

Chattopadhyay, A., & Alba, J. W. (1988). The situational importance of recall and inference in consumer decision making. *Journal of Consumer Research, 15,* 1–12.

Chen, H.-C., & Leung, Y.-S. (1989). Patterns of lexical processing in a nonnative language. *Journal of Experimental Psychology: Learning, Memory, and Cognition, 15,* 316–325.

Cheng, C.-M. (1981). Perception of Chinese characters. *Acta Psychologica Taiwanica, 23,* 137–153.

Cho, J.-R., & Chen, H. C. (1999). Orthographic and phonological activation in the semantic processing of Korean Hanja and Hangul. *Language and Cognitive Processes, 14,* 481–502.

Chomsky, N. (1986). *Knowledge of language: Origin, nature and use.* New York: Praeger.

Duncan, J. (1980). The locus of interference in the perception of simultaneous stimuli. *Psychological Review, 87,* 272–300.

Festinger, L., & Maccoby, N. (1964). On resistance to persuasive communications. *Journal of Abnormal and Social Psychology, 68,* 359–366.

Feuer, L. S. (1953). Sociological aspects of the relation between language and philosophy. *Philosophy of Science, 20,* 85–100.

Francis, W. (1999). Cognitive integration of language and memory in bilinguals: Semantic representation. *Psychological Bulleting, 125,* 193–222.

Hastie, R., & Park, B. (1986). The relationship between memory and judgment depends on whether the judgment task is memory-based or on-line. *Psychological Review, 93,* 258–268.

Heider, E. R., & Oliver, D. C. (1972). The structure of the color space in naming and memory for two languages. *Cognitive Psychology, 3,* 333–354.

Huey, E. B. (1908). *The psychology and pedagogy of reading.* New York: Macmillan.

Hung, D. L., & Tzeng, O. J. L. (1981). Orthographic variations and visual information processing. *Psychological Bulletin, 90,* 377–414.

Hunt, E., & Agnoli, F. (1991). The Whorfian hypothesis: A cognitive psychology perspective. *Psychological Review, 98,* 377–389.

Janiszewski, C. (1998). The influence of display characteristics on visual exploratory search behavior. *Journal of Consumer Research, 25,* 290–301.

Jiang, Y., Olson, I. R., & Chun, M. M. (2000). Organization of visual short-term memory. *Journal of Experimental Psychology: Learning, Memory, and Cognition, 26,* 683–702.

Johnson-Laird, P. N. (1983). *Mental models: Towards a cognitive science of language, inference and consciousness.* Cambridge: Cambridge University Press.

Jonides, J. (1995). Working memory and thinking. In E. E. Smith & D. N. Osherson, *Thinking* (pp. 215–265). Cambridge, MA: MIT Press.

Kosslyn, S. M. (1980). *Image and mind.* Cambridge, MA: Harvard University Press.

Lichtenstein, M., & Srull, T. K. (1987). Processing objectives as a determinant of the relationship between recall and judgment. *Journal of Experimental Social Psychology, 23,* 93–118.

Light, L. L., Berger, D. E., & Bardales, M. (1975). Trade-off between memory for verbal items and their visual attributes. *Journal of Experimental Psychology: Human Learning and Memory, 1,* 188–193.

Lutz, K. A., & Lutz, R. J. (1977). Effects of interactive imagery on learning: Applications to advertising. *Journal of Applied Psychology, 62,* 493–498.

McCusker, L. X., Hillinger, M. L., & Bias, R. G. (1981). Phonological recoding and reading. *Psychological Bulletin, 89,* 217–245.

Pan, Y., & Schmitt, B. (1996). Language and brand attitudes: Impact of script and sound matching in Chinese and English. *Journal of Consumer Psychology, 5,* 263–277.

Paivio, A. (1986). *Mental representations.* New York: Oxford Press.

Penney, C. G. (1989). Modality effects and the structure of short-term verbal memory. *Memory and Cognition, 17,* 398–422.

Perfetti, C. A., Bell, L., & Delaney, S. (1988). Automatic phonetic activation in silent word reading: Evidence from backward masking. *Journal of Memory and Language, 27,* 59–70.

Perfetti, C. A., & Zhang, S. (1991). Phonological processes in reading Chinese characters. *Journal of Experimental Psychology: Learning, Memory and Cognition, 17,* 633–643.

Petty, R. E., & Wegener, D. T. (1998). Attitude change: Multiple roles for persuasion variables. In D. T. Gilbert, S. T. Fiske, & G. Lindzey (Eds.), *The handbook of social psychology* (4th ed., vol. 1, pp. 323–390). New York: McGraw-Hill.

Petty, R. E., Wells, G. L., & Brock, T. C. (1976). Distraction can enhance or reduce yielding to propaganda: Thought disruption versus effort justification. *Journal of Personality and Social Psychology, 34,* 874–884.

Pinker, S. (1994). *The language instinct.* New York: Harper Perennial.

Reyes, R. M., Thompson, W. C., & Bower, G. H. (1980). Judgmental biases resulting from differing abilities of arguments. *Journal of Personality and Social Psychology, 39,* 2–12.

Sapir, E. (1929). Conceptual categories in primitive languages. *Science, 74,* 578.

Schmitt, B. H., Pan, Y., & Tavassoli, N. T. (1994). Language and consumer memory: The impact of linguistic differences between Chinese and English. *Journal of Consumer Research, 21,* 419–431.

Schmitt, B. H., & Tavassoli, N. T. (1994, June). *The influence of the writing system on brand perceptions in Japan.* Paper presented at the Asia Pacific ACR Conference, Singapore.

Schmitt, B. H., Tavassoli, N. T., & Millard, R. (1993). Memory for print ads: Understanding relations among brand name, copy and picture. *Journal of Consumer Psychology, 2,* 55–81.

Schmitt, B. H., & Zhang, S. (1998). Language structure and categorization: The role of classifiers in cognition, memory and ad evaluations. *Journal of Consumer Research, 25,* 108–122.

Shah, P., & Miyake A. (1996). The separability of working memory resources for spatial thinking and language processing: An individual differences approach. *Journal of Experimental Psychology: General, 125*, 4–27.

Smith, E. E., & Jonides, J. (1994). Working memory in humans: Neuropsychological evidence. In M. Gazzaniga (Ed.), *The cognitive neurosciences* (pp. 1009–1020). Cambridge, MA: MIT Press.

Tavassoli, N. T. (1998). Language in multimedia: Interaction of spoken and written information. *Journal of Consumer Research, 25*, 26–37.

Tavassoli, N. T. (1999). Temporal and associative memory in Chinese and English. *Journal of Consumer Research, 26*, 170–181.

Tavassoli, N. T. (2001). Color memory and evaluations for alphabetic and logographic brand names. *Journal of Experimental Psychology: Applied, 7*, 104–111.

Tavassoli, N. T. (2002). Spatial memory in Chinese and English. *Journal of Cross Cultural Psychology, 33*, 415–430.

Tavassoli, N. T. & Han, J. K. (2001). Scripted thought: Processing Korean Hancha and Hangul in a multimedia context. *Journal of Consumer Research, 28*, 482–493.

Tavassoli, N. T., & Han, J. K. (2002). Auditory and visual brand identifiers in Chinese and English. *Journal of International Marketing, 10*, 13–28.

Tavassoli, N. T., & Lee, Y.-H. (2001a). *Reading in Chinese and English: The effect of auditory and visual interference on memory, attitudes, and inferences.* Unpublished manuscript.

Tavassoli, N. T., & Lee, Y.-H. (2001b). *Recall order and memory-based judgments by Chinese–English bilinguals.* Unpublished manuscript.

Treisman, A., & Gelade, G. (1980). A feature integration theory of attention. *Cognitive Psychology, 12*, 97–136.

Unnava, H. R., Burnkrant, R. E., & Erevelles, S. (1994). Effects of presentation order and communication modality on recall and attitude. *Journal of Consumer Research, 21*, 481–490.

Van Dijk, T. A., & Kintsch, W. (1983). *Strategies of discourse comprehension.* New York: Academic Press.

Van Orden, G. C. (1987). A ROWS is a ROSE: Spelling, sound, and reading. *Memory & Cognition, 15*, 181–198.

Whorf, B. (1956). *Language, thought and reality: Selected writings of Benjamin Lee Whorf*, J. B. Carroll (Ed.). Cambridge, MA: MIT Press. (Original work published 1940)

Yee, P. L., Hunt, E., & Pellegrino, J. W. (1991). Coordinating cognitive information: Task effects and individual differences in integrating information from several sources. *Cognitive Psychology, 23*, 615–680.

Zhang, S., & Schmitt, B. H. (1998). Language-dependent classification: The role of classifiers in consumer cognition, judgment and choice. *Journal of Experimental Psychology: Applied, 4*, 375–385.

Zhang, S., & Schmitt, B. H. (2001). Creating local brands in multilingual international markets. *Journal of Marketing Research, 38*, 313–325.

Zhang, G., & Simon, H. A. (1985). STM capacity for Chinese words and idioms: Chunking and the acoustical loop hypothesis. *Memory & Cognition, 13*, 193–201.

Zhou, X., & Marslen-Wilson, W. (1999). Phonology, orthography, and semantic activation in reading Chinese. *Journal of Memory and Language, 41*, 579–606.

CHAPTER NINE

Visual and Linguistic Processing of Ads by Bilingual Consumers

David Luna
University of Wisconsin–Whitewater

Laura A. Peracchio
University of Wisconsin–Milwaukee

Today, most of the word's population speaks more than one language (Grosjean, 1982). For example, in many parts of the world, people speak English as a second language, so although there are only 322 million native English speakers worldwide, there are an estimated 1.3 billion people who speak English as a second language. In Western Europe alone, 77% of college students speak English well enough to carry on a conversation (Fox, 2000). People speak a second language in addition to their native language for a number of reasons: They may have moved to a different country, they may need to communicate with individuals from other cultures within their own country, or they may conduct business or travel for pleasure in countries where their native language is not spoken (Milroy & Muysken, 1995). The need to speak more than one language is intensifying as cross-national communications media and international migration and travel become more common.

In sum, one could argue that multilingualism is becoming the norm throughout the world. Even in the United States, a nation sometimes thought to be largely monolingual, the proportion of the total population that speaks a second language fluently is considerable and continues to increase due to migration and acculturation patterns. One of the largest bilingual segments in the United States is the Hispanic population. Over 72% of the 31 million Hispanics in the United States speak both English and Spanish (Levey, 1999). The increasing prevalence of bilingual individuals both in the United States and internationally intensifies the need to consider how bilingual individuals comprehend both visual and linguistic information. Particularly, studying how bilingual individuals understand messages presented in their first versus their second language is of crucial importance to those trying to communicate with a bilingual audience.

In this chapter, we examine how pictures can enhance text processing by bilingual individuals. Extant research in psycholinguistics helps us identify circumstances in which pictorial cues can improve bilingual individuals' understanding of a message. First, we examine how words and their meanings are represented in the minds of bilinguals and argue that bilinguals may have a particularly acute consciousness of the arbitrariness of language. This may lead bilinguals to prefer processing in a more reliable modality, for instance, visually. Therefore, we theorize that bilinguals prefer to think more visually than monolinguals. In addition, we discuss our finding that pictures seem to facilitate processing of messages in the bilingual's weaker language. Finally, we review the psycholinguistic literature relevant to the issue of the semantic or meaning representation of words across languages. Based on this review, we propose that pictures may improve the cross-language equivalence of written messages.

CONCEPT–WORD LINKS ACROSS LANGUAGES

Bilingualism Defined

We begin our discussion of bilingual concept representation by defining what we mean by a bilingual individual and bilingualism. Following prior work in psycholinguistics (Kroll & de Groot, 1997) and consumer behavior (Luna & Peracchio, 2001), we consider individuals to be bilingual if they have a relatively high level of proficiency in the languages they speak. For example, in the studies we describe in this chapter, we studied Spanish–English bilinguals living in Spain, Mexico, and the United States. Our research studies included respondents who scored in the middle to upper range of a language fluency scale in both Spanish and English. This language fluency scale was a self-report of respondents' proficiency in various tasks like reading newspaper headlines and writing a shopping list. The language in which respondents scored themselves as more (less) proficient was considered their first (second) language.

It is worth noting that in this chapter language proficiency or fluency is the construct used to conceptualize first and second language. Thus, the chronological order in which each language was learned is not used in the analyses. This is because it is possible that a person could have learned Spanish (English) first and yet be more proficient in the other language at the time of the research (Dufour & Kroll, 1995). In such a case, the models we present in this chapter would predict that the language learned chronologically first would suffer from weaker conceptual links and a smaller lexicon. Thus, it would be best described as second language. The language learned chronologically second would be the "dominant" language and would be best described as the first language. Therefore, in the rest of this chapter, *first language* denotes the language in which a bilingual is more fluent, and *second language* denotes the language in which a bilingual is less fluent.

Concepts and Their Representations

In cognitive psychology and psycholinguistics research, a distinction is often made between words and the concepts they represent. Thus, there is a separation between *form* (words) and *meaning* (concepts). Words can be thought of as labels for internal concepts or, alternatively, as internal mental constructs associated with the concepts (Francis, 1999). Information about words is contained in the lexicon, the vast inventory of words a person holds in memory. Information about concepts, or the meanings of words, is thought to be contained in a separate storage system for semantic memory that consists of a network of word meanings.

This conceptualization of the mental organization of words and concepts is consistent with a dual code approach to memory (Paivio & Desrochers, 1980). Dual-code theory holds that cognitive activity is mediated by two independent but interconnected symbolic systems that encode, organize, and store visual and verbal information. One system, the visual image system, is specialized for processing information concerning pictorial objects and events and for generating mental images of such items. The other system, the verbal system, is specialized for processing linguistic information and generating speech. Dual-code theorists would argue that knowledge about objects and events (semantic knowledge) is organized according to the way in which that knowledge is acquired. Hence, different underlying representations or meanings can be accessed by two surface forms: pictures and words. Pictures are thought to lead to superior recall relative to words (Paivio, 1971; Unnava & Burnkrant, 1991).

Paivio's dual code theory addresses the issue of separate systems for verbal and "conceptual" information, but his definition of the imaginal system does not completely coincide with the more recent theories in bilingual research regarding the separation of lexical (verbal) versus semantic (conceptual) memory (de Groot & Kroll, 1997). According to these psychological models, concepts are amodal representations. They are neither pictures nor words, and they are not coded in any specific language. Both words and pictures are surface representations of those underlying concepts. Although words do not necessarily require semantic processing, pictures do involve processing at the semantic level. However, operationally, both approaches would agree that pictorial information offers superior results with respect to measures such as recall (Paivio & Lambert, 1981; Snodgrass, 1984) and facilitates tasks such as word translation (La Heij, Hooglander, Kerling, & Van der Velden, 1996; Sholl, Sankaranarayanan, & Kroll, 1995). Hence, most bilingual researchers today would agree that, even if there are not two qualitatively different codes for the two different surface representations (words and pictures), pictures are able to access the conceptual system more effectively and/or directly than words, especially second language words (Kroll & de Groot, 1997; Sholl et al., 1995). This chapter offers further support for these assertions.

Bilingual Concept Representation

A recent and widely accepted model of bilingual concept representation is the revised hierarchical model, or RHM (Dufour & Kroll, 1995; Kroll & de Groot, 1997). This model builds on previous findings that suggest that there exist two levels of mental representation: the lexical (word) level and the conceptual (meaning) level. At the lexical level, each language is stored separately. However, at the conceptual level there is a unitary system in which words in each language access a common semantic representation or meaning (see Fig. 9.1).

The connections between words in different languages made at the lexical (or word) level are referred to as *word associations* or lexical links, whereas the connections in memory between lexical representations in either language and the concepts (or meanings) they represent are referred to as *conceptual links*. The model specifies a stronger lexical link from an individual's second language to his or her first language than from an individual's first language to his or her second language. This is a residual effect from the second-language acquisition process in which individuals begin learning words in their second language by relating them to words in their first language. Hence, words in the bilingual individuals' second language are closely associated with words in their first language. For example, a Mexican immigrant in the United States who is more proficient in Spanish than

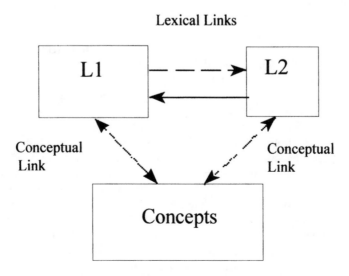

FIG. 9.1.   The revised hierarchical model from Dufour and Kroll (1995).

English may be able to lexically translate the word "friend" into Spanish faster than she can translate "amigo" to English because the word "friend" is connected more strongly to "amigo" than "amigo" to "friend."

The same residual effect accounts for the stronger conceptual links between the lexical representations in an individual's first language and the semantic representations in memory (concepts). For example, for a Mexican immigrant in the United States, the word "amigo" may be more easily linked to concepts related to its meaning like [having coffee] or [watching sports] than the word "friend." Conceptual links to the individual's second language are weaker than first language links because it is only after individuals have achieved a high level of proficiency in their second language that they rely less on their first language to gain access to meaning. Thus, the strength of both lexical and conceptual links is a function of the second-language proficiency of the individual in question. However, even after the individual has become fluent in both languages there is a residual asymmetry in both lexical and conceptual links (Dufour & Kroll, 1995; Kroll & de Groot, 1997).

The RHM also specifies that the second-language lexical store is smaller than the first-language store, which indicates a pervasive superiority of first-language vocabulary even for highly fluent bilinguals. From this research, we can conclude that the RHM suggests that processing a second-language message at the conceptual level is more effortful than processing a first-language message conceptually.

Bilingual Processing of Visual Information

Visual cues may be of particular importance for bilingual individuals. Bilinguals tend to have a higher level of awareness of the arbitrariness of language than monolinguals because they can use two different words to communicate the same concept (Bialystok, 1988, 1991). Therefore, bilingual individuals seem to prefer to rely on pictures, which are a language-independent representation that can aid information processing. Additionally, for bilinguals who must frequently switch from one language to another, it may not be efficient to rely solely on words or lexical representations for two reasons. First, knowing two languages may lead to interference between the two lexicons (Miljkovitch, 1980; Ransdell & Fischler, 1991). Second, as the RHM suggests, bilinguals processing either first- or second-language words may have to potentially translate those words to their other language using the indirect route through concepts before they can communicate their thoughts. This translation process involves two steps. For example, a person thinking in first-language words must match those words with their corresponding concepts, then match the concepts with their respective second-language words, and finally communicate the thoughts in his or her second language. Instead, bilingual individuals may prefer to use a language-independent form to process information: visual images (Paivio & Lambert, 1981). This would avoid the two-step translation process. Consequently, we propose that, compared with monolingual individuals, bilinguals are more likely to rely on imagery and visual representations as information-processing aids.

An empirical study was conducted to examine this proposition. In this study, bilingual individuals were compared to their monolingual counterparts in both the United States and Mexico. Respondents completed the Styles of Processing Scale (Childers, Houston, & Heckler, 1985). This measure distinguished individuals who prefer to process information visually from those who prefer to process verbally. The scale includes 22 items (e.g., "I generally prefer to use a diagram rather than a written set of instructions") rated on a 4-point scale (always true/ always false). Half the items measure the predisposition to process verbally and the other half measure the predisposition to process visually. The two scores (visual and verbal) were then used to compute a single Style of Processing score for respondents. The results of our analysis confirmed our expectations in that bilinguals in both countries tended to rely on imagery and visual representation as information processing aids. Figure 9.2 presents the results of the study.

Research in psycholinguistics also seems to indicate that visual cues can help process verbal stimuli. Studies testing the RHM have found that the accessibility to concepts of a second language text may be facilitated by manipulating visual components of the stimulus, such as whether a word is accompanied by a congruent picture. For example, La Heij et al. (1996) exposed bilingual subjects to words that had to be translated into a different language. In an experiment, words were accompanied by either congruent or incongruent pictures—for instance, the word SHARK in combination with a picture of a shark or a picture of a bottle. La Heij et al. (1996) found that translation of the written stimuli from second language to first language was facilitated by congruent pictures—translations were faster, whereas incongruent pictures resulted in slower translations. Thus, pictures seem to aid or hamper language processing, depending on their level of relatedness to the textual stimulus. Consistent with the RHM, La Heij et al. (1996) concluded that respondents are able to access concepts from second-language words, but do so with more effort than from first-language words. More importantly, the La Heij et al. (1996) findings imply that pictures may moderate the asymmetries described by the revised hierarchical model. That is, the weaker second-language conceptual links may be "strengthened" by a pictorial cue, which facilitates activation of the concept represented by the second-language word. This effect is consistent with extant research in marketing (e.g., Schmitt, Tavassoli, & Millard, 1993; Unnava & Burnkrant, 1991), which has employed mostly monolingual speakers as respondents.

Picture Effects in Advertising

A number of advertising researchers have examined the role of pictures in ad processing by monolingual individuals (Alesandrini, 1982; Holbrook & Moore, 1981; Houston, Childers, & Heckler, 1987; Lutz & Lutz, 1977; Schmitt et al., 1993).

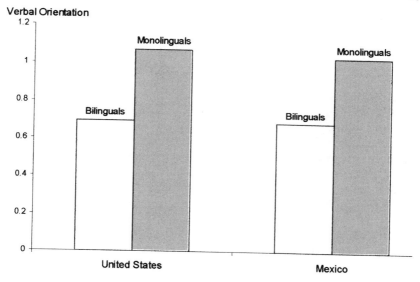

Means of Verbal and Visual scores

| | United States | | Mexico | |
	Verbal	Visual	Verbal	Visual
Monolinguals	2.23	2.92	2.26	2.94
Bilinguals	1.89	2.96	2.08	3.11

FIG. 9.2. Verbal versus visual orientation of monolinguals and bilinguals.

Several studies have theorized that pictures that are congruent with the brand name of the product featured in an ad (interactive pictures) facilitate processing of the message by providing a frame to process the ad claims (Houston et al., 1987; Lutz & Lutz, 1977).

In this chapter, we follow prior psycholinguistic and consumer behavior research in our conceptualization of picture–text congruity. We define congruity as the degree to which the picture and the text communicate the same message. For example, if the picture of a grocery-store ad depicts wonderfully fresh vegetables and the text talks about prompt delivery, the picture would be "incongruent," or irrelevant to the text. If the text talked about having the best fresh vegetables in the area, then the picture would then be "congruent," or relevant to the text. In such a case, the picture and the text communicate similar messages.

In addition to congruence between the brand name and the ad picture, the relationship or congruence between the product attribute described in the ad claims and the ad picture must also be considered. Thus, Schmitt et al. (1993) built on previous research (Edell & Staelin, 1983; Lutz & Lutz, 1977; Miniard, Bhatla, Lord, Dickson, & Unnava, 1991) to explain picture congruity effects on ad processing by monolingual consumers. Relying on the spreading activation paradigm (Anderson, 1983), they suggested that the ad picture activates a conceptual node, which then may become closely associated with the concept(s) described by the subsequent ad copy if there is a certain level of congruity of picture–text. The strong linkages between these sets of nodes then facilitate further processing, which in turn makes the links stronger. Picture–text congruity, therefore, seems to enhance memory.

Further support for this reasoning is provided by dual-code theory. Because pictures are more easily accessed in memory than verbal information (Paivio, 1986), the probability of a concept being retrieved is higher if it is closely associated with a picture (Unnava & Burnkrant, 1991). From this research, we can conclude that when the product attribute expressed in the ad claims and/or the product's brand name expresses the same (or similar) concepts as the ad picture, strong linkages will be formed in memory that will facilitate processing of these textual ad elements. Hence, memory will be enhanced when congruent text and pictures are employed.

Note that our conceptualization of congruity does not imply that incongruent pictures represent a visual metaphor of the text. In the stimuli we use in our research, individuals exposed to incongruent ads do not find a connection between the text and the picture. Individuals are not asked to resolve any incongruity—in our conceptualization, pictures are just not related to the text at all. Hence, in our case incongruity does not lead to deeper processing, higher levels of elaboration, or the pleasurable resolution of such incongruity (McQuarrie & Mick, 1999). Therefore, incongruity as described in this chapter should not lead to higher levels of memory. On the contrary, it is congruent pictures, those with a clear connection between picture and text, that should lead to greater processing in second language conditions.

Therefore, given the previous findings in consumer research and the La Heij et al. (1996) findings with bilinguals, it would seem that our conceptualization of congruity between the ad picture and textual ad elements may make retrieval of the second language information less cognitively effortful and enhance recall. Consequently, we propose that second-language ads in which the picture is congruent with the ad's claim will lead to higher recall than second-language ads without pictures or in which the picture is not congruent with the ad's claim. Luna and Peracchio's (2001) findings offer empirical support for this proposition. Figure 9.3 represents the results of that research. In an experiment, Luna and Peracchio tested the memory of bilingual subjects for several first- and second-language ads under conditions of low, moderate and high picture–text congruity. Memory was measured by having respondents write down as much of the text as they could remember for each of the ads presented (free recall). Between the ad exposure and memory test, respondents had to perform a 15-min unrelated task to clear their short-term memory. Here, we only focus on the key findings of that study. Interested readers may refer to Luna and Peracchio (2001) for further details.

The results reveal that second-language ads result in low memory when the pictures are not congruent with the ad's copy or when the pictures only exhibit a moderate degree of congruity with the copy. However, when the ad's picture is highly congruent with its copy, the study reveals an interesting result: Second-language ads can lead to a high level of memory, similar to first-language ads. These findings suggest that if constructed to include congruent pictures, ads in the consumers' second language can be as memorable as ads in their first language.

We next address the impact of visual cues and language with respect to a different set of dependent measures, attitudinal measures, and a different medium, the web. The issue of bilingualism is of paramount importance on the web, as a large number of web users around the world are bilingual (Fox, 2000).

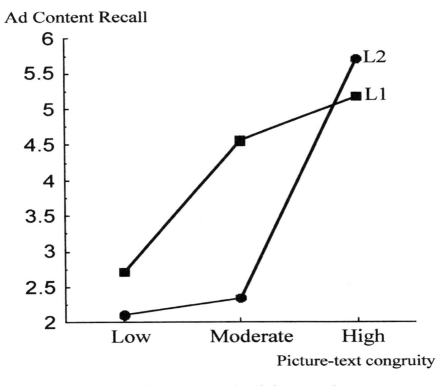

FIG. 9.3. Picture–text congruity and ad content recall.

Picture Effects in Cross-Language Web Sites

As with advertising, pictures that are congruent with the content of a web site are expected to facilitate processing of second-language web sites. This is particularly relevant if we take into account the global reach of the internet as a communications medium. Given that visitors from all over the world can access web sites regardless of where they may be hosted, it is clear that people can and do surf web sites in both their first and second languages.

Computer-mediated environments like the World Wide Web have a unique characteristic: interactivity. In such an environment, individuals may reach a state in which their attention is focused solely on the universe contained within the boundaries of their network navigation experience. This state is frequently evidenced by users' comments like "I forgot where I was," or "I completely lost track of time." This state has been labeled *flow* (e.g., Csikszentmihalyi & LeFevre, 1989). Recently, Hoffman and Novak (1996) defined flow in the context of web navigation as "the state occurring during network navigation, which is (1) characterized by a seamless sequence of responses facilitated by machine interactivity, (2) intrinsically enjoyable, (3) accompanied by a loss of self-consciousness, and (4) self-reinforcing" (p. 57). Hoffman and Novak's (1996) conceptualization of flow refers to a general state resulting from a positive Internet navigation experience. In this chapter, we adapt the flow concept to apply to individual web sites.

An e-commerce site's capacity to induce a state of flow in its visitors is an important attribute. Key consequences of flow for consumers are increased learning, exploratory and participatory behaviors, positive subjective experiences, and a perceived sense of control over their interactions in the computer-mediated environment. Antecedents of flow include (a) a balance between the demands, or challenges, of network navigation and the ability of visitors to navigate the site, (b) interactivity and vividness of the site, and (c) the intrinsic or extrinsic involvement of the visitor (Hoffman & Novak, 1996).

Language is expected to have an effect on whether a visitor to a web site reaches a state of flow. According to the revised hierarchical model, it is more effortful to process second-language stimuli than first-language stimuli. Therefore, second-language sites may excessively increase the demands or challenges for visitors and consequently reduce their likelihood of achieving flow. However, a site's language and certain site design elements may interact to influence whether the site's visitor achieves a flow experience. Hence, if a site is in the visitors' second language, it may generally be more effortful to experience flow in their second language than in their first language, but even second-language sites may be conducive to flow if they are designed so that pictorial cues help visitors process the verbal content of the site. Theoretical support for this proposed interaction is evident in the findings of the research described previously that examined the moderating effect of pictures on the asymmetry between first- and second-language conceptual link strength (La Heij et al., 1996; Luna & Peracchio, 2001). Pictures, therefore, can

Attitudes Toward Web Site

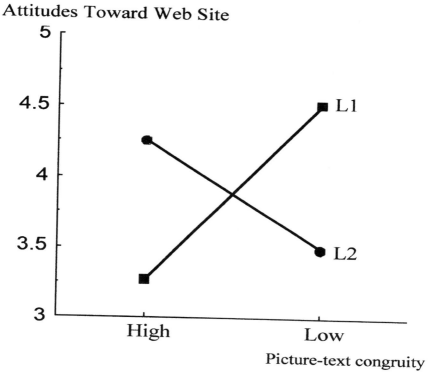

FIG. 9.4. Graphics–content congruity and attitudes toward the web site.

decrease the difficulty of processing second-language messages so that individuals are not excessively challenged by the message difficulty.

Consequently, we propose that web sites in the visitor's second language will be less likely to lead to the flow experience than web sites in their first language if the sites do not contain nonverbal or pictorial cues congruent with the site content. On the other hand, web sites in the visitor's second language will be as likely to lead to the flow experience as web sites in their first language if the sites contain nonverbal or pictorial cues congruent with the site's verbal content.

Luna, Peracchio, and de Juan's (in press) research offers support for these propositions. The results are represented in Fig. 9.4. In two empirical studies, Luna, Peracchio, and de Juan found that, if a web site's graphics do not closely follow the verbal content of the site (incongruent graphics), first-language sites result in more positive attitudes toward the site than similar second-language sites. On the other hand, when visual cues supported and were consistent with the sites' verbal content, second-language sites actually elicited more positive site attitudes than similar first-language sites. The superiority of second-language sites over first-language sites in the congruent condition may occur because the congruent first-language sites are too unchallenging to process, leading subjects to a state of boredom or tedium (Anand & Sternthal, 1990).

Further, the results of a path analysis (Cohen & Cohen, 1983) showed that attitude toward the site significantly mediated the effect of congruity on flow. In other words, positive attitudes toward the site were found to lead to a higher likelihood of achieving flow. In addition, a LISREL model revealed that the experience of flow makes visitors more likely to revisit and purchase from the site (Luna, Peracchio, & de Juan, 2002). Therefore, because positive attitudes toward the site lead to a higher likelihood of flow, we can infer that sites with highly relevant graphics may lead to flow more often in consumers' second language than in their first language.

From this research, we can conclude that provided a web site's content is supported by adequate nonverbal cues, it may not be necessary to translate a web site to each of its international visitors' respective languages. Indeed, an English site may even be more effective than its local-language versions when the site's visitors are fairly fluent bilinguals.

Both our advertising and our web site results are theoretically consistent with each other and with current research in consumer behavior, particularly with the resource-matching hypothesis and research suggesting that both too much and too little effort result in negative consequences. Our research results suggest that pictures can assist second-language processing by enhancing relational processing. In our web site study we apply similar principles to attitudinal measures. The findings converge with our advertising study in that congruent second-language sites do not become too unchallenging but congruent first-language sites do. On the other hand, in our studies, incongruent second-language sites can be too effortful to process, while incongruent first-language sites are not.

This section has examined the role of pictures in the processing of first- versus second-language messages. We observed that pictures seem to help reduce the cognitive capacity required to process second language messages. In the next section, we describe another model from psycholinguistic research, the conceptual feature model. We derive several additional predictions from this model regarding the role of visual cues in the cognitive processing of marketing messages by bilingual consumers.

CONCEPTS ACROSS LANGUAGES

We now explore a psycholinguistic model that describes how words are defined in the minds of bilingual individuals and how the lexical form of words maps onto a series of semantic, or conceptual, features. This model is introduced for several reasons: (a) It integrates the streams of literature discussed in this and previous sections; (b) it emphasizes the importance of the visual nature of certain words or expressions for cross-linguistic meaning equivalence; and (c) it can be used to make additional predictions about the effect of visual cues on linguistic processing and bilingual lexicosemantic representation.

Words and Concepts: I Say "Potato," You Say "Patata"

One of the issues most often researched in cognitive psychology studies of bilingualism is whether translation-equivalent words in two languages access the same conceptual representation (shared representation) or if there is a separate conceptual system for each language (independent representation). After numerous attempts to garner support for both views, most evidence seems to point to the view that the two languages of a bilingual tap a common semantic–conceptual system (Francis, 1999). Instead of the extreme views of shared versus independent systems, most evidence suggests that a model that allows simultaneously for some sharing and some independence seems to better account for previous findings.

One such model is the conceptual feature model or CFM (de Groot, 1992), in which words in each language known by a bilingual activate a series of conceptual features. These features, or concepts, are language independent and are distributed, so one word is connected to a number of concepts that ultimately define the subjective meaning of the word for each individual. For example, the features activated by the word "friend" are not necessarily the same features activated by its Spanish-language translation equivalent, "amigo." "Friend" may be associated with the concepts [McDonalds] and [honesty], while "amigo" may be associated with the concepts [honesty] and [male]. The difference in the conceptual features linked to each translation-equivalent word could be due to the different contexts in which the words are learned and normally used. Figure 9.5 shows the hypothetical links between two translation-equivalent words and the concepts with which they might be connected. As shown, the conceptual nodes connected to "friend" may not be the same as the ones connected to "amigo."

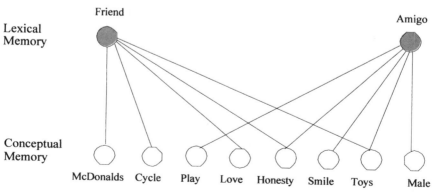

FIG. 9.5.   The conceptual feature model. Adapted from de Groot and Kroll (1997), with permission.

The example in Fig. 9.5 can be interpreted as depicting two language-specific knowledge schemas: the English "friend" schema, and the Spanish "amigo" schema. Luna and Peracchio (1999) showed that, although such schemas tend to be highly person specific, there exist certain categories of concepts that are more frequently connected to a word in one language than to its translation equivalent in another language. For example, emotion concepts tend to be elicited more often in response to words in Spanish than to their translation equivalents in English, and technical concepts tend to be elicited more often in English than in Spanish. Luna and Peracchio (1999) labeled this phenomenon the *cognitive duality* of the bilingual mind.

Tests of the CFM have found that concrete words (e.g., "window") share more conceptual features across languages than abstract words (e.g., "love"). This difference is apparent in that abstract words often do not seem to have an exact translation. De Groot (1992) theorized that the reason for this difference may be that, in contrast with the words representing abstract concepts, the visual representation, function, and appearance of concrete entities (e.g., apple, chair) tend to be more similar across different languages. Thus, the language learner creates a visual representation for a new concrete word that varies relatively little across languages. Abstract words do not have external referents that can be inspected during the learning process, so there is no guarantee that the content of the developing representations across languages will be similar. The meanings of abstract words have to be acquired from an objective source (e.g., a dictionary), or, more importantly, by deducing them from the contexts in which they are used. Because contexts are likely to differ between languages, or cultures, the meanings of these words are also likely to be different. Differences between concrete and abstract words also appear in monolingual settings. For example, in an experiment with monolingual subjects, de Groot (1989) found that concrete words have more and stronger links with the concepts they represent than abstract words.

It should be noted that the operationalization of word concreteness normally employed by psycholinguistic studies testing the CFM (de Groot & Hoeks, 1995; Luna & Peracchio, 1999; Paivio, Yuille, & Madigan, 1968) is based on asking individuals to rate words as to the ease or difficulty with which they arouse mental images. For example, any word that, in their estimation, arouses a mental image (i.e., a mental picture, or sound, or other sensory experience) very quickly and easily is given a *high imagery* rating and is high in concreteness; any word that arouses a mental image with difficulty or not at all is given a *low imagery* rating and is considered to be low in concreteness.

Empirical evidence is abundant regarding the impact of one particular type of abstract words, emotionally-charged words. Whether a word is emotionally charged or emotionally neutral has been found to impact the degree of overlap in conceptual features between translation-equivalent words (de Groot, 1992). There are two manifestations of this phenomenon: First, some languages have more emotion words than others, so a word in one language may cover the meaning of two or more words in another language. Second, even if the numbers of emotion words are similar in any two languages, the reference of corresponding words in the two languages may differ (Russell, 1991). We can conclude that emotionally charged words have less conceptual overlap between translation equivalents than emotionally neutral words (Kolers, 1963).

Another variable that has an impact on lexicosemantic organization is the cognate status of words. A word is a cognate when its translation equivalent sounds and looks like it. For example, "addiction" and "adicción" are cognates, while "book" and "libro" are noncognates. According to the CFM, cognates share a great deal more conceptual features across translation equivalents than do non-cognates. Cognate effects on lexicosemantic organization may be due to two factors: First, cognate translation-equivalent words are generally derived from the same root in a common parent language (e.g., Latin or Greek), so they have probably preserved the meaning of this root over time. Consequently, cognates may have similar meanings. Another reason for the cognate effect may be that second-language learners, noticing the form similarity between a cognate word and its translation, assume that the two also have a meaning similarity, conveniently linking the new second language word with the concept representation of the first language word (de Groot, 1992). Following this reasoning, we could infer that in a case in which a message is being devised to target speakers of different language families (e.g., Finnish and French), most words will be noncognates. Therefore, in such a case there will be little conceptual overlap between words in each language.

Theoretical Support for the CFM. The duality specified by the CFM finds support in a number of theories that help explain the underlying processes resulting in language-specific schemas. The repeated coupling of certain concepts with a first-language word, for example, the concept [play] and the Spanish word "amigo" (friend), during first-language learning and the life of the individual provides consistent and strong mappings from those concepts to the first language word (Kroll & de Groot, 1997; MacWhinney, 1997). These consistent mappings result in strong links between the first-language word and concepts. Different associations are likely to happen during second-language learning. Other concepts are likely to be consistently present when the individual learns second-language words, for example, the concept [McDonalds] and the English word "friend," so alternate links specific to the second language will be created between these nodes. This reasoning is consistent with the theory of spreading activation (Anderson, 1983; Collins & Loftus, 1975), which predicts that links that are "practiced," or observed, many times become stronger. Therefore, if we assume that the "amigo"–[play] link was practiced more than the "friend"–[play] link, the former will be stronger than the latter.

Also, according to spreading activation principles, encoding context plays a large role in the memory for an item. Anderson (1983) asserted that

The encoding context determines the sense of the word chosen [i.e., one of its mean-ings] and that a trace is formed involving that sense and, perhaps, the encoding con-text. When the subject is tested, context will again determine the sense chosen and activation will spread from the chosen sense. Probability of recognition will be greater when the same sense is chosen because activation will be spreading from a sense node directly attached to the trace. (p. 283)

The language of a message can be considered a contextual cue that helps a partic-ular word activate a series of nodes that would not be activated in another lan-guage, thus priming the language-specific schemas implied by the CFM. Note that this effect is similar to encoding specificity (Tulving & Thompson, 1971).

Barsalou's (1982) work also helps explain the notion of language-specific sche-mas. Properties, or concepts associated with a stimulus, become automatically activated by that stimulus after being frequently associated with it during process-ing. Frequent pairings of a stimulus and a concept cause an automatized relation between them to be established in memory. Barsalou indicated that there are two types of concepts likely to be frequently active during the processing of a stimulus: concepts having high diagnosticity ("gills" for "fish"), and concepts relevant to how people typically interact with instances of the respective stimulus ("edible" for "apples"). Hence, individuals' experiences may be a source of differences in cogni-tive structure. Because culture shapes human experience, cultural differences may give origin to different patterns of activation or cognitive structures in individuals.

We can conclude from this discussion that it is the cultural context in which a word is learned that determines which concepts will be associated with that word. Cultural context includes the language in which the word is coded. Later, when a person retrieves that word, language serves as a cue that activates context-specific concepts. Pictures, like words, may also be considered surface representations of concepts, so two pictures of the same rabbit may elicit different associations: If the rabbit is wearing a top hat and a clock, Western individuals will associate it to dif-ferent concepts than if the rabbit is seen in a pet store.

Dual Code Theory and the CFM. The CFM specifies that concrete words have a higher degree of conceptual overlap than abstract words, the latter including emotionally charged words. This is consistent with dual code theory, which argues that concrete words have a more direct relationship with their imaginal referents than abstract words. Hence, concrete words are more easily imagined as external objects that do not vary across languages. As a result, the conceptual features asso-ciated with concrete words will be more consistent across languages than the con-ceptual features of abstract words, as predicted by the CFM. An interesting ques-tion, however, arises when examining the use of rhetorical figures in speech, which may be combinations of concrete words but whose intended meaning is more abstract. For example, the phrase "piece of cake" is composed of two concrete nouns, but its composite meaning is certainly of a more abstract nature than that of its separate components. To make these figures of speech fit with the CFM, we could treat the phrase not as a collection of words but as a "word" or lexical entry itself, composed of several morphemes. In such case, we would treat it as an abstract, not a concrete entity.

Pictures and the CFM.   The CFM implies that, regardless of how well advertisers translate a word or text from one language to another, the meaning will not be exactly the same. The conceptual features activated by a word like "amigo" will likely not be the same as those activated by its translation equivalent "friend." Recent studies in consumer research support this statement (e.g., Luna & Peracchio, 1999). It seems, then, that if a higher degree of equivalency is sought in different languages (Douglas & Craig, 1984), we must ensure that our message is expressed by visual cues in addition to verbal cues. As discussed earlier, when compared to words, the pictures that represent them are less likely to vary in meaning across languages and are more directly linked to conceptual representations. Therefore, pictures may improve the cross-language equivalency of messages. However, as predicted by the CFM, this effect may be more (less) noticeable when the ad's claims are abstract (concrete), emotionally charged (emotionally neutral), or the two languages belong to different language families (the same language family). The latter effect may appear because languages of different language families (e.g., Finnish and French) should contain a lesser number of cognates between them than languages of the same language family (e.g., Spanish and French). Therefore, when targeting speakers of languages of different language families, ads in which visual cues express the same message as the verbal cues may achieve a higher level of cross-language conceptual equivalence than similar ads in which visual cues do not support the verbal cues. These propositions have been unexplored by empirical research, so unfortunately we cannot offer answers for the questions we raise.

An interesting topic related to language families and pictures is that of different writing systems—for example, phonographic versus logographic systems. Phonographic writing (e.g., English) represents the sounds of speech in graphic form. Logographic writing (e.g., Chinese) represents words and concepts in the form of symbols. Logographic symbols, therefore, resemble pictures. What is the impact of nonverbal cues on each of the different writing systems? Will Chinese benefit less than English from congruent pictures? Current research on the processing differences between individuals exposed to the two different writing systems has begun to explore this issue (e.g., Zhang & Schmitt, 2001), but more work is needed in order to fully understand the interaction of written language and pictures.

CONCLUSION

In this chapter we examined the effect of pictures on the processing of information by bilingual consumers. Previous research has found that pictures can strengthen the links between second-language words and their meanings. We reported evidence suggesting that pictures can help reduce the processing load involved in second-language versus first-language processing. Thus, the presence of congruent pictures can increase bilinguals' comprehension of second language messages. Our research applies these conclusions to web-site navigation and advertising.

The findings of our research can also be extended to other contexts in which verbal representations create difficult or effortful processing conditions. Thus, although our results apply to bilinguals for whom a second language is more effortful to process, conclusions similar to those described in this chapter could be applied to monolinguals who are exposed to texts written in technical jargon. It seems likely that monolinguals will use the strategy of becoming more "visual" and rely on nonverbal cues to help them comprehend the text. An example of this situation would be a monolingual who travels to a foreign country and doesn't speak the language. This person, too, will rely on nonverbal cues. Our chapter, however, does not examine this case. Our research focuses on relatively fluent bilinguals.

Additionally, our research utilizes a model from psycholinguistic research, the conceptual feature model (CFM), to suggest that pictures can help advertisers achieve cross-language message equivalence. The CFM implies that the meaning of translation-equivalent words may not overlap completely across languages, especially for abstract and noncognate words. Pictures can help bridge this lack of overlap by supplying an external objective referent. An interesting question for future researchers relative to the CFM is whether pictures, as surface representations of concepts, can also be examined within the paradigm advanced by the CFM. For example, consider the following two pictures: Apple Computer's trademark picture of a multicolor apple, and the picture of a regular red apple. A question worthy of further examination is whether one apple can be considered more abstract than the other and, consequently, whether two different pictorial representations of apparently similar objects can have different degrees of conceptual overlap across languages/cultures. Another question of interest relative to the CFM is the effect on between-language overlap of false cognates (e.g., Spanish "noticia" versus English "notice") or of words in language A that are related not to their translation equivalents but to other semantically related words in language B—for example, "libro" and "library."

It needs to be noted that we do not imply in this chapter that bilinguals have mental "codes" that are different from monolinguals, or that their mental code is visual or verbal. The finding that bilinguals are more likely to rely on imagery and visual representations than monolinguals does not mean that their mental code is more visual than that of monolinguals. Such a finding could be interpreted perhaps more accurately as a difference in processing strategies. Bilinguals tend to prefer visual processing whereas monolinguals prefer verbal processing, but both could easily shift their processing strategies. One question that remains unanswered by our research on bilinguals' style of processing is whether bilinguals rely more on visual imagery when they operate in their second language relative to when they operate in their first language. This proposition would be consistent with our findings regarding bilinguals' reactions to marketing communications and is an issue to be examined in future research.

We should also note that the research described in this chapter uses text and pictures that are moderately difficult to process. Results should therefore be interpreted with caution. For example, if really difficult web sites are developed, in which visitors must fully employ their navigational skills, first-language sites may never become too easy to navigate, and second-language sites may never become easy enough for visitors to navigate.

This chapter underscores the facilitating role of visual cues in messages targeting bilingual individuals. Considering that a large population of the world speaks more than one language, it is surprising that bilingual populations have received very little attention from consumer researchers. Further research must be conducted in order to understand whether existing models of information processing and consumer behavior need to be adapted to this important segment of the global population.

REFERENCES

Alesandrini, K. L. (1983). Strategies that influence memory for advertising communications. In R. J. Harris (Ed.), *Information processing research in advertising* (pp. 65–82). Hillsdale, NJ: Lawrence Erlbaum Associates.

Anand, P., & Sternthal, B. (1990). Ease of message processing as a moderator of repetition effects in advertising. *Journal of Marketing Research, 27,* 345–353.

Anderson, J. (1983). A spreading activation theory of memory. *Journal of Verbal Learning and Verbal Behavior, 22,* 261–295.

Barsalou, L. (1982). Context-independent and context-dependent information in concepts. *Memory and Cognition, 10,* 82–93.

Bialystok, E. (1988). Levels of bilingualism and levels of linguistic awareness. *Developmental Psychology, 4,* 560–567.

Bialystok, E. (1991). Metalinguistic dimensions of bilingual language proficiency. In E. Bialystok (Ed.), *Language processing in bilingual children* (pp. 113–140). Cambridge: Cambridge University Press.

Childers, T., Houston, M., & Heckler, S. (1985). Measurement of individual differences in visual versus verbal information processing. *Journal of Consumer Research, 12,* 125–134.

Cohen, J., & Cohen, P. (1983). *Applied multiple regression/correlation analysis for the behavioral sciences.* Hillsdale, NJ: Lawrence Erlbaum Associates.

Collins, A., & Loftus, E. (1975). A spreading-activation theory of semantic processing. *Psychological Review, 82,* 407–428.

Csikszentmihalyi, M., & LeFevre, J. (1989). Optimal experience in work and leisure. *Journal of Personality and Social Psychology, 56,* 815–822.

de Groot, A. (1989). Representational aspects of word imageability and word frequency as assessed through word association. *Journal of Experimental Psychology: Learning, Memory and Cognition, 15,* 824–845.

de Groot, A. (1992). Bilingual lexical representation: A closer look at conceptual representations. In R. Frost & L. Katz (Eds.), *Orthography, phonology, morphology, and meaning* (pp. 389–412). Amsterdam: Elsevier.

de Groot, A., & Hoeks, J. (1995). The development of bilingual memory: Evidence from word translation by trilinguals. *Language Learning, 45*(4), 683–724.

de Groot, A., & Kroll, J. (1997). *Tutorials in bilingualism: Psycholinguistic perspectives.* Mahwah, NJ: Lawrence Erlbaum Associates.

Douglas, S. P., & Craig, C. S. (1984). Establishing equivalence in comparative consumer research. In E. Kaynak, & R. Savitt (Eds.), *Comparative marketing systems* (pp. 93–113). New York: Praeger.

Dufour, R., & Kroll, J. (1995). Matching words to concepts in two languages: A test of the concept mediation model of bilingual representation. *Memory and Cognition, 23,* 166–180.

Edell, J. A., & Staelin, R. (1983). The information processing of pictures in print advertisements. *Journal of Consumer Research, 10,* 145–161.

Fox, J. (2000, September 18). The triumph of English. *Fortune,* pp. 209–212.

Francis, W. (1999). Cognitive integration of language and memory in bilinguals: Semantic representation. *Psychological Bulletin, 125,* 193–322.

Grosjean, F. (1982). *Life with two languages: An introduction to bilingualism.* Cambridge, MA: Harvard University Press.

Hoffman, D., & Novak, T. (1996). Marketing in hypermedia computer-mediated environments: Conceptual foundations. *Journal of Marketing, 60,* 50–68.

Holbrook, M. B., & Moore, W. L. (1981). Feature interactions in consumer judgments of verbal versus pictorial presentations. *Journal of Consumer Research, 8,* 103–113.

Houston, M. J., Childers, T. L., & Heckler, S. E. (1987). Picture–word consistency and the elaborative processing of advertisements. *Journal of Marketing Research, 24,* 359–369.

Kroll, J. F., & de Groot, A. (1997). Lexical and conceptual memory in the bilingual: Mapping form to meaning in two languages. In A. de Groot & J. Kroll (Eds.), *Tutorials in bilingualism: Psycholinguistic perspectives* (pp. 169–199). Mahwah, NJ: Lawrence Erlbaum Associates.

La Heij, W., Hooglander, A., Kerling, R., & Van Der Velden, E. (1996). Nonverbal context effects in forward and backward word translation: Evidence for concept mediation. *Journal of Memory and Language, 35,* 648–665.

Levey, R. H. (1999, May). Give them some credit. *American Demographics,* pp. 41–43.

Luna, D., & Peracchio, L. A. (1999, October). *What's in a bilingual mind? Examining bilingual conceptual representation.* Paper presented at the Association for Consumer Research annual conference, Columbus, OH.

Luna, D., & Peracchio, L. A. (2001). Moderators of language effects in advertising to bilinguals: A psycholinguistic approach. *Journal of Consumer Research, 28,* 284–295.

Luna, D., Peracchio, L. A., & de Juan Vigaray, M. D. (2002). *Estimating and validating a model of flow across specific web sites and cultures.* Manuscript submitted for publication.

Luna, D., Peracchio, L. A., & de Juan Vigaray, M. D. (in press). The impact of language and congruity on persuasion in multicultural e-marketing. *Journal of Consumer Psychology.*

Lutz, K. A., & Lutz, R. J. (1977). Effects of interactive imagery on learning: Application to advertising. *Journal of Applied Psychology, 62,* 493–498.

MacWhinney, B. (1997). Second language acquisition and the competition model. In A. de Groot & J. Kroll (Eds.), *Tutorials in bilingualism: Psycholinguistic perspectives* (pp. 113–144). Mahwah, NJ: Lawrence Erlbaum Associates.

McQuarrie, E. F., & Mick, D. G. (1999). Visual rhetoric in advertising: Text-interpretive, experimental, and reader-response analyses. *Journal of Consumer Research, 26,* 37–54.

Miljkovitch, I. (1980). Classement suivant des catégories sans etiquette verbale chez le bilingue. *Canadian Journal of Psychology, 34,* 359–369.

Milroy, L., & Muysken, P. (1995). *One speaker, two languages: Cross-disciplinary perspectives on code-switching.* New York: Cambridge University Press.

Miniard, P. W., Bhatla, S., Lord, K. R., Dickson, P., & Unnava, H. R. (1991). Picture-based persuasion processes and the moderating role of involvement. *Journal of Consumer Research, 18,* 92–107.

Paivio, A. (1971). *Imagery and verbal processes*. New York: Holt, Rinehart and Winston.

Paivio, A. (1986). *Mental representations: A dual coding approach*. New York: Oxford University Press.

Paivio, A., & Desrochers, A. (1980). A dual-coding approach to bilingual memory. *Canadian Journal of Psychology, 34*, 388–399.

Paivio, A., & Lambert, W. (1981). Dual coding and bilingual memory. *Journal of Verbal Learning and Verbal Behavior, 20*, 532–539.

Paivio, A., Yuille, J., & Madigan, S. (1968). Concreteness, imagery, and meaningfulness values for 925 nouns. *Journal of Experimental Psychology Monograph Supplement, 76*(1, part 2), 1–25.

Ransdell, S. E., & Fischler, I. (1991). Imagery skill and preferences in bilinguals. *Applied Cognitive Psychology, 5*, 97–112.

Russell, J. A. (1991). Culture and the categorization of emotions. *Psychological Bulletin, 110*, 426–450.

Schmitt, B., Tavassoli, N. T., & Millard, R. T. (1993). Memory for print ads: Understanding relations among brand name, copy, and picture. *Journal of Consumer Psychology, 2*, 55–81.

Sholl, A., Sankaranarayanan, A., & Kroll, J. (1995). Transfer between picture naming and translation: A test of the asymmetries in bilingual memory. *Psychological Science, 6*, 45–49.

Snodgrass, J. G. (1984). Concepts and their surface representations. *Journal of Verbal Learning and Verbal Behavior, 23*, 3–22.

Tulving, E., & Thompson, D. M. (1971). Retrieval processes in recognition memory: Effects of associative context. *Journal of Experimental Psychology, 87*, 116–124.

Unnava, H. R., & Burnkrant, R. E. (1991). An imagery-processing view of the role of pictures in print advertisements. *Journal of Marketing Research, 28*, 226–231.

Zhang, S., & Schmitt, B. H. (2001). Creating local brands in multilingual international markets. *Journal of Marketing Research, 38*, 313–325.

CHAPTER TEN

The Role of Imagery Instructions in Facilitating Persuasion in a Consumer Context

Gayathri Mani
Indiana University

Deborah J. MacInnis
University of Southern California

Mental imagery has long been recognized by psychologists as a potent tool to increase learning and memory. Consumer research, on the other hand, has more recently begun to examine the effects of mental imagery on persuasion. While the use of visual stimuli (such as pictures) is a common way to elicit mental imagery, imagery can also be evoked through the use of rich verbal descriptions or through specific verbal instructions to consumers to imagine particular products or situations. Are these techniques effective in persuading consumers? What circumstances determine their effectiveness? Answers to such questions represent the first step toward developing an understanding of the role of verbal stimuli in eliciting mental imagery and thereby enhancing persuasion.

Recent research in consumer behavior has yielded inconsistent effects from the use of verbal instructions to imagine on various persuasion-related outcomes. Nevertheless, given the small number of studies that has examined the issue and the impressive body of evidence from psychology documenting the impact of such imagery instructions on learning and memory (Paivio, 1971), it may be premature to dismiss this technique as relatively ineffective in persuasion. In this chapter, we (a) review extant literature on the effects of imagery instructions on persuasion in a consumer context and (b) make suggestions regarding whether and when imagery instructions might lead to persuasion.

In the section that follows, we introduce the notion of mental imagery and discuss various strategies used to elicit imagery. We focus next on imagery instructions as a technique for eliciting mental imagery and examine its meaning and charac-teristics. We then review empirical evidence regarding the effects of imagery instructions on persuasion. Next, we describe various circumstances under which imagery instructions might act as a persuasive tool. Finally, we explore some mea-surement issues relating to the effects of imagery instructions. We supplement our discussion in this chapter with findings from a recent study and with suggestions for future research.

MENTAL IMAGERY AND IMAGERY-ELICITING STRATEGIES

Mental imagery is a form of cognitive processing that evokes perceptual or sensory experiences in working memory instead of utilizing verbal or semantic means to process information (MacInnis & Price, 1987). Although mental imagery can be multisensory in nature, research has primarily focused on visual imagery, which involves the generation of mental pictures of external stimuli.

In general, three main strategies have been suggested to elicit mental imagery, namely, pictures, concrete words, and instructions to imagine (Alesandrini & Sheikh, 1983; Lutz & Lutz, 1978; MacInnis & Price, 1987). Pictures, by their very nature, provide external images that can be used as a source for mental imagery. Concrete words have tangible referents (e.g., apple), whereas abstract words (e.g., peace) do not. As a result, concrete words lend themselves more easily to the evo-cation of mental images. Instructions to imagine, of course, directly exhort con-sumers to visualize product information.

Considerable research in cognitive psychology has demonstrated the facilitative effects of these imagery-eliciting strategies on learning and memory (e.g., Bower, 1972; Paivio, 1969). One prominent explanation for these effects suggests that imaginal processing stimulates the encoding of information in both verbal and image formats and thereby increases its availability in memory (Paivio, 1971, 1986). Another stance also suggests greater information availability but attributes this to the increased extent of cognitive elaboration evoked by the imagery elicit-ing strategies (Kisielius & Sternthal, 1984, 1986). Thus, according to the first argu-ment, information processed through mental imagery is more available because it is mentally represented both in verbal as well as pictorial form, whereas according to the latter argument, imagery-evoking stimuli lead consumers to process the information more thoroughly.

Some researchers have suggested that the increased availability of information arising from imagery processing should also assist in persuasion (e.g., Lutz & Lutz, 1978). While research in this area is still in its infancy, support for Lutz and Lutz's position has been more forthcoming in the case of pictures or concrete words. Thus, some researchers in advertising have shown that the use of pictorial in-formation enhances ad and brand attitudes and behavioral intentions (Edell &

Staelin, 1983; Mitchell, 1986; Mitchell & Olson, 1981; Rossiter & Percy, 1978, 1980). Similarly, a few studies have shown positive effects on ad and brand attitudes as well as behavioral intentions using concrete words (Burns, Biswas, & Babin, 1993; Burns, Biswas, & Roach, 1991; McGill & Anand, 1989; Rossiter & Percy, 1978, 1980). In the case of imagery instructions, the evidence is not at all clear-cut. We address this issue in greater detail in a subsequent section.

One general precaution that should be noted is that persuasion is contingent on the favorableness of the imaginal processing that is undertaken. For instance, the stimuli in Kisielius and Sternthal (1986) appeared to evoke unfavorable processing and led to lower brand attitudes (although these results were reversed in a replication that used a more reliable attitude measure—Dickson, Burnkrant, Miniard, & Unnava, 1986). Babin and Burns (1997) suggest that most ads contain favorable information that is designed to evoke positive imagery. While this is often true, an individual's reaction to a stimulus (be it an ad or not) is not always predictable. For instance, a consumer could perceive an ad to be of inferior quality or react negatively to the persuasive intent of the ad itself. Yet, in general, burgeoning evidence seems to point to the two strategies discussed (i.e., pictures and concrete words) as fairly reliable persuasion tools.

MEANING AND CHARACTERISTICS
OF IMAGERY INSTRUCTIONS

Imagery instructions (or *instructions to imagine*—we use the two terms interchangeably) can be described as the provision of explicit verbal guidelines to undertake imaginal processing. Lutz and Lutz (1978) define imagery instructions as "a statement to the learner that directs him or her to form a mental picture of the concept to be learned" (p. 612).

Imagery instructions possess certain distinct features compared to other imagery-eliciting strategies. First, unlike pictures, which are restricted to visual media, imagery instructions (like concrete wording) can be used in a purely auditory format as well. Second, it is the only technique that is designed to evoke self-generated imagery (rather than imagery supplied by the communication). This has the potential to be more persuasive because the images generated may be more personally relevant and meaningful.

On the down side however, the absence of externally provided images places greater reliance on consumers' abilities to independently generate imagery for imaginal processing to occur. Further, because self-generated images are more idiosyncratic, the valence of the imagery may be more unpredictable; in other words, consumers have more latitude to generate negative as well as positive images. By contrast, pictures and concrete words may be better at channeling consumers' imagery in a specific direction.

EMPIRICAL EVIDENCE FOR
IMAGERY INSTRUCTIONS EFFECTS

Extensive research in psychology documents the facilitative effects of imagery instructions on learning and memory (see Paivio, 1971). In the context of persuasion however, the results are far from convincing. Rossiter (1982) proposed that providing advertising stimuli that are rich in imagery (i.e., through the use of pictures or concrete words) may be more effective than instructing consumers to imagine. Although his suggestion at the time was not based on empirical efforts examining persuasion, his prediction appears to be borne out by the body of evidence accumulated thus far.

Null Effects of Imagery Instructions on Persuasion

The earliest empirical studies on the impact of imagery instructions on persuasion in an advertising context did not find any significant effects (Mowen, 1980; Wright & Rip, 1980). In Wright and Rip (1980), high school students evaluated various colleges after reading advertising messages that either did or did not include imagery instructions. The presence of imagery instructions did not consistently enhance students' preference judgments for the colleges. However, research elsewhere has indicated that imagery is not effective when subjects are faced with new or difficult concepts (De Rose, 1976; Rigney & Lutz, 1976). Thus, the subjects' lack of experience with the product category may have impeded their ability to generate meaningful images. In Mowen (1980), subjects who were exposed to an ad that instructed them to imagine using a fictitious brand of shampoo reported no stronger intentions to try the product than subjects who saw an identical ad without the instructions. However, supplementary data on subjects' reactions to the ad revealed that the instructions were too blatant to be credible. Thus, the very statements used to elicit imagery may have affected the results.

Although explanations can be provided for the null findings of these two studies, a more recent study incorporated imagery instructions in the headline and closing statement of a print ad for automobiles but failed to produce any effects on ad or brand attitudes and intentions (Burns et al., 1993). Several other studies that examined the role of experimental instructions to subjects to engage in imagery also did not demonstrate any significant main effects for imagery instructions, although some interactions (with pictures or concrete words) were obtained (Dickson et al., 1986; Keller & McGill, 1994; Kisielius & Sternthal, 1984; McGill & Anand, 1989).

Positive Effects of Imagery Instructions on Persuasion

The first study to demonstrate positive effects was conducted by Gregory, Cialdini and Carpenter (1982). One group of individuals listened to a message instructing them to imagine themselves enjoying the benefits of cable television while another group simply heard a description of the benefits. The group who received imagery instructions exhibited more positive attitudes and behavioral intentions and was more likely to actually subscribe to the cable TV service. In a recent attempt, Babin and Burns (1997) used multiple instructions to imagine, embedding them throughout the copy of a print ad, and found significant effects on ad and brand attitudes (although the size of the effect was fairly modest).

Finally, we conducted a study in which 155 undergraduates were exposed to four ads for fictitious brands in different product categories (with an ad for jacuzzis being the target). One group of subjects was given explicit instructions to try to imagine the information conveyed in each ad while the other group was not. Within each group, we varied the modality in which the product information was presented (auditory vs. written) as well as the manner in which product information was described (as attributes of the product or as consumer benefits arising therefrom). Once subjects had been exposed to all the ads, dependent measures relating to attitudes and purchase intentions were administered, followed by various process checks and covariate measures. The results revealed significantly higher brand attitudes and purchase intentions (which were combined into a single composite measure) when imagery instructions were provided than when they were not ($F_{(1,142)} = 8.3$; $p < .006$).

IMAGERY INSTRUCTIONS AS A PERSUASIVE TOOL

We now turn to the circumstances under which imagery instructions might facilitate persuasion, given the body of evidence just described.

Interactions with Other Imagery-Eliciting Strategies

As we have mentioned, some interactions between imagery instructions and other imagery eliciting strategies have been observed. For instance, McGill and Anand (1989) found that attitudes were most favorable when subjects were instructed to imagine and the products had positive descriptions of concrete (as opposed to abstract) attributes. Thus, one stance might be to argue that imagery instructions have weak effects by themselves, but gain importance when used in conjunction with other eliciting strategies. Additional support for this notion is provided by the works of Bone and Ellen (1990, 1992), although their studies did not explicitly manipulate either imagery instructions or concrete wording, (i.e., all subjects received the instructions and concrete descriptions). Nevertheless, when the stimuli and procedures incorporate imagery instructions along with concrete wording, significant effects on behavioral intentions were observed in the initial study (Bone & Ellen, 1990). The follow-up study (Bone & Ellen, 1992) found effects on attitudes toward the ad but not on brand attitudes or purchase intentions.

Although these results support the view expressed by some (MacInnis & Price, 1987; Rossiter, 1982) that combining imagery instructions with other imagery elic- iting strategies may be helpful, this is not the only situation in which imagery instructions assist persuasion. As we have mentioned, a few studies (e.g., Babin & Burns, 1997; Gregory et al., 1982) have found facilitative effects from imagery instructions on persuasion (even in the absence of other eliciting strategies). A simple explanation, explored next, is that imagery instructions can work inde- pendently, but only under certain conditions.

Issues in the Provision of Imagery Instructions

Externally Versus Internally Provided Instructions. One issue that might impinge on the effectiveness of imagery instructions is the manner in which the instructions themselves are provided. For instance, the instructions may be pro- vided externally in the context of the experiment (i.e., through written and/or oral study instructions) or internally in the context of the stimulus (i.e., embedded within the ad or message). However, external instructions are less realistic because it is hard to directly translate them outside the experimental setting.

External validity issues aside, Wright and Rip (1980) suggest that external instructions constitute a direct command from an authority figure and hence may be more potent than instructions embedded within mass media communi- cations. When we add to this the fact that advertising messages, because of their intent to persuade, are often received with skepticism, Wright and Rip's con- tention seems doubly appealing. But, there is no empirical evidence to support their contention. While embedded instructions have been ineffective in facilitat- ing persuasion (Burns et al., 1993; Mowen, 1980; Wright & Rip, 1980), externally provided instructions have also failed to produce significant main effects (Dick- son et al., 1986; Kisielius & Sternthal, 1984; McGill & Anand, 1989). In fact, the few studies that have found facilitative effects from imagery instructions have used embedded instructions (Babin & Burns, 1997; Gregory et al., 1982). Never- theless, future research could more directly test this issue by varying the method of instructions provided (external vs. embedded) and examining the relative impact on persuasion.

One other possibility is, of course, to use both modes of instruction. This was the tactic employed in our study. Thus, our written instructions (which were also verbally reinforced) asked subjects to imagine the information conveyed in the ad and develop a mental picture of the product descriptions. In addition, the word 'imagine' preceded mention of the claims for the ads used in the imagery instruc- tions conditions. To the best of our knowledge, Bone and Ellen (1990, 1992) are the only other researchers to follow a similar procedure. However, comparisons with their studies are not fruitful because, as mentioned earlier, they did not manipulate imagery instructions.

Redundancy of Instructions. As we mentioned, we did find a significant effect of imagery instructions on attitudes and purchase intentions. If this is, in fact, due to the dual approach to providing instructions that was employed in our study, the question arises as to whether the critical aspect is the combination (external along with embedded) or the redundancy (two instructions, or three if the verbal reinforcements are considered). Although this issue cannot be definitively resolved, comparisons with other recent studies are revealing. For instance, Burns et al. (1993) used two repetitions of the instructions to imagine, placed in the headline and the closing statement of the copy. Although these locations were strategically chosen to be salient (as predicated by primacy and recency considerations), the study did not find significant effects. In the next attempt (Babin & Burns, 1997), the authors used five insertions of imagery instructions distributed throughout the ad copy and found significant effects. This suggests that redundancy may indeed be important.

However, in the Mowen (1980) study, five out of seven sentences in the ad included instructions to imagine. Although the absolute number of repetitions appears to be the same as in the Babin and Burns (1997) study, perhaps the imagery instructions component in the Mowen ad was greater in proportion to the total text in the ad copy. As mentioned earlier, subjects' reactions to the ad indicated that they found the instructions to be exaggerated and the study did not find any significant effects. Thus, it appears that a communication needs to tread a fine line between understatement and overstatement if the imagery instructions used are to be effective.

Focus of Instructions on Self Versus Others. Another aspect of the instructions that merits consideration is whether they instruct individuals to imagine themselves or to imagine others (assuming of course that some person-oriented imagery is involved). Bone and Ellen (1992) contend that self-imagery is likely to be generated more easily and vividly than other-imagery. As such, self-oriented imagery instructions should be more effective in persuasion than other-oriented instructions. However, the problematic issue (and one that the researchers faced) is that the orientation in the instructions is no guarantee that individuals will comply with them. Thus, the authors found that many subjects who were instructed to imagine others also imagined themselves (which in itself supports the contention that individuals may be more fluent at self-imagery).

Reconciling Effects on Learning Versus Persuasion Based on Issues in the Provision of Imagery Instructions. A broader issue that needs to be addressed is the discrepancy between the powerful effects of imagery instructions on learning and the conflicting effects on persuasion. In other words, why are imagery instructions more reliably effective in psychological studies of learning but not in studies of persuasion in an advertising context? In this regard, it should be noted that the learning effects were obtained by eliciting imagery primarily through external experimental instructions. Thus, Wright and Rip (1980), given their stance that embedded instructions are less potent, attribute the learning effects obtained to the method of imagery instructions employed. However, as we mentioned, external instructions have not proved to be superior in effecting persuasion. Thus, Wright and Rip's speculation does not satisfactorily explain the discrepancy.

Another potential explanation stems from the availability–valence hypothesis proffered by Kisielius and Sternthal (1984, 1986). According to this explanation, imagery-eliciting strategies evoke elaborative imagery and thereby increase the availability of information in memory. However, the effects on attitudes are contingent on the valence of the imaginal elaboration. Thus, if the elaboration is favorable, positive associations to the stimulus are made in memory and attitudes toward the stimulus are correspondingly enhanced, whereas if the elaborative processing is unfavorable, attitudes may be adversely affected.

Consistent with this explanation, we find positive effects on learning and memory for imagery instructions (as well as for the other two imagery-eliciting strategies). However, as mentioned earlier, imagery instructions may lead to more idiosyncratic processing than other eliciting strategies. When more idiosyncratic associations are evoked, the valence of the elaboration is more uncertain. By contrast, in the case of pictures or concrete words, the elaboration is likely to be more consistently favorable because it is closely tied to the information contained in the message (which is almost always positive in nature). Thus, we find conflicting effects on persuasion for imagery instructions but more clearly facilitative effects for pictures or concrete words. One way to overcome the idiosyncratic nature of consumers' imaginal processing in response to imagery instructions might be to vary the type of instructions provided to subjects and thereby channel the valence of their imagery in a single direction. Thus, if individuals are provided instructions that specify the nature of the imagery to be undertaken (favorable vs. unfavorable), we would expect persuasion to be correspondingly enhanced versus undermined.

Role of Other Facilitating Factors

Thus far, we have discussed some issues in constructing the imagery instructions themselves that may play a role in their efficacy in persuasion. Other factors may also be helpful in enhancing the persuasive capability of imagery instructions. We next identify some of these factors under four categories, based on whether they represent aspects of the ad, the product, the individual, or the situation.

Ad Factors.   Several aspects of the ad (the message, medium, various executional elements, etc.) may contribute to its imagery evoking potential. Alesandrini and Sheikh (1983) suggest that the use of a scenario can be helpful because it provides a context for the imagery. While we used a constant scenario for each product in our study, Bone and Ellen (1992) varied the plausibility of the scenario and found that more plausible scenarios increased the fluency of mental imagery generation.

Another aspect of the ad message that may be relevant is whether ad claims are described in the form of attributes or benefits (i.e., the physical features of the product or the advantages that the features offer to the consumer). We speculate that benefit-oriented ads may be more conducive to imagery generation because they portray information in terms that are more meaningful to the consumer. Yet another pertinent factor is the medium (modality) in which the ad is provided. Because reading an ad and engaging in visual imagery both involve visual information processing, presenting an ad visually tends to interfere with imagery production (Brooks, 1967; Levin & Divine-Hawkins, 1974; Unnava, Agarwal, & Haugtvedt, 1996). Thus, the auditory mode (i.e., radio) is more likely to facilitate imagery generation. With regard to these predictions, it is noteworthy that the first study to reveal significant effects of imagery instructions on persuasion variables (Gregory et al., 1982) presented the message to subjects aurally and in the form of benefits.

Product and Individual Factors.   Product and individual factors are discussed together because many product characteristics can be examined only in relation to specific consumers. Two such characteristics, knowledge and familiarity with the product, are key prerequisites for imagery generation (MacInnis & Price, 1987). In the context of new products, Oliver, Robertson, and Mitchell (1993) found that imaginal processing was enhanced by the perceived novelty of the new product. Another aspect of the product that may be relevant is whether it is functional or hedonic in nature. MacInnis and Price (1987) suggest that hedonic consumption experiences lend themselves more readily to imagery and thus, imagery may be especially important for hedonic products. As mentioned earlier, we used a highly hedonic product (jacuzzis) as the target for our study and found that most subjects had no difficulty engaging in imagery for the product.

Finally, some relevant individual factors include gender, and individual differences in imagery ability, and preference for visual versus verbal processing. Rossiter and Percy (1978) found gender differences in the attitude generated by ads with pictures and concrete copy, with higher ratings for women. They attributed this to the tendencies of women (more so than men) to be bilateral (both visual and verbal) processors. More generally, individual differences in preferences for visual versus verbal processing, as in imagery ability, can be assessed using standard scales (such as the Style of Processing scale—Childers, Houston, & Heckler, 1985; Betts Questionnaire Upon Mental Imagery—Sheehan, 1967; etc.).

Situational Factors.   At least one important situational factor has been indicated to impact imagery evocation, namely, time available for processing (MacInnis & Price, 1987). Because imaginal processing is a form of cognitive elaboration, imposing time constraints hinders such elaborative activity (Kisielius & Sternthal, 1984).

Role of Imagery Instructions Vis-à-Vis Other Facilitating Factors. While we have reviewed various factors that appear to facilitate imagery generation, our specific concern is with whether these factors moderate the impact of imagery instructions on persuasion. However, a systematic examination of these factors in conjunction with the use of imagery instructions is yet to be undertaken in consumer research and represents an important avenue for future endeavor.

The next logical question that arises is whether the presence of these facilitating factors obviates the need for imagery instructions itself. For instance, in our study, several subjects who were not provided instructions to imagine still reported the use of imagery. Wright and Rip (1980) suggest that many individuals might have naturally developed the practice of generating imagery as a means to process information and thus may spontaneously generate imagery while processing "interesting messages," even in the absence of specific instructions to do so. If the default method of processing information is primarily visual for most individuals, this may explain the lack of significant effects due to the manipulation of imagery instructions in various studies. In a similar vein, Lutz and Lutz (1978) note that, even if the "nominal treatment of imagery instructions" fails, reported use of mental imagery may still be effective.

The implication of this argument is that instructions to imagine are effective (or even necessary) only when individuals would not otherwise engage in imaginal processing. If, on the other hand, the circumstances are conducive to the automatic generation of imagery (i.e., various facilitating factors are present), specific instructions are not needed. Before this reasoning can be conclusively confirmed or refuted, additional testing (by varying the presence vs. absence of both imagery instructions as well as various facilitating factors) is warranted.

However, some findings in our study contradict the view that imagery instructions are superfluous when the conditions are conducive to mental imagery. For instance, even though many subjects in our study engaged in imaginal processing independent of the provision of imagery instructions, instructions to imagine did have a significant impact on attitudes/purchase intentions. Thus, imagery evoked through instructions had a greater tendency to affect persuasion than imagery generated spontaneously. This would suggest that there is a greater likelihood of affect generated from imaginal processing to transfer to the brand when the advertiser explicitly instructs the individual to engage in mental imagery. However, this interpretation is undoubtedly speculative, and additional research is needed to systematically examine the various differences between spontaneous imagery and imagery generated in response to specific instructions.

MEASURING THE ROLE OF IMAGERY INSTRUCTIONS

Thus far, we have implicitly assumed that any persuasion-related effects arising from the use of imagery instructions derive from their ability to evoke mental imagery. However, to establish that imaginal processing was, in fact, the cause of any observed effects, manipulation and process checks are required. Several issues arise in this regard. Some researchers have argued that imagery may not be adequately captured through written responses, as sensory experiences may be difficult to verbalize (Morris & Hampson, 1983). Further, all retrospective measures (be they written responses or scales) are criticized on the grounds that they measure only respondents' memory for images and not the images themselves. On the other hand, concurrent measures interrupt subjects while they are engaged in imaginal processing. Researchers also need to be sensitive to the issue of demand effects while constructing their manipulation and process check measures. In other words, the measures should not lead subjects to falsely indicate that they engaged in imagery simply in order to provide an "acceptable" response. Thus, an important avenue for future research is the development of more refined and nonintrusive measurement techniques to obtain evidence of imaginal processing.

SUMMARY

The purpose of this chapter was to review and reconcile the body of evidence relating to the role of imagery instructions in persuasion. We began by clarifying the concepts of mental imagery and imagery instructions and exploring the mechanisms implicated in their use. We then described the inconsistent findings regarding the impact of imagery instructions and identified circumstances under which instructions to imagine might be persuasive. Thus, we explored various issues in the provision of the instructions that might influence their capacity to enhance persuasion. We also suggested that imagery instructions might be persuasive in conjunction with other imagery-eliciting strategies or facilitating factors. Finally, we discussed some issues relating to the measurement of mental imagery evoked through instructions to imagine. In each section, we described relevant findings from a recent study and identified possible avenues for future research in the area.

REFERENCES

Alesandrini, K., & Sheikh, A. (1983). Research on imagery: Applications to advertising. In A. Sheikh (Ed.), *Imagery: Current theory, research and application* (pp. 535–556). New York: John Wiley.
Babin, L. A., & Burns, A. C. (1997). Effects of print ad pictures and copy containing instructions to imagine on mental imagery that mediates attitudes. *Journal of Advertising, 26*(3), 33–44.
Bone, P. F., & Ellen, P. S. (1990). The effect of imagery processing and imagery content on behavioral intentions. In M. E. Goldberg, G. Gorn, & R. W. Pollay (Eds.), *Advances in consumer research* (vol. 17, pp. 449–454). Provo, UT: Association for Consumer Research.
Bone, P. F., & Ellen, P. S. (1992). The generation and consequences of communication-evoked imagery. *Journal of Consumer Research, 19*, 93–104.
Bower, G. (1972). Mental imagery and associative learning. In L. Gregg (Ed.), *Cognition in learning and memory.* New York: John Wiley.

Brooks, L. R. (1967). The suppression of visualization in reading. *Quarterly Journal of Experimental Psychology, 19,* 289–299.

Burns, A. C., Biswas, A., & Babin, L. A. (1993). The operation of mental imagery as a mediator of advertising effects. *Journal of Advertising, 22,* 71–85.

Burns, A. C., Biswas, A., & Roach, S. (1991). The effects of advertising stimulus concreteness and familiarity on consumer attitudes and intentions. In R. L. King (Ed.), *Developments in marketing science* (vol. 14, pp. 17–20). Richmond, VA: Academy of Marketing Science.

Childers, T. L., Houston, M. J., & Heckler, S. E. (1985). Measurement of individual differences in visual vs. verbal processing. *Journal of Consumer Research, 12,* 125–134.

DeRose, T. M. (1976). *Pictorial and verbal strategies in children's reading comprehension.* Paper presented at the meeting of the American Research Association, San Francisco.

Dickson, P. R., Burnkrant, R. E., Miniard, P. E., & Unnava, H. R. (1986). If it isn't a duck then why did it quack? Competing explanations for an observed effect of illustrations in an advertisement. In R. J. Lutz (Ed.), *Advances in consumer research* (vol. 13, pp. 153–157). Provo, UT: Association for Consumer Research.

Edell, J. A., & Staelin, R. (1983). The information processing of pictures in print advertisements. *Journal of Consumer Research, 10,* 45–61.

Gregory, W. L., Cialdini, R. B., & Carpenter, K. M. (1982). Self-relevant scenarios as mediators of likelihood estimates and compliance: Does imagining make it so? *Journal of Personality and Social Psychology, 43,* 89–99.

Keller, P. A., & McGill, A. L. (1994). Differences in the relative influence of product attributes under alternative processing conditions: Attribute importance versus attribute ease of imagability. *Journal of Consumer Psychology, 3*(1), 29–49.

Kisielius, J., & Sternthal, B. (1984). Detecting and explaining vividness effects in attitudinal judgements. *Journal of Marketing Research, 21,* 54–64.

Kisielius, J., & Sternthal, B. (1986). Examining the vividness controversy: An availability–valence interpretation. *Journal of Consumer Research, 12,* 418–431.

Levin, J. R., & Divine-Hawkins, P. (1974). Visual imagery as a prose-learning process. *Journal of Reading Behavior,* 23–30.

Lutz, K. A., & Lutz, R. J. (1978). Imagery-eliciting strategies: Review and implications of research. In H. K. Hunt (Ed.), *Advances in consumer research* (vol. 5, pp. 611–620). Ann Arbor, MI: Association for Consumer Research.

MacInnis, D. J., & Price, L. L. (1987). The role of imagery in information processing: Review and extensions. *Journal of Consumer Research, 13,* 473–491.

McGill, A. L., & Anand, P. (1989). The effect of vivid attributes on the evaluation of alternatives: The role of differential attention and cognitive elaboration. *Journal of Consumer Research, 16,* 188–196.

Mitchell, A. A. (1986). The effect of verbal and visual components of advertisements on brand attitudes and attitudes toward the advertisement. *Journal of Consumer Research, 13,* 12–24.

Mitchell, A. A., & Olson, J. C. (1981). Are product attribute beliefs the only mediator of advertising effects on brand attitude? *Journal of Marketing Research, 18,* 318–332.

Morris, P. E., & Hampson, P. J. (1983). *Imagery and consciousness.* London: Academic Press.

Mowen, J. C. (1980). The availability heuristic: The effect of imagining the use of a product on product perceptions. In R. Bagozzi, K. Bernhardt, P. Busch, D. Cravens, J. Hair, & C. Scott (Eds.), *Educators' Conference Proceedings* (pp. 140–142). Chicago, IL: American Marketing Association.

Oliver, R. L., Robertson, T. S., & Mitchell, D. (1993). Imaging and analyzing in response to new product advertising. *Journal of Advertising, 22,* 35–49.

Paivio, A. (1969). Mental imagery and associative learning and memory. *Psychological Review, 76,* 241–263.

Paivio, A. (1971). *Imagery and verbal processes.* New York: Holt, Rinehart & Winston.

Paivio, A. (1986). *Mental representations: A dual coding approach.* New York: Oxford University Press.

Rigney, J. W., & Lutz, K. A. (1976). Effect of graphic analogies of concepts in chemistry on learning and attitude. *Journal of Educational Psychology, 68,* 305–311.

Rossiter, J. R. (1982). Visual imagery: Applications to advertising. In A. A. Mitchell (Ed.), *Advances in consumer research* (vol. 9, pp. 101–106). Ann Arbor, MI: Association for Consumer Research.

Rossiter, J. R., & Percy, L. (1978). Visual imagining ability as a mediator of advertising response. In H. K. Hunt (Ed.), *Advances in consumer research* (vol. 5, pp. 621–629). Ann Arbor, MI: Association for Consumer Research.

Rossiter, J. R., & Percy, L. (1980). Attitude change through visual imagery in advertising. *Journal of Advertising, 9,* 10–16.

Sheehan, P. (1967). A shortened form of Betts' questionnaire upon mental imagery. *Journal of Clinical Psychology, 23,* 386–389.

Unnava, H. R., Agarwal, S., & Haugtvedt, C. P. (1996). Interactive effects of presentation modality and message-generated imagery on recall of advertising information. *Journal of Consumer Research, 23,* 81–86.

Wright, P., & Rip, P. (1980). Product class advertising effects on first-time buyers' decision strategies. *Journal of Consumer Research, 7,* 176–188.

CHAPTER ELEVEN

The Contribution of Semiotic and Rhetorical Perspectives to the Explanation of Visual Persuasion in Advertising

Edward F. McQuarrie
Santa Clara University

David Glen Mick
University of Virginia

There are many ways to conceptualize the role of the visual element in advertising. In this chapter we address this issue from the perspectives of semiotics and rhetoric, and attempt to articulate their distinctive contributions, along with supporting empirical evidence. From semiotics we draw the ideas of *sign* and *text*. A sign is anything that can stand for something else. Text refers to any purposeful assemblage of signs, whether written or spoken, linguistic or pictorial. In light of this, pictures can be read as texts composed of signs. From rhetoric we draw the idea of a *figure of speech*. As developed here, figures need not be embodied in language, but can be defined more abstractly in terms of sign structure, so that visual figures are possible. To appreciate more fully the specific contribution of rhetorical and semiotic perspectives, it may be useful first to sketch briefly some of the alternative perspectives available.

ALTERNATIVE PERSPECTIVES ON ADVERTISING VISUALS

Human System or Ad System?

Perhaps the most basic distinction among perspectives is whether one focuses on the human system that processes the visual elements, or on the visual elements contained within the ad system. In turn, this distinction tends to drive the choice of which elements will be the focus of theoretical differentiation, as compared to elements that will be treated in a simplified manner, held constant, or tacitly assumed. For instance, in the study of ad visuals, a focus on the human system might be anchored in, and most concerned to differentiate, perceptual processes as revealed by contemporary research on the physiology of the brain, the retina, the optic nerve, and so forth. This approach would seek to explain visual persuasion in advertising in part by the distinct brain processes associated with visual as opposed to, say, auditory perception. Conversely, a focus on the ad system might address the comparative effects of color versus black-and-white images, photographic versus drawn representations, or similar distinctions, and link these directly to persuasion outcomes, without addressing perceptual processes per se.

A focus on the human system can also be played out in other ways. For example, one might examine traits that differentiate consumers, and use these to explain why visual elements may play a large or small role in determining the persuasion outcomes of some set of advertisements. Thus, consumers might be differentiated according to their propensity to process visual stimuli (Childers, Houston, & Heckler, 1985).

Yet another example where the focus lies primarily on the human system is the well-known distinction between central versus peripheral processing (along with the cognate distinction between systematic and heuristic processing), as seen in Petty, Cacioppo, and Schumann (1983), Maheswaran and Chaiken (1991), and others. Here the visual element in ads is categorized as prone to being processed by one aspect of the human system (peripheral, heuristic) as opposed to another. The visual character of these elements is relatively unimportant in this approach; ad visuals serve only as an example of material prone to one or another type of ad processing.

The point to be emphasized is that when a research approach focuses primarily on the response of the human system, with or without an emphasis on personal or situational moderators, it tends to pay relatively less attention (if any) to differentiations within the set of visual elements. In contrast, the distinctive contribution of rhetorical and semiotic approaches is precisely to deepen our understanding of how best to parse and comprehend the role of particular visual elements within the ad system. Rhetoric and semiotics are *text-centered* disciplines (McQuarrie, 1989; Mick, 1986). As such, they make relatively simple and straightforward assumptions about the human system, concentrating instead on the development of elaborate structures that can be used to differentiate types of visual content in advertisements.

It bears mentioning that the human system/ad system contrast is not a facsimile of any other extant attempt to distinguish among approaches to consumer or marketing research. In particular, it does not line up with the positivist versus interpretivist distinction. For instance, reader-response approaches to advertising, as described by Scott (1994b) and others, are clearly interpretive, but they are equally clearly focused on the response of the human system—here dubbed the reader—to the visual element. The kinds of possible readings, the depth to which these readings may be taken, and the means whereby competing readings are negotiated constitute the focus of reader-response theory; differentiations within the texts being read are not as central.

Ultimately, in our view, the goal of consumer advertising research must be to integrate the human system and the ad system, weaving together conceptually rich insights within and across each. It can be argued that historically consumer research as a whole has tended to emphasize the human system; text properties, visual or otherwise, have not been the central focus. This follows directly from the naming of the discipline in terms of consumers (i.e., human systems), and from its deep roots in social psychology. Rhetoric and semiotics offer a very different approach to consumption phenomena, in focusing their differentiation efforts away from the consumer, and on to the sign systems of ads that the consumer confronts. It is our hope that a "return to the text," coupled with the decades of insight accumulated within human psychology, broadly construed, can significantly advance the progress of the field toward an integration of ad systems with human systems.

Differentiation of the Visual Element

In human systems approaches, the visual element tends to remain a poorly differentiated "black box," defined primarily in opposition to other kinds of elements: thus, visual versus verbal, or visual versus auditory. Initial attempts to differentiate the visual elements found in ads, which date back many years and continue today, have been largely mechanical and atheoretical (Assael, Kofron, & Burgi, 1967; Greenberg & Garfinkle, 1963; Motes, Hilton, & Fielden, 1992). Examples include the amount of each page devoted to visuals; size of typeface; or types of layout of picture, headline, and other components. Similar but more subtle distinctions have also been investigated, especially by Meyers-Levy and Peracchio (e.g., 1992, 1995, 1996; Peracchio & Meyers-Levy, 1994). These include camera angle and use of color, among others.

Mechanical distinctions are very real and some, such as color, have a long history of discussion that even predates the advent of modern advertising. Moreover, empirical evidence can be adduced that distinctions at the mechanical level among types of visual element do in fact influence consumers' processing of ads. However, an important shortcoming of mechanical distinctions, at least as currently pursued, is their atheoretical nature. Each distinction stands on its own without any conceptual links to any other distinction. Each is backed by common sense or has some foundation in perception research, and some are supported in laboratory studies, but none is generated from a theoretical specification or nomological network. Because of the lack of an overarching theoretical structure, there is no generativity—there is no way to tell if there are 5 five more such distinctions worthy of study, or 50, or 500, and no way to specify what the next five distinctions worthy of investigation might be.

A more sophisticated approach to the visual element can be found in Scott (1994a), who draws on art theory, among other disciplines, to differentiate advertising visuals. Perhaps most important, Scott introduces the concept of *style* to discussions of consumption phenomena. Style is a central idea in art theory, as seen in such common phrases as "Picasso's style," or "Renaissance style." Style can be thought of as a global attribute of a visual depiction. As such, it highlights the atomistic nature of such mechanical distinctions as color or degree of photographic cropping. Style is also an inherently integrative idea: To speak of the style of any single advertising visual is automatically to link it to certain other visuals, and to differentiate it from still other kinds. The mantra of stylistics is, "style is difference." Thus, Renaissance style emerges when it is counterposed to Baroque style, just as Picasso's style emerges when it is counterposed to Monet's; moreover, the factors that constitute Picasso's style emerge most clearly when one views multiple instances of his work.

Another contribution of Scott (1994a) was to lay bare the impoverished, if not altogether mistaken, theory of visual depictions tacitly held by many Western social scientists, consumer researchers included. This *copy theory* holds that a picture is a straightforward representation of the object(s) it depicts. Hence, in the context of an advertising experiment, when describing a visual stimulus, it is sufficient to say "sunset" or "kitten," that is, to name the object depicted. Scott took the authors of these two examples (Miniard, Bhatla, Lord, Dickson, & Unnava, 1991, and Mitchell & Olson, 1981, respectively) to task as follows: There can be no picture of a sunset per se—there can only be a depiction of a sunset in one style or another, such as the Hallmark card style, the travel poster style, the New Age style, and so on. Nor can the picture be thought of as a simple stimulus trigger tied to a feeling. The same object depicted in different styles will produce different feelings; moreover, feelings will not be the only consumer response to such stylized pictures.

A sunset in the travel poster style will lead to one kind of reading and one set of associations, whereas one in the New Age style will be assimilated to a different stock of cultural knowledge and will point the reader in a different direction when constructing meanings for the brand being advertised. The metaphor of consumer as reader suggests that complex inferences may be drawn from an ad, and legitimates the idea that differences in the style of the visual depiction will be consequential. In contrast, the notion of pictures serving primarily as a means for transferring positive affect to the brand, and its predecessor the classical conditioning model, suggests cognitive processes more at the level of a pigeon.

How does the approach outlined in Scott (1994a, 1994b) compare to the rhetorical and semiotic approaches developed later in this chapter? Scott avowed that her approach is most definitely rhetorical, but chose to position it away from semiotics. Closer reading shows that a narrowly structuralist semiotics is the source of this disaffection. We believe a broader approach to semiotics, in the mold of Eco (1976), is quite compatible with the approach taken by Scott. To the extent that there is a distinction between the approach of Scott and the one taken in our work, it concerns the level of systematization applied to the visual element. The global and subtle character of the notion of artistic style, in the hands of a skilled analyst such as Scott, allows for a deep and complex reading of how the pictures in an ad contribute to persuasive impact. The problem, of course, is that apprehending and interpreting stylistic characteristics of this sort depend so heavily on the ability and skill of the interpreter.

Our own approach to visual rhetoric, shaped by the semiotic tradition, is intended to be more analytic and systematic in its focus on particular sign structures within the visual image, and not so dependent on the interpretive and scholarly abilities of the analyst. (For a different approach to systematizing rhetorical figures that draws more heavily on psychological ideas, see McGuire, 2000.) The sign structure that has been the focus of our work is the *rhetorical figure*. In the next section we review conceptual work on the rhetorical figure; we then discuss processes and outcomes to be expected when a consumer encounters a rhetorical figure in an ad, and then we describe possible boundary conditions (moderating factors). Finally, we examine the likely impact of visually embodied as opposed to verbally delivered figures.

THE RHETORICAL PERSPECTIVE

Rhetorical approaches in general have two distinguishing features. The first is their focus on method or manner—the "how" rather than the "what" of utterances, statements, or texts. The root idea is that any proposition can be expressed in multiple ways, and that some of these expressions will be more effective than others. The focus on impact or effectiveness is the second distinguishing feature of rhetoric. In linguistic terms, rhetoric concerns the pragmatics of speech—the actions or events that are supposed to occur as a result of an utterance. In the narrower arena of speech acts, rhetoric concerns the illocutionary force of utterances—what the listener is supposed to do or experience in response to the speaker. Fundamentally, one looks to rhetoric for advice on how to communicate so as to bring about some desired outcome in the world.

Historical Perspective

Rhetoric has a long and tangled history in Western thought, and not every scholar would agree with the way we have positioned rhetoric in the preceding paragraph. In fact, the modern corpus of rhetoric is so vast and sprawls across so many scholarly disciplines that complete agreement on definitions is unlikely (Bender & Wellbery, 1990). The assessment of rhetoric's place in the grand scheme of things is

further complicated by the vicissitudes of its history and the controversies associated with it. In ancient Greece and Rome, and also in Medieval and Renaissance
Europe, rhetoric was a fundamental building block in the school curriculum. It
encompassed everything we would now classify as persuasion, much of what we
would call communication, and a good portion of aesthetics (Sperber & Wilson,
1990).

Later, as the scientific revolution gathered momentum, rhetoric became firmly
aligned, in the minds of many scientists, with the most reactionary and unenlight-
ened sectors of the old Establishment. Science concerned the search for truth; rhetoric concerned clever arrangements of words. Science rested on real facts; rhetoric
offered only embellishments, ornaments, and artifice. This uneasy relationship between rhetoric and truth actually goes back much further in history. For instance,
many of the Greek sophists were teachers of rhetoric, and the notions of "sophisti-
cal" and "rhetorical" have always been semantic neighbors. There is, in the end,
an extremely complicated and contentious relationship between the truthful and
the persuasive (e.g., see Peter & Olson, 1983), unfortunately the only fundamental
commitment of rhetoric is to the achievement of persuasion. Hence, as scientific
reasoning grew to dominate the search for observable and provable truth in Western thinking, the prominence and prestige of rhetoric sank apace. By the end of the
19th century, rhetoric had been reduced to an epithet or term of opprobrium, as in
"empty rhetoric."

For reasons whose history has yet to be written, rhetoric enjoyed a revival early
in the 20th century, especially in Europe. Scholars, particularly in the humanities,
once more began to draw on rhetoric for ideas and concepts useful for explaining
text structure. By the 1980s, the stream of books, journals, and articles, on both
sides of the Atlantic, and in both the social sciences and the humanities, had grown
steadily in volume. Nonetheless, as McGuire (2000) argued, the social sciences
have not as yet gone very far in exploring the rich vein of accumulated craft knowledge of persuasion embodied over the centuries in works on rhetoric.

In light of this, our positioning of rhetoric as "strategies for achieving impact"
might be best thought of as simply a useful definition from the standpoint of consumer and advertising research. What rhetoric offers the study of advertising visuals is the same thing that rhetoric offers consumer research, broadly speaking:
guidance in differentiating text properties and linking these differentiations to
consumer processing outcomes.

The Rhetorical Figure

One of the key contributions of the rhetorical perspective to advertising is the idea
of a rhetorical figure, which can be defined as an artful deviation. Perhaps the best
known rhetorical figure is metaphor, but rhyme is also a figure, as are puns, irony,
and antithesis, along with other more obscure devices, such as ellipsis, metonym,
and antimetabole. The idea of a rhetorical figure is a fundamentally stylistic notion

that concerns a particular method or manner of expressing proposition(s). The rhetorical figure, as we have defined it, is a potent device for influencing consumer processing of advertisements. Hence, this line of work is in the same vein as Scott, in arguing for the importance of stylistic analysis for understanding how advertising is experienced by the consumer.

Although the simple definition of rhetorical figures in terms of artful deviation has the advantage of being readily grasped, we intend the rhetorical figure to serve as a scientific construct capable of anchoring a theoretical framework. Hence, a more detailed exposition may be helpful, centering on the meaning of deviation. While the idea of a figure is a fundamentally rhetorical notion, the semiotic aspects of our treatment will emerge as we further articulate its definition.

Properties of Rhetorical Figures

The deviation that constitutes a figure does not refer to anything abnormal, and it certainly does not imply something defective. It has the more neutral connotations of "swerve" or "departure." The deviation that constitutes a figure functions to mark out a segment of a text or utterance. The importance of text marking was discussed at length by the semiotician Mukarovsky (1964). For purposes of analogy, consider what happens, for the author and reader, when a word is *italicized* or put in **boldface**. The author intends this word to be treated differently. He or she expects the reader to notice the marking, and to respond in accordance with the author's intention. Similarly, the reader knows to emphasize the italicized word, and understands more generally that the interpretation of the sentence hinges on or revolves around the italicized word, so that it should anchor the reading.

Thus, one way to think of rhetorical figures is to regard them as a kind of italicized text. Figures contain within themselves instructions that they are to be treated differently than the surrounding text. Conversely, readers are knowledgeable about the conventions that govern how text marked in this way is to be read. (That is, most readers are knowledgeable about conventions; the absence of such knowledge, as in the case of individuals from a very different cultural background, emerges as an important boundary condition, as developed later.) Although the convention with respect to italicized text is to give it emphasis, the convention with respect to rhetorical figures is to consider why the author was not content with a straightforward literal assertion of the underlying proposition. In other words, rhetorical figures encourage reinterpretation, or reading in additional meaning.

An alternative perspective on figurative deviation, with roots in the psychology of aesthetics (Berlyne, 1971), would approach it as a kind of incongruity. Like ambiguity and other collative properties of aesthetic objects, incongruity is arousing. More generally, incongruity tends to provoke cognitive elaboration. One can think of this as a kind of exceptions processing—incongruity requires resolution, and the reader brings processing resources to bear in order to deal with the incongruity. The link between deviation and incongruity, as further developed later, provides a bridge between the semiotic and rhetorical perspectives and the more familiar (within consumer research) cognitive and experimental psychological perspectives.

A third perspective on rhetorical figures rests on the artfulness of their deviation. Like all aesthetic phenomena, rhetorical figures have the potential to provide pleasure. The specific pleasure is what semioticians refer to as "the pleasure of the text" (Barthes, 1985). The idea is that it pleases a reader to encounter a text that sets multiple meanings into motion. These meanings are not ambiguous or unstable in the negative sense of an uncomfortable uncertainty, but playful in a positive sense. Rhetorical figures allow readers to play with their interpretation, and to cocreate their meanings, as they search out the sender's intent (Sperber & Wilson, 1986).

Taxonomy of Rhetorical Figures

These three ideas—text marking, incongruity, and pleasure of the text—are central to our understanding of the artful deviation that constitutes a rhetorical figure. They can be integrated with yet other ideas to form the basis of a taxonomy discussed in detail elsewhere (McQuarrie & Mick, 1996) and recapitulated later in this chapter. Of course, we are not the first, and probably not the last (cf. McGuire, 2000), to propose a taxonomy of rhetorical figures. Efforts to organize the sprawling compendia of rhetorical tips and tricks go back at least to Quintillian in Roman times. The revival of rhetoric in the 20th century was accompanied by renewed attempts to differentiate and integrate the corpus of rhetorical figures, ranging from the relatively simple distinctions of Jakobson (1971) and Burke (1950) to the complex, multidimensional classification schemes of Dubois et al. (1970) and Durand (1987). However, none of these prior efforts, except Durand's, focuses on the ad system per se, and Durand does not attempt to integrate psychological ideas. Moreover, none of these earlier taxonomies is concerned to derive causal propositions about consumer processing from their analytic categorizations of rhetorical figures. As argued earlier, only thus can the human and ad systems be effectively integrated.

The purpose of the taxonomy is to identify properties shared by some but not all rhetorical figures, or possessed to a varying degree by different figures, and then to use these properties to group figures into distinct categories (see Fig. 11.1). These categorizations can then be linked to consumer processing and outcomes, as developed subsequently. An initial distinction concerns the amount or degree of deviation present in a particular case. Individual instances of rhetorical figures can be more or less deviant, both as a function of random variation in the population of figures, and as a function of systematic variation among types of figures, as discussed later. However, the deviation must be above some threshold for a figure to be present. For example, "frozen" metaphors, which have become clichés (e.g., a tire that hugs the road), are (no longer) rhetorical figures by our definition.

As shown in Fig. 11.1, the next subdivision concerns what we have called the mode of figuration, or the type of deviation at issue. From the beginning of scholarly discussion of rhetoric in ancient times, two different kinds of figure have been distinguished, under the headings of scheme and trope. Each constitutes a distinctive kind of deviation: Schemes are excessively regular or ordered, whereas tropes are irregular or disordered. Among schemes, rhyme provides a ready example. The unnecessary echo of syllables and sounds is an instance of excessive order or regularity. Among tropes, the pun serves as an illustration. When context allows a word to carry two different meanings, or when a word can be interpreted in two very different ways, we have an instance of the irregularity or disorder that underlies any trope. Both schemes and tropes function as text marking, both produce incongruity, and both provide a pleasure of the text, but they do so using different means.

Two additional semiotic ideas can be used to give insight into the workings of each mode, and a third more psychological notion is also introduced. The first semiotic idea concerns the linguistic distinction between *combination* constraints and *selection* constraints. Texts must combine signs in certain ways to be comprehensible, and at any place within a combination, texts must select from a limited set of permissible items to fill that place. From this perspective, schemes constitute deviant combinations, whereas tropes constitute deviant selections. A rhyme combines too many of the same sounds; a pun selects a term that is "wrong" for

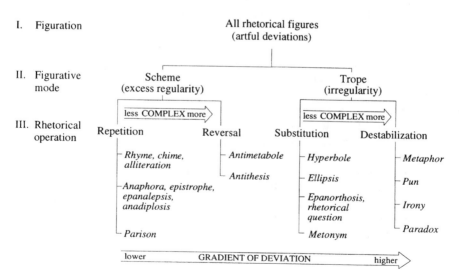

FIG. 11.1. A taxonomy of rhetorical figures in advertising. *Note.* Reproduced from McQuarrie, E. F., and Mick, D. G. (1996). Figures of rhetoric in advertising language. *Journal of Consumer Research, 22*, p. 426. © University of Chicago Press. Used by permission.

the combination, but that is nonetheless comprehensible. (For those conversant with Saussurean linguistics, combination constraints equate to the syntagmatic axis of communication analysis, whereas selection constraints equate to the paradigmatic axis.)

Another way of approaching schemes and tropes is to consider them as over-coded and undercoded text, respectively (cf. Eco, 1979). Schemes carry an excess of information, in the form of repetition or other patterning on the surface of the text. They possess internal redundancy, which offers multiple instructions for how they are to be interpreted. Tropes are undercoded or incomplete. The reader has to fill in what is missing to make sense of the violation of selection constraints. Both schemes and tropes permit multiple readings, but we might say that schemes *push* these meanings onto the reader, where tropes *pull* them out of the reader. The distinction between over- and undercoding leads readily to a more psychological perspective, in terms of depth of processing. Because schemes represent deviations that occur on the surface of the text, they are generally more *sensory* than tropes. Conversely, tropes function exclusively at the level of meaning, rendering them more *semantic* than schemes. Childers and Houston (1984) have shown that semantic alterations are processed at a deeper level than sensory alterations.

To summarize, the two figurative modes exhibit both qualitative and quantitative differences, in some cases representing a different kind of process, in others systematically exhibiting more or less of some property. In turn, these differences can be translated into empirical hypotheses concerning differential processes and outcomes, as discussed later. The final level of the taxonomy makes an internal distinction within both schemes and tropes, each having simple and complex varieties. Crossing complexity with mode of figuration generates four rhetorical operations, as described in McQuarrie and Mick (1996). Variations in complexity, and also variation in the degree of deviation, together place varying demands on the processing resources of the reader, in the sense of Anand and Sternthal (1990), allowing figures to be utilized in diverse settings, while still hopefully matching the resources available to the reader. (Resource availability emerges as a crucial moderating factor determining the impact of rhetorical figures in specific advertising situations, as developed later in this chapter.) In general, complexity and deviation can be expected to have additive effects, suggesting that simple schemes on the one hand, and complex tropes on the other, will show the sharpest distinctions in empirical work. Although this third level of the taxonomy is key to mapping its conceptual structure onto the named figures inherited from the classical tradition, space constraints prevent us from pursuing it further here (for additional discussion, see McQuarrie & Mick, 1996).

Contribution of the Taxonomy

Some kind of taxonomy is required if the rhetorical figure is to be rescued from the Tower of Babel into which it had descended over the centuries. As an idea with prescientific roots, knowledge of rhetorical figures, as handed down over the centuries, took the form of sprawling compendia of names, categorizations and illustrations. By the Middle Ages, the total number of named figures easily exceeded 100. In our view, one of the most important contributions of the taxonomy is that it shifts the focus away from the individual named figure to the underlying structural properties associated with that figure because of its place within the taxonomy. If valid, there is no longer any great need to ascertain the causal properties of metaphor as compared to irony, or metaphor as compared to metonym or ellipsis; one can simply speak of two complex tropes in the first instance, and of a complex trope as compared to two simple tropes in the second instance. True, irony is not the same as metaphor, and the one or the other may be a better choice in a particular persuasion endeavor, but if the taxonomy is correct, then in each case the bulk of the causal impact will be a function of their shared status as complex, tropic figures.

Thus, the taxonomy obviates the need to theorize about the specific impact of dozens of individual figures, contributing to a more parsimonious explanation of rhetorical phenomena. Conversely, it sets a high standard for work focused on any of the more common figures, such as metaphor. To continue with metaphor as an example, in our view the bane of studies on this named figure is an inability to distinguish between properties and outcomes that are peculiar to metaphor, properties and outcomes that are shared by all complex tropes, and properties and outcomes that can be expected from any rhetorical figure whatsoever. The taxonomy thus imposes a discipline on studies of any individual figure, in requiring both a differentiation of, and integration with, other kindred rhetorical figures. In this way, the taxonomy promotes a more scientific approach to rhetorical phenomena.

The taxonomy provides a similar benefit to the study of visual persuasion. It inveighs against a haphazard approach that would simple investigate a plethora of unrelated stylistic devices. It similarly protects one from a fruitless attempt to build a model of, say, visual metaphor from scratch. Instead, it argues that we already understand a great deal about visual metaphor, simply by apprehending it as the particular kind of rhetorical figure known as a complex trope (Forceville, 1995; Phillips, 1997). In turn, the virtue of this approach is that it frees the investigation to focus more tightly on the question of what difference it makes, if any, when a complex trope is presented in visual form.

The taxonomy as just set out has several additional advantages as we turn toward understanding visually expressed rhetorical figures. First, nothing about the conceptual apparatus used to construct the taxonomy is specifically linguistic. The semiotic and psychological concepts used can be applied to pictures as well as words. Pictures can incorporate artful deviance, and pictures can be simple or complex. Conversely, empirical studies of visual figures have much to offer as far as validation of the rhetorical and semiotic perspectives and the taxonomy itself is concerned. If the taxonomy can succeed in predicting empirical results obtained with visual as well as verbal figures, then its claim to be part of a general theory of rhetoric is strengthened. Furthermore, the claim of rhetoric itself to be a general theory of persuasion via stylistic variation is also supported. In that sense, the taxonomy, as an explanation, and visual figures, as a phenomenon requiring explanation, are mutually supportive.

A final virtue of the taxonomy is that it illustrates how text-centered and consumer psychological concepts, the ad system and the human system, can be fused into a single account. This is seen in ideas such as deviation, which links the semiotic notion of text marking to the psychological concept of incongruity. We firmly believe that both perspectives must be brought together if the scientific understanding of visual persuasion in advertising is to advance.

RHETORICAL FIGURES: PROCESSING AND OUTCOMES

The mutual articulation of the human system and the ad system requires that the taxonomy just presented be linked to consumer processing and related outcomes. The failure to make this link, in our view, has prevented text-centered approaches from receiving their due in consumer research. Without this link, conceptual frameworks like the taxonomy are difficult to evaluate—there is no ready means of determining whether any one framework is superior to another. However, once linked to processing outcomes, the taxonomy becomes testable. Experiments can be devised for determining whether rhetorical figures in advertising have the persuasive powers claimed. Similarly, visual figures may be empirically distinguished from verbal figures, as appropriate. We have investigated the properties of rhetorical figures, both visual as well as verbal, in a series of conceptual papers and experiments over the past dozen years (McQuarrie, 1989; Mick & Politi, 1989; McQuarrie & Mick, 1992, 1996, 1999), and this work is ongoing. In this section we lay out, in more detail than before, the consumer processing mechanisms and outcomes associated with rhetorical figures, and summarize some of the supporting evidence. A subsequent section looks at boundary conditions. Then, issues specific to visual figures will be examined. Throughout, avenues for future research will be indicated.

The impact of rhetorical figures can be discussed in terms of a series of processes and outcomes, with earlier outcomes and processes providing input to subsequent processes and outcomes. In our view, rhetorical figures can alter a consumer's initial encounter with an ad, shape that consumer's online response, and then affect the residue left by the ad encounter. As we show, some processes and outcomes are common across all figures, inasmuch as they derive from properties common to all. Other processes and outcomes vary by figurative mode. Finally, there may be additional outcomes that are specific to the four rhetorical operations, and perhaps even to specific named figures, but these are not addressed here. One caveat applies throughout this discussion: All of the assertions concern the hypothetical average instance of each type of figure (see the Boundary Conditions section for more on this point).

Attention

By attention we refer primarily to the *selection* of some particular ad or ad component for processing. The related idea of *degree* of attention, sometimes termed looking time, is a much more problematic notion, of uncertain value to the advertiser. That is, if one thinks of circumstances where looking time is prolonged, these are at least as likely to involve negative responses such as puzzlement or confusion (How do I make Excel calculate this value?) as to involve positive responses, as in the case of contemplation of a beautiful object. Hence, in retrospect it does not seem surprising that in one of our earliest experiments, using a relatively crude technique for assessing looking time (an event recorder), we found no difference in degree of attention paid to ads with or without a rhetorical figure (McQuarrie & Mick, 1992).

A stronger argument can be made in favor of rhetorical figures as a means of attracting attention—that is, causing the consumer selectively to attend. Under field exposure conditions, a consumer is free to attend to or ignore any ad (this is particularly true in the case of print media, which lack the intrusiveness of broadcast media). For an ad to be noticed, something must draw and at least minimally hold the consumer's attention. Here the motivational quality of rhetorical figures comes to the fore.

First, as incongruous stimuli, figures tend to motivate further processing; second, as pleasurable stimuli, figures also motivate processing. As an incongruity that requires resolution, any rhetorical figure offers a certain incremental boost to motivation, over and above whatever the ad achieves by being personally relevant or by using more raw forms of attention-getting design elements (bright colors, etc.). In addition, because rhetorical figures have been pleasurable to process in the past, and on the assumption that consumers are pleasure seekers, rhetorical figures beckon to consumers. Thus, the incongruity that underlies a rhetorical figure, plus the promise of the pleasure to be had from resolving this particular kind of incongruity, combine to provide the consumer with motivation to process. Moreover, and this may be among their most important advantages relative to other attention-getting devices, figures have a cognitive component—one cannot pleasurably resolve the incongruity without interpreting and arranging the set of meanings engendered by the signs displayed. If the figure has been properly chosen, these meanings will serve to enhance the brand. Hence, unlike some other attention-getting devices (e.g., humor), the risk of distraction—winning attention but squandering it on the wrong subject matter—may be noticeably less in the case of (well-conceived and well-constructed) figures.

The effect of rhetorical figures on consumer attention to an ad can be further differentiated by means of the scheme–trope distinction. Because tropes are undercoded, or incomplete, they draw attention and invite elaboration. Hence, the motivational argument introduced earlier applies particularly well to tropic figures. Deviation, and hence incongruity, is also greater in the case of tropes; thus, the pleasure of the text achieved during processing tends to be greater as well. The case for schemes is rather different. They benefit to a lesser degree from the property of deviation, in accordance with the lesser amounts of deviation present in the case of schemes. Rather, the benefit of schemes will lie in their robustness under conditions of minimal attention. By minimal attention, we mean that strictly speaking consumer attention to ads is not all or none, but a matter of thresholds. If an ad attracts enough processing from a consumer, that is, passes an initial threshold, we say that it has been attended to; as more resources are put into processing the ad, it becomes more convenient to talk about depth of processing rather than attention per se (Greenwald & Leavitt, 1984). Given this line of argument, there will be many cases where an ad is barely attended to—it has registered, the consumer did attend, but only barely. Here the overcoded and internally redundant character of schemes may offer an advantage.

Figure 11.2 may be useful in clarifying these points. The first thing to note is that with the possible exception of the effects hypothesized for tropes, the typical forced-exposure paradigm used in laboratory experiments on advertising does not provide a very suitable test of any of our contentions concerning rhetorical figures and attention. By definition, a paradigm that forces subjects to attend to ads cannot measure the impact of figures on attention. Assuming a design with unforced exposure, in terms of Fig. 11.2 the general prediction regarding rhetorical figures is that they facilitate the move from Zone 2, where attention is uncertain, to Zone 3, where the attention threshold has been securely crossed. The more specific prediction for schemes is that they help consumers surmount the Zone 3 threshold; to put it another way, schemes produce a pattern of results for Zone 2 consumers that approximate the pattern that normally only appears for an ad that has crossed the attention threshold and reached Zone 3. Thus, schemes *survive inattention*. In turn, the specific prediction for tropes is that they pull the consumer through Zone 3 toward Zone 4 and beyond. Thus, tropes *secure attention*.

This analysis also suggests a key factor that may moderate the overall impact of tropes versus schemes on ad effectiveness. It is important to keep in mind that the presence of a rhetorical figure is but one of many factors that contribute to an ad's effectiveness. Similarly, contextual factors independent of the ad's text may loom very large in determining the impact of a particular ad. It follows from the above that whether an ad achieves Zone 2, Zone 3, or Zone 4, and its rough position within those zones, may be fixed by other factors having nothing to do with rhetorical figures. Therefore, we predict a scheme–trope interaction such that schemes will be most effective for ads at the boundary between Zone 2 and Zone 3, whereas tropes are most effective for ads likely to achieve Zone 3. The liability of tropes is that their invitation to process can be refused, and may be most likely to be refused when processing resources are constrained or absent (as when an ad falls into

Zone 2, or is at the border of Zone 2 and Zone 3). Conversely, the liability of schemes is that their relatively small amount of deviation may lack the power to move a consumer into or within Zone 3; however, precisely because they require fewer processing resources, in being less deviant, they are more robust than tropes as the consumer falls toward to the bottom of Zone 3, or fails to quite surmount the Zone 2 to Zone 3 threshold.

Finally, this analysis has intriguing implications for comparisons of visual and verbal figures. To this point we have not been specific about where within an ad the rhetorical figure is located. It seems to us that figures that appear within the body copy of an ad are unlikely to have much of a measurable impact under any circumstances, and are certainly unlikely to affect attention, inasmuch as whether an ad will be attended to at all is probably determined before processing of the body copy begins. The remaining possibilities for figure placement are, one, locating it within the headline, subhead, or tagline, that is, presenting it in a large typeface prominently located within the ad, or two, making it part of the advertisement's visual element. We posit that if any part of an ad is going to achieve Zone 2 processing or above, it will be the visual element; more generally, when an ad only

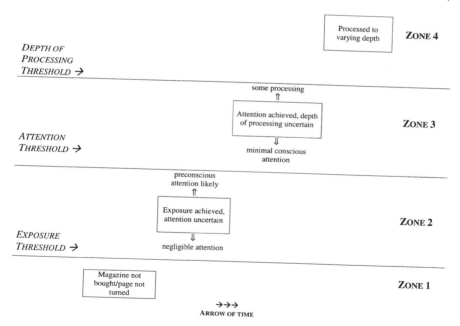

FIG. 11.2.   Stages of selective attention to rhetorical figures in advertising. *Note.* To be read from bottom left to upper right. Boxed text indicates four possible outcomes for processing of ads containing rhetorical figures. Processing may terminate at any point; there is no guarantee that a particular ad will surmount any of the thresholds shown.

achieves Zone 2 or Zone 3, the bulk of what is attended to will be the visual element—hence, the value of embedding a rhetorical figure in the picture of an ad.

Elaboration

Once a threshold of attention has been achieved, an ad may be processed at greater depth. For our purposes, deeper processing is synonymous with greater degree of elaboration. Because both constructs are widely used in the literature, with many shades of meaning, it is important to specify what is meant by *elaboration* and *depth of processing* in the present context. An ad is elaborated when it is linked to other cognitive structures or sign complexes already present in the mind of the consumer (cf. MacInnis & Price, 1987). The greater the number of these linkages, the more central the structures to which the ad is linked, and the larger and more complex these structures, the greater is the elaboration (cf. Mick, 1992).

There would appear to be two fundamental explanations for why elaboration might be greater in the case of a particular ad stimulus. Either there were aspects of the ad that forced elaboration, that is, guaranteed it or supplied it ready-made, or there were aspects that allowed, invited, or encouraged elaboration by the consumer. In the second case a host of contingencies will govern; that is, factors outside the ad, associated with the consumer or the exposure situation, may determine whether the invitation to elaborate is accepted and taken up, and to what degree.

The two routes to elaboration roughly align with the distinction between schemes and tropes. However, all rhetorical figures that receive attention, by the nature of the artful deviation that constitutes them, probably force some minimal degree of elaboration. It is the involuntary character of this elaboration that makes rhetorical figures so appealing to an advertiser who seeks to compel a response. Although all rhetorical figures have this property, the distinction between schemes and tropes is important and can be developed further in terms of its testable implications.

As noted earlier, the deviation that underlies a scheme is in part sensory, that is, the sound that echoes in a rhyme, or the contour that is repeated in a picture, or the physically identical words in a scheme of repetition (e.g., anaphora). A scheme contains its own links, and these links involve the sensory level. The claim that schemes supply a ready-made elaboration rests on two foundations. First, the impact of incongruity is essentially involuntary. The human system is designed, for sound evolutionary reasons, to respond to discrepancies. Second, a rhyme, if attended to at all, is unavoidable. The two words are linked by a common sound; once processed at all, that link exists. Because it is incongruous (excessively regular), the rhyme will be explored—there must be a reason these words are linked.

Now stepping back a little, by and large we are skeptical that the human system can be forced to do much or compelled to respond in any very specific way in the context of advertising. This suggests that schemes should have a robust but limited impact on elaboration: robust, because the involuntary character of the elaboration evoked by schemes indicates that there will be few contingencies that can disrupt or eliminate the effect (as long as attention has been achieved). Conversely, because of the sensory component, and because the deviation that constitutes a scheme tends to be less than in the case of tropes, elaboration, on average, *ceteris paribus*, will be less in the case of schemes as compared to tropes.

Complementary predictions can be made in the case of tropes. Greater deviation, hence greater incongruity, suggests greater elaboration. The more semantic nature of tropes similarly suggests an opportunity for greater depth of processing. More specifically, because tropes are, in a fundamental sense, incomplete, undercoded, or ill-specified, they require the cognitive participation of the consumer if they are to be meaningfully resolved. This is both a strength and a weakness from the perspective of advertising. The advantage of tropes is that the consumer can participate to almost any degree. Such participation may be powerfully persuasive, as the research on omitted conclusions and self-generated inferences attests. The disadvantage of tropes is that they are vulnerable to disruption by any number of contingencies. Factors specific to the consumer or to the exposure situation may forestall or inhibit the consumer's participation in resolving the trope. In sum, a trope carries the potential for a much greater impact on elaboration than a scheme. Simultaneously, a trope is much more vulnerable to the disruptive impact of contextual factors.

Study 1 in McQuarrie and Mick (1999), which used visual figures, provides supporting evidence for the proposed impact on elaboration. Here elaboration was measured by six 7-point semantic differential scales that tapped both discursive and imagistic elaboration (MacInnis & Price, 1987). Results showed that the presence of a figure led to increased elaboration. In nominal terms, the trope effect was larger than the scheme effect, but this finding did not achieve significance. Study 2 and Study 3 in that paper (discussed later) suggested that the trope effect had probably been disrupted by the inclusion of foreign-born students, who did not accept the invitation to elaborate, probably because they could not do so in view of their less developed semantic capacity (knowledge structures) for American advertising, relative to the U.S. students.

Ad Liking

As suggested earlier, every rhetorical figure that is successfully processed yields a quantum of pleasure. This pleasure in turn can be expected to produce a more positive attitude toward the ad. Before exploring the nature of the pleasure offered, it is important to examine the hedge in the first sentence just given. At the one extreme, if the rhetorical figure goes unnoticed because the ad is not attended, then of course no pleasure can result. At the other extreme, it is possible for a rhetorical figure to be excessively deviant. Incongruity, like many of the other arousal factors investigated by Berlyne (1971), has an impact that conforms to an inverted U pattern. In the present case, too small an incongruity (i.e., insufficient deviation) implies that no figure is present; too large an incongruity means that the figure will not be successfully resolved. That is, as deviation becomes more extreme, the probability of its being incomprehensible goes up accordingly, and there is nothing pleasurable about a message that defies comprehension—instead, frustration or irritation is likely. Experiment 2 in McQuarrie and Mick (1992) provides supporting evidence. Here we selected figures that would be difficult or impossible for most subjects to resolve. As predicted, the positive effect on ad liking otherwise obtained for figures disappeared.

Given a moderate degree of deviation, what is the nature of the pleasure produced by rhetorical figures in advertisements? Here the semiotic phrase "pleasure of the text" is evocative. The argument is simply that any sign structure that resists immediate decoding, while showing the way to its ultimate resolution, will be intrinsically pleasurable to process. Keep in mind that rhetorical figures are artful deviations, deviations with a purpose. The art lies in showing the way to resolution of the incongruity. The first source of the pleasure offered by rhetorical figures, then, is akin to the satisfaction experienced when one solves a puzzle. Per Berlyne (1971), apprehension of the incongruity creates arousal, which is then released once the resolution is found. This arousal–release sequence, of course, is a fundamental component of many pleasure experiences.

There is another source of the pleasure to be gained from rhetorical figures. Figures are artful, clever constructions. As with any art object, aesthetic appreciation may result. This pleasure is no different in kind from that received upon encountering a graceful old building, a lovely Impressionist painting, or a melody by Mozart.

To complete the link to consumer processing, the pleasure experienced on encountering and resolving an artful deviation should, *ceteris paribus*, produce a more positive attitude toward the ad (Aad). This finding has been robust across stimuli, subject populations, and studies. We demonstrated a positive Aad effect for one set of figures across two experiments conducted with student and with adult populations (McQuarrie & Mick, 1992). We demonstrated it again using a different set of stimuli, this time consisting of visual figures (McQuarrie & Mick, 1999).

It may also be the case that the pleasure associated with rhetorical figures can transfer to the brand, as shown in McQuarrie and Mick (1992). However, such brand attitude effects may only be a secondary result of the Aad effect just discussed. An autonomous effect of rhetorical figures on brand attitude has to be regarded as tentative at this point; it may be most likely when the figure incorporates a direct reference to the brand.

We have hypothesized that tropes will have a greater impact on Aad than schemes. Both types of figure generate pleasure by their artfulness. However, deviation or incongruity, and the potential pleasure from the resolution of same, should be greater in the case of tropes. The fundamentally semantic character of tropes also suggests that greater pleasure of the text can be expected.

The superiority of tropes demonstrated in McQuarrie and Mick (1999) was subject to an important contingency. We found that the figure effect, in the case of tropes, disappeared for foreign born subjects (most of whom grew up in Asian countries, at a considerable cultural distance from the world of American advertising). This finding harks back to the comments made earlier about the disruptibility of tropes. The elaboration occasioned by and the pleasure offered by tropic figures have the same source—the artful deviation that constitutes the figure. If elaboration does not occur, because the consumer was unable or unwilling to accept the invitation proffered by the trope, then pleasurable processing cannot result. It appears that the foreign-born students tended not to "get" the tropes, and hence did not experience the pleasure of resolving the incongruity. Follow-up interviews supported this explanation, laying bare the difficulties foreign-born students had as they attempted to engage the tropes.

As an aside, this finding supports a crucial point long championed by Scott (1994a), who argued that visual images are not automatically available and comprehensible to any human subject, but instead require the same sorts of learned, cultural competencies as any other text. This is tantamount to arguing that all visual images have semantic components and implications. Our claim to have manipulated and experimentally examined visual tropes rests on the same presupposition—that visual images have semantic components, which in turn can only be accessible to someone who has acquired the cultural competency in which these semantic components, as always, must be embedded.

Memory

Rhetorical figures should be more memorable than comparable text lacking figures. The argument is based again on the expected impact of the elaboration that results from encountering artful deviation. Greater elaboration means more mental connections, and more mental connections imply a higher probability of retrieval. In consequence, will there be a trope superiority effect for memory, as was the case for elaboration and pleasure? Insufficient evidence exists to give a ready answer. It is entirely possible that either tropes or schemes may have a superior impact on memory, depending on the kind of boundary conditions discussed in the next section. Tropes will be more effective under conditions that favor the extra elaboration occasioned by the undercoding characteristic of tropes; schemes will be more effective under conditions that favor the redundancy associated with the overcoded character of schemes.

GENERAL BOUNDARY CONDITIONS

In the preceding section we discussed processes and outcomes likely to follow from the inclusion of a rhetorical figure in an advertisement. These were derived from either the fundamental stimulus properties of figures, drawing on the psychology literature, or from the underlying sign structure, drawing on semiotics. Essentially we claimed that rhetorical figures make advertisements more effective across a broad front, gaining attention, inviting elaboration, producing pleasure, and leaving a stronger memory trace. The purpose of the current section is to examine the limits on this broad claim in a more systematic way, beyond the occasional contingency mentioned in passing.

The two fundamental limits or bounds that constrain assertions concerning the contribution of rhetorical figures to advertising effectiveness might be summed up as "*ceteris paribus*" and "on average." By *ceteris paribus,* we mean that the presence of a rhetorical figure is only one of countless factors contributing to the overall effectiveness of a given ad. In the laboratory it is possible to arrange pairs of stimuli that are virtually identical except for the presence or absence of a figure, and to demonstrate under controlled conditions the incremental effectiveness of the ads containing rhetorical figures. In the field, an ad with a rhetorical figure may fail terribly, whereas an ad lacking a figure succeeds brilliantly, due to other differences between the two ads, that is, better choice of key attribute, body copy that was more personally relevant, exposure conditions that were more favorable, and so on. Many factors determine ad effectiveness, and rhetorical figures, although almost always a candidate for consideration, are unlikely to be the most important determinant of success in most situations.

The second fundamental limit is particularly apropos to the assertions comparing schemes and tropes. All of these assertions should be read with the qualifier, "for the average or typical scheme (trope)." On average, tropes are more deviant than schemes; on average, schemes have more robust processing impacts. However, individual schemes (tropes) may be all over the map as far as deviation and robustness is concerned. Any specific scheme or trope used in empirical work can be regarded as a sample drawn from the population of schemes and tropes; hence, sampling variance is inevitable.

A limitation or constraint that is specific to comparisons of schemes and tropes might be stated as "the assumption of equivalent causal power." That is, whenever we have argued that schemes will have an advantage in one context, while tropes will have an advantage in another, we have necessarily assumed that the cognitive assist provided by the redundancy of schemes can have, in principle, an impact on ad processing that is equal to the motivational impact provided by the incongruity of tropes. Whether this kind of cognitive assist can be equated to that kind of motivational lure, in the context of ad processing, is an empirical question. If, instead, it is far more important that an ad be deviant than redundant, then empirical studies may show tropes to have an advantage over schemes across a much wider variety of situations, beyond the prototypical case where the consumer has ample processing resources available to elaborate upon the trope. This is a priority topic for future research into this level of the taxonomy.

A final caveat is that ad repetition may moderate many of the impacts suggested in this chapter; thus, the impact of a single exposure to an ad containing a rhetorical figure may not be the same as the impact after multiple exposures, and in turn, a moderate number of exposures may not produce the same impact as a heavy schedule of repetition (McQuarrie, 1998). This caveat is particularly apropos to comparisons of schemes and tropes. For instance, repetition may favor the cognitive assist provided by redundant schemes, even as it dulls the motivational allure provided by tropes, producing a reversal of effect sizes as compared to the single exposure case. To our knowledge, there have been no studies of the impact of rhetorical figures under varying schedules of repetition, and this is a promising avenue for future research.

Specific Contingencies Affecting Processing and Outcomes

We have argued overall that trope outcomes will be more subject to contingencies than scheme outcomes; however, even the robustness of schemes has its limits. Nonetheless, the contingencies discussed next are particularly pertinent to tropes. Following MacInnis, Moorman, and Jaworski (1991), Batra and Ray (1986), and others, these contingencies can be grouped according to whether they alter the consumer's *ability, opportunity,* or *motivation* to process an ad that contains a rhetorical figure. In some cases, empirical evidence exists to support the supposed contingency, as cited; in other cases, the argument is from plausibility.

Ability to Process. As shown in McQuarrie and Mick (1992), Experiment 2, tropes at least can be constructed to be so deviant as to defy the consumer's ability to process the meanings set in play. The latitude of acceptable deviation, however, may be quite wide; notably, in that study only one of our two attempts to design an excessively deviant trope succeeded.

Here it is worth emphasizing that there is nothing intrinsically difficult about rhetorical figures; that is, they are not intrinsically more effortful to process than comparable non-figurative texts. At least, the extra processing provoked or evoked by figures is not consciously experienced by subjects as an energic drain. This was demonstrated in McQuarrie and Mick (1999) using scale items anchored by "difficult" and "confusing." We found that the presence or absence of a figure had no effect on these measures. Part of the appeal of rhetorical figures, from the standpoint of advertisers, is that they can convey more information, or carry richer meanings, without any subjectively experienced costs. It can reasonably be argued that figures require incremental resources to process, but this line of argument properly falls under the heading of opportunity to process—a state variable quite different than the trait variable presupposed by "ability."

Perhaps the clearest example of a case where consumer processing ability served as a contingency concerns the results reported for foreign born subjects in McQuarrie and Mick (1999), Study 2. It appears that these individuals lacked the cultural competency to appreciate or engage in the pleasure of the text offered by the visual tropes in that experiment. In other words, a consumer must be equipped with a variety of socially and culturally conveyed understandings in order to effectively process a tropic figure. This finding may generalize to other cultural, subcultural, and social groupings. Thus, a rhetorical figure readily apprehended by a consumer who is an expert in a particular product category may be missed by a novice; a figure that works well with an educated segment may bomb with the merely literate; and a figure readily grasped by a frequent listener to hip-hop music may be opaque to a member of mainstream culture.

As noted earlier, foreign-born subjects in McQuarrie and Mick (1999) were more able to appreciate the visual schemes than the tropes. We would argue in general that the more limited the abilities of the consumer, the greater is the effectiveness of schemes relative to tropes, and also the greater is the probability that a trope will simply fail, even as a scheme continues to provide some incremental benefit.

Opportunity to Process.   These opportunities can be externally supplied, or may result from an internal predisposition of the consumer. Interestingly, the manipulations of externally driven opportunities most commonly seen in the literature *restrict* opportunity relative to some baseline or normal level (we are not aware of any manipulations in the consumer or marketing literatures that rest on a claim to have heightened or expanded opportunity). Examples of manipulations used to restrict opportunity include: (a) introduction of intrusive, distracting stimuli that compete for attention; (b) speeded up presentation rates and/or very constrained time allowances; or (c) instructions to concentrate on some task remote from the advertisement. Essentially, such manipulations reduce the probability that an ad or ad component will be attended to, or processed, or processed to any depth, by constricting the resources available to the consumer.

For these externally driven opportunity constraints, the general prediction is that rhetorical figures will survive moderate to moderately severe restrictions on the opportunity to process, provided they are prominently featured in the ad (dominant picture, larger type headlines, etc.). The reasoning is that incongruity compels attention, so that the probability that the rhetorical figure will garner some of the meager resources available is good. In addition, we would expect schemes to do better than tropes under opportunity constraints, in accordance with the general argument from robustness.

Greater opportunity to process an ad may also result from a predisposition toward processing certain kinds of stimuli, as captured by the term *propensity.* Thus, Childers et al. (1985) drew on the idea that there may be a propensity to process either visual or verbal stimuli to construct their Style of Processing (SOP) scale. If a consumer has a propensity to process certain kinds of stimuli, then ad components belonging to that stimulus class will have more opportunity to be processed. The SOP scale is clearly relevant to comparisons of visual and verbal rhetoric. (It has also been argued that there may be a propensity to process figurative language [see Yarbrough, 1991]; however, problems with the face validity of items in this scale have made us reluctant to use it.) Nonetheless, propensity effects may be easily drowned out by other factors. McQuarrie and Mick (1999), Study 2, examining visual figures, did not show any moderating effect for visual style of processing. This may be because the forced-exposure paradigm they used gave every subject plenty of opportunity to process the ads.

At some point, propensity to process shades into the desire or urge to process stimuli of a particular sort—that is, motivation to process. A construct that straddles this boundary is tolerance for ambiguity (TOA). This refers to the consumer's comfort with, and willingness to engage, ambiguous, contradictory, or uncertain situations where multiple interpretations are possible (Norton, 1975). Given the role that pleasure of the text plays in the proposed impact of rhetorical figures in advertising, early on TOA presented itself to us as a relevant individual difference variable, and we incorporated it in our initial experiments (McQuarrie & Mick, 1992). Surprisingly, TOA failed to emerge as a significant moderator in Experiment 1, perhaps due to the limited variation present in a homogeneous student population. A significant moderating effect did appear in Experiment 2, which involved a partial replication conducted with a more diverse adult population. The interaction was driven by the most deviant of the several kinds of tropes used in that study, indicating that TOA, for an individual consumer, may be predictive of the level of deviation beyond which incongruity becomes excessive and counterproductive. Although not yet empirically investigated, the results suggest that TOA is unlikely to moderate the impact of schemes, inasmuch as demonstration of an effect for TOA required particularly deviant examples of a kind of figure, the pun, that itself lies at the high end of the gradient of deviation.

Motivation to Process. Although figures in general, and tropes in particular, motivate additional processing, it still seems possible that some consumers will be more motivated to process figures in ads relative to other consumers. A good candidate for such a trait variable would appear to be need for cognition (Cacioppo, Petty, Feinstein, Jarvis, & Blair, 1996). The specific prediction concerns an interaction between mode of figuration (scheme vs. trope) and Need for Cognition (NCOG). That is, when NCOG is high, tropes should be particularly effective, relative to both schemes and nonfigurative controls. Because the pleasure of the text is greater in tropes, a consumer who delights in thinking might particularly appreciate the play of meanings set in motion by a trope.

The prediction just made is straightforward. Close examination of the items in the NCOG scale, however, suggests a very different argument, wherein NCOG would not moderate the impact of figures or of tropes and schemes. The reasoning is as follows. A number of items in the NCOG scale suggest a taste for mental challenge, a preference for effortful mental tasks, and a disinclination to be satisfied with simple, ready-made solutions. If this interpretation of the scale governs (i.e., it actually measures "taste for expenditure of mental effort"), then there should be no moderating effect on rhetorical figures in general, because figures do not require effortful processing. Empirical work will be required to determine which of these interpretations of Need for Cognition governs.

Summary. The contingencies just suggested are only a sampling from what is presumably a much larger set. Perhaps the most notable fact, however, is the relatively weak supporting evidence thus far available. Although many moderators can be imagined for rhetorical figures, it remains possible to maintain, given present evidence, that the impact of rhetorical figures in an ad on consumer processing is quite robust. If so, then although we may reasonably expect a variety of factors modestly to enhance or attenuate the impact of figures, we should not expect this impact to be eliminated under any but the most extreme circumstances.

If validated by future work—and it would take many years of effort to support the robustness claim, because it is ultimately an assertion of a negative proposition—the robustness of the figure effect would at least square with the prevalence of rhetorical figures in print advertising, as documented by Leigh (1994) and McQuarrie and Mick (1996). It is more parsimonious to suppose that a widely used device, with a 2,500-year pedigree, is robust in its impact, than to assert the contrary.

Of course, other explanations for the prevalence of rhetorical figures can be envisioned. Interestingly, however, none of the early theories of advertising response make any mention of rhetorical figures; in fact, stylistic device in general is notable by its absence. To compound the mystery, scholars outside of marketing and consumer research have been mining advertisements as a rich source of examples of rhetoric for decades (Corbett, 1990; Sheldon, 1956). We confront the enigma of a device that is widespread in actual advertisements, whose prevalence in advertising has long been noted in other scholarly disciplines, but that has been neglected for decades in the very discipline that is presumably most in search of theoretical explanations of advertising. How can this be?

Rhetorical Figures and Naturalistic Viewing Conditions

Three explanations can be adduced for this conundrum of long term theoretical neglect. First, mainstream theories of advertising response are heirs to the social psychological tradition in modern social science, as seen in the work of Hovland, Janis, and Kelley (1953) and others. This tradition in turn is very much a child of the Enlightenment, which in turn has always been hostile to anything rhetorical, as an insult to reason. As a consequence rhetoric, and stylistic device in general, is naturally thought of as mere embellishment, undeserving of theoretical attention (if noticed at all).

More subtly, mainstream work in advertising response tends to emphasize manipulations of the body copy in ad stimuli. It is the body copy that contains the strong or weak arguments, the important or unimportant brand attributes, and so forth. Body copy lends itself to rational argumentation, and is a natural focus for a tradition that was initially concerned with political discourse on major topics of the day. Unfortunately, stylistic devices are most commonly found in, and most potently enhance, the headline or picture in an advertisement. Hence, the first two explanations for the neglect of rhetorical figures, and of style per se, are one, that these irrational appeals are at variance with the intellectual tradition from which consumer research springs, and two, that style is most important with respect to two components of an advertisement that until recently were not the focus of either experimental manipulation or theoretical attention.

The third and somewhat more fundamental explanation is that rhetorical figures may represent an adaptation to an exposure condition rarely found in experimental work on advertising. We term this condition *unforced exposure,* and contrast it to both *forced exposure* and *forced nonexposure* paradigms. That is, the conventional laboratory advertising experiment, as is well known, forces exposure to advertising stimuli. Subjects are notified that they will be shown ads and asked to read them carefully; in fact, free-standing ads may be the only stimuli included in the experiment. Some years ago, when the concept of low-involvement consumer behavior was introduced, an alternative paradigm, forced nonexposure, came into vogue as the appropriate contrast to forced exposure conditions. In forced non-exposure, a subject is either motivated to ignore or dismiss ads (e.g., Petty et al., 1983), or subjected to a variety of distractions, or otherwise given little or no opportunity to process.

The problem with both of these conditions, as far as understanding advertising in the world is concerned, is their forced character. Conversely, the distinctive characteristic of mass-media advertising, relative to virtually any other category of persuasion or influence attempt, is that exposure and processing are at the option of the audience. Under conditions of unforced exposure, ads must simultaneously win attention, and be persuasive. Success at this dual task can be elusive, as research on the potentially distracting effect of humor has shown. That is, tactics capable of winning attention may be so distracting as to nullify persuasion, whereas tactics capable of effecting persuasion may be so boring that they cannot gain attention.

In short, we argue that rhetorical figures are prevalent in print advertising because they solve a problem specific to field conditions of advertising exposure, where attention is never guaranteed, and one and the same message must both gain attention and be persuasive. The artful deviation that constitutes a figure provides an efficient means of achieving both goals. The problem of unforced exposure is rarely faced in conventional advertising experiment designs, hence, the invisibility of this problem, in the eyes of mainstream theory, may explain the neglect of rhetorical figures, and of stylistic device generally.

VISUAL RHETORIC

The gist of much of this chapter has been that there is nothing special about the visual modality. Pictures can be signs, and semiotic theory explains the communicative function of pictures using the same constructs that explain the function of words. Pictures can take the form of rhetorical figures, and rhetoric explains the function of these figures using the same tools as for words. Last, pictures present many possibilities for stylistic variation, but so do words. In short, at the level of scientific theory, whether something is visual or verbal, pictorial or auditory, may be of little consequence. At the extreme, perhaps "visual" is only an Aristotelian category, a prescientific idea that, although intuitively clear, is not actually linked to distinct causal processes of the sort featured in scientific theory.

However, this complete reduction of the visual distinction to an epiphenomenon probably goes too far. It seems more likely that visual means of persuasion afford some opportunity, provide some advantage, or suffer from some constraint, even if these come only at the margin. Similarly, visual rhetoric may afford some opportunity or advantage, or suffer from some constraint, relative to verbal rhetoric. At least five such distinctive characteristics can be identified.

Visual Rhetoric Is More Tacit

All rhetorical figures benefit from their tacit character—figures are not the sort of direct assertions that stimulate counterargument. In fact, McQuarrie and Mick (1992) showed that ads with figures led to less counter-arguing relative to their controls. It seems to us that visual figures must be among the most tacit of all. The tacit quality of advertising visuals has been noted almost since the beginnings of advertising science early in the 20th century (Marchand, 1985). The tacit nature of visual assertions has advantages for the advertiser while posing complementary perils for public policy and regulation. For the advertiser, it appears that rhetorically structured visuals enable particularly stealthy persuasion attempts, which may be of interest when a plain or direct assertion would be rejected out of hand. For the regulator, operating under a legal framework rooted in the Enlightenment, and optimized for dealing with verbal statements, tacit visual persuasion poses knotty problems of detection and enforcement, as noted by Marchand (1985), Messaris (1992), Stern (1992), and others.

Visual Rhetoric Is Effected on Contact

Assume once more that naturalistic viewing conditions obtain. Now consider the typical magazine ad, containing picture, headline(s), body copy, and logo. On the further assumption that most ads encountered under these conditions receive only brief, cursory attention, and minimal processing, it seems likely that if anything will be processed in the ad, it will be the picture. To read and comprehend something, even a brief headline, requires more processing resources than a brief scene scan of the picture. Hence, visual persuasion generally, and visual rhetoric specifically, may be particularly effective, relative to verbal persuasion, under naturalistic viewing conditions.

Visual Rhetoric Enjoys Greater Prominence

To grasp the nature of this prominence, consider first the ratio of verbal content to pictorial content within the articles and other editorial content of a magazine, using a metric such as square inches of page coverage. This ratio will vary by publication, ranging from 1:1, or less, in the case of a magazine like *People*, to 2:1, or 5:1, or more, in the case of publications such as *Business Week* and *Atlantic Monthly*, where words predominate over illustrations. Now consider the same ratio in the case of the ads appearing in the magazine. Here the words-to-picture page coverage ratio will almost always be less than 1:1, and sometimes much less, on the order of 1:10, or even less, if fashion ads make up a large portion. Put another way, in ads, illustrations dominate. In fact, according to Pollay (1985), the word-to-picture ratio in ads grew steadily smaller over much of the 20th century.

Taking all four quantities into account, the following inequality should obtain in the case of most magazines.

$$\frac{\text{Ad pictures}}{\text{Total magazine pictures}} > \frac{\text{Ad words}}{\text{Total magazine words}}$$

This suggests that persuasion attempts made via pictures have less competition, as far as visual processing resources is concerned, relative to verbal persuasion attempts with respect to verbal processing resources. The typical magazine reader is exposed to a great deal of verbal material with which advertising verbals must compete. Ad pictures have much less competition from other pictures in the magazine. Once again, this disparity should be particularly important under naturalistic viewing conditions.

Visual Memory Is Stronger

Human memory for pictures, particularly recognition memory, is so strong that it poses real difficulties for experimentation, lest ceiling effects wipe out the differences of interest. Cluttered exposure environments, limits on opportunity to process, and delayed measurement are often used to manage the challenge of ceiling effects for memory of visual stimuli. The same characteristics, of course, are typical of naturalistic viewing conditions. Under these conditions, the greater memorability of ad visuals acts to accentuate the other advantages of tacit quality, immediacy, and prominence.

Visual Messages Are More Difficult To Craft

The implicit assertion of this chapter, that ad visuals are highly meaningful to consumers, does not imply that these meanings are all or mostly under the control of the advertiser, or that pictorial meanings can be easily devised or shaped to meet the needs of a particular marketing strategy. There are good reasons why alphabets and ideographs replaced pictographs! No other modality can match the semantic fluency or protean quality of words. Despite all the advantages of visual persuasion just discussed, in many concrete advertising situations it may be difficult or impossible to craft the desired message in a pictorial format.

Summary

On balance, we are skeptical that attempts to distinguish visual persuasion as a separate category of persuasion rest on much more than an intuitively appealing Aristotelian categorization, convenient for quick communication but not particularly fruitful for building a scientific theory. However, as described earlier, it certainly seems to be the case that ad visuals in general, and visual rhetoric in particular, will be subject to a somewhat different set of contingencies with respect to ad effectiveness. Most notably, these contingencies loom largest under naturalistic viewing conditions, testifying again to the dangers of adapting, without scrutiny and reflection, experimental traditions inherited from academic social psychology. Advertising science has different needs and may require a distinct kind of experimental procedure (McQuarrie, 1998).

CONCLUSION

We have described how a combination of semiotics and rhetoric can serve to build a general theory of persuasion able to address visual as well as verbal modalities. The distinctive advantage of a semiotic, rhetorical approach is the analytic tools it provides for identifying and explaining the impact of stylistic variation in advertising. The specific focus of our work has been on the rhetorical figure, a stylistic device that lends itself to conceptual and causal analysis. We have developed a taxonomy of rhetorical figures that brings order to what had been an amorphous catalog accumulated over centuries (McQuarrie & Mick, 1996). The taxonomy links semiotic and rhetorical ideas (e.g., deviation) to psychological constructs (e.g., incongruity). The taxonomy also generates testable causal hypotheses linking different properties of rhetorical figures (e.g., over- and undercoding) to important consumer processes and outcomes (e.g., elaboration, ad liking). Empirical studies over the years have demonstrated that: (a) ordinary consumers notice and reproduce the distinctions underlying the taxonomy (McQuarrie & Mick, 1996); (b) rhetorical figures lead to increased elaboration, more positive Aad, and better memory (McQuarrie & Mick, 1992, 1999); and (c) visual rhetorical figures appear to have the same sorts of impact on consumers as predicted for rhetorical figures in general (McQuarrie & Mick, 1999).

This chapter afforded an opportunity to further develop and go into more detail concerning the specific consumer processes and outcomes to be expected from an encounter with rhetorical figures. We particularly distinguished the impact to be expected from schematic versus tropic figures. In addition, we discussed a wide range of contingencies that might accentuate or diminish the processes and outcomes to be expected from these different figures. Here, naturalistic viewing conditions emerged as a key factor in explaining why rhetorical figures are so prevalent in print advertising. Finally, we articulated the specific advantages, opportunities, and constraints posed by visual rhetorical figures.

As awareness of the analytic power and generative possibilities of semiotics and rhetoric diffuse more widely, we hope they will be applied to yet other aspects of advertising style, especially visual style. The ultimate goal of any such application should be to integrate the ad system with the human system, so as to articulate causal hypotheses that connect text properties to consumer processes and outcomes.

REFERENCES

Anand, P., & Sternthal, B. (1990). Ease of message processing as a moderator of repetition effects in advertising. *Journal of Marketing Research, 27*, 345–353.

Assael, H., Kofron, J., & Burgi, W. (1967). Advertising performance as a function of print ad characteristics. *Journal of Advertising Research, 7*, 20–26.

Barthes, R. (1985). The rhetoric of the image. *The responsibility of forms* (pp. 21–40). New York: Hill and Wang.

Batra, R., & Ray, M. L. (1986). Situational effects of advertising repetition: The moderating influence of motivation, ability, and opportunity to respond. *Journal of Consumer Research, 12*, 432–445.

Bender, J., & Wellbery, D. E. (1990). Rhetoricality: On the modernist return of rhetoric. In J. Bender & D. E. Wellbery (Eds.), *The ends of rhetoric: History, theory, practice* (pp. 3–39). Stanford, CA: Stanford University Press.

Berlyne, D. E. (1971). *Aesthetics and psychobiology.* New York: Appleton-Century-Crofts.

Burke, K. (1950). *A rhetoric of motives.* Englewood Cliffs, NJ: Prentice Hall.

Cacioppo, J. T., Petty, R. E., Feinstein, J. A., Jarvis, W., & Blair, G. (1996). Dispositional differences in cognitive motivation: The life and times of individuals varying in need for cognition. *Psychological Bulletin, 119*, 197–253.

Childers, J. L., & Houston, M. J. (1984). Conditions for a picture superiority effect on consumer memory. *Journal of Consumer Research, 11*, 643–654.

Childers, J. L., Houston, M. J., & Heckler, S. E. (1985). Measurement of individual differences in visual versus verbal information processing. *Journal of Consumer Research, 12*, 125–134.

Corbett, E. P. J. (1990). *Classical rhetoric for the modern student.* New York: Oxford University Press.

Dubois, J., Edeline, F., Klinkenberg, J. M.., Minguet, P., Pire, F., & Trinon, H. (1970). *A general rhetoric.* Baltimore, MD: Johns Hopkins University Press.

Durand, J. (1987). Rhetorical figures in the advertising image. In J. Umiker-Sebeok (Ed.), *Marketing and semiotics: New directions in the study of signs for sale* (pp. 295–318). New York: Mouton.

Eco, U. (1976). *A theory of semiotics.* Bloomington: Indiana University Press.

Eco, U. (1979). *The role of the reader.* Bloomington: Indiana University Press.

Forceville, C. (1995). IBM is a tuning fork: Degrees of freedom in the interpretation of pictorial metaphors. *Poetics, 23*, 189–218.

Greenberg, A., & Garfinkle, N. (1963). Visual material and recall of magazine articles. *Journal of Advertising Research, 3*, 30–34.

Greenwald, A. G., & Leavitt, C. (1984). Audience involvement in advertising: Four levels. *Journal of Consumer Research, 11,* 581–592.

Hovland, C. I., Janis, I. L., & Kelley, H. H. (1953). *Communication and persuasion: Psychological studies of opinion change.* New Haven, CT: Yale University Press.

Jakobson, R. (1971). Language in relation to other communication systems. In R. Jakobson (Ed.), *Selected writings* (vol. 2, pp. 570–579). Mouton: The Hague.

Leigh, J. H. (1994). The use of figures of speech in print ad headlines. *Journal of Advertising, 23,* 17–34.

MacInnis, D. J., Moorman, C., & Jaworski, B. J. (1991). Enhancing and measuring consumers' motivation, opportunity and ability to process brand information from ads. *Journal of Marketing, 55,* 32–53.

MacInnis, D. J., & Price, L. L. (1987). The role of imagery in information processing: Review and extensions. *Journal of Consumer Research, 13,* 473–491.

Maheswaran, D., & Chaiken, S. (1991). Promoting systematic processing in low motivation settings: Effect of incongruent information on processing and judgment. *Journal of Personality and Social Psychology, 61,* 13–25.

Marchand, R. (1985). *Advertising the American dream: Making way for modernity, 1920–1940.* Berkeley: University of California Press.

McGuire, W. J. (2000). Standing on the shoulders of ancients: Consumer research, persuasion, and figurative language. *Journal of Consumer Research, 27,* 109–114.

McQuarrie, E. F. (1989). Advertising resonance: A semiological perspective. In E. C. Hirschman (Ed.), *Interpretive consumer research* (pp. 97–114). Provo, UT: Association for Consumer Research.

McQuarrie, E. F. (1998). Have laboratory experiments become detached from advertiser goals? A meta-analysis. *Journal of Advertising Research, 38,* 15–26.

McQuarrie, E. F., & Mick, D. G. (1992). On resonance: A critical pluralistic inquiry into advertising rhetoric. *Journal of Consumer Research, 19,* 180–197.

McQuarrie, E. F., & Mick, D. G. (1996). Figures of rhetoric in advertising language. *Journal of Consumer Research, 22,* 424–437.

McQuarrie, E. F., & Mick, D. G. (1999). Visual rhetoric in advertising: Text-interpretive, experimental, and reader-response analyses. *Journal of Consumer Research, 26,* 37–54.

Messaris, P. (1992). Visual "manipulation": Visual means of affecting responses to images. *Communication, 13,* 181–195.

Meyers-Levy, J., & Peracchio, L. A. (1992). Getting an angle in advertising: The effect of camera angle on product evaluations. *Journal of Marketing Research, 29,* 454–461.

Meyers-Levy, J., & Peracchio, L. A. (1995). Understanding the effects of color: How the correspondence between available and required resources affects attitudes. *Journal of Consumer Research, 22,* 121–138.

Meyers-Levy, J., & Peracchio, L. A. (1996). Moderators of the impact of self-reference on persuasion. *Journal of Consumer Research, 22,* 408–423.

Mick, D. G. (1986). Consumer research and semiotics: Exploring the morphology of signs, symbols and significance. *Journal of Consumer Research, 13,* 196–214.

Mick, D. G. (1992). Levels of subjective comprehension in advertising processing and their relations to ad perceptions, attitudes, and memory. *Journal of Consumer Research, 18,* 411–424.

Mick, D. G., & Politi, L. G. (1989). Consumers' interpretations of advertising imagery: A visit to the hell of connotation. In E. C. Hirschman (Ed.), *Interpretive consumer research* (pp. 85–96) Provo, UT: Association for Consumer Research.

Miniard, P. W., Bhatla, S., Lord, K. R., Dickson, P. R., & Unnava, H. R. (1991). Picture-based persuasion processes and the moderating role of involvement. *Journal of Consumer Research, 18,* 92–107.

Mitchell, A. A., & Olson, J. C. (1981). Are product attribute beliefs the only mediator of advertising effects on brand attitude? *Journal of Marketing Research, 18,* 318–322.

Motes, W. H., Hilton, C. B., & Fielden, J. S. (1992). Language, sentence, and structural variations in print advertising. *Journal of Advertising Research, 32*(5), 63.

Mukarovsky, J. (1964). Standard language and poetic language. In P. L. Garvin (Ed.), *A Prague School reader on esthetics, literary structure, and style* (pp. 17–30). Washington, DC: Georgetown University Press.

Norton, R. W. (1975). Measurement of ambiguity tolerance. *Journal of Personality Assessment, 39*(6), 607–619.

Peracchio, L., & Meyers-Levy, J. (1994). How ambiguous cropped objects in ad photos can affect product evaluations. *Journal of Consumer Research, 21,* 190–204.

Peter, J. P., & Olson, J. C. (1983). Is science marketing? *Journal of Marketing, 47*(4), 111–125.

Petty, R. E., Cacioppo, J. T., & Schumann, D. (1983). Central and peripheral routes to advertising effectiveness: The moderating role of involvement. *Journal of Consumer Research, 10,* 135–146.

Phillips, B. J. (1997). Thinking into it: Consumer interpretations of complex advertising images. *Journal of Advertising, 26*(2), 77–86.

Pollay, R. W. (1985). The subsidizing sizzle: A descriptive history of print advertising, 1900–1980. *Journal of Marketing, 48,* 24–37.

Scott, L. M. (1994a). Images in advertising: The need for a theory of visual rhetoric. *Journal of Consumer Research, 21,* 252–273.

Scott, L. M. (1994b). The bridge from text to mind: Adapting reader response theory to consumer research. *Journal of Consumer Research, 21,* 461–480.

Sheldon, E. K. (1956). Some pun among the hucksters. *American Speech, 31,* 13–20.

Sperber, D., & Wilson, D. (1986). *Relevance: Communication and cognition.* Cambridge, MA: Harvard University Press.

Sperber, D., & Wilson, D. (1990). Rhetoric and relevance. In J. Bender & D. E. Wellbery (Eds.), *The ends of rhetoric: History, theory, practice* (pp. 140–155). Stanford, CA: Stanford University Press.

Stern, B. (1992). "Crafty advertisers": Literal versus literary deceptiveness. *Journal of Public Policy and Marketing, 11*(1), 72–81.

Yarbrough, D. B. (1991). The reliability and validity of a measure of reported affinity for figurative language. *Creativity Research Journal, 4*(4), 317–335.

CHAPTER TWELVE

Invoking the Rhetorical Power of Character to Create Identifications

Michael S. Mulvey
Carmen Medina
Rutgers, the State University of New Jersey

His character may almost be called the most effective means of persuasion he possesses. (Aristotle, *Rhetoric*, I.2.1356.10)

Advertisers use numerous tactics to gain advantage through their communications. Perhaps the most popular is the strategic use of characters; myriads of ads use characters to deliver the persuasive message. Characters are cast in a variety of roles including the narrator who reports information, the witness who testifies personal experience, and the performer who acts in a dramatic play. Clearly, advertisers recognize the ability of characters to produce a major portion of the meaning conveyed in communication.

Scholars working on the consumer response to advertising, however, have not yet tested this assumption by means of empirical research, although several have hypothesized the ways readers interpret and respond to character (McCracken, 1989; Scott, 1991, 1994a, 1994b; Stern, 1988, 1991, 1994). The objective of this research, therefore, is to take Aristotle's concept of "character" to the workbench, using reader-response data to test its persuasive powers. Bringing to the question a key concept of Kenneth Burke's 20th-century approach to rhetoric, we then look at how (and whether) viewers form "identifications" with advertising characters (Burke, 1969). Our focus ultimately is on how consumers "make sense" of ads showing diverse types of characters. The investigation analyzes the formal properties of the ads and pays heed to the cultural and historical context within which consumers' interpretations are formed. Our goal is to enrich our understanding of the role of character in advertising and the process of identification by studying actual consumers.

CONVEYING CHARACTER

Characters in advertising convey their message to the audience using an extensive array of persuasive devices including speech, tonality, and gesture. The way characters speak contributes greatly to the depiction of an easily recognizable human type (Esslin, 1979). For instance, consider how characters' ways of speaking often correspond to distinctions of age (child or elderly), emotional state (happy or angry), outlook (optimistic or pessimistic), or demeanor (nervous or confident). The advertising genre requires typecasting to communicate swiftly (30 s for most TV commercials) and clearly to ensure that audience interpretations are largely shared. The characters' actions and appearance (clothing, grooming, possessions), the setting of the action, and the system of visual cues (typeface, motion, colors) and sound cues (music, sound effects) also contribute to the characterization to produce a persuasive communication designed to elicit a particular response from an audience.

The characters in ads take many forms. Because ads must communicate swiftly and unambiguously, they often contain fictional characters drawn from easily recognized human/mythic types (Dyer, 1982; Esslin, 1979) or celebrities who are potent sources of cultural meanings (McCracken, 1989; Scott, 1991). Firms also create trade characters—animate persons (Betty Crocker, Marlboro cowboy) or animated beings (Jolly Green Giant, Mr. Clean)—to give meaning to the brand (Phillips, 1996b). Even animals (Joe Camel, Tony the Tiger) may assume human qualities and function as characters in advertising (Phillips, 1996a). Characters give voice to the product and are capable of transferring complex bundles of meaning to consumers (McCracken, 1989). Advertisers strive to match qualities of the product to the character. Hence, the casting of characters is rarely accidental: it is scripted.

The process of "delivering" meanings to the consumer consists of an elaborate series of choices (Dyer, 1982, McCracken, 1989). Once the message strategy has been clearly specified, the creative director combines words, sounds, images, and motion to craft an execution that is capable of transmitting the idea clearly, quickly, and economically (O'Toole, 1985). Most ads combine telling (verbal elements) with showing (visual elements) to make claims about what the product can do and how the consumer should feel (Deighton & Hoch, 1993). When advertisers include characters in the ad, they must make choices regarding the actors' appearance (age, gender, national and racial, hair, body, size, looks), manner (facial expression, eye contact, pose, clothes), quality of voice (tone, rhythm, words used), and the activities they're engaged in (touch, body movements, positional communication). Of course, the creative strategy must adapt to the sensory characteristics (sight, sound, smell, feel) of the medium (print, radio, TV, web).

READING AND RESPONDING TO CHARACTER

The topic of impression formation—how people integrate and combine information about other people—has been studied by the likes of Asch, Kelly, and Rosenberg. Social psychologists and anthropologists concur that character is revealed by what one says, and how one says it. In fact, all actions—both verbal and nonverbal—are evidence of the doer's character. Few researchers have formally examined the process of how consumers assign meaning to the behaviors observed in ads. By behavior, we are referring to observable events (e.g., smiling, screaming) as well as unobservable events (e.g., thinking, feeling), and intentional events (e.g., studying, imagining) as well as unintentional events (snoring, worrying). People can derive meaning from all of these events by "drawing on knowledge of human motivation and emotion, mapping it onto the events of the story" (Deighton & Hoch, 1993, p. 10).

Characters' emotional profiles tell us much about the consumption experience. The vivid imagery in TV commercials relies heavily on nonverbal cues to represent the sensory pleasure, cognitive stimulation, and emotional payoffs derived from consuming the product. Reading an ad requires imaginative thought; it is an active creative process that calls on consumers to construct meaning from the ad through the act of interpretation (McCracken, 1987; Scott, 1994a). Comprehension of the ad fiction involves finding answers to such questions as: What do the characters feel? Why do they have these feelings? Were the characters predisposed to these feelings, or are they the result of external causes? Surprisingly little research has studied the process of how people make causal inferences in viewing commercials, despite Stern's (1994) appeal for research in this area.

The persuasiveness of an ad message may be enhanced by encouraging consumers to identify with one or several of the characters in an ad: "You can persuade a man only insofar as you can talk his language by speech, gesture, tonality, order, image, attitude, idea, *identifying* your ways with his" (Burke, 1969, p. 55, italics in original). In other words, the advertiser can make a message more persuasive by casting characters that display qualities of the target consumers. Identification may be established by communicating common interests, opinions, values, goals and other personal characteristics (Burke, 1969). Kover (1995) offered evidence that copywriters implicitly heed this theory. In many agencies, copywriters are given a creative brief that includes a description of the target consumer (Wansink, 1987). Copywriters use this information to craft a message to "mesh with viewers' lives and needs," to "connect with the other," and to "strike an appropriate emotional chord" (Kover, 1995, pp. 601–602). Character identification has been hypothesized to generate empathy with characters and to encourage vicarious participation in the characters' experiences (Stern, 1988). In this chapter, we explore the rhetorical power of identification by examining how consumers perceive similarities (and differences) between aspects of their own self-identity and those depicted by characters in ads.

POSSIBLE DIFFERENCES IN CHARACTER ASSESSMENT

To produce an effective communication, advertisers must understand that "the same rhetorical act could vary in effectiveness, according to shifts in the situation or in the attitudes of audiences" (Burke, 1969, p. 62). First, cultural conventions prescribe appropriate behavior in the consumption context of interest. Consider the act of "demonstrating appreciation" at the opera compared to at a professional wrestling match. Although it is perfectly normal to hoot, holler, and shout approval at the wrestling match, the same behavior would be scorned at an operatic performance. Conversely, it would be equally strange to clap politely and exclaim "bravo!" ringside as the grapplers tussle. Models of advertising must incorporate the role of the broader cultural context within which advertising characters perform and viewers' impressions are formed (McCracken, 1989; Scott, 1994b).

Second, audiences differ in their experiences and understandings and these differences may affect their ability to assign a common meaning to a sign (Mick & Buhl, 1992). People who have been acculturated in similar social conditions and relations (e.g., collectivities based on gender, class, race/ethnicity, generation, occupation) or who share a dominant interactional community (e.g., subcultural groups such as those described by Hebdige, 1979) often derive similar interpretations of advertisements (Grier & Brumbaugh, 1999; Holt & Mulvey, 2000). As a result, members of the target audience may differ from non-target consumers in the meanings they attribute to characters in advertisements. For instance, the meanings of an ad message delivered by Wayne Gretzky (regarded by many as the greatest hockey player of all time) would likely be moderated by audience characteristics including their level of enthusiasm for the sport, nationality, and media exposure. The words of novelist Anaïs Nin ring true: "We don't see things as they are, we see them as we are." Nonetheless, divergent assessments of character may emerge from individuals within a group due to the diversity of personal understandings and experiences. For instance, membership in multiple communities may increase a person's repertoire of interpretations (Scott, 1994a). Also, members of a target audience may generate idiosyncratic meanings that diverge from the norm (see Mick & Politi's 1989 discussion of the "hell of connotation"). Ultimately, the effectiveness of a persuasive attempt delivered by a character is an empirical issue—one that can only be resolved by studying consumers' reactions to the communication.

AN INVESTIGATION INTO THE PROCESS
OF CHARACTER IDENTIFICATION

To illustrate and explore the concept of character identification, we conducted an empirical study designed to answer the following questions:

1. Are consumers able to name the feelings and emotions that imply character?
2. How do consumers' assessments of character enhance or detract from the "main point" of the persuasive message?
3. In what ways do the characters in ads encourage identification?

The cast of characters appearing in advertisements is huge, appearing in ads for all sorts of goods and services. Different kinds of characters may portray different kinds of experience within a product category. This study focuses on a single industry: online stock trading. By confining our scope to one industry we create an opportunity to compare consumers' reactions to a variety of characters that promote the practice of online trading. In the following sections we give details of the online trading phenomenon, describe the sample of respondents, explain the selection of the ads used in the study, and review the data collection and analysis procedures.

Setting the Historical Context

Do-it-yourself (D-I-Y) trading has arrived. With a simple click of the mouse, ordinary consumers can become self-directed investors. Technological innovations have reduced the costs of trading, increased access to information, and simplified the process of making trades by eliminating the need to consult a stockbroker. The dream of trading stocks in the comfort of one's home has become a reality for the average consumer. The surge in popularity of personal investing in our culture is reflected and shaped by the media on new financial networks (CNNfn, CNBC) and programming (MarketWatch, Money Talks, Your Money), in magazines (Kiplinger's, Money, Worth), and on web sites (Fool.com, TheStreet.com). D-I-Y investors have plenty of role models they call look up to for advice and inspiration: business tycoons like Warren Buffett and Peter Lynch, Wall Street gurus, and financial journalists, not to mention the multitude of characters that populate online brokerage advertising. In 1999, the industry spent a reported $1.2 billion on advertising to spread news of the virtues of online trading (Vickers & Weiss, 2000). Few persons could escape the buzz of the online trading revolution.

The data analyzed in for this study was collected during the longest bull market run in history. The fall of 1999 was a period of unprecedented growth, especially in the technology sector where the value of the NASDAQ doubled in less than a year. Recent stock market gains by the investing public were well publicized in the media prompting legions of consumers to seek their fortune by trading online. The SEC Chairman at the time, Arthur Levitt (1999, para. 7), remarked: "In 1994, not one person traded over the Internet. In the next few years, the number of online brokerage accounts will roughly equal the metropolitan populations of Seattle, San Francisco, Boston, Denver, Miami, Atlanta and Chicago, combined." Thus, in the present study, consumers' interpretations of the ad characters were formed in the historical context of a bullish socioeconomic environment that motivated millions of people to become D-I-Y investors.

Respondents

Fifty-three undergraduate business students participated in the study. We do not suggest that our respondents are representative of the target markets for the advertised firms; hence the results have little bearing on the commercials' effectiveness in the marketplace. What the study provides is a glimpse into the processes of character assessment and identification. We thought the participants would serve as a reasonable proxy for consumers who are predisposed to investing. First, we expected that business students would exhibit a greater interest in finance than their peers (nonbusiness students or nonstudents). Second, half of the sample consisted of finance majors enrolled in a program with a reputation for placing graduates on Wall Street. Results of the questionnaire confirmed the respondents' predisposition toward investing. More than 10% of respondents currently used, or had used online brokerage services. The choice of a full-service broker or on-line broker was viewed as a high-involvement decision (Foote, Cone, & Belding Involvement Subscale scores of 5.90 and 5.14 on a 7-point scale). Finally, our respondents perceived the activity of investing as important and interesting (90% of respondents scored greater than 50 out of 70 points using the Revised Personal Involvement Inventory; McQuarrie & Munson, 1991).

Selection of TV Commercials

Within a product category, the characters appearing in ads function as role models from whom consumers learn the motives and methods of engaging in consumption-related activity. We chose three TV commercials as case studies. The selection of ads used in the study was based on the goal of maximizing the diversity of character types. Points of difference between characters included: the firms they represented (Ameritrade, Suretrade, DLJdirect), age (20s, 30s, and 55+), mode of communication (performance, testimonial, lecture), dress and appearance (punk, casual, business), and ostensible level of experience (low, moderate, high). Most importantly, the characters appeared to have distinct personalities that affected the way they delivered their message. Together, the characters possess numerous qualities to establish potential identifications with viewers. Next we review the content and formal properties of the ads. Photoboards of the ads are reproduced in Fig. 12.1.

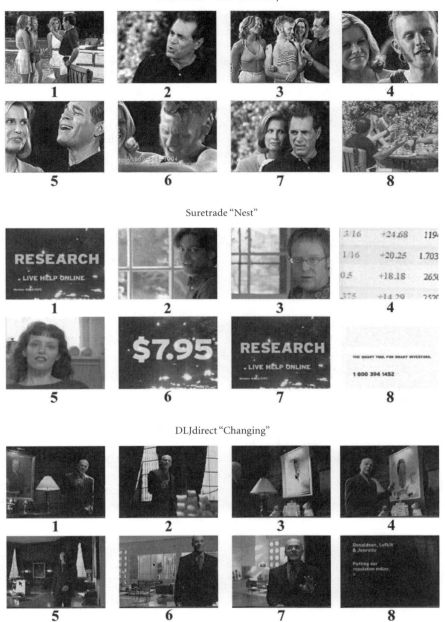

FIG. 12.1.   TV commercial photoboards.

Case 1: Ameritrade "Family." This commercial presents a variation on the classic "meet the parents" plotline by telling the story of Stuart, a young online trader who joins his girlfriend's family for dinner for the first time. The scene unfolds poolside on a patio in the backyard of a large mansion. Cinematographic techniques of camera angle, cropping, and motion create the perspective of participant-observer, drawing the viewer into the scene to feel as if he or she is a guest at the family gathering. The soundtrack includes background sounds of birds chirping and wind blowing in background to highlight the outdoor setting. Sounds of barking dogs metaphorically signal Stuart's arrival into potentially hostile territory. To most people, the prospect of making a good first impression with a romantic partner's parents is a precarious situation, even at the best of times. However, Stuart—the energetic, orange-haired punked-out protagonist—does not appear daunted by the task. The script of the dialogue follows:

Carol the Maid:	Pssst . . .
Girlfriend:	Daddy, Stuart's here!
Stuart:	G-mornin'!
Carol the Maid:	Little freak.
Girlfriend:	Mom, Dad, this is Stuart.
Girlfriend's Mother:	Oh, so you're Stuart.
Girlfriend:	Oh Dad you guys have so much in common!
Girlfriend's Father:	OK. Stuart, what are your plans for the future?
Stuart:	Well, I wouldn't mind livin' here.
Girlfriend's Father:	[laughs politely] No, what's your passion Stuart?
Stuart:	I like to trade online.
Girlfriend's Father:	Oh online trading. [aside to his wife] It's only a fad.
Stuart:	Have you ever heard of Ameritrade?
Girlfriend's Father:	I'm a stockbroker, son.
Girlfriend:	Dad, he only pays eight dollars per trade.
Girlfriend's Father:	You know, you give a kid a computer and he thinks he can beat the market.
Girlfriend's Mother:	Oh dear!
Stuart:	I don't want to beat the market. I want to grab it, sock it in the gut a couple of times, turn it upside down, hold it by pants, shake 'em out 'til all those pockets empty out . . . all of that spare change and then grab it for me! [pause] Let's eat.
Girlfriend:	I want to have his baby!
Narrator:	[jingle of drums, bass and xylophone herald the narrator's call] Call toll-free 1–888–345–7004. Ameritrade. Believe in yourself.
Carol the Maid:	[to Stuart] Well, what do you think about utilities?
Girlfriend's Father:	Carol!

To understand this drama, we, as readers, are expected to recognize the irony of the situation. The use of irony by the advertiser implies that the ad message can mean two things, its apparent meaning and the exact opposite. For instance, when the father asks, "What are your plans for the future?" Stuart replies, "I wouldn't mind livin' here." This answer can be taken in two ways. First, Stuart is a slacker who would like to freeload off his girlfriend's parents. Second, the remark signals Stuart's ambition to live in a mansion like the father's in the future. Several visual and verbal cues work to move the reader to adopt the more positive impression of Stuart. Most significantly, Stuart's punk hairdo, tattoos, and clothing signal his membership in youth counterculture (according to the maid, he looks like a "little freak"). The "us versus them" plotline is a timeless tale of young adults having difficulty earning the respect of their elders. However, unlike James Dean, Stuart is a modern-day rebel with a cause whose goals are clear. Stuart's youthful approach to investing epitomizes the enthusiasm and ambition of the "new generation" of D-I-Y online investors. Yet these ways appear strange to the father, who belongs to the "old generation" of traditional full-service brokers. Thus, successful reading of this ironic ad requires the reader to disregard elements of the literal truth in favor of the figurative truth, making it possible for readers to support the underdog's pursuit of the American Dream.

Case 2: Suretrade "Nest."   This commercial consists of a montage of video clips lasting no longer than 3 s each. This rapid-fire style of editing is reminiscent of music videos, a genre renowned for infusing viewers with copious doses of visual and aural stimulation. The flow of the ad oscillates back and forth between brief customer testimonials and visual images that echo the users' sentiments. For example, the ad opens with an image of a mother bird bringing a worm to the nest of chicks followed by a woman stating: "We're not relying on the government." The customer scenes take place in home offices with the characters seated at their computers. The message is clear: You can invest in the comfort of your own home. The up-tempo synthesized soundtrack repeats several times, adding a new instrument with each repetition. The rhythm builds and repeats to symbolize the legions of individuals that constitute the growing community of Suretrade users (the "we" referred to by the characters in the ad). The interplay between visual images and dialogue unfolds as follows:

Image:	[photo: bird feeding a worm to chicks in nest]
Woman1:	We're not relying on the government.
Image:	[photo: individuals executing trades online]
Man1:	We're not relying on the company.
Image:	[photo: empty boardroom table]
Man2:	We're not relying on a big fat inheritance.
Image:	[photo: elderly man standing next to an enormous ball of string]
Man3:	We trade online.
Image:	[photo: hands typing at computer]
Woman2:	We're betting on ourselves.
Narrator:	$7.95 stock trades. Low margin interest rates. Comprehensive research. Suretrade.com: The smart tool for smart investors.

The barrage of sound, video, and dialogue is directed at persuading viewers to take control of their financial futures by becoming self-reliant D-I-Y investors. Conversely, Suretrade supports individuals' quests for financial independence by providing the essential technological tools at bargain prices.

Case 3: DLJdirect "Changing." In this commercial, a man wearing a suit and tie walks around a large, luxurious executive office and speaks directly to the audience. Camera position points up to the speaker, a technique often used by cinematographers to suggest heroism, power, and authority. As he speaks about the company's movement into the Internet age, elements of the office decor (e.g., desk, table, paintings) transform from traditional to modern style. The transformations are initiated by a computer mouse cursor that is superimposed on the video scene. Computer-generated sound effects accompany the changes. The instrumental background music is a synthesized orchestral piece suggesting technological sophistication. The speaker draws upon the Socratic method of questioning to deliver his lesson, presenting ideas that establish the firm's value proposition.

> Man: What do you get when you combine the expertise of an investment bank that's been on Wall Street for 40 years with the speed of the Internet? The best of both worlds. Welcome to DLJdirect, an online brokerage designed to give investors the tools they need to make serious investment decisions. DLJdirect will change your expectations of online broker.
> Narrator: Donaldson, Lufkin and Jenrette. Putting our reputation online.

Investing is serious business. The ad message employs several cues to convey the firm's expertise and reputation. The speaker's conservative manner of delivery underscores the importance of using reliable information from a trusted source to make investment decisions with confidence.

Data Collection and Analysis

The research was conducted over the course of 2 weeks during 1-hour time slots, in groups of about 12 participants. First, the respondents completed a questionnaire that measured demographic characteristics, usage and involvement with investing, and ad and brand awareness/recognition/attitude. Next, the respondents were shown the three television commercials for online trading services. The order of ad presentation was rotated between groups. After viewing each ad, the subjects answered a series of open- and closed-ended questions. In this chapter, we focus on the responses relating to the following open-ended questions:

- What is the "main point" of the ad?
- Describe the feelings and emotions experienced by the main character in the ad. (Be specific!) Why did the main character experience these feelings and emotions?
- Can you relate to the main character in the ad? Detail the reasons why you can and/or can't relate to the character.

Most of the participants elected to type their open-ended responses into a computer; a few opted to write out their answers by hand (these answers were later transcribed into a computer file). The volume and richness of consumers' responses motivated the use of a computer program (ATLASti; Muhr, 2001) to facilitate data coding and retrieval. Coding procedures blended formal typologies with inductive procedures associated with discovery-oriented research. A popular survey instrument (Richins, 1997) was adapted to code consumers' impressions of the ad characters' feelings and emotions (see Mulvey & Medina, 2000). The authors coded the data independently and met to discuss the coding scheme. Additional codes were added to account for complex characterizations that were not included on the original list. Interrater reliability was high; we negotiated all discrepant assignments to reach complete agreement on the final coding. Similar procedures were employed to code consumers' attributions of causality and dimensions of character identification. The final stage of analysis, performed by the first author, involved distilling the findings into concise characterizations.

RESULTS

We present the results of our study from two perspectives. First we summarize consumers' impressions of the ad characters and identify the convergences and divergences in their responses. Our purpose is to describe the overall tendencies of consumers' interpretations; the focus is on shared understandings rather than individuals' personal idiosyncratic readings. Next, we compare consumers' propensity to identify with the various ad characters. These results are derived from a more detailed coding-and-counting approach that reveals patterns through quantification. We expect to produce a more comprehensive account by combining the two methods of data reduction.

Consumers' Impressions of Ad Characters

In spite of the brevity of the commercials, the respondents had no difficulty forming cohesive impressions of the ad characters. The verbatim quotes appearing in Table 12.1 provide evidence to support our synopses of the overall trends across responses.

Case 1: Ameritrade "Family."   The respondents agreed on the main point of the ad: "Anyone can do it." Ameritrade offers all people, regardless of age and income (and possibly intelligence), the opportunity to participate in the exciting new trend of online trading. The firm makes trading convenient, easy, and affordable so everyone has the opportunity to achieve financial success.

Although the respondents agreed on the main point of the ad, they did not share the same view of Stuart. Stuart's character drew a favorable response from viewers who recognized his excitement, passion, and confidence. Viewers believed

TABLE 12.1
Examples of Respondents' Impressions of the Main Point and Character

	Ad Character		
	Ameritrade Stuart	*Suretrade Ensemble*	*DLJdirect Man*
Main point	"Shows online trading as an alternative to the traditional, stuffy investing of the past. It emphasizes the point that anyone can invest, not just stockbrokers, and the most unlikely people can be successful at it." "It does not matter your age, everyone can log in to the Internet and use trading online. It can be any type of a person."	"You are in control of your money. You don't have to rely on anyone but yourself when you do online trading." "The ad tries to show that by online trading, you are in control of your financial future. You don't rely on firms, inheritance, government, etc."	"The main point of the ad is to give you the idea that DLJ Direct is a 'direct' extension of their firm on Wall Street. That fact should give you confidence in their superior service." "To advertise DLJ, the on-line brokerage firm which has both investment bank expertise and cutting-edge computer technology."
Primary invocations of character	"He felt independent, proud, excited, very enthusiastic, passionate about trading. He also didn't care about what others thought about him." "He seems very confident about himself and what he thinks of his future. He also seems to have a very humorous side to him. Then later on in the ad he shows how intensely involved he is about trading online."	"They are confident in themselves. They refuse to let others influence their financial situations. They choose to take action and invest." "The main character is confident in his ability to trade. And it is a feeling of independence and sort of 'No one can hold me down' attitude." "They are fresh, excited and ready to do things for themselves to make themselves more successful.	"He feels very secure, mature. He knows what he is talking about and is very professional." "The main character in the ad feels very confident about the product (DLJ Direct). He feels that the product is the best out there. He has a strong passion for the product." "Seemed very calm and confident, as if he has already attained some measure of success from using this company. Also

(Continued)

TABLE 12.1 (*continued*)

	Ad Character		
	Ameritrade Stuart	*Suretrade Ensemble*	*DLJdirect Man*
Primary invocations of character (*continued*)	"Stewart probably has seen great results by using Ameritrade's online services and thus is even more excited about future investments he can make."	They seem individualistic, optimistic and positive. They seem to mirror the attitudes of the American people."	seems very nonchalant in showing how easy it is to attain success."
Contrainvocations of character	"He is very aggressive. His description of investing is almost violent. He is also very confident, not caring what the stockbroker father thinks at all. He shows immaturity, too." "Annoying and brash. I wanted to smack him in the head a couple of times." "Ruthless, crass, rabid and competitive greed."	"Don't trust anybody, scared, worried, afraid, and lonely. They just care about themselves." "They seemed a little angry and it is if they are trying to get back at someone who wronged them in some way." "It seems that they are a bunch of bums who are into trading just to get rich quick and gamble."	N/A

his confidence was rooted in past success and that he must be somewhat competent and knowledgeable in matters of investing. His "nothing can go wrong" attitude conveys his optimism and eagerness to succeed. Online trading is his passion; he is intensely involved with the activity. Stuart's excitement reflects his ambition to win big—he will achieve great financial success.

The ad also elicited contrainvocations of character from certain viewers who considered Stuart's behavior to be extreme. Consequently, his extreme confidence is understood as cockiness and arrogance. Similarly, his intense excitement and eagerness are viewed as brash, immature, and annoying. As one participant put it: "He's an idiot."

Case 2: Suretrade "Nest."   The Suretrade ad communicated a succinct main point to respondents: "You can't rely on others: Do it yourself." Readers' retelling of the main pointed centered around three ideas. You can't trust others to take care of your interests. Take control to make the important financial decisions that shape your financial future. Suretrade offers the tools to make online trading easy and affordable so ordinary people can become D-I-Y investors.

The majority of respondents shared similar views of the character ensemble, anchored to the impression of confidence. The ad characters' confidence is credited to their proactive decision to assume control of their investments to achieve financial success. The idea of independence and "not relying on others" reinforces this notion, as do attributions of a solid work ethic and financial savvy. The characters also appear responsible, satisfied, and proud of their decision to become do-it-yourself investors.

However, the readers did not achieve consensus in their assessments of character. Specifically, a minority of readers theorized that the ad characters had difficulty trusting others. Noting an angry tone in the characters' delivery, respondents suspected that a negative experience filled the characters with resentment that fueled their desire for independence. Perhaps their quest was motivated by a selfish desire for vengeance against the party who did them wrong. According to some readers, the ensemble also showed symptoms of being scared, worried, and lonely. Also, the characters' air of confidence may be illusory, masking their true inner feelings of myopic hope.

Case 3: DLJdirect "Changing."   Respondents' interpretations of the main point of the DLJdirect ad centered on the idea: "A reputable Wall Street firm is using their expertise to offer serious investors new technology to trade online." People have trusted DLJ's investment banking expertise for over 40 years. Now they can have same confidence in the brokerage's leading-edge technological tools as they begin trading online.

Unlike the Ameritrade and Suretrade ads, respondents' impressions of the DLJ ad character were remarkably uniform. The DLJ man exudes confidence, pride, and calmness. The character is viewed as an emblem of the firm, a professional who is smart, knowledgeable, educated, and experienced. Viewers believe that the character has reason to be confident based on his apparent wealth and success. His demeanor demonstrates maturity and competency; his calmness and composure are befitting of an established expert in finance. The man's candid style of delivery reflects his pride in the firm: he believes in its offerings.

Cross-Case Analysis of Consumers' Identifications With Ad Characters

The results just reported display the significant role played by visual and nonverbal cues in influencing consumers' perceptions of the main point of an ad. The results also demonstrate consumers' ability to read and ascribe meaning to ad characters. Now we turn our attention to exploring the persuasive role of character identification by answering the questions: Which characters do respondents identify most with? What characteristics are most successful at establishing identifications? Table 12.2 contains verbatim quotes that demonstrate episodes of audience identification with ad characters. We encourage readers to review these typical responses as they shed light on the aggregate results presented next.

On the whole, respondents were far more likely to identify with the Suretrade ensemble and Ameritrade's Stuart than with the DLJ man (see Table 12.3). Reaction to the Suretrade ensemble was clearly divided among consumers who could and could not identify with the characters. In contrast, Stuart and the DLJ man drew a greater number of respondents who had mixed feelings about identifying with the character. Closer examination of the respondents' essays offers greater

TABLE 12.2

Examples of Respondents' Identifications with the Ad Characters

	Ad Character		
	Ameritrade Stuart	*Suretrade Ensemble*	*DLJdirect Man*
Positive identifications	"I can relate to Stuart because he is a kid around my age who seems to be a fun guy and confident in what he is doing." "I can definitely relate . . . it seems that people today are only talking about making money through the market. I am very anxious to make use of this market as well." "Yes I can relate, we all want to belong and be part of the new age, modern culture. If everyone else is doing it, I should too!"	"I can relate because if I was investing my money I would want complete control over the decisions regarding my money." "I can relate to the characters more in this ad because they are everyday kinds of people . . ." "Yes, controlling your own personal business is part of the American viewpoint. We like to be in control of ourselves and don't like to always rely on others to make important choices for us."	"I can relate to the main character in the ad because he represents a character that I will like to be in the future . . . he knows Wall Street and he is very professional." "I can relate . . . in the way of wanting to invest from home, and want specific services, etc. I also relate in the way of not being obsessed or excited about it either." "Yes, a little, I think eventually I want to be like him, very business and professional like, good career."

(Continued)

TABLE 12.2 (*continued*)

	Ad Character		
	Ameritrade Stuart	*Suretrade Ensemble*	*DLJdirect Man*
Negative identifications	"I cannot relate to the character because I don't possess the knowledge he has about online trading." "No, I don't really relate to the character because he is shown as a really wild and rebellious type of guy."	"I cannot relate to the main character because I have never traded on line. Also, this group seems to be aimed at college graduates." "I can't relate because I work hard, and I'll make my money by hard work and knowledge, not luck."	"No, he seems cold and unfriendly. I wouldn't feel comfortable with him." "No, he seemed to know a lot more about online brokerage than I do and it was slightly intimidating."
Mixed identifications	"Yes, in a way . . . he is a young person, with probably a low amount of money to be spending on trading, which is exactly what I am. His personality differs from mine by quite a bit and I really don't have the intensity that he has about trading online." "I can relate to him somewhat because he's young and probably taught himself what he knows about the market. However he's a little too wild for me, but I can definitely relate to making the job fun."	"Sure, I want to make money too, and I am not counting on anybody but myself. But, it bothered me a little when the women said we are betting on ourselves, that sound like gambling." "I suppose I can relate because I like being in control and doing things for myself. However I really can't say I identified with the people in the ad or felt any sort of connection."	"In some ways I can relate because he is the type of role model that I would like to follow. Yet, I cannot relate because he is much older and his lifestyle is very different than mine. He already seems successful and that is what I aspire to be." "No, I can't relate to this old guy because he is boring, however I can relate to the technology which he is selling. But I think this ad is focused at like 50 year old business men, like my father."

insight into the bases of identification. Respondents' identifications with ad characters were organized along the following dimensions: demographic characteristics, level of participation with the activity of online trading, and character dispositions.

Table 12.4 identifies the number of respondents who identified with the ad characters in terms of common demographic characteristics. Stuart drew the greatest number of positive identifications, mainly because of his age-related affinity with the college-aged respondents. Fewer respondents could identify with the Suretrade ensemble, and almost none could identify with the demographic

TABLE 12.3
Number of Respondents Identifying With Ad Characters

| | Ad Character | | | |
	Ameritrade Stuart	Suretrade Ensemble	DLJdirect Man	Total
No	10	17	29	56
Mixed	8	3	6	17
Yes	27	30	11	68
N/A	8	3	7	18
Total	53	53	53	

TABLE 12.4
Number of Respondents Identifying With Ad Characters' Demographics

| Dimension | Valence | Ad Character | | | |
		Ameritrade Stuart	Suretrade Ensemble	DLJdirect Man	Total
Age	+	19	6	0	25
	−	0	6	13	19
Career	+	0	2	3	5
	−	0	0	1	1
Education	+	2	2	0	4
	−	0	1	1	2
Financial status	+	1	3	0	4
	−	0	3	3	6
Typical person	+	0	5	0	5
	−	0	0	0	0
Atypical person	+	3	0	0	3
	−	0	0	0	0
Total	+	25	18	3	46
	−	0	10	18	28
Grand total		25	28	21	74

characteristics of the DLJ man. Although age played an important role in establishing identifications with the audience, it was not a necessary condition. Respondents do not focus exclusively on the present (who they are); they also consider the future (who they aspire to become). Being a student is temporary, and some respondents can identify with older characters because they aim to become self-directed investors who work at home (like the Suretrade ensemble) or Wall Street experts (like the DLJ man). Respondents also identified matches and differences with characters' financial status, level of education, and typicality.

Table 12.5 offers insight into consumers' propensity to identify with the ad characters' involvement in the activity of online trading. The Suretrade ad was the most successful at generating positive identifications by effectively communicating the principle of "do it yourself." Respondents seem to identify with characters that display a level of participation that matched their own ambitions. In the eyes of many respondents, the Suretrade ensemble and Amertrade's Stuart are proof positive that people like themselves could become self-directed investors. However, the DLJdirect man (and the Suretrade ensemble to a lesser extent) displayed advanced skills and expertise that alienated numerous respondents who felt deficient in matters of finance. These ads drew positive identifications only from the few respondents who aimed to become professional investors. Thus, it appears that consumers weigh information concerning their own capabilities in the consumption domain in processing the ad character's message.

Table 12.6 reports identifications with the ad characters' dispositions. The aggregate results are consistent with our earlier findings. Ameritrade's Stuart and the Suretrade ensemble attracted the greatest number of positive identifications as a majority of respondents related to qualities of the characters' dispositions. The

TABLE 12.5
Number of Respondents Identifying With Ad Characters' Participation
With the Activity

| Dimension | Valence | Ad Character | | | Total |
		Ameritrade Stuart	Suretrade Ensemble	DLJdirect Man	
Do-it-yourself	+	6	15	3	24
	−	0	4	0	4
Experienced	+	0	0	1	1
	−	3	7	12	22
Professional	+	0	0	1	1
	−	0	0	4	4
Total	+	6	15	8	29
	−	3	11	13	27
Grand total		9	26	21	56

TABLE 12.6
Number of Respondents Identifying With Ad Characters' Disposition

Dimension	Valence	Ad Character			Total
		Ameritrade Stuart	Suretrade Ensemble	DLJdirect Man	
Independence	+	2	17	0	21
	−	0	1	0	1
Enthusiasm	+	12	0	0	12
	−	8	0	0	8
Confidence	+	5	5	2	12
	−	0	1	2	3
Goals	+	9	1	3	13
	−	0	0	2	2
Work ethic	+	1	6	1	8
	−	0	0	0	0
Calmness	+	0	2	1	3
	−	0	1	2	3
Fun-loving	+	4	0	0	4
	−	0	0	0	0
Not respected by adults	+	4	0	0	4
	−	0	0	0	0
Other[a]	+	3	3	1	7
	−	3	2	4	9
Total	+	40	34	8	82
	−	11	4	10	25
Grand total		51	38	18	107

[a]Other category includes miscellaneous identifications that were not widely shared by respondents (mentioned by fewer than three respondents).

Suretrade ensemble drew mostly favorable associations. The audience appreciated the characters' sense of independence and desire to not rely on others. The respondents also respected the confidence that emanated from the ensemble's work ethic. Many respondents also identified with Stuart's enthusiastic ways of following his passions. Like Stuart, the respondents recognized the importance of having clearly defined goals and pursuing them with ambition. The character also elicited favorable identifications for his confidence and fun-loving nature and for being a young adult who—in spite of merit—has not earned the respect of his elders. Not all respondents shared praise for Stuart's demeanor. His extreme level of enthusiasm exceeded the tolerance of viewers who could not identify with his radical ways. Finally, although the respondents shared similar views of the DLJdirect man's character, few could identify with his disposition.

CONCLUSIONS

A new perspective on the rhetorical role of character in ads has been developed. We suggested that a considerable portion of ad meaning derives from how a message is delivered by characters in the ad. The manner of presentation often tells the audience much more than words alone. This research recognizes that ad comprehension and persuasion requires consumers to construct meaning from the ad through the act of interpretation. We presented the results of a study that demonstrates the communication potential of characters in ads. We began by detailing how consumers assigned meaning to the ad characters, and then we examined consumers' capacity to identify with the ad characters.

The concept of identification may require refinement to accommodate the unique properties of the advertising genre. Burke's (1969) discussion of identification is based on the assumption that effective persuasion derives partly from "shared substance" or "cosubstantiality" between actor and spectator. Audiences will pass favorable judgment upon characters whose qualities that are identical to their own. Hence, "it is not difficult to praise the Athenians among an Athenian audience" (Aristotle quoting Socrates, in *Rhetoric*, I, 9). This raises the question: Can an ad be effective if the ad characters have little in common with the viewer? Consider the online trading ads examined in the study. Each ad contained characters designed to serve as role models for people who aspired to become do-it-yourself traders. Suppose the consumer had no desire to manage investments alone and preferred to delegate responsibility to a professional. Is it possible to establish meaningful identifications with a service provider who does not share common qualities (demographic characteristics, involvement in the activity, or demeanor)? We surmise that identification may be possible in accordance with the role expectations that define the service relationship. For instance, an investor who prefers to delegate responsibility may identify with Peter Lynch, Fidelity's father-like figure who dispenses financial advice with authority to needy clients. Here, the basis of identification is a matching of roles that constitute the relationship. In the investment industry, firms differ significantly in the level of input required from the customer and the firm (Mulvey & Padgett, 2001). Future research might explore this issue to clarify the process of role identification for experiences along the self-service to full-service continuum.

Three particular limitations to this study need to be mentioned. First, the results obtained from our exploratory analyses apply exclusively to ads that use characters to deliver a persuasive message; the results have little bearing on ads that do not feature characters. Second, this research accepted McCracken's (1989, p. 319) challenge to develop "an instrument that allows us to determine methodologically the meanings that inhere in celebrities" (or, by extension, ad characters). Our analysis used open-ended questions and content analysis to detect and survey these meanings. Future research may devise survey instruments that further refine the data collection and analysis process (Mulvey & Medina, 2000). Third, the extent to which our results generalize across product categories needs to be examined. Almost certainly, the assortment and dimensionality of consumers' identifications with characters will vary according to the consumption experience depicted in the ad. Future research might examine a broader spectrum of ads and audiences to develop a more comprehensive typology of identifications.

The principal contribution of this research is the demonstration of how character enhances (or occasionally detracts from) a persuasive message. This finding draws attention to the strategic importance of casting and coaching the performers who act in ads. Characters make human values salient; they are a vital part of the executional framework that brings the ad message to life. Although researchers have presented frameworks to specify ad strategy (e.g., Olson & Reynolds's MECCAS model, 1983), very few researchers have addressed the process of translating strategy into creative message elements (for a notable exception, see Gengler & Reynolds, 1995). Characters contribute considerably to brand image and positioning; research should examine if the ad characters accomplish the communication objectives for which they were designed. Future research ought to bridge the gap between strategy and creative execution by giving further consideration to the rhetorical power of character. This research may proceed in several directions.

First, how do characters' emotion displays affect persuasion? The present study demonstrated consumers' ability to attribute reasons to characters' feelings and emotions. According to social constructionist theory, one of advertising's roles is to teach the consumer "how to have" an emotion (Deighton & Hoch, 1993). For instance, the Suretrade ensemble showed viewers how they could experience feelings of independence by not relying on others, by taking control of their finances, and by trading online. Persuasion of this sort derives from communicating the intangible benefits or "emotional payoffs" (Young & Feigin, 1975) resulting from the proposed consumption experience. Other paths to persuasion may be too subtle to be detected by consumers. Theories of emotional contagion posit that consumers may unknowingly mimic the feelings displayed by liked others (Howard & Gengler, 2001). Perhaps some of our respondents caught Stuart's enthusiasm and excitement. Ideally, the measurement of emotional response should use unobtrusive approaches that don't require retrospection or rationalization. For example, researchers could study viewers' emotional reactions as revealed by facial feedback (recorded real-time on video as participants view the commercial).

Other unanswered questions include: What is the optimal intensity of an emotion display? Perhaps more respondents could identify with Stuart if his level of excitement was toned down a bit. Alternatively, the change might adversely affect the audience's impression of character if they understood the rhetorical purpose of his exaggerated delivery. What happens if the character displays feelings or emotions that are outside the audience's repertory? Consumers may have difficulty appreciating or identifying with the character until they've acquired personal experience in the consumption domain (consider the skydiving experience: see Celsi,

Rose, & Leigh, 1993). How do recurrent characters that appear in a series of ads affect audience impressions? Our study examined people's reactions to single ads, not ad campaigns or vignette advertising. Different ad forms employ characters in different ways that may subtly alter the impression formation process (Stern, 1994). How do antiheroes, villains, and negative role models function in terms of identification? Dissuasion is a common goal of social marketing where the aim is to discourage certain consumer behaviors. Finally, perhaps the most important question of all: Which sorts of identifications have the greatest motivational force? This research lays the groundwork to encourage exploration of these important issues.

REFERENCES

Burke, K. (1969). *A rhetoric of motives.* Berkeley, CA: University of California Press.

Celsi, R. L., Rose, R. L., & Leigh, T. W. (1993). An exploration of high-risk leisure consumption through skydiving. *Journal of Consumer Research, 20*(2), 1–23.

Deighton, J., & Hoch, S. J. (1993). Teaching emotion with drama advertising. In A. A. Mitchell (Ed.), *Advertising exposure, memory, and choice* (pp. 261–281). Hillsdale, NJ: Lawrence Erlbaum Associates.

Dyer, G. (Ed.). (1982). *What do advertisements mean?* London: Methuen.

Esslin, M. (1979). Aristotle and the advertisers: The television commercial considered as a form of drama. *Kenyon Review, 1*(4), 96–108.

Gengler, C. E., & Reynolds, T. J. (1995). Consumer understanding and advertising strategy: Analysis and strategic translation of laddering data. *Journal of Advertising Research, 35*(4), 19–33.

Grier, S. A., & Brumbaugh, A. M. (1999). Noticing cultural differences: Ad meanings created by target and non-target markets. *Journal of Advertising, 28*(1), 79–93.

Hebdige, D. (1979). *Subculture: The meaning of style.* New York: Routledge.

Holt, D. B., & Mulvey, M. S. (2000). *Adscapes: Diagnosing the strategic effectiveness of ads through sociosemiotic analysis.* Working paper. Cambridge, MA: Harvard Business School, Department of Marketing.

Howard, D. J., & Gengler, C. (2001). Emotional contagion effects on product attitudes. *Journal of Consumer Research, 28*(2), 189–201.

Kover, A. J. (1995). Copywriters' implicit theories of communication: An exploration. *Journal of Consumer Research, 21*(4), 596–611.

Levitt, A. (1999). *Speech by SEC Chairman: Plain Talk About On-line Investing.* U.S. Securities & Exchange Commission. Available: http://www.sec.gov/news/speech/speecharchive/1999/spch274.htm (accessed 26 August 2001).

McCracken, G. (1987). Advertising: Meaning or information? In P. Anderson & M. Wallendorf (Eds.), *Advances in consumer research* (vol. 14, pp. 121–124). Provo, UT: Association for Consumer Research.

McCracken, G. (1989). Who is the celebrity endorser? Cultural foundations of the endorsement process. *Journal of Consumer Research, 16*(3), 310–321.

McQuarrie, E. F., & Munson, J. M. (1991). Revised product involvement inventory: Improved usability and validity. In J. F. Sherry & B. Sternthal (Eds.), *Advances in consumer research* (vol. 19, pp. 108–115). Provo, UT: Association for Consumer Research.

Mick, D. G., & Buhl, C. (1992). A meaning-based model of advertising experiences. *Journal of Consumer Research, 19*(3), 317–338.

Mick, D. G., & Politi, L. G. (1989). Consumers' interpretations of advertising imagery: A visit to the hell of connotation. In E. C. Hirschman (Ed.), *Interpretive Consumer Research* (pp. 85–96). Provo, UT: Association for Consumer Research.

Muhr, T. (2001). *ATLAS.ti* (Version 4.2). Berlin: Scientific Software Development.

Mulvey, M. S., & Medina, C. (2000). *How does it feel? Reading the emotions displayed by characters in ads.* Unpublished manuscript. Piscataway, NJ: Department of Marketing, Rutgers University.

Mulvey, M. S., & Padgett, D. (2001). *Experiential positioning: Strategic differentiation of customer–brand relationships.* Unpublished manuscript. Piscataway, NJ: Department of Marketing, Rutgers University.

Olson, J. C., & Reynolds, T. J. (1983). Understanding consumers' cognitive structures: Implications for advertising. In L. Percy & A. Woodside (Eds.), *Advertising and consumer psychology* (vol. 1, pp. 77–90). Lexington, MA: Lexington Books.

O'Toole, J. (1985). *The trouble with advertising: A view from the inside.* New York: Times Books.

Phillips, B. J. (1996a). Advertising and the cultural meaning of animals. In *Advances in consumer research* (vol. 23, pp. 354–360). Provo, UT: Association for Consumer Research.

Phillips, B. J. (1996b). Defining trade characters and their role in American pop culture. *Journal of Popular Culture, 29*(4), 143–158.

Richins, M. L. (1997). Measuring emotions in the consumption experience. *Journal of Consumer Research, 24*(2), 127–146.

Scott, L. M. (1991). The troupe: Celebrities as dramatis personae in advertisements. In R. H. Holman & M. R. Solomon (Eds.), *Advances in consumer research* (vol. 18, pp. 355–363). Provo, UT: Association for Consumer Research.

Scott, L. M. (1994a). The bridge from text to mind: Adapting reader-response theory to consumer research. *Journal of Consumer Research, 21*(3), 461–480.

Scott, L. M. (1994b). Images in advertising: The need for a theory of visual rhetoric. *Journal of Consumer Research, 21*(2), 252–273.

Stern, B. B. (1988). How does an ad mean? Language in services advertising. *Journal of Advertising, 17*(2), 3–14.

Stern, B. B. (1991). Who talks advertising? Literary theory and narrative point of view. *Journal of Advertising, 20*(2), 9–22.

Stern, B. B. (1994). Classical and vignette television advertising dramas: Structural models, formal analysis, and consumer effects. *Journal of Consumer Research, 20*(4), 601–615.

Vickers, M., & Weiss, G. (2000, April 3). Wall Street's hype machine: It could spell trouble for investors. *Business Week*, pp. 112–126.

Wansink, B. (1987). Developing useful and accurate customer profiles. In L. R. Kahle & L. Chiagouris (Eds.), *Values, lifestyle, and psychographics* (pp. 183–197). Mahwah, NJ: Lawrence Erlbaum Associates.

Young, S., & Feigin, B. (1975). Using the benefit chain for improved strategy formulation. *Journal of Marketing, 39*(3), 72–74.

CHAPTER THIRTEEN

Promises, Promises: Exploring Erotic Rhetoric in Sexually Oriented Advertising

Jacqueline Lambiase
University of North Texas

Tom Reichert
University of Alabama

The pleasure of the text is that moment when my body pursues its own ideas—for my body does not have the same ideas I do. (Barthes, 1994, p. 17)

Wise advertisers will always attempt to find out first what it is that we are after and then fashion a campaign with which to position their product. Only a fool, soon to be bankrupt, attempts to change our patterns of desire. (Twitchell, 1996, p. 14)

Sex, in its many cultural guises, stands as a rhetorical commonplace or topoi in much American advertising in the 20th century's last decade. Although advertising producers and consumers alike would probably avow the selling power of sexual images, findings from academic empirical research fail to lend much support to this perception. Some researchers even have warned advertisers to avoid using "overtly seductive, nude, or partially clad models" (Courtney & Whipple, 1983, p. 118), because these appeals can distract, cause offense, or result in negative evaluations of brands (for review, see Belch, Belch, & Villareal, 1987). Despite the findings from this body of research, sexual appeals continue to be employed by advertisers. Recent evidence even suggests that mainstream advertising is increasingly explicit with regard to clothing and sexual interaction (Reichert, Lambiase, Morgan, Carstarphen, & Zavoina, 1999). Most quantitative sexual appeal research is located in the advertising and consumer behavior literatures, as opposed to theoretical work on this topic performed by scholars in the humanities, such as Freudian, semiotic, rhetorical, or literary analyses.

Empirically discerning the precise impact of sexual appeals may be difficult for several reasons. For one, sexual ad research suffers from demand effects because it is often conducted in an artificial setting utilizing a one-exposure test model. Another reason, one central to the present rhetorical analysis, is that researchers have primarily approached this phenomenon from an information-processing paradigm. Although this perspective is vital given that advertisements are persuasive messages, more examination is needed of the arguments advocated in sexual appeals. Frequently, these ads offer promises, both implicitly and explicitly through words and images, of sexual fulfillment or attractiveness if the brand is used. Considered alongside these implicit or explicit promises will be: an audience member's individualized perception and perspective toward a sexual appeal; the many alternative readings available for any given appeal; and even whether the ad may be considered sexual at all.

This project examines the verbal and visual arguments used in sexually oriented advertising to discover the benefits promised by such advertising, to uncover the cultural work performed, and to understand the discourse community engaged by the rhetoric of ads with sexual content. By stepping away from empirical exploration of sexually oriented ads—and by drawing from the rhetorical and communication theories of Kenneth Burke and others—new places for both critical discussion and empirical research will emerge. Although "sex sells" has become a commonplace, even if disputed by research, it is important to ask exactly what sex does attempt to sell consumers. Research has shown that sexual images and words can attract attention and can affect associations with product brands, but perhaps sex sells itself more than any product associated with sexual appeals, when it serves as a discourse frame in advertising.

PAST EMPIRICAL ANALYSIS
OF SEXUALLY ORIENTED ADVERTISING

A commonly studied form of sexual appeal is the investigation of female "nudity," in which nudity is typically defined as the amount and style of clothing worn by models in ads (e.g., LaTour, 1990). In these studies, female models in various stages of undress are tested against a control ad to gauge effectiveness (Alexander & Judd, 1978; Grazer & Keesling, 1995; Judd & Alexander, 1983; LaTour, 1990; LaTour & Henthorne, 1993; Steadman, 1969). For example, Alexander and Judd (1978) found that ads with pastoral scenes (no female model) stimulated higher levels of unaided brand name recall than ads featuring nude models. Reid and Soley (1981, 1983), examining existing market data, found that male viewers paid greater attention to ads featuring decorative models, but were no more likely to read the ads. The results of these studies suggest that sexual appeals increase attention to the ad, but that the increased attention is diverted to the sexual image with little carryover effect to the brand. Other than exploring the effect of information processing variables, these studies offer little evidence that sex is effective for selling products.

Researchers also have examined the impact of emotion evoked by sexual imagery on evaluations of the ad and the brand (Jones, Stanaland, & Gelb, 1998; LaTour, 1990; LaTour & Henthorne, 1993; Severn, Belch, & Belch, 1990; Smith, Haugtvedt, Jadrich, & Anton, 1995). Findings from these studies suggest that the relationship between evaluations and sexual imagery is complex and depends on contextual and individual difference variables. For example, evaluations can depend on the gender of the respondent and model/actor in the ad (LaTour, 1990), level of explicitness (LaTour & Henthorne, 1994), and relevance to the brand (Simpson, Horton, & Brown, 1996). Overall, it appears that viewers who like the sexual content are more apt to like the ad and the brand, whereas the opposite is true for those who do not like the sexual content. Otherwise, the research into emotional responses to sexual appeals provides little evidence about the power of sexual ads to encourage purchases.

A recent study provides some evidence that sexual appeals can be persuasive. Reichert, Heckler, and Jackson (2001) tested the effectiveness of sexual appeals for 13 social marketing topics. The comprehensive study analyzed the effects of sexy public service announcements on a series of advertising variables (e.g., attention, likeability, emotional impact, cognition, and persuasion). Overall, the sexy ads were found to be more attention-getting, more liked, and more persuasive than the nonsexy ads, whereas the nonsexy ads stimulated more critical analysis of the ad message. The researchers reasoned that the positive emotional response to sexual content was persuasive by preventing respondents from thinking deeply about the topic. Although persuasion did occur, it appeared to be a temporary effect and easily changed. Based on this study and those previously cited, there is little empirical evidence that sex sells.

Aside from the empirical research just described, there has been little examination of the meaning in sexual ads. Although most ads contain some form of selling message—frequently described as benefits to the consumer—no efforts have been made to examine, much less test, the "appeals" made in sexual ads. Even in review articles (Belch, Belch, & Villareal, 1987; Percy & Rossiter, 1992), little is mentioned beyond the previously mentioned processing and emotion-based studies. An exception is work by Mick and Politi (1989) and Stern and Holbrook (1993), in which interpretive strategies were employed to uncover the construction of consumer meaning in sexually suggestive ads. Both studies analyzed consumer interpretations of romantic but somewhat ambiguous ads. Although respondents provided a variety of interpretations for the interaction in each ad, there was a pronounced gender difference in both studies. In the Mick and Politi study, male respondents viewed the interaction as sexual. In the Stern and Holbrook study, both men and women viewed the relationship as sexual, but they differed in their interpretations of the narrative and qualities of the characters. These studies indicate that interpretations of ads, even of sexy ads, can vary widely.

RHETORICAL ANALYSIS AND ADVERTISING

What has been neglected in previous empirical research is not the role of sexual information on processing or ad evaluations, but the meanings and rhetorical arguments constructed in tandem by these advertisements and their audiences. Other disciplines also tend to ignore this collaborative rhetorical approach. For example, Freudian theorists usually ignore product type and consumer response when discussing embedded or subliminal sexual images (Williamson, 1978). Wilson Key (1973) popularized identifying sexual embeds throughout media, without regard for a creator's intention or a viewer's focus. In contrast, rhetorical approaches do take into account the product type, consumer response, and media context. McQuarrie and Mick (1996) suggest that meaning in advertising language may be discovered through a language-centered approach to advertising analysis by first creating a taxonomy of common rhetorical figures and then defining them as "artful deviations" or "gaps" that "invite elaboration by the reader" (p. 429).

Rhetorical analysis, then, recognizes strategies that persuade readers and viewers, while engaging them to construct meaning from a text when culturally salient figures of speech are used. Rhetoric at its most basic is defined by Aristotle as an ability "to see the available means of persuasion" (trans. 1991, p. 36). Its scope has been enlarged by Kenneth Burke (1950/1969) to include the notion of persuasion as identification and the expansion of persuasion "to include the unconscious intent, the self as audience, and nonverbal elements that have meaning for an audience" (Foss, Foss, & Trapp, 1991, p. 180). Formulating a discourse theory that would certainly include advertising, Burke (1967a) argued for a large scope for rhetorical analysis:

> Words are aspects of a much wider communicative context, most of which is not verbal at all. Yet words also have a nature peculiarly their own. And when discussing them as modes of action, we must consider both this nature as words in themselves and the nature they get from the nonverbal scenes that support their acts. (p. xvii)

In *Understanding Media,* McLuhan (1964) believed consumers interpret advertising through its visual rhetoric, because advertising's imagery "offers a way of life that is for everybody or nobody" (p. 205). Ad copy, he believed, distracts an audience "hypnotized" by images. "Since the advent of pictures, the job of the ad copy is as incidental and latent as the 'meaning' of a poem is to a poem, or the words of a song are to a song" (p. 205). These theorists suggest that nonverbal elements of advertising are especially appropriate for rhetorical analysis. Just as empirical analysis has limitations in uncovering all of an ad's meaning, so does language analysis alone.

Scott (1994) made a similar argument in favor of analyzing visual rhetoric and saw advertising as "one of the richest symbolic institutions of our time" (p. 271). She believed "[c]onsumers draw on a learned vocabulary of pictorial symbols and employ complex cognitive skills even in the simplest response. Thus, advertising images can be understood as a discursive form, like writing, capable of subtle nuances in communication or, like numbers, capable of facilitating abstraction and analysis" (p. 264). Her system of visual rhetoric drew on three of the classically defined parts of rhetoric: invention, arrangement, and delivery (the other two parts are style and memory). Through this rhetorical framework, she believes, advertising's visual appeals may be analyzed using theories of cognitive processing, affective response, interpretive research, and other methods. In acknowledging the larger discourse community in which advertising operates, Scott wrote that "[i]nterpretive efforts might seek to explain the use of particular images, cultural trends, and the practical situation being addressed by the advertiser" (p. 271).

Burke's Dramatistic Pentad and Sexual Appeals

Through his dramatistic pentad, Burke offers a rhetorical tool for discerning multiple meanings (Table 13.1). This theoretical tool becomes an invention machine, one that may be applied to an advertisement to gauge just how many meanings are available for its varied audience members. The pentad does this by providing perspective on the process of storytelling or the analysis of attitude or motive in advertising. It is a way of reading a text by analyzing word or symbol choices and then seeing those choices in light of their meanings for particular discourse communities. Burke (1967b) defined the five parts of the pentad as act, agent, scene, agency, and purpose, and described them thusly: "For there to be an act, there must be an agent. Similarly, there must be a scene in which the agent acts. To act in a scene, the agent must employ some means, or agency. And there cannot be an act, in the full sense of the term, unless there is a purpose" (p. 332).

The pairing or ratio of scene/act provides a fruitful perspective for analyzing advertising. For example, viewers may see truth in the scene or image (being persuaded by, or as Burke would say, identifying with, the agents embedded in this

TABLE 13.1
Burke's Dramatistic Pentad

As a tool of rhetorical analysis, the pentad:
- May be used to find motive in "stories, plays, poems, the rhetoric of oratory and advertising, mythologies, theologies, and philosophies" (Burke, 1990, p. 1035).
- Offers five terms as generating principles: act, scene, agent, agency, purpose.
- Is useful for locating rhetorical gaps, such as the multiple benefits promised by advertising's narratives. The Jewelry.com ad is one explicit rendering of suggested benefits from sexually oriented appeals (Fig. 13.1); Burke's pentad is most useful for teasing out meanings, motives, and benefits from sexually oriented appeals that do not explicitly depict sexual acts.
- Allows two perspectives: an *intrinsic* reading for interpreting the narrative in the ad itself, as well as an *extrinsic* reading, which considers the "outside" narrative of the producer of the ad (agent) and its viewers (who interpret the scene).

scene), and then move to project the act (with the product as agency). In other words, it is possible to understand a whole with a part, or one thing (the act of sexual intercourse) with another (a sexually suggestive scene). Burke scholar W. H. Rueckert (1963) addressed this method of representation by way of the pentad:

> Burke moves from the assertion that the act is caused by the scene, agent, agency, and purpose to the assertion that the act is equal to the scene, agent, agency, and purpose. The logic is: since "caused by" therefore "equal to." This reductive or synecdochic logic is thoroughly characteristic of Burke. (p. 82)

Burke's pentad provides a method for analyzing advertising that contains more images than words, and it is especially useful for analyzing sexually oriented advertising in mainstream media, in which sexual intercourse cannot be explicitly represented but may be understood by another image.

Rhetorical Patterns in Sexually Oriented Advertising

The need for another way to analyze sexual appeals became clear to the authors while conducting a content analysis of sex in advertising several years ago. For that analysis, over 2,500 full-page ads from mainstream magazines were coded to assess sexual content in advertising. One of several findings, reported in *Journalism Quarterly* (Reichert et al., 1999), revealed that in 1993, of all women and men in ads, 40% of women and 28% of men were dressed in a sexual manner. In addition, 53% of heterosexual couples in ads were engaged in unmistakable sexual interaction with each other. The majority of sexualized models appeared in women's (*Cosmopolitan* and *Redbook*) and men's (*Playboy* and *Esquire*), compared to general-interest, magazines (*Time* and *Newsweek*). The authors employed a well-cited protocol, based on work by Soley and Reid (1988) and Soley and Kurzbard (1986), to measure sexual content in advertising: style and amount of clothing worn by models, and physical interaction between models. Although this method captured one aspect of sexual appeals, others were evident, but not able to be included because sexual content is not always related to dress or interaction. The models' poses and facial expressions can contribute, but weren't captured in the analysis. And in many instances, unclothed models are not portrayed sexually, and fully clothed models can be very sexual. Of course, sexual orientation of the viewer also is not taken into account, nor is the pleasure that heterosexuals derive from seeing people of their own sex displayed in ads.

Although coding can be stabilized and made to conform to definitions established by researchers, there is always content in advertising that cannot be quantified. Yet patterns of verbal and visual discourse could be identified from hundreds of these previously studied ads from the mid- to late 1990s. Six advertisements—some which are sexually explicit and some which are less explicit—were chosen for this rhetorical analysis because they represent a larger pattern and because they provide examples of meaning within advertising that cannot be captured by con-

TABLE 13.2
Themes of Benefits Promised in Sexually Oriented Advertising

Producers of ads create narrative scenes offering promises for consumers to consider, which may include these interpretations:

1. Sexual attractiveness: Wear this, consume this, smoke this, apply this, and you will be more sexually attractive to others.
2. Likely engagement in sexual behavior (and more enjoyment from these encounters): Wear this, consume this, smoke this, apply this, and you will be more likely to engage in sexual behavior and will also enjoy it more.
3. Feelings of sex-esteem: Wear this, consume this, smoke this, apply this, and you will boost your own feelings of sexiness and sensuality.

---

tent analysis or empiricism alone. Furthermore, this analysis demonstrates how this type of rhetorical analysis might be conducted to discern benefits and to explore multiple meanings.

In this present analysis, sexually oriented appeals are defined as appeals containing overt sexual language or visual sexual information (e.g., nudity and/or suggestiveness; Reichert et al., 2001). Of particular interest are sexual appeals that either implicitly or explicitly offer the promise of sexual benefits. These three benefits may be considered as subsets of an appeal to conform to idealized and gendered appearance and/or sexual performance. They are: (a) sexual attractiveness for the consumer, (b) likely engagement in sexual behavior (and more enjoyment from these encounters), and (c) sex esteem, or feelings of being sexy or sensual (Table 13.2). For example, the Jewelry.com ad (Fig. 13.1) is an explicit rendering of suggested benefits from sexually oriented appeals. In the ad, a man embraces a woman wearing jewelry, the advertised product, clearly exemplifying the second benefit shown in Table 13.2, that of likely engagement in sexual behavior. After all, ads seek to prompt particular behavior from consumers, including awareness, recognition, positioning, buying, and perhaps most interesting for this analysis, identification, or placing themselves into the "scene" part of Burke's pentad. Producers of advertising are taught especially to make benefits of products explicit to audiences, which have come to expect benefits from products, whether as "added value" or "magic" (Twitchell, 1996).

The Jewelry.com advertisement provides a simple example for applying Burke's pentad, because the ad's meaning at first seems explicit. This is an "intrinsic" reading of the ad's imagery, taking it at face value by using only the verbal and visual rhetoric available. The act is sexual contact between two agents (a woman and a man), with a scene that's at once clear: The woman has capitulated, the man has triumphed. The scene may also be interpreted as ambiguous: The woman is in a powerful position above the man, receiving both jewelry and sexual pleasure, or she is "paid off" to serve the man. The agency is the jewelry itself, with the purpose being pleasure for both man and woman, but perhaps on different planes of meaning; it is here, in purpose, that an ad's promise of benefits may be discerned.

FIG. 13.1.   Jewelry.com.

An "extrinsic" reading is equally important, perhaps more important to the present analysis, for "[w]ithout this information, there is nothing to associate the act portrayed in the visual image with the advertiser" (Rutledge, 1994, p. 210). In an extrinsic interpretation of the Jewelry.com advertisement, the act is the production of an image and its placement in print media by Jewelry.com's advertising agents who serve as designers/publishers. Agents would be the designers or publishers of the ad, with agency as the technology used to transmit the information (such as a printed page). Scene is the ad itself, but it is a scene coupled with an active viewer interpreting visual and verbal information by linking it to culture, personal preferences, and other contexts that this active viewer brings to such an interpretation. Does the viewer find identification in this scene, or is she or he repulsed by its message? Purpose in the Jewelry.com ad is its motive, which is selling jewelry to audiences of a national news weekly magazine that serves mostly upper-class, college-educated readers. Although the purpose of the agents may be to sell, it is the scene and a viewer's glancing interpretation of that scene that will determine whether "selling" of the message or its implicit benefits has occurred.

Of the six ads in this study, three fragrance advertisements—Bernini (for men), Yves Saint Laurent's Opium (for women), and Gravity (for men)—use both words and images to communicate sexual benefits to their audiences, much as the Jewelry.com ad does. Meanings are less ambiguous in these advertisements when compared to ads in which images carry the primary message; meanings must also take into consideration the producers and consumers of the ads, using Burke's extrinsic pentad. And plausibility of any so-called benefits would be based on an individual's experience, cultural cues, and a viewer's willing suspension of disbelief when that viewer engages with the scene of these advertisements.

In the ad for Bernini, a men's fragrance ad that appeared in a men's magazine, the upper body of a nude woman lies in bed, with a sheet barely covering her nipples (Fig. 13.2). She is an actor in a scene that suggests a sexual encounter. Her head rests on pillows, with the top of her head and eyes cropped from view. At bottom right, a round-topped fragrance bottle is superimposed over a sheet that covers the woman's hips. Across her breasts and bare upper body is this headline: "Sometimes she recalled his scent so vividly, she would lie there, aroused by her own imaginings." This text, which makes the act more explicit, may prompt male readers to come to at least one conclusion: Use Bernini and be sexually attractive to an idealized and sexualized woman. This would fall into the conventional wisdom of "sex sells" a particular product for an expected result. Perhaps most importantly, the Bernini ad provides a sexual pleasure of its own, a use of sex for sex's sake. Twitchell (1996) asserted that ad agencies produce ads such as this one and the Calvin Klein series for clothing "in active collusion with the male viewers" (p. 232); he believed "[i]f there were no printed text, we would decode these ads as mild pornography" (p. 233). Indeed, if these ads were stripped of the signs of a marketing pitch, then the photo illustration would fit easily into the editorial style set by men's magazines such as *Maxim, Playboy,* and *Esquire.* Although targeted to a generalized male readership, the Bernini ad undergoes an interpretive transformation when its scene is engaged by heterosexual women, lesbians, or gay men. Although these other audiences may recognize the scene and its intended stereotyped message, they may resist that message or read through that message for alternative meanings. Stereotyped interpretations assumed by most

FIG. 13.2.   Bernini of Beverly Hills.

empirical studies are not likely in these sorts of extrinsic readings by outsider viewers, even some heterosexual men.

The second sexually oriented fragrance ad, for Opium Parfum, which appeared in a women's magazine, also features a female actor, à la odalisque (Fig. 13.3). She looks directly at the audience and is suggestively draped in luxurious fabric and jewelry, with one shoulder and leg exposed as she lounges on furniture that is also draped, in silk. Again, at bottom right, is a superimposed perfume bottle. At top right are the words "Opium: Sensuality to the extreme." Benefits suggested by this scene include promises to female viewers that they, too, will feel sexy, will be sexually desirable, and will be able to conform to an idealized image of what constitutes a sexy woman. Less explicit is the benefit for female viewers of being more likely to engage in sex. Because the scene itself mimics an opium den, a viewer's identification with or repulsion by such as scene will be based on her or his appetite for decadence relating to clothes, sex, food, and consumption in general.

The third fragrance ad, for a men's product called Gravity, appearing in a men's magazine, features a profile shot of a man dressed in demure business attire, sitting in a reclined chair (Fig. 13.4). He is looking up at a woman who is bending over him; she is dressed in high heels and a short dress with straps. In this ad, the fragrance bottle is rectangular and not upright, but instead rests at bottom left and tilts to right, forming a line of movement up through the man and into the enclosed space made by the woman's body as she bends over the man. Although the scene of this ad is not the intimacy of a bed or boudoir, the headline at the top of the advertisement leaves little ambiguity about the benefits promised. It says, "The force that pulls you closer." The expressed verbal benefit has more to do with sexual attractiveness than with sexual intercourse, but the visual rhetoric of this scene reinforces that promise.

When discussion of interpretation turns to a larger discourse community and to the elements of Burke's pentad for extrinsic analysis (e.g., factors outside the obvious narrative of an ad), then tidy meanings are harder to come by. A viewer's interaction with the scene determines its message, and although viewer interpretations may be stereotyped by ad producers or agents, some viewers will resist identification with an ad's scene. Producers may embed meanings for viewers in a depicted act, but viewers may not be "media-savvy and hip" (Messaris, 1997) or may simply resist or ignore a deliberate meaning constructed by an ad's producer. Placement of a Bernini or Gravity ad in the context of a men's magazine may help to ensure that particular benefits promised are more obvious. These same ads in a foreign context, such as a general interest magazine like *Time*, may lose that meaning entirely for many in the audience.

Meaning is harder to fix in ads without text, making multiple interpretations even more likely. An ad for Baileys Original Irish Creme Liqueur that appeared in a women's magazine includes only the words "Baileys, Yum, The Original," with a close-up of a young woman's face, her eyes closed and her lips parted (Fig. 13.5). In the bottom right corner is a superimposed image of a glass of Baileys being

FIG. 13.3. Opium perfume by Yves Saint Laurent.

THE FORCE THAT PULLS YOU CLOSER.

FIG. 13.4.   Gravity fragrance for men.

poured. The intrinsic scene in this ad is one of oral pleasure, or the thought of it. This interpretation could arguably be extended to a female agent involved in orgasmic pleasure, with the benefit of Baileys ostensibly that of adding more pleasure to sexual intercourse or increasing the possibility of sex. Because of the growing taboo against associating alcohol with sex, the visual syntax makes connections that cannot be made with explicit words or images (Messaris, 1998, pp. 76–77). When an extrinsic pentad is constructed, however, the agent becomes an ad producer seeking to show enjoyment of a product, and the scene engaged by the ad's viewer is a beautiful face experiencing innocuous pleasure. The extrinsic purpose suggests a mundane reading of the ad: that of a photo of a person enjoying a product so viewers will make a positive association with Baileys.

An ad for Lucky Strike Cigarettes appearing in a men's magazine (Fig. 13.6) subtly uses a sexual appeal: Good-looking women flirt with men smoking Lucky Strikes. The only headline in the ad is the name "Lucky Strike," appearing as a logo on the back wall of the scene in a diner. The act is one of a relaxed conversation between a man smoking and a waitress, wearing a suggestively short uniform with apron. Yet the act in this Lucky Strike ad can also be seen as an open scene, created so that the audience feels it is invited to complete the narrative, with or without sexual overtones. O'Barr (1994) believed that some contemporary advertising is open to interpretation, with

> the advertisers inviting the audience to participate, aware that what they intended may not help at all in the consumers' comprehension of the meaning. It may simply be that the intention of the maker was to create an advertisement that we would use as a skeleton to which we would add flesh and into which we would breathe life. (p. 8)

Advertising, like other symbol-using social institutions, is rarely if ever language or image neutral, even when consciously developing a skeleton on which the audience hangs meaning. Although there may be more than one narrative path for the Lucky Strike ad, there still is one narrative path that is more likely than others because of the visual vocabulary chosen by its producers. In a culture that now professes to consider smoking negatively, this ad's message may simply be that a man smoking a cigarette is still attractive to a beautiful woman, especially when pairing the product name, Lucky Strike, with the act of two people interacting.

Unlike the Lucky Strike ad, three of the advertisements in this study feature explicitly sexual images: First is the Jewelry.com ad, with a woman straddling and being carried by a man and wearing expensive jewelry; the Bernini ad with its "aroused" and bare female model, barely covered by a sheet; and, to a lesser degree, the Opium ad with its "Sensuality to the extreme" headline and decadent scene. If these ads were to be included in a content analysis, coding of visual elements based on nudity, sex-role portrayals, and degree of sexual contact would adequately register their sexual content. However, if the other three advertisements were subjected to empirical coding schemes, the existence of sexual content becomes more difficult to determine. In the Baileys ad, for example, a woman's face

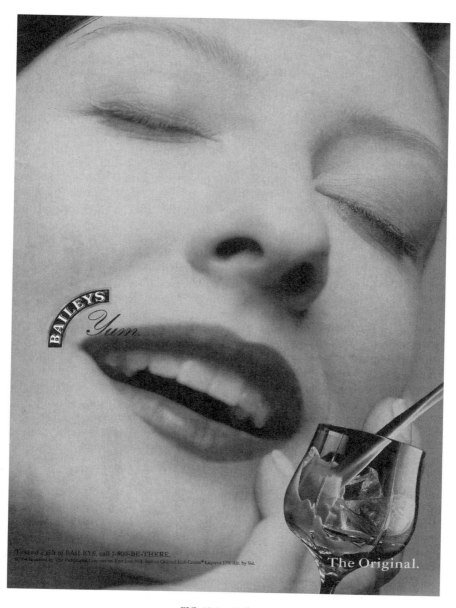

FIG. 13.5. Baileys.

FIG. 13.6.   Lucky Strike cigarettes.

serves as the primary image. It would be difficult to address the breadth of its sexual content without rhetorical analysis, for there is no sexually suggestive physical contact with another person and there is no sign of nudity. Based on sex-role portrayals, we could classify the woman's face as merely decorative, for women are being used in increasingly decorative ways in magazine advertising, as are men to a lesser degree (Lambiase et al., 1999). In much the same way would empirical coding capture part, but not all, of the sexual content of the Gravity and the Lucky Strike ads. All this is to say that Burke's pentad provides a strategy for teasing a fuller meaning, and perhaps a different reading, from sexually suggestive advertising.

FUTURE RESEARCH ABOUT SEXUAL NARRATIVES IN ADVERTISING

As stated earlier in this chapter, rhetorical analysis exposes the gaps in empirical research and helps to interpret the narratives and meanings that sometimes go undetected by scientific scrutiny. Conversely, an empirical approach provides rich data that in their turn prompt other places for rhetorical analysis to do its work. Content analysis of benefits promised by sexual appeals in women's and men's magazines could provide grist for feminist and gender theory perspectives. Kenneth Burke's ideas about rhetoric's ability to provide new identity could prove useful in further analyzing sexually suggestive appeals and how they might transform or affect audience identity.

An important area for future research of sexually oriented appeals would be to document the prevalence and nature of these appeals, as they are constructed to argue for buying the brand. This research would build on the arguments made in this present study by laying an empirical foundation that could serve as a springboard for further critical analysis. In so doing, several important variables could be reliably and validly assessed.

A central question would be to determine how common these appeals are compared to other types of sexual appeals. Do ads using sex as a benefit represent a fraction of sexual ads or do they represent a majority of these appeals? Presently, there are no reliable estimates. Such an analysis would provide guidance for effects research in this area, because if ads using sex as a benefit are prevalent, the effectiveness and believability of this type of ad need to be assessed. Currently, there is no research to suggest whether consumers "buy" the arguments made in these ads.

The nature of the appeal, or the rhetorical approach, would also be important to assess. For instance, do most of these ads encourage the consumer to use the brand to be sexually attractive to others, or do most appeals feature people as an object of sexual conquest? This could be examined by analyzing the nature of the appeals in ads in men's and women's magazines. According to research that has examined sex-role portrayal in the media, one would assume that ads directed toward women use arguments designed to convince women that the brand will enable them either to have a "lasting impression" on men or to attract their attention. On the other hand, ads targeted toward men may be more likely to suggest that women are the "prize" for those who use the advertised brand.

Roland Barthes's (1994) challenge to consider the "pleasure of the consumer" provides another place, by no means a commonplace, from which to address meaning in sexually suggestive advertising. Barthes adopted a strategy similar to

Burke and his pentad invention strategy, that of focusing on a consumer's identification with the scene of an ad:

> Imagine an aesthetic (if the word has not become too depreciated) based entirely (completely, radically, in every sense of the word) on the pleasure of the consumer, whoever he may be, to whatever class, whatever group he may belong, without respect to cultures or languages: the consequences would be huge, perhaps even harrowing. (Barthes, 1994, p. 59)

CONCLUSION

Although three of the more explicit ads in this study demonstrate the circulation of a shared vocabulary for sexually oriented appeals, two of these three could be easily interpreted as parody (Jewelry.com) or as an extreme consumer's dearest dream (Opium). When these ads are grouped together and interpreted as part of the "scene" of women's and men's magazines, they can appear as a magnification of sexual foreplay, ostensibly to define the ultimate benefit of a product. That benefit might be a higher probability of sexual encounters or feelings of sexuality, if the ads are interpreted in intrinsic ways of interpreting scene as act. More important are extrinsic interpretations that use the pentad to analyze and dissect busy, distracted, and varied audience members who may have desires and ideas of their own when they interact with an ad. In this way, the pentad opens up an advertisement to doubled interpretations and more.

As a common vocabulary develops for both words and images in sexually oriented advertising, it gains currency and its use increases, but this vocabulary or grammar should not be viewed as static or narrow. Burke's pentad offers a multiplicity of interpretations, unlike other interpretive strategies adopted by Freudians, semioticians, and others, because the pentad does not close down possibilities into one interpretation. Burke and his theories do not propose to unlock hidden meaning, but instead to expose many meanings available to many audiences. Erotic appeals in advertising make many promises, and they may help to sell products. Yet proving or disproving the conventional wisdom of "sex sells" may be less important than the collaborative efforts of empiricists and rhetoricians, working together to devise new ways to trace the discourse communities surrounding sexually oriented ads and their varieties of meanings.

REFERENCES

Alexander, M. W., & Judd, B. (1978). Do nudes in ads enhance brand recall? *Journal of Advertising Research, 18,* 47–50.
Aristotle. (1991). *On rhetoric: A theory of civic discourse* (G. A. Kennedy, Trans.). New York: Oxford University.
Barthes, R. (1994). *The pleasure of the text* (R. Miller, Trans.). New York: Hill/Wang.

Belch, G. E., Belch, M. A., & Villarreal, A. (1987). Effects of advertising communications: Review of research. In J. Sheth (Ed.), *Research in Marketing* (vol. 9, pp. 59–117). New York: JAI Press.

Burke, K. (1967a). *The philosophy of literary form: Studies in symbolic action* (2nd ed.). Baton Rouge: Louisiana State University Press.

Burke, K. (1967b). Dramatism. In L. Thayer (Ed.), *Communication: Concepts and perspectives* (pp. 327–360). Washington, DC: Spartan Books.

Burke, K. (1969). *A rhetoric of motives*. Berkeley: University of California Press. (Original work published 1950)

Burke, K. (1990). Language as symbolic action. In P. Bizzell & B. Herzberg (Eds.), *The rhetorical tradition: Readings from classical times to the present*, (pp. 1034–1041). Boston: Bedford Books.

Courtney, A. E., & Whipple, T. W. (1983). *Sex, stereotyping and advertising*. Lexington MA: Heath.

Foss, S. K., Foss, K. A., & Trapp, R. (1991). *Contemporary perspectives on rhetoric* (2nd ed). Prospect Heights, IL: Waveland Press.

Grazer, W. F., & Keesling, G. (1995). The effect of print advertising's use of sexual themes on brand recall and purchase intention: A product specific investigation of male responses. *Journal of Applied Business Research, 11*(3), 47–58.

Jones, M. Y., Stanaland, A. J., & Gelb, B. D. (1998). Beefcake and cheesecake: Insights for advertisers. *Journal of Advertising, 27*(2), 33–51.

Judd, B., & Alexander, M. W. (1983). On the reduced effectiveness of some sexually suggestive ads. *Journal of the Academy of Marketing Science, 11*(2), 156–168.

Key, W. B. (1973). *Subliminal seduction: Ad media's manipulation of a not so innocent America*. New York: Signet.

Lambiase, J., Reichert, T., Morgan, S., Carstarphen, M., Zavoina, S., & Callister, M. (1999). Gendered bodies still thrive in (post)modern magazineland. In M. Carstarphen & S. Zavoina (Eds.), *Sexual rhetoric: Media perspectives on sexuality, gender and identity* (pp. 149–158). Westport, CT: Greenwood.

LaTour, M. S. (1990). Female nudity in print advertising: An analysis of gender differences in arousal and ad response. *Psychology and Marketing, 7*(Spring), 65–81.

LaTour, M. S., & Henthorne, T. L. (1993). Female nudity: Attitudes toward the ad and the brand, and implications for advertising strategy. *Journal of Consumer Marketing, 10*, 25–32.

LaTour, M. S., & Henthorne, T. L. (1994). Ethical judgments of sexual appeals in print advertising. *Journal of Advertising, 23*, 81–90.

McLuhan, M. (1964). *Understanding media: The extensions of man*. New York: Signet.

McQuarrie, E. F., & Mick, D. G. (1996). Figures of rhetoric in advertising language. *Journal of Consumer Research, 22*, 424–438.

Messaris, P. (1997). *Visual persuasion: The role of images in advertising*. Thousand Oaks, CA: Sage.

Messaris, P. (1998). Visual aspects of media literacy. *Journal of Communication, 28*(1), 70–80.

Mick, D. G., & Politi, L. G. (1989). Consumers' interpretations of advertising imagery: A visit to the hell of connotation. In E. C. Hirschman (Ed.), *Interpretive consumer research* (pp. 85–96). Provo, UT: Association for Consumer Research.

O'Barr, W. (1994). *Culture and the ad: Exploring otherness in the world of advertising*. Boulder, CO: Westview.

Percy, L., & Rossiter, J. R. (1992). Advertising stimulus effects: A review. *Journal of Current Issues and Research in Advertising, 14*, 75–90.

Reichert, T., Heckler, S. E., & Jackson, S. (2001). The effects of sexual social marketing appeals on cognitive processing and persuasion, *Journal of Advertising, 30*, 13–27.

Reichert, T., Lambiase, J., Morgan, S., Carstarphen, M., & Zavoina, S. (1999). Beefcake and cheesecake: No matter how you slice it, sexual explicitness in advertising continues to increase. *Journalism & Mass Communication Quarterly, 76*(1), 7–20.

Reid, L. N., & Soley, L. C. (1981). Another look at the "decorative" female model: The recognition of visual and verbal ad components. In J. H. Leigh and C. R. Martin, Jr. (Eds.), *Current Issues and*

Research in Advertising (pp. 122–133). Ann Arbor: University of Michigan Graduate School of Business Administration.

Reid, L. N., & Soley, L. C. (1983). Decorative models and the readership of magazine ads. *Journal of Advertising Research, 23,* 27–32.

Rueckert, W. H. (1963). *Kenneth Burke and the drama of human relations.* Minneapolis: University of Minnesota Press.

Rutledge, K. E. (1994). Analyzing visual persuasion: The art of duck hunting. In R. Fox (Ed.), *Images in language, media, and mind* (pp. 204–218). Urbana, IL: NCTE.

Scott, L. M. (1994). Images in advertising: The need for a theory of visual rhetoric. *Journal of Consumer Research, 21,* 252–273.

Severn, J., Belch, G. E., & Belch, M. A. (1990). The effects of sexual and non-sexual advertising appeals and information level on cognitive processing and communication effectiveness. *Journal of Advertising, 19,* 14–22.

Simpson, P. M., Horton, S., & Brown, G. (1996). Male nudity in advertisements: A modified replication and extension of gender and product effects. *Journal of the Academy of Marketing Sciences, 24*(3), 257–262.

Smith, S., Haugtvedt, C. P., Jadrich, J. M., & Anton, M. R. (1995). Understanding responses to sex appeals in advertising: An individual difference approach. *Advances in Consumer Research, 22,* 735–739.

Soley, L., & Kurzbard, G. (1986). Sex in advertising: A comparison of 1964 and 1984 magazine advertisements. *Journal of Advertising, 15*(3), 46–54, 64.

Soley, L. C., & Reid, L. N. (1988). Taking it off: Are models in magazine ads wearing less? *Journalism Quarterly, 65,* 960–966.

Steadman, M. (1969). How sexy illustrations affect brand recall. *Journal of Advertising Research, 9*(1), 15–19.

Stern, B. B., & Holbrook, M. B. (1994). Gender and genre in the interpretation of advertising text. In J. A. Costa (Ed.), *Gender issues and consumer behavior* (pp. 11–41). Thousand Oaks, CA: Sage.

Twitchell, J. B. (1996). *Adcult USA: The triumph of advertising in American culture.* New York: Columbia University Press.

Williamson, J. (1978). *Decoding advertisements.* New York: Marion Boyers.

CHAPTER FOURTEEN

"Uncle Sam Wants You!": Exploring Verbal–Visual Juxtapositions in Television Advertising

Amy A. Wiggin
Christine M. Miller
California State University, Sacramento

Excellent careers for excellent young men. (U.S. Army Recruiting brochure, 1952)

. . . we help ordinary young men and women become better. (http://www.goarmy. com, 2001)

Millions of tiny dots blend, creating a clear and distinct image. Bright colors flash across the screen, grabbing one's attention. Famous people lure in devoted viewers week after week. It is the phenomenon of television and it has become a dominating medium in the lives of many Americans. Television has come to serve as a source of information and entertainment, as an agenda setter, and as an aid in the socialization process (Gamble & Gamble, 1999; Vande Berg et al., 1998). Television also is used as a means to persuade viewers (Gamble & Gamble, 1999). The television industry is created and maintained by people whose primary goal is to make money (Vande Berg et al., 1998). Thus, advertisements function as a significant factor in television and are created as a means to persuade audience members to purchase or "buy into" a given product (Vande Berg et al., 1998).

Although many television commercials are aimed at selling a product, image, or service, some television commercials seek to recruit members to groups or organizations. Such advertisements have also been called "classified advertisements" and are aimed at recruiting new employees. The goal of both the product advertising television commercials and the recruitment television commercials is to persuade audience members to "buy into" what the advertisers are selling. The difference is that the recruitment television commercials are asking people to make life-changing decisions (to change jobs or join a particular organization), whereas product advertisements are merely seeking the purchase of a product or service. The scope of behavior change being asked of the audience in the recruitment commercials is significantly larger than in the product advertising, thus making highly persuasive techniques a must in recruitment advertising.

The purpose of this study is to explore visual and verbal techniques used in television commercials intended to recruit new members. This chapter uses U.S. Army television commercials from the 1999–2000 advertising campaign as a case study in visual persuasion. The goal is to determine how the blending of visual images and verbal texts can help to accomplish the task of recruiting. Thus, constructs related to visual persuasion offer points of access into the analysis of the Army television recruitment commercials.

The U.S. military is an entity that relies on television advertising as one method of reaching its target audience. The primary goal of military advertising is to persuade prospective recruits to join a branch of the military within the Department of Defense: the Army, Navy, Air Force, or Marines (the Coast Guard is part of the Department of Transportation; D. J. Johnson, Freedom of Information Act Officer, personal communication, 17 August 1999). The military faces a difficult task in its advertising because the target audience is being asked to make a lifestyle change, not just simply to purchase a product, like most other advertising. Thus, military television commercials seek to persuade a potential recruit to consider the military as a lifestyle option.

The armed forces hope that advertising will help fill their ranks. Typically, all military branches, excluding the Marines, struggle to meet their quotas.[1] In 1999, the Army was only able to recruit 68,209 enlistees, failing to meet its recruiting goal of 74,500 (*Armed Forces,* 2000), thus making 1999 one of the toughest years to recruit in the history of the All-Volunteer Force (AVF) (Bandow, 2000; *Louis Caldera,* 2000).

Efforts to expand enlistment have included increased military advertising budgets (Asch et al., 1999; Murray & McDonald, 1999). The Army's advertising budget, which is the highest of the five branches, rose from $85 million in 1998 to $115 million in 2000 (D. A. Johnson, Freedom of Information Act Officer, personal communication, 17 August 1999; Myers, 2000). But although advertising budgets have increased, little is known about the effectiveness of current advertising efforts. In 1999, political consultants Mike Murphy and Carter Eskew conducted an analysis of the military's recruiting strategies under the order of Secretary of Defense Cohen (*U.S. Representative Steve Buyer,* 2000). The consultants concluded that the military services used ineffective advertising strategies and needed to emphasize traditional patriotic themes and intangible benefits of serving in the military (*U.S. Representative Steve Buyer,* 2000). Although the findings of the review addressed

---

[1] However, the terrorist attacks on the World Trade Centers and the Pentagon that took place on 11 September 2001 have since helped all military branches meet their quotas, at least temporarily.

the military's advertising strategies in general and did not address specific rhetorical strategies used in the advertising, it was clear the military needed to make adjustments to its advertising. Hence, the Army has begun making major changes in its approach to advertising, including the dismissal of the catchy "Be All You Can Be" jingle and slogan (*U.S. Representative Steve Buyer*, 2000) as well as the termination of its contract with Young & Rubicam, the Army's official advertising agency for the last 12 years.

The consultants' review also criticized the military for spending its advertising dollars poorly (*U.S. Representative Steve Buyer*, 2000). The Murphy–Eskew review noted that, for instance, the military would broadcast advertisements on telecasts of national sporting events rather than on syndicated or cable programs that are geared toward niche markets (Myers, 2000). The review recommended that the services reevaluate their advertising efforts because the services were "yielding inefficient advertising strategies" (*U.S. Representative Steve Buyer*, 2000, p. 13). Such findings bring to light the need to review and critique how the military is spending its advertising budget, and on what, whether it be the military's choice of media or the content of its advertisements.

In 1998 and 1999, 76% of the Army's media budget went to television advertising (USA Recruiting Command, 1999). The Army has found television advertising to be the most successful because it is the medium most consumed by the target audience it hopes to reach, it generates the best recall rates, and it is the medium most effective in initiating Army awareness (USA Recruiting Command, 1999). However, the USA Recruiting Command (1999) noted that military recruitment commercials do not necessarily cause people to join the military; rather, they are designed to position the military as an option in the minds of prospective recruits. Thus, exploring the various persuasive techniques featured in the television commercials may provide insight into how this goal is achieved.

Little scholarly research has focused on the persuasive strategies used to encourage consideration of enlistment in military recruitment advertisements. In particular, the literature on Army advertising is sparse and extremely limited in scope (Harkey et al., 1988; Keck & Muller, 1994). More generally, the research on recruitment advertising focuses exclusively on the print medium (Knoch, 1990; Highhouse et. al., 1998; Martin, 1987; Magnus, 1986; Stoops, 1984) and fails to address television recruitment advertising. This study begins to address a gap in research related to the ways in which television advertising persuades potential recruits. It examines six Army commercials from the 1999 to 2000 advertising campaign and one from the 1997–1998 campaign: "The Difference" (from 1997–1998 ad campaign), "Step Up," "Find Out," "Do You Know," "Technology," "Get to Work," and "Are You Ready?" (see Appendix for a transcription of the verbal text and a description of the visual images for each commercial). This chapter explores the use of a specific rhetorical strategy that an institution can use in its television advertising to recruit new members: the blending of visual images and verbal text in a metaphoric relationship intended to influence the viewers' perception of the institution.

This notion of blending the visual with the verbal deserves closer scrutiny. Visual images often must be accompanied by verbal labels in order to distinguish certain elements (such as temporal progressions between scenes; Messaris, 1998). Messaris (1998) used an example of two magazine print advertisements that have the same visual structure (a nature scene with flowers, trees, and a field), but where the implied relationship between the product and the image is completely different in the two advertisements (p. 75). The first print advertisement was for a nutritional supplement (Echinacea), with the nature scene representing the natural element of the supplement, whereas the other ad was for an allergy medicine (Loratadine) which used the nature scene to indicate what the medicine combats. Therefore, the advertisements must rely on the verbal text to distinguish them from one another. Such a distinction is useful for the current study because the Army commercials rely on the same visual structure, but each scene is differentiated by the verbal text that accompanies it. Additionally, Messaris's article addresses the fact that visual images often need the help of verbal symbols to convey the intended message effectively. Such is the case with the Army recruitment advertisements that blend the visual and verbal components. It seems that in order to understand the full meaning of the visual images in the commercials the verbal text is needed. Similarly, it is also necessary to consider the visual images fully to understand the meaning of the verbal texts.

Messaris (1994) helps to clarify the nature of the relationship that exists between the visual images and the verbal texts in his discussion of visual–verbal juxtapositions. Messaris (1994) explained that visual–verbal juxtapositions are the positioning of visual images in opposition to verbal texts. He contended that such juxtapositions serve to extend the receiver's ability to think abstractly. He drew on a Smucker's fruit preserves television commercial as an example of visual–verbal juxtaposition. Within the commercial, there are visual images as well as verbal texts. Examples from the commercial include a narrator stating, "If you could taste time," with the visual image of a man walking across a wide expanse of cultivated land; and "If you could taste the sun," coupled with the visual image of cherries glistening in the sunlight (Messaris, 1994, p. 130). This commercial is a good illustration of how the viewer is asked to think in abstract terms. In reference to what the voice-over is stating and what is visually represented, the viewer must make the connection between an abstract concept (time) and the concrete image portrayed on the screen (the expansive land). This type of abstract thinking (the use of visual and verbal juxtaposition) is a technique that the Army also employs in its advertising in an attempt to sell its "product" to the viewer.

In the same vein as Messaris's example, the Army's commercials may be considered figurative in that the verbal text has a different meaning than the images depicted visually. For example, in one Army ad, the verbal text "learn to dance" is juxtaposed with the image of a person in a boxing ring. When presented with the notion of learning how to dance, most people would not conjure up visions of people wearing boxing gloves and fighting in a ring. It seems the combination of the verbal text with the visual images is meant to create a figurative relationship rather than literal. Hence, it can be argued that this Army commercial, and the others being analyzed, are examples of metaphors.

As this example illustrates, metaphor is a device used to promote abstract thought by forging unique relationships between two objects or ideas. Once looked on as a characteristic found only in verbal language, metaphor is now acknowledged as a device also used in visual communication (Dent & Rosenberg, 1990; Forceville, 1996; Kaplan, 1992; Phillips, 1997; Whittock, 1990). Most scholars treat visual metaphor as consisting only of visual images. However, Forceville (1996) offered a unique perspective on visual metaphor by also looking at the role the verbal or written text plays when combined with a visual image. He argued that visual metaphors can exist not only when two terms are presented visually, but when one term[2] is presented visually and the other textually (Forceville, 1996).

Charles Forceville (1996) is a pioneer in the exploration of visual metaphors[3] in advertising, choosing to focus solely on advertisements because they have "an unambiguous purpose: to sell or promote a product or service . . . [and] thus advertising has a great commercial interest in having its intentions recognized" (p. 65). Hence, analyzing the visual metaphors within the Army television commercials is appropriate because recruiting commercials have the unambiguous aim of promoting membership in the organization. When that objective is met by combining verbal text and visual imagery in an associational matrix, exploring the visual metaphors created allows insight into the organization's intentions.

Furthermore, Forceville (1996) provided a framework for analyzing visual metaphors which will serve to guide the evaluation of the Army commercials. He asserted that investigating visual metaphors should be approached with certain criteria in mind. First, one should determine what the two terms of the metaphor are and explain how this was decided. Second, one must conclude which is the tenor (the primary subject or focus of the metaphor) and which is the vehicle (the secondary subject or frame of reference of the metaphor),[4] followed by an explanation of how one came to this conclusion. Finally, Forceville (1996) suggested

---

[2]Although it is arguable that a visual image would not necessarily be a "term" but rather a concept, Forceville (1996) referred to the word used to summarize the visual image as a "term." Hence, this chapter uses the phrase *term* in reference to the word selected to represent the visual image that functions as a component of the metaphor.

[3]Forceville (1996) referred to metaphors where both the tenor and the vehicle are rendered visually as "pictorial" metaphors. He does not explain his choice for the word *pictorial*. Other scholars (Dent & Rosenberg, 1990; Kaplan, 1992) referred to such a phenomenon as "visual" metaphors. The term *pictorial* implies picture-based metaphors, which seems limited to artifacts where the image is static, as with a photograph or print advertisement. *Visual* is an all-encompassing term and would more likely include the rapid and complex images found in a television commercial. Therefore, it seems more appropriate to use the term *visual metaphors*.

[4]The terms *tenor* and *vehicle* were first used by I. A. Richards (1936) in his book *The Philosophy of Rhetoric* (Oxford: Oxford University Press).

exploring what can be said about the feature(s) of the secondary subject (vehicle) that are imposed on to the primary subject (tenor).

Although both verbal and visual metaphors share some similar properties, there is an important aspect of visual metaphors in advertising that distinguishes them from verbal metaphors. Such a distinction, as addressed by Kaplan (1992), concerns the question of "direction in metaphorical expressions" (p. 201). Kaplan provides an example of the verbal metaphor "encyclopedias are gold mines" as an illustration of the directionality present in verbal metaphor, noting that "the identity created between the two subjects results in a metaphor in which the schema for encyclopedias is revised to the context of the properties of gold mines" (p. 201). However, he argued that to reverse the metaphor to read "gold mines are encyclopedias" would be an ineffective metaphor in most regards, and thus illustrates the importance of unidirectionality in verbal metaphors.

Some scholars (Forceville, 1996; Kaplan, 1992) asserted that visual metaphors in advertising also rely on unidirectionality similar to that found in verbal metaphors. However, unlike verbal metaphors, visual metaphors in advertising are constricted by the product that is advertised. Forceville (1996) argued that in the case of metaphors in advertising, the tenor "is, or is connected to, the product advertised" because the primary focus of any advertisement will be the product, and thus the focus of the metaphor (p. 69). Additionally, Kaplan (1992) noted that "visual metaphors used in advertising can be considered a special case wherein the advertiser's rhetorical intent *requires* the target [tenor] to be the product or service" (italics added) (p. 204). Hence, the generation and analysis of the metaphors present in the Army commercials will deviate from traditional analysis of verbal metaphors in that the tenor of each metaphor must always be the term focused on or connected to the Army, rather than the familiar or expected term, as with verbal metaphors.

It should also be noted that in this analysis the two terms of the metaphors will be, by necessity, articulated verbally, because it is impossible to reproduce the images in the commercials. Although the verbal term used to describe the visual images is only representative of those images and should not be confused with the verbal component on the metaphor, it is necessary to reduce the visual images down to a single term in order to describe the metaphors in this chapter. Furthermore, the two terms of the metaphor will be determined based on the proximity of the verbal component with the visual image. The cue established by the verbal component will indicate which visual images are significant and thus which terms to select as a means to generate the metaphor.

Once the metaphors are generated in this way, Forceville's (1996) criteria for analyzing visual metaphors guides the critique of the Army commercials. In addition, the works of other scholars (Lakoff & Johnson, 1980; Osborn & Ehninger, 1962; Phillips, 1997; Scott, 1994; Sperber & Wilson, 1986; Whittock, 1990) are used to develop our understanding of how the visual metaphors within the 1999–2000 Army television commercials fulfill the criteria put forth by Forceville. The next section provides a general overview of the distinction between literary and visual metaphors. A discussion of how people process and interpret metaphors, which provides an explanation of how the metaphors function to create meaning, follows.

In a literary metaphor, the tenor and the vehicle are both rendered verbally. An example of a literary metaphor is TIME IS MONEY. In this example, the tenor is TIME and the vehicle is MONEY. By exploring various features of MONEY, we come to understand more about TIME (i.e., how it can be *spent* or should be *saved*). A visual metaphor, in contrast, depicts both the tenor and the vehicle pictorially. Scott (1994) provided an example of a visual metaphor in her discussion surrounding a Clinique ad, which featured a lipstick immersed in a cold glass of soda water with a lime wedge. She argued that the visual metaphor is CLINIQUE LIPSTICK IS A REFRESHING GLASS OF SODA WATER (Scott, 1994). The tenor in this example would be the Clinique lipstick, whereas the vehicle is the glass of soda water, with both terms being visually depicted.

When a person encounters a metaphor like the ones described in the previous paragraph, there is a mental process he or she goes through in an attempt to create meaning from two disparate terms that don't have a literal relationship. Osborn and Ehninger (1962) termed this the "process of metaphor" (p. 226). They argued that a viewer (reader/listener) goes through a response sequence when he or she is confronted with a metaphor, which includes the *error, puzzlement–recoil,* and *resolution* stages. First, the viewer (reader/listener) recognizes there is an *error* in the information presented. The viewer (reader/listener) then becomes puzzled by the combination of the terms, which is followed by agitation and uncertainty because his or her "normal expectancy of meaning is crossed" (Osborn & Ehninger, 1962, p. 227). He or she recoils because of the agitation and uncertainty he or she experiences, thus completing the *puzzlement–recoil* stage. The *recoiling* in turn "is the spring that motivates him [or her] to solve the puzzle . . . and seek a proper understanding," which is the *resolution* stage (p. 227). Osborn and Ehninger's (1962) discussion of the processes by which a metaphor is comprehended serves as an explanation of how they function in creating meaning. Understanding this process is important for the rhetorical critic who seeks ultimately to account for the effect that metaphoric discourse may have on an audience.

The process was further explained by Phillips (1997), who noted that viewers (readers/listeners), when confronted with a metaphor, interpret and transfer relevant properties from one term to another while ignoring inapplicable similarities. The consequential meaning of the metaphor is called the "implicature" (Forceville, 1996, p. 92). Sperber and Wilson (1986) define an implicature as information that is communicated to the viewer (reader/listener) implicitly. The implicatures are inferred by the audience in order to interpret a message.

Implicatures may be either weak or strong. According to Forceville (1996), a strong implicature would be the primary meaning in a message, or the most obvious meaning. In contrast, a weak implicature would be less obvious, forcing the viewer to jump to conclusions in an effort to create meaning. For instance, in the

TIME IS MONEY metaphor, a strong implication is that one should *invest* wisely in how one *spends* time. By comparison, a weak implicature still establishes some connection between the two things being compared, but the connection does not leap immediately to mind and requires the drawing of more convoluted inferences. In the TIME IS MONEY example, a weak implicature could be that the *exchange rate* favors foreigners whose *spending power* lasts a long or a short time, depending on the currency. This implicature is derived by searching the metaphor for less obvious associations that can be created between ideas. Most likely, such an association would not be the immediate connection a person would make between time and money, and so it is a weak implicature.

Forceville (1996) suggested exploring both the weak and strong implicatures present in a metaphor. He argued that "the more strongly an assumption is communicated, the more the communicator [creator of the message] takes responsibility for having it derived by the addressee [viewer/reader/listener]; the weaker an assumption is communicated, the more the addressee takes responsibility for deriving it" (Forceville, 1996, p. 93). Understanding both the strong and the weak implicatures allows the critic to offer insight into a range of possible audience interpretations. Therefore, the analysis of the Army television commercials includes a discussion surrounding the implicatures that may be derived from the metaphors.

As a starting point for this analysis, it is useful to categorize the Army commercials based on the types of metaphors used. In particular, the blending of the visual and the textual components in these commercials suggests the presence of a specific subcategory of visual metaphors identified by Forceville (1996). He argued that there are four distinguishable subtypes of visual metaphors, delineated based on how the two terms [tenor or vehicle] are presented (Forceville, 1996). Three of the four subtypes focus specifically on metaphors that are formed only by visual images (e.g., the Clinique ad), which is not the case with the Army commercials. However, Forceville's (1996) final subtype is a verbo-pictorial metaphor, which is structured so one term is rendered textually and the other is depicted visually. In the case of a verbo-pictorial metaphor, if one term is removed the metaphor is lost.

It became clear that the metaphors in the Army commercials were verbo-pictorial metaphors based on the characteristics offered by Forceville (1996). The metaphors within the Army commercials only exist through the combination of verbal text and the visual images. Additionally, three kinds of metaphors seemed to be present in the Army commercials. These metaphors can be grouped to reflect figurative associations between the Army and (a) skill building, (b) personal growth, and (c) career development. Examining individual metaphors by looking at the blending of the visual images and textual components in each group illuminates how the metaphors function collectively.

Based on Forceville's (1996) framework, each metaphoric example includes a discussion of what two terms are featured in the metaphor, which term is the tenor and the vehicle, and what can be said about the features of the vehicle that are imposed onto the tenor. After the application of Forceville's schema, there is a discussion of how the television commercials within this campaign serve the Army's recruiting purposes.

SKILL METAPHORS

Many of the metaphors in the Army commercials seem to express various skills that could be developed in the Army. Within this group of metaphors, the tenor is always presented visually, while the vehicle is presented verbally. One example is found in the commercial "Step Up." The narrator states, "Learn to dance," while the visual images on the screen depict two men boxing. It seems that no literal relationship can be established between BOXING and DANCING, so there must be a metaphoric or figurative relationship between the two terms.

Forceville (1996) then suggests determining which term is the focus of the metaphor and which is the frame. In "Step Up," it is important to note that immediately before the scene of the men boxing in the ring, there is the depiction of a different boxer throwing a punch at the camera, followed by a person doing a lay-up with a basketball. It seems the visual depictions in this portion of the commercial (surrounding the "Learn to dance" statement) deal primarily with sports that are aggressive. Furthermore, it is unlikely that the Army will be teaching soldiers how to ballroom dance, but instead will encourage more physical and combative activities like boxing. It can be concluded that the tenor is BOXING and the vehicle is DANCING, with the tenor portrayed visually and the vehicle rendered verbally. The viewer is being invited to understand BOXING in relation to a DANCE, resulting in the metaphor BOXING IS A DANCE.

Whittock (1990) expanded on Osborn and Ehninger's error stage, noting that the shock of the metaphor makes the connection in thought possible because thought itself is metaphoric and can be restructured by metaphor. The idea that metaphor influences the way in which thought is processed, interpreted, and recalled gives rise to the question of why the Army decided to use the words "learn to dance" while depicting boxing and other aggressive sports. One possible reason may be so the viewer, the potential recruit, might come to understand some of the Army's beliefs and values though the use of the metaphor.

Lakoff and Johnson (1980) argued that metaphors help people to understand concepts by downplaying some aspects and highlighting others. What are the features of dancing being highlighted when compared to boxing? Dancing requires quick, precise, and fluid movements. It also places physical demands on the body. Similarly, these are qualities that the Army values in a soldier who may be on a battlefield. Yet if the Army's purpose is only to suggest that they are seeking people capable of quick, precise, and fluid movement, which can be found in both boxing and dancing, wouldn't it be more straightforward to state literally "learn to box" rather than "learn to dance"? It seems another reason for the use of a figurative comparison may be more insightful.

Within American culture, "let's dance" is a colloquialism understood by some as an invitation to fight. This may help explain why the Army chose to state the figurative term "dance" instead of the literal term "box." However, this could be taken a step further. The Army may very well be a place where one could learn to "fight" or "box," but it is the very nature of the Army to instill in its people the ability to "fight" or engage in war. The purpose of the Army is to train soldiers to be prepared to go to war. The verbo-pictorial metaphor BOXING IS A DANCE goes far beyond these activities to express one of the basic skills one will be expected to learn in the Army, which is to learn to fight in combat.

The commercial "Find Out" offers another example of a skill metaphor. The narrator states, "Learn to swim," which is juxtaposed with the visual images of several soldiers, dressed in full military gear and flippers, sitting on the edge of a helicopter hovering about 20 feet above the water. The soldiers throw large backpacks (which are tied to them) into the water and jump in after them. Because a person would already have to know how to swim in order to participate in such a mission, no literal meaning can be articulated between the two subjects. One must then assume it is a figurative relationship, specifically metaphorical.

Based on the narrator's statement, SWIM is one of the terms in the metaphor. On the other side of the metaphoric equation, the visual images depict a group of soldiers, or a unit, jumping out of a helicopter. This activity is called "helicasting" and is the act of covertly infiltrating enemy territory via helicopter. The unit is dropped down in this fashion because it is more secretive than if they were to arrive by parachute. Therefore, the second term of the metaphor is HELICASTING.

In order for a person to be part of a helicasting mission, he or she would already have to know how to swim. These soldiers are obviously skilled at swimming, so capable that they can swim while carrying heavy gear. Therefore, it is clear that the focus is on HELICASTING, which makes it the tenor of the metaphoric relationship. Based on the strong implicature of the visual images, the metaphor would be HELICASTING IS SWIMMING. How might this metaphor be interpreted?

The act of swimming requires one to propel oneself forward in an effort to stay afloat. The characteristics of propelling oneself forward can be applied to the tenor HELICASTING. A soldier who is assigned the duty of helicasting would need to possess the physical skills and mental strength necessary to complete such a mission. The features of swimming, propelling oneself forward to stay afloat, would be representative of a soldier who is prepared, both mentally and physically, to keep moving forward (propelling) until the mission is safely accomplished (staying afloat). This metaphor suggests that the Army is a place where one will learn the skills necessary to avoid drowning, maintain forward progress, and achieve goals. The Army teaches a soldier how to fight against adversities, such as things that weigh one down, and to do so effectively.

A look at the common metaphor "sink or swim" may be helpful in suggesting a weaker implicature of HELICASTING IS SWIMMING. The "sink or swim" metaphor implies that a person "swim" (i.e., be productive) or "sink" (i.e., flounder in the current situation). Essentially, this commonly used metaphor refers to one's ability to succeed or fail. It can be argued that the Army commercial draws on this metaphor by using the statement "Learn to swim." The "sink or swim" metaphor, which may be conjured up, helps to provide another possible interpretation of the HELICASTING IS SWIMMING metaphor present in the Army commercial.

Literally, the heaviness of the gear attached to the soldiers during the helicasting jump represents something that would "sink" the ordinary person. "Learn to swim," then, could be interpreted as "learn to succeed," because most people would not be able to succeed in a situation where they jumped off a helicopter with 40 or more pounds of gear attached to them. Success, then, would be a weak implicature derived from the juxtaposition of the visual images of helicasting and the verbal statement "Learn to swim." The weak implicature of this metaphor suggests that the Army will provide the skills needed to succeed in a most difficult situation (where one might otherwise "sink").

The final example of a skill metaphor comes from the commercial "Are You Ready?" In the beginning, the narrator states, "Are you ready . . . to learn how to drive?" Based strictly on the verbal text, one might infer that the Army offers driver's education courses such as those available in high school. While the narrator is making this verbal statement, the visual image on the screen depicts a tank leading other tanks through muddy, rough terrain, followed by a shot of a soldier within the tank talking into a headset, giving orders. There is no literal relationship that exists between the visual images and verbal text because presumably to drive a tank one would already have acquired driving skills. Therefore, there must be a metaphoric relationship.

Based on the visual images and the verbal text, it is clear that the first term is DRIVING. The second term pertains to the tank and the rough terrain, because that is what is depicted. More specifically, there is one tank leading the rest of the tanks and they are moving quickly while maintaining their formation. It is clear that the tank being featured in the commercial is the leader of the unit. The second term, then, appears to be TANKING. Since the Army is not encouraging people to join so they can learn how to drive, the vehicle of the metaphor would be DRIVING, making the tenor TANKING. The viewer is being asked to understand TANKING in terms of features related to driving. The metaphor, then, can be verbalized as TANKING IS DRIVING. Because the vehicle is the secondary term of the metaphor, which helps to frame the tenor, or primary term, it is important to consider what features of DRIVING can be mapped onto TANKING to help interpret the metaphor.

DRIVING begins with a starting point and ends with a destination, and suggests the process of getting from point A to point B. Some people may drive for the sake of pleasure or adventure, but most people drive with a purpose. It can be implied, then, that TANKING, like driving, has a purpose. Although the purpose of TANKING might also be to get from point A to point B, it is more likely that the purpose is to conquer difficult obstacles. Tanks are used in situations where other vehicles would be ineffective or unable to gain access. The vehicle DRIVING suggests a purpose, which highlights that aspect of TANKING, rather than other aspects. Hence, an implicature of the metaphor is that the Army is a place where soldiers learn the skills needed to get from point A to point B, regardless of the difficult obstacles that may be present.

A weak implicature of the metaphor suggests that "tanking" is leadership. The visual images depict one tank leading the rest of the unit. Furthermore, the soldier in the tank is giving orders to the personnel in the other tanks. It is clear that he is the leader of the tank mission, which supports the idea that tanking represents leadership. Additionally, it is implied that being in the "driver's seat" gives one control over various situations. This implicature suggests that the Army can help foster leadership skills and give a person the ability to take control, or be a leader, in given circumstances.

The metaphors analyzed in this cluster focused specifically on skill development. BOXING IS A DANCE was the first metaphor addressed, which implied that the Army is a place to learn the skill of fighting. The second metaphor, HELICASTING IS SWIMMING suggested that learning how to survive difficult situations was a skill one could learn in the Army. Finally, the TANKING IS DRIVING metaphor indicated that the Army provides a soldier with the skills to conquer obstacles with ease.

These three skill metaphors serve as representative examples. There are other examples that exist in the campaign, including the metaphor in the commercial "Are You Ready?" In this example, the verbal statement "Learn how to fly" accompanies the visual image of several soldiers jumping from an airplane. "Step Up" offers another example of a skill metaphor. In this commercial, the narrator states, "Learn to draw," while the visual images depict a soldier sitting at a computer, using the mouse to zero in on a target within a "drop zone." These examples are also verbo-pictorial metaphors, meeting the criteria put forth by Forceville (1996), and further illustrate the presence of skill metaphors in the Army commercials.

PERSONAL GROWTH METAPHORS

In addition to the cluster of metaphors relating to skill development, the notion of developing the self also seemed to be a prevalent theme in metaphors within the Army television commercials. This group of metaphors presented the tenor verbally, while presenting the vehicle visually.

One example of a personal growth metaphor is in the commercial "Are You Ready?" Specifically, the narrator states, "Are you ready to find yourself?" The visual images that accompany the verbal statement depict a motorcycle driving quickly through muddy, rugged terrain, filmed so that the viewer sees things through the eyes of the driver. What sense can be made of the statement "Are you ready to find yourself?" Driving a motorcycle is not what most people would think of when asked if they were ready to find themselves. One might imagine therapy, long conversations with friends, or other situations where there is self-reflection. Therefore, it seems there is no literal relationship that can be concluded from the visual images and the verbal text. The relationship, to make sense, must then be a metaphorical one.

The verbal statement "Are you ready to find yourself?" questions the viewer's willingness to be introspective, to discover who he or she is on the inside, to explore the true spirit of one's being. Thus, the first term in the metaphor could be labeled SOUL-SEARCHING. The second term, generated in juxtaposition with the verbal text, is A MOTORCYCLE DRIVE, because the commercial depicts a motorcycle nego-tiating a muddy and rugged environment.

Because the Army is a place where many young people often go in search of structure and discipline in their lives, it is likely that the tenor is SOUL-SEARCHING. Forceville (1996) argued that an advertisement has a clear and specific purpose, which is aimed at selling or promoting a product or service. Given this assumption, it is unlikely that the Army would spend its advertising budget on informing view-ers that they will go for motorcycle rides if they enlist in the Army. Consequently, A MOTORCYCLE DRIVE is the vehicle of the metaphor, designed to create figurative associations, through which a better understanding of the tenor can be gained. The metaphor can be verbalized as SOUL-SEARCHING IS A MOTORCYLE DRIVE.

Having determined the tenor and the vehicle, let us look at how the features of A MOTORCYCLE DRIVE can be mapped onto SOUL-SEARCHING in an effort to under-stand how meaning is interpreted. Motorcycles, as portrayed in the commercial, frequently drive "off-road," or on more rugged and rough ground than the city streets most drivers are accustomed to. This could be seen as difficult task. The same, then, can apply to soul-searching: There may be times when one encounters rugged, muddy obstacles that make the process of discovering one's true self more difficult.

Another aspect of A MOTORCYCLE DRIVE that could be mapped onto SOUL-SEARCHING is responsibility. If a person is driving, he or she is responsible for other people who are on the road. A person must be careful about her or his decisions and actions because irresponsibility could result in loss of life. Therefore, it can be implied that soul-searching requires one to be responsible. One should approach the task of learning about oneself thoughtfully and carefully. Based on this meta-phor, it could be argued that the commercial implies the Army will teach a person how to be accountable, and the ability to be responsible will lead the person to a deeper understanding of who he or she is.

The use of the verbo-pictorial metaphor SOUL-SEARCHING IS A MOTORCYCLE DRIVE helps to highlight aspects of the Army. The viewer is invited to engage in metaphoric thinking in an effort to make sense of the verbal text and the visual images. In doing so, the viewer may begin to see the Army as a place where he or she can learn more about him- or herself as a person.

The commercial "The Difference" provides another example of a personal growth metaphor. In this ad, a narrator who has a distinctive Spanish accent says, "The Army has taught me to see the world through different eyes." Several quick scenes flash while this statement is made. The first visual image is that of a person in a camouflage uniform running through water. This scene is shot through night vision gear, giving the appearance that the viewer is the one with the night vision goggles watching the situation unfold. This is followed by similar shots of tanks and other soldiers going through the water. Finally, a soldier wearing night vision gear is shown taking the goggles off. Because night vision gear serves as a tool for seeing, but is not literally one's own eye, a figurative relationship between the verbal statements and the visual images is created.

Considering this, the first term could be stated as SEEING. The visual images depict a night mission and the use of night-vision gear (night goggles). The focus is primarily on looking through the night goggles at what is taking place. The viewer is even invited to look though the goggles because this portion of the commercial is filmed in green. Therefore, the second term would be LOOKING THROUGH NIGHT GOGGLES.

Although the act of looking through night goggles may be something a soldier in the Army does, the term SEEING does little to deepen our understanding of the metaphoric relationships. Little can be learned about NIGHT GOGGLES by mapping the features of SEEING onto the term. In contrast, features of NIGHT GOGGLES provide insight into the term SEEING. Therefore, the metaphor can be verbalized as SEEING IS LOOKING THROUGH NIGHT GOGGLES.

What, then, might be some features of LOOKING THROUGH NIGHT GOGGLES that could be highlighted to help interpret the metaphor? Night goggles are used to see in darkness or in other situations when one would not ordinarily be able to see. Night goggles illuminate the darkness, providing "enlightenment" in an otherwise veiled situation. Based on the features of the vehicle, the tenor SEEING can be understood as a person being enlightened, or open to a different perspective.

Another possible interpretation of the metaphor could be that by "seeing" or being "enlightened," one becomes aware of different people and their cultures. The verbal text mentions "seeing the world through different eyes." The word "world," as well as the marked accent of the narrator, suggests different cultures. LOOKING THROUGH NIGHT GOGGLES allows a person to "see" things differently. SEEING things differently, then, leads to acceptance of differences in people throughout the world. The weak implicature of the metaphor suggests that the Army is a place where one will be given an opportunity to experience different cultures and to grow by being exposed to diversity. Based on the enlightenment aspect of the metaphor, the Army is a place to discover things that were unknown before (like what was occurring in the darkness) by providing the "night vision," or the opportunity to learn about the unknown.

The final example of a personal growth metaphor is in the commercial "Do You Know." Within this commercial, the narrator makes the statement "do you know

. . . where in your soul to find character?" The visual images depicted include a woman, who is outdoors, reaching up as though she is climbing something. This visual image occurs while the narrator is stating "where in your . . ." The following visual image, which is depicted during the statement ". . . soul to find character," is of several men jogging in unison on a tarmac. They are all dressed in jogging clothes, with the word "ARMY" on their shirts.

Based on the two very different visual images depicted during the verbal statement, it is more difficult to determine the two terms that make up the metaphor. It seems the focus of the verbal statement surrounds "character." The rest of the verbal statement leads up to the idea of finding character within oneself. Therefore, the first term, based on the verbal text, would be DEFINING CHARACTER. The visual images of the woman reaching and soldiers jogging accompany the verbal statement regarding character. Since the visual images focus predominately on the soldiers jogging, the second term can be identified as JOGGING.

Although jogging is something soldiers regularly participate in, there is nothing unique or important about highlighting this activity as part of being in the Army. Hence, the vehicle of the metaphor would be JOGGING, while the tenor would be DEFINING CHARACTER. The metaphor can be verbalized as DEFINING CHARACTER IS JOGGING.

Looking at the visual images may offer insight into interpretations of the metaphor. The first image is of a woman reaching up to climb something. This image features physical exercise. Next is the image of several male soldiers jogging in unison. They are all in perfect formation and do not seem strained by the exercise. They seem to have the strength and the ability to endure the physical demands. So how does this help to interpret the tenor DEFINING CHARACTER?

The fact that the soldiers are running in unison, and not physically taxed by the jog, implies they are running for conditioning. The jog is a means of keeping the soldiers fit and ready to respond to future challenges. It seems reasonable that because they do not appear to be fatigued as they run, one might assume they jog regularly to stay in top physical condition.

With respect to defining one's character, personal growth demands developing the strength and ability to endure psychological and emotional challenges. To "build character," one must seek out opportunities to "condition" one's character by embracing mental challenges. Such conditioning could be approached just like an exercise regimen, with regular, sustained activities to keep one's character "in shape."

Furthermore, jogging requires discipline. The Army joggers are clearly regimented and uniform in their movements. Discipline is also a quality many people wish to bolster in themselves, and may be a quality one would want when seeking to discover aspects of one's character. The Army is certainly a place where discipline is both valued and demanded. The metaphor gives the implicit message that the Army will facilitate the defining of character by providing potential recruits with the ability to endure challenges and be disciplined.

The metaphors in this cluster focused specifically on personal growth. SOUL-SEARCHING IS A MOTORCYCLE DRIVE implied that the Army is a place to learn how to overcome difficulties, gain direction and develop responsibility. SEEING IS LOOK-ING THROUGH NIGHT GOGGLES suggested that different perspectives on people, situations, and cultures could be gained in the Army. Finally, the metaphor DEFIN-ING CHARACTER IS JOGGING indicated that the conditioning needed to build one's character could be found in the Army.

These three metaphors are representative examples of personal growth metaphors. There are other examples that exist in this campaign as well, such as the metaphor in the commercial "Do You Know." In this example, the narrator states, "Do you know the shortest line to a college degree is a straight line called discipline? Do you know how to walk it?" The visual images depicted are of soldiers sitting in a classroom, with a military instructor lecturing at an overhead projector. This is followed by two soldiers repelling down a tall wooden wall, with the focal point being the straight lines of the two ropes. Finally, there is the visual image of a soldier's boots walking across a tightrope. "The Difference" offers another example of a personal growth metaphor. The verbal statement "The Army has taught me . . . to find the road I am looking for" accompanies the visual images of a female soldier flagging a tank, then walking down a road. These examples also meet Forceville's (1996) criteria, rendering them verbo-pictorial metaphors. They provide further support for the assertion that the Army uses personal growth metaphors in its television recruiting commercials.

CAREER METAPHORS

So far, clusters of metaphors relating to skill development and personal growth have been identified in the 1999–2000 Army advertising campaign. The last cluster of metaphors used in the commercials draws figurative associations between opportunities in the Army and career paths that one might pursue. Many people who enlist or become officers in the Army make the job a career.

The first example is found in the commercial "Get To Work." The narrator states, "There are other ways to get to work . . . but nahhh!" The visual images featured in this commercial show Army soldiers, dressed in flight gear, preparing to jump from an airplane. They are then shown jumping from the plane and falling through the sky. The soldiers are shown hanging from their open parachutes and then finally walking on the ground packing up their parachutes.

The verbal statement "other ways to get to work" suggests a commute. Therefore, the first term of the metaphor seems to be COMMUTING. With respect to the visual images, the viewer infers that the airplane is dropping the soldiers off to engage in their work—the completion of a mission or training. Such an activity often occurs when there is a need for the soldiers to be dropped into places secretly. Therefore, the second term would be A PARACHUTE DROP.

Which of the terms is the tenor and which is the vehicle? Between the two terms, it is more likely that the primary focus of the ad is A PARACHUTE DROP. The Army would not be interested in advertising a commute as an aspect of military life. Going on parachute drops would be a more exciting element of the Army to feature in the commercial. Therefore, the metaphor can be stated as A PARACHUTE DROP IS COMMUTING. Commuting suggests traveling to get to work. To relate COMMUTING to A PARACHUTE DROP, then, is to imply that a parachute drop is a means of getting to work. This is strongly implied by the metaphor.

The interpretation of the metaphor can be taken further to suggest that the Army is a career option. The visual image of a parachute drop challenges the typical notion of a commute, which usually suggests sitting in traffic to get to and from work. The metaphor invites the viewer to perceive the Army as an alternative career option to the "9 to 5," working-in-a-cubical career. The use of the visual images depicting the parachute drop implies that this is how the viewer would get to work should he or she join the Army, in contrast to sitting in traffic for hours in order to get to work. The "commute" in the Army will be filled with action and excitement, as will a career in the Army.

The metaphor A PARACHUTE DROP IS COMMUTING may also conjure up the notion of a judge, governor, or president commuting a prisoner's sentence from, for example, the death penalty to life imprisonment. Although this is a rather weak implicature, the interpretation is that the Army commutes a potential recruit's sentence from a "dead-end job" to a job full of fun and adventure.

An additional example of a career metaphor is found in the commercial "Technology." In this commercial, the narrator states, "Applicants wanted. High-tech jobs. Window offices. No experience necessary." The visual images that accompany the verbal text depict people standing in front of the flag, taking an oath ("applicants wanted"). Then there are several shot of x-rays, computer banks, and a satellite dish ("high-tech jobs"). Then there is a shot of a soldier in a tower on a ship at sea, looking through binoculars out large windows ("window offices"). The commercial finishes with close-up shots of several younger people dressed in various military uniforms ("no experience necessary").

In attempting to apply Forceville's (1996) criteria to the "Technology" example, it became clear that the commercial did not fit. Forceville (1996) suggested identifying the tenor and the vehicle, terms that originate from literary metaphor research. Although "Technology" is a verbo-pictorial metaphor, the two terms are not easily reducible to a tenor and vehicle. The difficulty in determining the tenor and the vehicle stems from the presence of eight terms in the commercial that produce four different metaphors. Dissecting the commercial in this manner negates the cumulative meaning. The whole of the commercial is greater than the sum of its parts.

However, Whittock (1990) offered some insight into how one might interpret the metaphoric aspects of the commercial "Technology." He argues that "there is no reason to suppose the effect of cinematic metaphors may be captured in words without loss"[5] (Whittock, 1990, p. 49). Although "Technology" is not a cinematic metaphor but a verbo-pictorial metaphor, attempting to capture the metaphor entirely in words may result in a loss of meaning. Because this particular verbo-pictorial metaphor relies on a series of visual images juxtaposed with a series of words, it is appropriate to look at the commercial as a whole in order to understand the greater meaning of the metaphor.

In an effort to organize his discussion of cinematic metaphors, Whittock (1990) generated 10 metaphoric formulas that help to understand how they function. One metaphoric formula, substitution, seems useful in analyzing the "Technology" commercial. Metaphoric substitution is when one term is replaced by another term (Whittock, 1990). What the audience anticipates seeing is replaced with something quite different, but intended to stimulate metaphoric thought. Whittock (1990) noted that "an audience, in order to recognize a substitution [in a film], must have an expectation of what should appear so they can perceive something has been put in its place" (p. 54). Whittock (1990) provided an example of substitution that comes from Satyajit Ray's film *Pather Panchali*. Whittock (1990) described an occasion "when a father comes home from a long absence only to learn that his daughter is dead. We see him uttering a cry of lament, but what we hear on the soundtrack is the wail of a flute" (p. 55). In this example, the flute serves as a substitution for the wail of the father, and, as Whittock (1990) argued, functions to distance and universalize the father's grief. When analyzing the commercial "Technology," it is important to identify some of the possible expectations a viewer may have when confronted with the terms of the metaphors in an effort to determine how the substitution functions to create the metaphor.

The verbal components of the "Technology" commercial are structured like a classified advertisement, including common terms used in an ad promoting a job. The viewer, on hearing the verbal text, may have the expectation of visual images depicting people turning in applications and résumés to an office filled with computers. Furthermore, the expectation of a "window office" would be that of a private office with a great view seen through large windows, as opposed to a small cubicle like those featured in Dilbert cartoons.

However, what is depicted in the commercial is very different, challenging the expectation of the viewer by using substitutions. Instead of people turning applications in to an office building, there is the visual depiction of many people lined up in front of a United States flag, taking an oath. Satellite dishes, x-rays. and computer banks take the place of the computer-filled cubicles. Rather than an office with large windows, the viewer is shown a man standing in the tower of a ship at sea, looking through binoculars out large windows.

The effect of this substitution is the implication that the Army, like other organizations, is a place for career opportunities. The commercial seems to be designed

---

[5]Whittock (1990) focused specifically on metaphors in film, and thus identified visual metaphors present in films as "cinematic metaphors."

to appeal to people who have been looking for a career, possibly even scouring the classified ads looking for a job. The verbal text relies on the structure of a "typical" classified ad to grab the attention of viewers, hoping to remind them that the Army is an option for employment. In essence, the structure of the commercial implicitly states, "The Army is hiring!"

In contrast, the images that were substituted suggest a very different career opportunity than what one might find if pursuing leads from the classified ads. The visual images depict an exciting and adventurous career cruising the ocean, creating graphic designs, sending satellite transmissions, or taking x-rays. The use of the visual images as substitutions for what one would expect when confronted with a conventional classified ad challenges the viewers' perception of what a career "looks" like, and offers an alternative to the uneventful 9-to-5 office job.

The metaphors analyzed in this cluster focused specifically on career development. A PARACHUTE DROP IS COMMUTING was the first metaphor addressed, which implied that the Army is a career option and offers more excitement than other careers may. The second metaphor, which was different in structure, was the classified ad metaphor. This example served as a reminder that the Army is "hiring," and offered an alternative to the traditional 9-to-5 job via the visual images depicted.

These two career development metaphors are examples. Although the other clusters of metaphors had several other examples, there was only one other career development metaphor present in this campaign. One possible reason for the imbalance may be that the entire commercial "Technology" was focused on career development, whereas the other commercials featured different metaphors within a given commercial. The commercial "The Difference" features the other example. In this commercial, the narrator states, "The Army has taught me . . . to build bridges towards my future." This statement accompanies the visual images of soldiers working to assemble a portable bridge and then extend the bridge across a river. This example is a verbo-pictorial metaphor similar to that of the PARACHUTE DROPPING IS COMMUTING metaphor and provides another example of a career metaphor in the Army commercials.

The purpose of this essay was to explore the ways in which visual images and textual components could be blended metaphorically as a persuasive technique in recruiting. A select group of Army commercials served as an example from which conclusions were drawn. Specifically, this chapter explored groups of metaphors that were present in the Army commercials, which were categorized as skills, personal growth and career metaphors.

The skills and career metaphors both featured the vehicle verbally (DANCING, SWIMMING, DRIVING, and COMMUTING) while depicting the tenor visually (BOXING, HELICASTING, TANKING and PARACHUTE DROP). In contrast, the personal growth metaphors relied on a visually depicted tenor (SOUL-SEARCHING, SEEING, and DEFINING CHARACTER) and a verbal vehicle (MOTORCYLE DRIVE, NIGHT GOGGLES, and A JOG). One possible reason for the discrepancy between the structure of the terms in personal growth metaphors versus the other two clusters may be due to the theme of the metaphor. In the personal growth metaphors, the tenor may have been verbally stated because it would be difficult to depict visually. For example, "soul-searching" and "building character" are abstract concepts rather than concrete activities. As the tenor becomes more abstract, then, it may become more challenging to communicate the intended interpretation via visual images. The skill and career metaphors were aimed at expressing more concrete aspects of the Army, and consequently featured the primary focus of the commercial visually.

Both the skill metaphors and the career metaphors seem to rely on terms that are basic aspects of the human experience. For example, learning to swim is an activity many people engage in early in their lives. Most people have had the experience of learning to swim, so when this statement is made, there is a specific expectation about what can be visually depicted.

Verbo-pictorial metaphors are an important subtype of visual metaphors because they are common, and seem to be more easily identifiable than other types of visual metaphors because the text provides some clues as to how to process the metaphor. They are a rhetorical technique that stimulates abstract thinking by the juxtaposition of a visual image with a verbal text. Past research (Forceville, 1996) addressed how verbo-pictorial metaphors functioned within static advertisements. This chapter expands the research regarding verbo-pictorial metaphors in advertising by focusing on television commercials. The examples analyzed illustrate that verbo-pictorial metaphors can also be used as a rhetorical technique in television commercials. Furthermore, the examples demonstrate that verbo-pictorial metaphors may exist in clusters that can be grouped based on specific themes of the metaphors.

An institution may employ many techniques in its advertising. The set of Army commercials analyzed in this chapter highlights how verbo-pictorial metaphors function as a rhetorical technique useful in advertising designed to recruit new members. The role played by verbo-pictorial metaphors in the recruitment commercials was to illustrate how the Army could benefit the potential recruit (i.e., skill building, personal growth, and career development). The verbo-pictorial metaphors also expressed some of the Army's values, which could be extracted from the implicatures of the metaphors.

Advertising alone may not cause a person to join the Army or become a member of an organization, but it can position the organization as an option in the mind of the potential recruit. Rhetorical techniques that grab the attention of the potential recruit are more likely to begin the persuasive process. For example, a verbo-pictorial metaphor may cause the viewer to engage in abstract thinking in an effort to figure out the error that has occurred in the relationship suggested between the two terms. After the viewer has processed the metaphor, he or she may feel content, having "solved the puzzle." The viewer is more likely, then, to view the advertisement positively and thus transfer that positive feeling to the institution producing the advertising.

Additionally, visual metaphors serve to restructure the viewer's perception of the Army or other institutions. The use of verbo-pictorial metaphors, as well as fast-paced and complex images, highlights fun and exciting aspects of the Army, while downplaying the violent and destructive aspects. Verbo-pictorial metaphors, then, can be an effective rhetorical technique used by an institution seeking to promote a particular image of itself in order to recruit new members.

Visual persuasion is a rich area for research. Visual images are complex and multifaceted and often feature layers of meaning. However, meaning is not always easily discerned from visual images, and often requires the use of verbal texts to fully convey the message. In contrast, verbal texts may rely on visual images in an effort to develop deeper meanings. The Army commercials provide a compelling example of how verbal texts and visual images can be juxtaposed to serve a particular rhetorical purpose, while at the same time illustrating the complexity of visual rhetoric.

REFERENCES

Armed forces recruiting: Hearing before the Senate Armed Services Personnel, 106th Cong., 2d Sess. (2000) (testimony of David Ohle, Deputy Chief of Staff for Personnel, U.S. Army).

Asch, B. J., Kilburn, M. R., & Klerman, J. A. (1999). *Attracting college-bound youth into the military.* Santa Monica, CA: RAND.

Bandow, D. (2000). Mend, never end, the All-Volunteer Force. *Orbis, 44,* 463–476.

Dent, C., & Rosenberg, L. (1990). Visual and verbal metaphors: Developmental interactions. *Child Development, 61,* 983–994.

Forceville, C. (1996). Pictorial metaphors in advertising. New York: Routledge.

Gamble, T. & Gamble, M. (1999). *Communication works.* Boston, MA: McGraw-Hill College.

Harkey, W., Reid, L., & Whitehill King, K. (1988). Army advertising's perceived influence: Some preliminary findings. *Journalism Quarterly, 65,* 719–732.

Highhouse, S., Beadle, A., Gallo, A., & Miller, L. (1998). Get 'em while they last! Effects of scarcity information in job advertisements. *Journal of Applied Social Psychology, 28,* 799–795.

Kaplan, S. (1990). Visual metaphors in the representation of communication technology. *Critical Studies in Mass Communication, 7,* 37–47.

Kaplan, S. (1992, June). *An empirical investigation of the tension in visual metaphors.* Paper presented at the Sixth Annual Visual Communication Conference, Flagstaff, AZ.

Kaplan, S. (1994). A conceptual analysis of form and content in visual metaphors. *Communication, 13,* 197–209.

Keck, G. & Mueller, B. (1994). Intended vs. unintended messages: Viewer perceptions of United States Army television commercials. *Journal of Advertising, 34,* 70–77.

Knoch, J. (1990). Apple ads reflect target intellect. *Personnel Journal, 69,* 107–114.

Lakoff, G., & Johnson, M. (1980). *Metaphors we live by.* Chicago: The University of Chicago Press.

Louis Caldera holds Special Defense Department briefing on recruiting: Hearing before the Defense Department, 106th Cong., 2d Sess. (2000) (testimony of Louis Caldera, Secretary of the U.S. Army).

Magnus, M. (1986). Recruitment ad-vantages. *Personnel Journal, 65,* 58–80.

Martin, B. (1987). Recruitment ad ventures. *Personnel Journal, 66,* 46–60.

Messaris, P. (1994). *Visual literacy: Image, mind, & reality.* San Francisco, CA: Westview Press.

Messaris, P. (1998). Visual aspect of media literacy. *Journal of Communication, 48,* 70–80.

Murray, M. P., & McDonald, L. L. (1999). *Recent recruiting trends and their implications for models of enlistment supply.* Santa Monica, CA: RAND.

Myers, S. (1998, November 3). Fewer teens feel the pull of "Be all that you can be." *The Sacramento Bee, 284,* p. A1.

Myers, S. (1999, September 27). Drop in recruits pushes pentagon to new strategy. *The New York Times,* pp. A1, A14.

Myers, S. (2000, January 8). Army, its recruiting not all it could be, decides to overhaul its advertising. *The New York Times,* p. A9.

Osborn, M. M., & Ehninger, D. (1962). The metaphor in public address. *Speech Monographs, 29,* 223–234.

Phillips, B. J. (1997). Thinking into it: Consumer interpretation of complex advertising images. *Journal of Advertising, 26,* 77–88.

Scott, L. M. (1994). Image in advertising: The need for a theory of visual rhetoric. *Journal of Consumer Research, 21,* 252–273.

Sperber, D. & Wilson, D. (1986). *Relevance: Communication and cognition.* Oxford, UK: Blackwell.

Stoops, R. (1984). Recruitment ads that get results. *Personnel Journal, 59,* 24–26.

United States Army (USA) Recruiting Command. (1999). Power Point presentation and business packets. (Received October, 1999).

U.S. Representative Steve Buyer (R-IN) holds hearing on the All-Volunteer Force: Hearing before the Personnel Subcommittee of the House Armed Services Committee, 106th Cong., 2d. Sess. (2000).

Vande Berg, L., Wenner, L., & Gronbeck, B. (1998). *Critical approaches to television.* Boston, MA: Houghton Mifflin Company.

Whittock, T. (1990). *Metaphor and film.* New York: Cambridge University Press.

APPENDIX

General Description of Visual Metaphors in Army Commercials
(1999–2000)

1. The Difference: (:30) (from 1997–1998 ad campaign)

Narrator's Statements	Visual Images
The Army has taught me to see the world through different eyes.	The camera looks through a night vision scope at someone running in the water. A soldier is seen using the night vision scope, which is followed by the same soldier looking though the night vision at a tank.
To know how to take the leap.	There is a tank being directed by a soldier atop the tank.
To build bridges towards my future.	A bridge is being constructed. Several soldiers help with the construction.
To find the road I am looking for.	A soldier is shown motioning a tank down a dirt road.
Your career tomorrow begins today.	A radar screen is depicted. Soldiers work on a helicopter.
In the Army, you can learn valuable skills while earning up to $40,000 to continue your education.	College GI bill information is presented on the screen. An Army officer receives commendation.
Take a step forward.	Soldiers are seen taking a step forward, and then walking with happy looks on their faces. A stern-looking soldier is shown looking though a camera.
Be all that you can be.	Army logo appears on screen followed by the phone number for a recruiting office.

2. Step Up: (:30)

Narrator's Statements	Visual Images
Step up . . .	A man is getting up into starting position for a race. A woman is pulling herself up an Army training structure. Pilots look at the sky, followed by an image of a radar screen. A helicopter is shown taking off and flies with the radar screen superimposed over it. Army logo then appears on screen, along with a white star, the phrase "be all you can be," and the phone number for a recruiting office.

Learn to see farther.	A soldier looks through binoculars in a control room while a helicopter flies by in the background.
Learn there are teachers who won't allow you to fail.	A person wearing an ARMY t-shirt tosses a basketball back and forth. A gym with people pledging allegiance to the flag is depicted. A paratrooper officer checks the gear of his soldiers.
Learn to dance.	A man practices boxing in a ring. Women are doing jumping jacks. Two men box together in a ring.
To draw.	An image of radar screen, then a close-up of the screen which reads "Drop Zone."
Learn that the real challenge doesn't come from the outside . . . *but from within . . .*	Army motorcycle convoy. Man getting out of pool. Paratroopers preparing to jump out of an airplane. Soldiers as a group are shown jumping out of the plane. Paratroopers are shown falling through the sky. There is a progression of a few seconds as the paratroopers fall farther from the plane. Paratroopers fall closer to camera located below the falling group as they have jumped from the plane. Tanks on maneuvers, man typing on computer in tank, tank firing.
and that there is more to you than you ever knew . . .	Soldiers of different color and gender are depicted looking into the camera. A woman plays soccer in an Army t-shirt.
Be all that you can be.	Army logo appears on screen, followed by a white star and the phone number for a recruiting office.

3. Find Out: (:30)

Narrator's Statements	*Visual Images*
Are you ready to make real noise?	A man bowls. Women look across a crowded room at camera. Soldier in field on phone. Man choosing a bowling ball. Tank gun firing. Bowling friends cheering.
To make new friends?	Men playing basketball in gym with large American flag in background. Men wearing Army t-shirts are lined up in front of flag.
To take sharper pictures?	Two army officers are shown looking at P.E.T. scans of the brain. An Army surveyor looks at blueprints.

Are you ready to build bridges?	Soldiers and machinery are shown crossing a bridge. A man shaves his head with a razor.
Learn diplomacy?	A soldier holds a female child while standing next to a Hispanic woman. Two soldiers play with some children while chickens run around. An Army officer is shown getting married. A young man wearing an Army shirt sits on his bed in his bedroom. Soldiers are shown on a train. The soldiers laugh together.
Learn to swim?	Two soldiers jump out of helicopter into water (helicasting). Soldiers look through a sniper scope while lying in tall grass. A young girl runs into the arms of a soldier leaving an Army helicopter on a tarmac.
Are you ready to turn what you want to do into what you will do?	Soldiers climb a wall with ropes. A soldier looks up at the sky (a satellite dish is depicted behind him). A soldier stands in front of a radar screen. Men are shown cheering and laughing. A man is seen wearing boxing gloves, with a tired expression on his face. A soldier walks with a forlorn look on his face.
Are you ready?	A close-up of a soldier in camouflage looking away from camera.
Be all that you can be.	Army logo then appears on screen, followed by a white star and the phone number for a recruiting office.

4. Do You Know: (:30)

Narrator's Statements	Visual Images
Do you know how to drive?	An officer shown at his wedding while an older officer takes pictures. A bride and groom in convertible, with Army officers in dress uniforms and women in summer dresses standing in the background. Army vehicles are a shown being driven in sandy area.
How to say "hey that's a foul" in Japanese?	Men play football in the mud. Men play basketball in gym under an American flag. A stationary satellite dish is shown in time-lapse photography while clouds fly by overhead.

Do you know where in the heavens to find a human voice?	A keyhole camera lens depicts soldiers in front of banks of computers in a small room. A soldier holds a smiling baby in the air. A soldier, who stands in front of a satellite dish, looks up at the sky. A red sky is depicted along with several soldiers jumping over the camera.
Where in your soul to find character?	A man is shown sweating. A woman climbs a rock. Soldiers wearing Army t-shirts run in unison on a barren tarmac with overcast sky in the background. Soldiers jump from a helicopter into water below. Soldiers wearing Army t-shirts stand in front of a large American flag. A man runs behind a camouflage net. A computer screen is depicted. A woman laughs to herself.
Do you know the shortest distance to a college degree is a straight line called discipline?	An officer stands beside an overhead projector while teaching a class. Soldiers read blueprints. In unison, two soldiers repel down a wall that reads "Airborne." A close-up shot of an Asian soldier, which is followed by a soldier reading.
Do you know how to walk it?	A soldier is shown walking a tight rope as camera looks up from below the rope at the soldier. Close-up of soldier wearing face paint.
Be all that you can be.	Army logo then appears on screen, followed by a white star and the phone number for a recruiting office.

5. Get To Work: (:15)

Narrator's Statements	*Visual Images*
There are other ways to get to work . . .	Pilot with oxygen mask is shown looking around a corner. A soldier has his hand on a lever. Close up of rear of parachute divers as they prepare of jump. A group of soldiers jump out of a plane. Paratroopers fall to the camera as the plane flies out of the shot.
But. . .nahhh!	A progression of a few seconds is shown as the paratroopers fall further from the plane and from the camera. The paratroopers pack up their gear up on the ground as the

plane flies over them. Camera follows plane as it flies overhead.

Army logo then appears on screen, followed by a white star and the phone number a for recruiting office.

6. Technology: (:15)

Narrator's Statements	Visual Images
Applicants wanted.	Men and women lined up in front of flag in a gym as they take an oath (right hands held in the air).
High-tech jobs.	A soldier, who stands in front of a satellite dish, looks up at the sky. Two soldiers are shown looking at a P.E.T scan. Computer banks within a small room are depicted. A soldier stares at a computer with an elaborate radar screen. A helicopter taking off, followed by a soldier working at a computer.
Window offices.	A soldier is seen looking though binoculars, while a helicopter flies by in the background. Soldiers salute. Soldiers of different races look at the camera.
No experience necessary.	A man is seen playing basketball and then standing in front of radar and computer screens. A soldier looks up at the sky while standing in front of a satellite dish.
	Army logo then appears on screen, followed by a white star and the phone number for a recruiting office.

7. Are You Ready?: (:60)

Narrator's Statements	Visual Images
Are you ready?	A man is shown crouching down, preparing to run. A soldier, who stands in front of a satellite dish, looks up at the sky. There is a close-up of the runner's face, which is sweaty. Soldiers laugh together. A soldier is seen talking on a telephone in the field. Men are playing football in the mud. A woman wearing an Army t-shirt hits a

soccer ball with her head. The same woman is seen with comrades smiling and laughing, while holding the soccer ball. Soldiers laugh and cheer. Another close-up of the runner with sweat on his face. Soldiers are shown looking content after a soccer game. A woman is depicted climbing a rock.

To learn how to drive?

An officer receives a diploma in front of an American flag; he then hugs his parents. Military vehicles drive through a sandy environment. A soldier is seen working at her computer.

To swim?

Men jump from a helicopter into the water below.

To dance?

Men box under an American flag. Soldiers are shown running over the camera.

Are you ready . . .

A close-up shot of soldiers of different races. Calvary soldiers in dress uniforms on horses are depicted. Soldiers run in unison on a tarmac, while a black man leads the group. Men are seen standing on a tank, which is silhouetted against the sky. A progression of the clouds is shown.

. . . to find yourself?

A soldier looks up at sky with a satellite dish in the background. A soldier stands in front of radar screens. Men wearing face paint ride motorcycles in the fog. A baby is shown holding small American flag. There is a close-up of a man with a forlorn look. A helicopter is superimposed over a radar screen. Soldiers and vehicles are depicted crossing a bridge.

To prove yourself?

Soldiers climb with ropes. Soldiers stand on the peak of a mountain. Swimmer emerges from pool.

To learn how to fly?

Paratroopers are shown jumping out of an airplane and falling from the sky. Men play basketball in front of an American flag in a gym.

Are you ready to make noise?

Tanks are shown moving and firing. A woman does a bicycle kick.

To play hard?

Men cheer while the woman finishes the bicycle kick, landing on the ground.

Are you ready?

Women laugh, while a woman holds a soccer ball. Soldiers are depicted repelling, in unison, down a wall with an "Airborne" logo on it.

Be all that you can be.

Army logo then appears on screen, followed by a white star and the phone number for a recruiting office.

CHAPTER FIFTEEN

Understanding Visual Metaphor in Advertising

Barbara J. Phillips
University of Saskatchewan

Imagine having a dream in which ordinary objects blend and merge into fantastic hybrids. In the dream, you reach for a pot on the stove, only to snatch your hand back when you discover the pot handle has turned into a cactus. After slipping into one shoe, you find that the other has morphed into a sleek black sports car. Hoping to escape the dream, you race to your car but as you place your luggage into the trunk, the car burps. You slide behind the wheel and find a bottle of dishwashing liquid hanging from your rearview mirror.

Welcome to the world of visual metaphor in advertising—a place where products undergo strange, dreamlike transformations in order to persuade consumers to purchase commodities. The cactus pot handle from your dreams is the central image in an ad for Advil pain reliever, an ad for Tod's shoes places its loafer side-by-side with a sports car, the Toyota Echo eats your luggage "whole," and dishwashing liquid takes the place of a car's air freshener in an ad for Cascade. Although visual metaphor has been appearing in ads for at least 50 years, researchers are just starting to understand this rhetorical figure. Some researchers have chosen to focus on the literary and interpretive aspects of the arresting imagery in visual metaphor ads; others have concentrated on examining the cognitive effects of this ad execution. This chapter reviews what we know about visual metaphor and poses questions to provoke thought and spur new research that can build a deeper understanding of the impact of visual metaphor in advertising.

A DEFINITION OF VISUAL METAPHOR

A metaphor is a rhetorical figure—an artful deviation from audience expectation that occurs at the level of style, not content, and is not judged as an error by the audience (McQuarrie & Mick, 1996). Metaphor is one type of rhetorical figure known as a trope, a category that also includes irony, pun, and other literary devices. Tropes are incomplete and undercoded and require closure by the audience (McQuarrie & Mick, 1996); they are used to present advertising messages in unusual ways to gain attention and persuade consumers to consider the ad's proposition (Scott, 1994a).

The difference between metaphor and other tropes is that metaphor compares two objects through analogy by suggesting that one object is figuratively like another, although they are literally quite different (Stern, 1990; Ward & Gaidis, 1990). Once the comparison is made, the similarity between the two objects becomes understood as reasonable (Salomon, 1979). For example, an ad for Johnson's bath oil suggests, "Turn your baby's bath into a lullaby." Consumers who encounter this ad do not think that the advertiser has made an error. Instead, consumers feel invited to metaphorically compare bath oil to a lullaby to find what the two objects have in common. This analogy is conventionally represented as, "BATH OIL IS LULLABY" (e.g., Forceville, 1996) and can be understood to be making the statement, "bath oil is like a lullaby because both are soothing to children and help put them to sleep."

The Johnson bath oil ad, which relies exclusively on words to relate bath oil to a lullaby, provides an example of a verbal metaphor. Other ads use *images* to present two objects for association and comparison—a visual metaphor. In the Tod's shoe ad discussed earlier, for example, the image of a shoe is compared to the image of an automobile. This visual metaphor could be read as, "LOAFER IS SPORTS CAR because both are elegant and stylish." Although most published research examines verbal metaphor, a small but growing body of research examines visual metaphor. Interest in visual metaphor was initiated through seminal articles by Scott (1994a, 1994b), who argued that images in advertising are not merely peripheral cues or representations of reality but visual symbols that provide meaning to consumers as elements of persuasive rhetoric.

To guide the exploration of visual metaphor, advertising researchers have assumed an equivalence between the visual and verbal forms of metaphor. This assumption of equivalence is supported by authors who assert that metaphor does not occur at the level of surface language, but at the level of thought (Forceville, 1996; Hitchon, 1997). That is, it is not words or images that define a metaphor but instead the nonliteral character of the underlying comparison. Indirect empirical support for this argument comes from Smith (1991), who concludes that a consumer's interpretation of an advertising message can be similar whether it is based on images or words.

Countering the assumption of equivalence is the work of Morgan and Reichert (1999), who measured consumers' comprehension of six unaltered magazine ads that contained visual or verbal metaphors. One of the findings of their study is that subjects comprehended the advertiser's intended meaning more often for visual metaphor ads than for verbal metaphor ads. The authors speculate that a verbal metaphor is turned into a mental image by consumers during ad interpretation. With a visual metaphor, the work that is required to turn the words into images has already been done, simplifying the processing task and increasing comprehension.

In a similar experiment, McQuarrie and Mick (2002) measured attitude toward the ad and recall of print ads containing visual or verbal metaphor and other forms of rhetoric. One of their conclusions is that visual rhetoric is better liked and recalled than verbal rhetoric under normal magazine viewing conditions. The stronger effects they attribute to visual rhetoric suggest that the two forms of metaphor may not be equivalent in terms of consumer response.

Both of the studies by Morgan and Reichert (1999) and McQuarrie and Mick (2002) focus on other aspects of rhetoric and metaphor beyond the visual/verbal dichotomy. To achieve their goals, neither study was able to compare the same metaphors expressed both visually and verbally; instead, the "visual" and "verbal" categories of ads they used contained different products, different selling features, and different metaphors. In addition, to create realistic ads, the "visual" ads in both experiments contained verbal copy that could help explain the meanings of the visual metaphors. Consequently, further work is required to identify and distinguish the effects of visual versus verbal metaphor.

Given these opposing theories and findings regarding the equivalence of visual and verbal metaphor, the remainder of this chapter discusses metaphor research with the implicit assumption that findings regarding verbal metaphor in advertising are equally descriptive of visual metaphor in advertising. It is an open question whether this assumption of equivalence will be supported over time as further evidence is uncovered.

Research question 1: How are visual and verbal advertising metaphors similar or different in their impact on consumer interpretation and response?

THE CATEGORIZATION OF VISUAL METAPHOR

Beyond defining visual metaphor, researchers have attempted to categorize it through typologies and examples. One of the most complete categorizations has been developed by Forceville (1996) based on his judgment of modern print ads. Forceville described four types of visual metaphor: (a) metaphors with one pictorially present term, (b) metaphors with two pictorially present terms, (c) pictorial similes, and (d) verbo-pictorial metaphors. These categories are represented by the ad examples discussed in your dream. A metaphor with one pictorially present term (MP1) compares the image of an object to an implied secondary object that is not shown. For example, the Cascade ad suggests that, "DISHWASHING DETERGENT IS AIR FRESHENER because both have a fresh scent." The bottle of dishwashing detergent is pictured hanging from the rearview mirror of a car, a place one would normally find an air freshener. In addition, the bottle of detergent is flattened to look like an air freshener. However, the air freshener is not pictured.

A metaphor with two pictorially present terms (MP2) compares two objects that are both at least partially pictured. The objects are fused together into a hybrid object such as the cactus-handled pot in the Advil ad. The metaphor can be read as, "POT HANDLE is CACTUS because both cause pain when held (when one has arthritis)." A pictorial simile is similar to an MP2 in that both objects are pictured in the ad. However, the objects are not combined together but are presented separately as in the Tod's shoe ad where the loafer and the sports car are pictured side by side.

Forceville's final category, verbo-pictorial metaphor, relies on a comparison between a visual object and verbal object where the visual object is usually an image of the product. For example, the Toyota Echo ad pictures the open trunk of a car. By adding the word "Burp" to the ad, the metaphor is developed: "TRUNK is STOMACH because both can hold a lot." Removing the words from a verbo-pictorial metaphor removes the metaphorical meaning of the ad. This is not the case for the other three categorizations of metaphor that can stand on their own without verbal copy.

Investigations of the number of occurrences of these types of visual metaphors are rare. Kaplan (1992) examined 464 current print ads for automobiles and alcoholic beverages and found that 31% of the ads in his sample contained visual metaphors. He classified 29% of the visual metaphors as "identity" metaphors (similar to Forceville's MP2s) and 71% as "juxtaposition" metaphors (similar to Forceville's pictorial similes).

In terms of relative effectiveness, Forceville argues that pictorial similes have weaker persuasive effects than the other types of metaphor because the images are not combined. He believes that this makes the comparison between the images more explicit, thereby requiring less work from the reader and making the metaphorical comparison less interesting and pleasurable. His views are consistent with those of other advertising researchers who have contended that verbal (Stern, 1990) and visual similes (McQuarrie & Mick, 1999) weaken the possible effects of metaphorical comparison because these similes are less deviant and less figurative than metaphors.

An alternative view is that pictorial similes ought to be just as persuasive as MP1s and MP2s if metaphors operate at the level of thought instead of language (Hitchon, 1997). That is, there should be little difference between a metaphor (e.g., LOAFER is SPORTS CAR) and its corresponding simile (e.g., LOAFER is *like* a SPORTS-CAR) if it is the analogous comparison, and not the form of the images, that is driving the impact of the visual metaphor. Although several authors have categorized visual metaphor based on descriptive differences in appearance, there is little empirical evidence that these differences matter. A rich understanding of visual metaphor awaits the researcher who can match the form of a metaphor with its effects.

Consistent with the assumed equivalence of verbal and visual metaphor in the preceding section, the remainder of this chapter will assume equivalence between

MP1s, MP2s, pictorial similes, and verbo-pictorial metaphors; the term "visual metaphor" will continue to be used regardless of the forms of the comparative objects in the ads. Research is clearly needed to test the validity of this assumption.

Research question 2: What influence does the form of a visual metaphor have on consumer interpretation and response? How do the effects of form interact with the effects of visual or verbal modalities?

THE INTERPRETATION OF VISUAL METAPHOR

In the definitions and examples of visual metaphor presented in this chapter, visual metaphor ads have been discussed as if they had one clear and unambiguous meaning. This often is not the case because visual metaphors have to be interpreted by consumers. MacCormac (1985, p. 76) noted: "Metaphors force us to wonder, compare, note similarities and dissimilarities, and then seek confirmation or disconfirmation of the suggestions posed by the metaphors." This interpretive process creates a consumer's comprehension of the meaning of the advertising metaphor; thus, the ad's created meaning may differ between individuals.

The first step in making sense of a visual metaphor ad is to understand that the ad's images cannot be read literally—as representative pictures used to express concrete objects and events (MacCormac, 1985). Instead, consumers use the images' deviance from expectation to start thinking about figurative ways of understanding the ad's images (McQuarrie & Mick, 1999; Scott, 1994a). For example, seeing a bottle of dishwashing detergent hanging from a car's rear view mirror in an ad is odd and unusual and should prompt figurative processing. In a study based on interviews with real consumers (Phillips, 1997), I found that consumers use deviance from expectation in visual metaphor ads to skip over literal interpretations (e.g., Cascade can be used to wash my car) and light on metaphorical interpretations (e.g., Cascade has a fresh scent like air freshener).

Sperber and Wilson (1986) used relevance theory to explain how consumers interpret the meaning of a metaphor. They proposed that the reader is guided by her awareness that the sender of the ad is trying to be relevant to her. The reader finds the first plausible interpretation of the metaphor that seems relevant to the message. In the Cascade example, other possible similarities between dishwashing detergent and air fresheners are that their containers are both made of plastic and each is bought infrequently. However, these interpretations are less likely to be elicited given that they are less relevant in an advertising context, where products are usually associated with positive benefits (Forceville, 1996). Consumers have been shown to use their knowledge of advertiser intent (e.g., to sell a product) and advertising formats (e.g., before-and-after ads), knowledge of typical product benefits commonly portrayed (e.g., pain relief for Advil), and knowledge of cultural sayings and clichés (e.g., "eats luggage whole" for Toyota) to complete metaphorical interpretations (Phillips, 1997; Scott, 1994a, 1994b).

A metaphorical association between visual objects may entail more than the transfer of a single, clear attribute, such as "fresh scent" for the Cascade ad. Consider the ad for Tod's shoes that compares the loafer to the sports car. The meaning of this metaphor has been stated above as, "LOAFER is SPORTSCAR because both are elegant and stylish." However, a "fuzzy set" of similarities exists between the two objects so that the attributes they could possibly share range from more to less common (MacCormac, 1985). Consumers may interpret the ad as saying that Tod's shoes are "expensive" or "for an individual who is concerned with a high-class image"; these are plausible overlapping attributes of the fuzzy set of similarities. In fact, metaphors have been noted for their efficiency at transferring rich detail from one object to another; these "chunks of characteristics" may not be capable of being expressed in literal words (Ortany, 1975, p. 49). For example, the feeling of driving a powerful and attractive sportscar and gaining the respect and envy of onlookers is transferred to the act of wearing a pair of shoes by the Tod's ad; this feeling is not readily captured in the verbal attributes "elegant and stylish."

Given that a visual metaphor provides an implicit set of messages that rely on the interpretation of consumers, it is clear that different interpretations of the ad's metaphor will exist. It is by asking consumers for their interpretation that the ad's meaning can be clarified. Previous research has shown that consumers can converge on one meaning for the ad, sometimes called the "strong implicature" because it is strongly implied by the sender (Sperber & Wilson, 1986), such as "Cascade has a fresh scent" (Phillips, 1997). For other ads, several plausible meanings emerge, called "weak implicatures" because they are only weakly implied, such as "Tod's shoes are elegant" and "Tod's shoes are expensive." Finally, consumers may completely miss the advertiser's intended meaning for the ad and create a meaning that is idiosyncratic to them, such as "Tod's shoes can be used for running because, like a sports car, they go fast." Although advertisers would label the latter interpretation incorrect, consumers who successfully complete the metaphor are satisfied with their interpretations and may even defend their conclusions when challenged (Phillips, 1997). If several consumers interpret the metaphor "incorrectly" in the same way, their interpretation becomes a valid weak implicature, underscoring the fact that it is the consumer and not the advertiser who ultimately controls the meaning of the visual metaphor (Scott, 1994b). If consumers cannot complete any interpretation for the visual metaphor, they will dislike the ad and stop trying to understand it (McQuarrie & Mick, 1992).

Tanaka (1994) contends that advertisers use visual metaphors with multiple weak implicatures to appeal to a heterogeneous audience; each consumer can interpret the metaphor to suit him- or herself. In contrast with this view, I found that the "creatives" who designed the visual metaphors I used in one study (Phillips, 1997) were amused and dismayed at the multiple meanings attributed to their ads. They intended to convey one clear benefit through their use of visual metaphor and felt that consumers would come to the "correct" interpretation through viewing the same ad repeatedly over time or through viewing similar ads in the same campaign. I interviewed only three creatives for the study, so these conclusions cannot be considered to invalidate Tanaka's supposition. Further research in this area will have to take note of Kover's (1995) finding that the informal theories underlying the creation of ads can be implicit and unarticulated.

Research question 3: Under what conditions do advertising creatives attempt to elicit multiple meanings through the use of visual metaphor?

THE BENEFITS OF VISUAL METAPHOR— ATTENTION AND ELABORATION

Visual metaphor has been and continues to be a popular ad execution choice for advertisers (Kaplan, 1990, 1992); in a study of rhetorical figures over time, we found that visual metaphors appeared in ads in all of the time periods of our print ad sample, from 1954 to 1999 (Phillips & McQuarrie, 2001). Previous research has identified three main reasons why advertisers benefit when they use visual metaphor: attention, elaboration, and pleasure. McQuarrie and Mick (2002) find that ads with visual rhetoric, including visual metaphor, are more likely to be noticed by consumers under the normal cluttered viewing conditions of low-involvement magazine reading. They suggest that it is the deviation from expectation in these ads that spurs greater consumer attention.

Because visual metaphor ads require completion by a consumer, they also elicit greater elaboration. To state the metaphorical interpretation process in more cognitive terms, a consumer comprehends a visual metaphor by drawing an inference from the ad's images. This inference occurs through elaboration, using message information to generate assumptions and integrate them with prior knowledge (Malaviya, Kisielius, & Sternthal, 1996). Consumers will search for a simple inference that associates the two objects; if no simple inference can be found, consumers will entertain alternatives. However, the limited capacity of working memory is likely to restrict the number of possible inferences considered (Sawyer & Howard, 1991).

The cognitive effort expended in drawing an inference from a visual metaphor improves accessibility of the inference in memory; accessible inferences are held with more confidence, exert a strong influence on behavior, and are resistant to change (Kardes, 1993). In addition, if consumers are expending cognitive effort on forming inferences, they have fewer cognitive resources to use counterarguing the ad's claims (Kardes, 1993), increasing acceptance of the ad's message.

The attention and elaboration benefits attributed to visual metaphor presuppose that consumers perceive the metaphor to be a deviation from expectation. One type of metaphor, called a *dead metaphor,* does not provide this deviation. A dead metaphor is one that's use is so widespread and common that individuals no longer consider it metaphorically; instead, it becomes part of ordinary language

(Hitchon, 1997; MacCormac, 1985). MacCormac provides an example of a dead verbal metaphor in "the birth of the Roman empire." Although "birth" is technically metaphorical in this statement, the use of the word "birth" to represent the beginning of a nonliving entity is so common and accepted that this verbal metaphor is dead. MacCormac suggests that we can measure the death of a verbal metaphor by the extent to which one can find the metaphorical definition of the word enshrined in the dictionary as an alternate meaning.

Unfortunately, we have no dictionary of visual meaning. Therefore, it is difficult to know whether or not visual metaphors can die. Consider a recent ad for Brita water filtration pitchers as a possible dead metaphor; it juxtaposes the image of the Brita pitcher against the image of a waterfall. This visual metaphor can be read as, "PITCHER IS WATERFALL because both provide clean, clear water." This metaphor is scarcely novel, however. We have seen waterfalls and streams used metaphorically to sell other filtration systems, bottled water, and even beer. Is it possible that this metaphor is so commonplace that it has ceased to be read as a metaphor by consumers? One way to explore whether a visual metaphor is alive or dead might be to examine the pleasure consumers take in the metaphor; although living metaphors provide pleasure, as explained later, dead metaphors should provide no more pleasure than literal images.

Research question 4: Can visual metaphors die? How can we tell?

THE BENEFITS OF VISUAL METAPHOR— PLEASURE AND LIKING

The benefits of using visual metaphors in ads accrue when consumers try to interpret the advertising message from the images presented in the ad. However, advertising research has shown time and again that consumers are uninterested in, ignore, and actively avoid processing advertising messages (e.g., Friestad & Wright, 1994; Hawkins & Hoch, 1992; Krugman, 1965; Scott, 1994b). Why, then, would we expect consumers to expend cognitive effort drawing inferences from visual metaphors? The main reason is because it is fun.

Many consumers enjoy and get a sense of pleasure from figuring out the meaning of visual tropes (Peracchio & Meyers-Levy, 1994). The entertainment value of the puzzle inherent in all tropes is the reason that consumers attend to and think about these ads. McQuarrie and Mick (1999) found that ads with visual tropes, including visual metaphor, produced deeper elaboration and a more positive attitude toward the ad than similar ads without these images.

Visual metaphors are most pleasurable if they are perceived as apt—clever, appropriate, and insightful (Ward & Gaidis, 1990). Ward and Gaidis (1990) stated that the most pleasurable metaphors show a large number of overlapping attributes between two widely separate domain categories (cf. Rossiter & Percy, 1997). Metaphors that compare two objects with closely related domains are seen as trite and obvious. For example, DICTIONARY is GOLDMINE is a more pleasurable metaphor than DICTIONARY is ENCYCLOPEDIA.

The problem with apt metaphors is that because they compare widely different objects, they are less likely to be comprehended as the advertiser intended than less apt, obvious metaphors (Ward & Gaidis, 1990). Tropes, such as visual metaphor, that cannot be comprehended by consumers are not liked by consumers (McQuarrie & Mick, 1992, 1999). Therefore, the difficulty for advertisers who wish to employ visual metaphors is to make them sufficiently apt to induce pleasure in solving the puzzle in the ad, but simple enough so that they can be easily comprehended. One way to resolve this trade-off between comprehension and pleasure is to anchor the visual metaphor in the ad with verbal copy.

Barthes (1977) was one of the first researchers to theorize that words can anchor, or fix in place, the implicit meanings of images in press photos and ads (Dyer, 1982; McCracken, 1986; Pollay, 1983). Verbal anchoring can make visual metaphors easier to understand because the explicit verbal cues provide a link to stored knowledge in memory and reduce the amount of elaboration needed to complete the inference (Alba & Hutchinson, 1987). As the amount of effort required to interpret the ad's message decreases, the likelihood of understanding the advertiser's desired meaning increases (Kardes, 1993). Therefore, adding explanatory verbal copy to a visual metaphor gives advertisers the best of both worlds. The apt visual metaphor provides pleasure and the verbal anchoring promotes comprehension. For example, the Toyota Echo ad in your dream implies that "TRUNK is STOMACH because both can hold a lot." The accompanying copy anchors this interpretation by stating that the Echo "eats luggage whole."

Given the above explanation, it is surprising that we have noted a decrease in the amount of anchoring copy used in visual metaphor ads over time (Phillips & McQuarrie, 2001). In a content assessment of magazine ads from 1954 to 1999, we described a decreasing trend in the amount of anchoring copy that accompanies visual metaphors; visual metaphor ads at the beginning of the time period tend to use verbal copy that fully explains the meanings of the metaphors, while more recent ads have much less explanatory copy or none. We theorize that, over time, advertisers have perceived that consumers are growing more competent in understanding and interpreting visual metaphor in ads. Consequently, advertisers have reduced the amount of verbal anchoring offered to consumers to help them comprehend visual metaphor. But why would advertisers risk the noncomprehension of their ads by reducing the amount of verbal anchoring?

One explanation comes from previous research that tested the effects of adding verbal anchoring to visual metaphor ads (Phillips, 2000). Experimental results show that although verbal anchoring increases consumers' comprehension of the advertising message, fully explaining the visual metaphor in literal words decreases the pleasure consumers get from the visual metaphor ad. This suggests that if consumers enjoy solving the puzzle in the ad's image, they may dislike verbal anchoring that gives away the "answer" to the puzzle. Thus, although verbal anchoring increases comprehension, which is necessary for pleasure in the ad, it also *decreases* pleasure by providing help when none is needed. Note, however, that this conclusion comes from adding literal words to a visual metaphor. The Toyota Echo ad uses metaphorical words (e.g., "eats luggage whole") to anchor the ad's message. The effect of adding a verbal metaphor to a visual metaphor has not been tested.

Research question 5: What factors influence consumer pleasure in a visual metaphor ad? Do different forms of visual metaphor in an ad, such as MP1s or visual similes, require different amounts of verbal anchoring? What happens to consumer pleasure if we add rhetorical words, such as verbal metaphors or puns, to visual metaphor ads?

THE SEGMENTATION OF VISUAL METAPHOR

Although many consumers take pleasure in visual metaphor ads, previous research has identified "literalists"—individuals who do not like the flights of fancy presented in this type of advertising (Phillips, 1997). Searching for literalist consumers may not be fruitful for advertisers, however, as those identified as literalists do not appear to argue against all visual metaphor ads. Literalists dislike specific ad examples yet like others, suggesting that the literalist label is idiosyncratic and situationally dependent. Other segmenting variables that may hold more promise for segmenting consumer response to visual metaphor include age and gender.

Most previous research in visual metaphor examines responses from college-aged students or adults. However, a few studies suggest that age may be a factor that affects the interpretation of these ads. The findings from research that explores children's responses to metaphor are mixed. Pawlowski, Badzinski, and Mitchell (1998) tested verbal metaphors in ads with children in second, fourth, and sixth grade. They found that children of all ages had difficulty comprehending the ad metaphors; therefore, metaphorical ads were recalled and liked less than literal ad executions. They caution advertisers that metaphorical ads are not likely to be effective with children.

On the other hand, Epstein and Gamlin (1994) presented children with visual and verbal metaphors that were not part of advertisements. Children aged 3 to 5 were shown 10 sets of three objects; two of the objects were metaphorically related and one was not related. The objects were presented as either pictures or words. The children were told to select the two objects from each set that were alike and explain why. The authors found that children as young as 3 years old could not only recognize metaphoric relations between objects but also explain the relationship. Children were better at translating visual as opposed to verbal metaphor. In addition, children were more likely to understand explicit metaphors—those where the association between the two objects is physically apparent because they look the same (e.g., EYE is BUTTON because both are round) than implicit metaphors—those where the association between the two objects is not appearance based (e.g., HORSE is BICYCLE because both are ridden).

Combining the findings from these two studies starts to reveal the boundaries of children's comprehension of visual metaphor in advertising. Unlike Epstein and Gamlin (1994), who used explicit, non–ad-based visual metaphors and found positive effects with children, Pawlowski et al. (1998) used one implicit and one explicit verbal, ad-based metaphor in their experiment and found negative effects. Further work can examine whether it is the implicit comparison, the verbal metaphor, or the ad setting that negatively affects children's response.

No researchers have examined the use of visual metaphor at the other end of the age continuum. Interesting findings from related work in consumer behavior, however, suggest possible avenues for exploration. Law, Hawkins, and Craik (1998) examined the influence of age on the "truth effect"—a label used to describe repetition-induced increases in belief in fictitious statements. The authors show that elderly consumers are more likely than younger consumers to think that facts are true after repeated exposure to them. However, if consumers are asked to form a mental picture of a fact while processing it, the differences between elderly and younger consumers disappear. The authors interpret these findings as suggesting that mental imagery can compensate for memory deficits in elderly consumers; advertisers who wish to facilitate recall in elderly consumers should consider providing strong visual information. Although not directly related to visual metaphor, this study offers an intriguing hint as to the possible effectiveness of visual metaphor ads for older consumers.

Beyond age, gender also may influence the interpretation of visual metaphor. Previous research has supported the idea that men and women interpret the meanings of visual images in ads differently based on their different world views (Mick & Politi, 1989). In addition, women are more likely than men to make inferences from narrative text (Stern, 1993) and advertisements (Edens & McCormick, 2000). One reason for this difference was suggested by Morgan and Reichert (1999), who showed that individuals who are naturally more likely to use both hemispheres of their brains (i.e., integrative processors) find advertising metaphors easier to comprehend than individuals who rely mainly on one or the other hemisphere. Current thought in neurobiology supports the contention that women are more likely to be integrative processors for several cognitive tasks (e.g., Iaccino, 1993; Kimura, 1998). Taken together, this evidence suggests that women may be more likely to comprehend and draw inferences from visual metaphors than men.

Research question 6: What influence do age and gender have on consumer response to visual metaphor?

UNDERSTANDING VISUAL METAPHOR

This chapter provides an introduction to visual metaphor by explaining what visual metaphor is, how it can be categorized, how it is interpreted by different types of consumers, and what benefits it offers to advertisers, and by providing research questions to provoke further thought on these topics. Beyond those explored in this chapter, other avenues of inquiry exist that may advance the study of visual metaphor, including conceptual metaphors, involvement, and presentation medium. Conceptual metaphors are used by individuals to frame situations and make sense of the world (Kaplan, 1990; Lakoff & Johnson, 1980), such as characterizing life as a journey or the human brain as a computer. Conceptual metaphors promote many points of correspondence between the two objects in the metaphor and may even limit one's ability to think beyond the metaphor to new possibilities (MacCormac, 1985). The study of conceptual metaphor appears to have implications for both the creation and interpretation of visual metaphor.

Involvement is another factor that impacts the study of visual metaphor, because it has been shown to have an effect on inference generation (Sawyer & Howard, 1991; Toncar & Munch, 2001) and metaphorical processing (Ottati, Rhoads, & Graesser, 1999). And although almost all studies of visual metaphor in advertising examine print ads, researchers are starting to question whether studies of visual metaphor in film (e.g., Whittock, 1990) could be applied to visual metaphor in TV ads. Space does not permit the exploration of these and other related topics in this chapter.

Researchers are starting to patch together the information needed for a complete understanding of visual metaphor in advertising. Many pieces are still missing. The key to continued discovery is the explicit, systematic breaking down of "metaphor" into meaningful categories such as visual versus verbal modalities, dead versus alive metaphors, and differing forms of visual presentation. Exploration should follow both qualitative and quantitative routes to examine the metaphorical outcomes of interpretation and meaning, elaboration and comprehension, attention and recall, and pleasure and liking. Finally, the broadest possible audience for visual metaphor in advertising will provide the best test of theories, comparing young with old, men with women, and consumers with the creatives who design the ads.

REFERENCES

Alba, J. W., & Hutchinson, J. W. (1987, March). Dimensions of consumer expertise. *Journal of Consumer Research, 13*, 411–454.

Barthes, R. (1977). *Image music text.* New York: Hill and Wang.

Dyer, G. (1982). *Advertising as communication.* New York: Routledge.

Edens, K. M., & McCormick, C. B. (2000). How do adolescents process advertisements? The influence of ad characteristics, processing objective, and gender. *Contemporary Educational Psychology, 25,* 450–463.

Epstein, R. L., & Gamlin, P. J. (1994). Young children's comprehension of simple and complex metaphors presented in pictures and words. *Metaphor and Symbolic Activity, 9*(3), 179–191.

Forceville, C. (1996). *Pictorial metaphor in advertising.* New York: Routledge.

Friestad, M., & Wright, P. (1994, June). The persuasion knowledge model: How people cope with persuasion attempts. *Journal of Consumer Research, 21,* 1–31.

Hawkins, S. A., & Hoch, S. J. (1992, September). Low-involvement learning: Memory without evaluation. *Journal of Consumer Research, 19,* 212–225.

Hitchon, J. C. (1997). The locus of metaphorical persuasion: An empirical test. *Journalism and Mass Communication Quarterly, 74*(1), 55–68.

Iaccino, J. F. (1993). *Left brain–right brain differences: Inquiries, evidence, and new approaches.* Hillsdale, NJ: Lawrence Erlbaum Associates.

Kaplan, S. J. (1990, March). Visual metaphors in the representation of communication technology. *Critical Studies in Mass Communication, 7,* 37–47.

Kaplan, S. J. (1992). A conceptual analysis of form and content in visual metaphor. *Communication, 13,* 197–209.

Kardes, F. R. (1993). Consumer inference: Determinants, consequences, and implications for advertising. In A. A. Mitchell (Ed.), *Advertising exposure, memory, and choice* (pp. 163–191). Hillsdale, NJ: Lawrence Erlbaum Associates.

Kimura, D. (1998). Sex, sexual orientation, and sex hormones influence human cognitive function. In L. R. Squire & S. M. Kosslyn (Eds.), *Findings and current opinion in cognitive neuroscience* (pp. 155–159). Cambridge, MA: MIT Press.

Kover, A. J. (1995, March). Copywriters' implicit theories of communication: An exploration. *Journal of Consumer Research, 21,* 596–611.

Krugman, H. E. (1965, Fall). The impact of television advertising: Learning without involvement. *Public Opinion Quarterly, 29,* 349–356.

Lakoff, G., & Johnson, M. (1980). *Metaphors we live by.* Chicago: University of Chicago Press.

Law, S., Hawkins, S. A., & Craik, F. I. M. (1998, September). Repetition-induced belief in the elderly: Rehabilitating age-related memory deficits. *Journal of Consumer Research, 25,* 91–107.

MacCormac, E. R. (1985). *A cognitive theory of metaphor.* Cambridge, MA: MIT Press.

Malaviya, P., Kisielius, J., & Sternthal, B. (1996, November). The effect of type of elaboration on advertisement processing and judgment. *Journal of Marketing Research, 33,* 410–421.

McCracken, G. (1986, June). Culture and consumption: A theoretical account of the structure and movement of the cultural meaning of consumer goods. *Journal of Consumer Research, 13,* 71–84.

McQuarrie, E. F., & Mick, D. G. (1992, September). On resonance: A critical pluralistic inquiry into advertising rhetoric. *Journal of Consumer Research, 19,* 180–197.

McQuarrie, E. F., & Mick, D. G. (1996, March). Figures of rhetoric in advertising language. *Journal of Consumer Research, 22,* 424–438.

McQuarrie, E. F., & Mick, D. G. (1999, June). Visual rhetoric in advertising: Text interpretive, experimental, and reader-response analyses. *Journal of Consumer Research, 26,* 37–54.

McQuarrie, E. F., & Mick, D. G. (2002). *Visual and verbal advertising rhetoric under directed processing versus incidental exposure.* Manuscript submitted for publication.

Mick, D. G., & Politi, L. (1989). Consumers' interpretations of advertising imagery: A visit to the hell of connotation. In E. Hirschman (Ed.), *Interpretive consumer research* (pp. 85–96). Provo, UT: Association for Consumer Research.

Morgan, S. E., & Reichert, T. (1999). The message is in the metaphor: Assessing the comprehension of metaphors in advertising. *Journal of Advertising, 28*(4), 1–12.

Ortany, A. (1975). Why metaphors are necessary and not just nice. *Educational Theory, 25*(1), 45–53.

Ottati, V., Rhoads, S., & Graesser, A. C. (1999). The effect of metaphor on processing style in a persuasion task: A motivational resonance model. *Journal of Personality and Social Psychology, 77*(4), 688–697.

Pawlowski, D. R., Badzinski, D. M., & Mitchell, N. (1998). Effects of metaphors on children's comprehension and perception of print advertisements. *Journal of Advertising, 27* (2), 83–98.

Peracchio, L. A., & Meyers-Levy, J. (1994, June). How ambiguous cropped objects in ad photos can affect product evaluations. *Journal of Consumer Research, 21,* 190–204.

Phillips, B. J. (1997). Thinking into it: Consumer interpretation of complex advertising images. *Journal of Advertising, 26*(2), 77–87.

Phillips, B. J. (2000). The impact of verbal anchoring on consumer response to image ads. *Journal of Advertising, 29*(1), 15–24.

Phillips, B. J., & McQuarrie, E. F. (2001, June). *Change and constancy over time in the rhetorical style of advertisements.* Paper presented at the European Association for Consumer Research Conference, Berlin, Germany.

Pollay, R. W. (1983). Measuring the cultural values manifest in advertising. In J. H. Leigh & C. Martin, Jr. (Eds.), *Current issues and research in advertising* (pp. 71–92). Ann Arbor: University of Michigan School of Business.

Rossiter, J. R., & Percy, L. (1997). *Communications & promotions management* (2nd edition). New York: McGraw-Hill.

Salomon, G. (1979). *Interaction of media, cognition, and learning: An exploration of how symbolic forms cultivate mental skills and affect knowledge acquisition.* San Francisco, CA: Jossey-Bass.

Sawyer, A. G., & Howard, D. J. (1991, November). Effects of omitting conclusions in advertisements to involved and uninvolved audiences. *Journal of Marketing Research, 28,* 467–474.

Scott, L. M. (1994a, September). Images in advertising: The need for a theory of visual rhetoric. *Journal of Consumer Research, 21,* 252–273.

Scott, L. M. (1994b, December). The bridge from text to mind: Adapting reader-response theory to consumer research. *Journal of Consumer Research, 21,* 461–480.

Smith, R. A. (1991). The effects of visual and verbal advertising information on consumers' inferences. *Journal of Advertising, 20*(4), 13–24.

Sperber, D., & Wilson, D. (1986). *Relevance: Communication and cognition.* Oxford, UK: Basil Blackwell.

Stern, B. B. (1990). Beauty and joy in metaphorical advertising: The poetic dimension. In M. E. Goldberg, G. Gorn, & R. W. Pollay (Eds.), *Advances in consumer research* (vol. 17, pp. 71–77). Provo, UT: Association for Consumer Research.

Stern, B. B. (1993, March). Feminist literary criticism and the deconstruction of ads: A postmodern view of advertising and consumer responses. *Journal of Consumer Research, 19,* 556–566.

Tanaka, K. (1994). *Advertising language: A pragmatic approach to advertisements in Britain and Japan.* London, UK: Routledge.

Toncar, M., & Munch, J. (2001). Consumer response to tropes in print advertising. *Journal of Advertising, 30*(1), 55–65.

Ward, J., & Gaidis, W. (1990). Metaphor in promotional communication: A review of research on metaphor comprehension and quality. In M. E. Goldberg, G. Gorn, & R. W. Pollay (Eds.), *Advances in consumer research* (vol. 17, pp. 636–642). Provo, UT: Association for Consumer Research.

Whittock, T. (1990). *Metaphor and film.* Cambridge, UK: Cambridge University Press.

V. IMAGE AND OBJECT

CHAPTER SIXTEEN

Color as a Tool for Visual Persuasion

Lawrence L. Garber, Jr.
Eva M. Hyatt
Appalachian State University

Color is considered to be the most salient and the most "resonant and meaningful" visual feature of those seen in early vision (Hilbert, 1987, p. 2; Sacks, 1995). This makes color a compelling visual cue for persuasive communications purposes, such as conferring identity, meaning, or novelty to an object or idea.

An interesting example that illustrates the powerful and complex workings of color in a persuasive communications context is Pepsico's early 1990s introduction of a clear form of Pepsi, called Crystal Pepsi (cf. Triplett, 1994). It failed. Pepsi was trying to take advantage of a new product color phenomenon, clearness, pioneered at that time by Ivory dishwashing liquid. Ivory had successfully changed the color of its liquid soap from its signature milky white color to a clear form, in order to capitalize on the very eye-catching-ness and excitement of this vivid and surprising departure from the familiar and expected. Pepsico, along with many other consumer packaged good companies in a variety of product categories, believed it could piggyback on the clear visual phenomenon by hurrying its own clear product, Crystal Pepsi, onto the market. However, Pepsi had failed to understand that product color conveys more than sensory experience, as, in this case, clearness connotes more than a distinctive, eye-catching appearance to the cola drinker. Among other things, it creates flavor and other performance expectations. Consumers expected a clear cola to have a lighter, cleaner flavor with fewer calories. However, upon tasting Crystal Pepsi, consumers' expectations were disconfirmed: They got the original Pepsi Cola strength of taste rendered unpalatable by a mere change of color! Even loyal Pepsi fans didn't like it! The moral of the story is that there is a relationship between food color and flavor in color-associated foods, and to change one is to risk changing the other. Ivory Liquid had succeeded because the new color did not change the meaning of the brand: clearness in a dishwashing liquid meant purity and mildness to the consumer, as did the milky color of Ivory before it.

This example illustrates that, as much as color is a powerful and salient persuasive communications tool, it is as well a complex, multidimensional phenomenon, poorly understood yet difficult to examine, making individual response to color exposure notoriously hard to explain or predict (Sharpe, 1975). Given that all individuals are also consumers, marketing communications, whose constant intent is persuasion, provide a good domain, a natural experiment, from which to study the general effects of color as a persuasive communications tool. Marketers intuitively understand that color should enhance the appeal of and satisfaction with products, especially foods, for which we seem to have a particular acuity (Bruce & Green, 1990, pp. 200, 343; Danger, 1969, p. 128).

In particular, although color may only be a single visual element, color experience is more than sensory phenomenon (Duncker, 1939; Garber, Burke, & Jones, 2000; Hine, 1996; Scott, 1994a), though many would assume otherwise (Scott, 1994a); for example, in a packaging context, color is also a cultural artifact that holds (often subtle and deep) personal meanings for an individual, due to a lifetime of prior experience (Scott, 1994a). Color is known to carry important symbolic and associative information about the product category and about specific brands (Hine, 1996, p. 216). Such meanings overlay direct sensory experience, thereby mediating, and at times dominating, color response (Garber, Hyatt, & Starr, 2000). This duality to the color phenomenon means that both its sensory and cognitive aspects must be considered for color as a persuasive communications tool to be correctly understood or properly framed (Marr, 1982). In this chapter, as an aid to the researcher and the practitioner, we review the conceptual issues that arise over the effects of persuasive color, particularly those stemming from color's dual nature, and present a research method that disentangles and separately measures color's sensory and cognitive aspects. In particular, we: (a) review the literature on color; (b) present research results in a food color context that graphically illustrate the cognitive processing of color and show the dominating role that prior knowledge can play in perception and choice; (c) present two conceptual frameworks that explicitly consider the respective roles that the sensory and cognitive aspects of color play in specific contexts; and (d) present an empirical methodology that decomposes and estimates the sensory and cognitive effects of color exposure.

LITERATURE REVIEW

Color Thought

In seeking to understand the role of color for persuasive communications purposes, one might think that it would be helpful to understand what color is, in general. Unfortunately, color is still not fully understood (Marr, 1982). A very old but ongoing discussion concerns whether color is primarily a physical phenomenon endowed in the object that is being viewed, or a product of the lengths of the reflected light waves that strike the retina (Helmholtz, 1962; Marr, 1982; Newton, 1979), or a subjective phenomenon that is endowed in the viewer, making it a product of our sensory apparatus and/or of the processing and interpretation that takes place in the brain (Goethe, 1988; Land, 1977; Locke, 1975; Zeki, 1980). For good overviews of this discussion from writers in various disciplines, see Bruce and Green (1990), Crick (1994), Hilbert (1987), Sacks (1995), and Swirnoff (1989).

Concerning the latter point, that color is the product of the brain's interpretation of the visual sensory information that it receives, Scott (1994a), while speaking of visual imagery in an advertising context, made an elegant argument for how and why applied researchers have overlooked this dual nature to visual stimuli. Scott pointed out that visual imagery (and, we argue, color, too, as one of several visual elements that the brain integrates to compose recognizable objects and images) acquires (at times very rich) meaning through learned contexts and schemas that are culturally and historically based:

> To understand the message, consumers must interpret the picture as a symbolic summary of a past event . . . visuals are social, rather than logical, code and an elaborated rather than restricted system. Therefore, we would not expect exact, concrete correspondences of meaning but rather provisional, contextually situated, meanings that are highly sensitive to differentiation and relationships. . . . Consumers draw on a learned vocabulary of pictorial symbols and employ complex cognitive skills even in the simplest response. Thus, advertising images can be understood in a discursive form, like writing, capable of subtle nuances in communication, or, like numbers, capable of facilitating abstractions and analysis . . . consumer research reflects a bias in Western thinking about pictures that is thousands of years old: the assumption that pictures reflect objects in the real world. From the vantage of this ethnocentric stance, the frankly rhetorical nature of advertising imagery is either purposively overlooked or criticized as a distortion of reality. (pp. 252, 264–265)

Such interpretation in the processing of advertising imagery is also evident in the processing of food color in marketing communications (Garber, Hyatt, & Starr, 2000) and color used in marketing communications (Garber, Burke, & Jones, 2000). (For a trenchant and definitive discussion of the processing of visual information, see Marr, 1982.)

The Complexity of Color

Complicating matters is the fact that color is a highly interactive, relative, and context-dependent phenomenon, reliant for its effects on the entire visual field in which it is perceived, the larger sensory environment in which it is encountered, and the circumstances, situation, disposition and cognition of the viewer. Land (1977), for instance, demonstrated that color determination depends, "not . . . solely on the wavelengths entering the eye from that patch but also on the wavelengths entering from the other regions of the visual field" (Crick, 1994, p. 53).

In particular, color has been shown to depend for its effect on an interaction with adjacent colors (Albers, 1963; Cheskin, 1957; Swirnoff, 1989). For example, red is made to look redder when it is surrounded by green, its complement, as when a red Lava Soap pack sits next to a green pack of Irish Spring. And red appears less salient when surrounded by red, its analogue, as when Lava soap sits next to a red Lifebuoy pack.

Moreover, color effect is highly interactive with the other visual features of which an object is composed, all of which must be integrated before an object or image can be recognized and its meaning to the viewer established (Bruce & Green, 1990; Crick, 1994; Davidoff, 1991; Marr, 1982; Triesman, 1991; Triesman & Gelade, 1980). An example would be Crystal Pepsi, discussed earlier, whose change of color caused consumers to reformulate their thoughts about product performance, as well as the product itself. For example, transparency makes the bottle form appear lighter in weight, whereas regular Pepsi, with its opaque dark color, appears heavier and denser than its erstwhile counterpart (Garber & Buff, 2000). Indeed, there are those who argue that color cannot be perceived and understood independently of form (Collinson, 1992, p. 145).

In addition, there are cultural, social, and personal dimensions to color and its meaning. Hine (1996) described the cultural dimension as visual conventions that have built up over time in respective societies. The usual example of differences in the symbolic meaning of color across cultures is that black is the color of death in Western societies, whereas the color of death is white in many Asian countries. And in Japan, brighter colors are reserved for packages representing products from foreign countries, whose people the Japanese consider to be brash in nature, and the more subtle, soft gray hues are reserved for their own products. The meaning of color is also highly situational, changing over time, as in fads and fashion (Danger, 1969; Sharpe, 1975), and depends on the subject category in whose context it is considered (Bruce & Green, 1990, p. 190; Marr & Nishihara, 1978). To illustrate the latter, Hine (1996, p. 221) reported that a 1987 study showed that residents of four American cities believed in general that red means love, safety, danger, strength, and warmth; however, when asked to think about red in relation to products, they stated that it means Coca-Cola.

Finally, color, along with visual perception in general, is known to interact with the other senses, in that color sensation may make an impression in another sense altogether, an effect known as synesthesia (Ball, 1965; Bullough, 1910; Nelson & Hitchon, 1995; Sharpe, 1975). Therefore, the effect that a color has on a person may be couched in terms of temperature (red is hot, blue is cool), weight (dark colors are heavy, light colors are light), sound (loud, soft), or smell (fresh, stale).

A deliberate approach to the selection of color for persuasive communications purposes must consider all these dimensions, for they are expressed, though not altogether clearly, in the receiver's response to color exposure. For example, in a commercial frame, color exposure may come in the context of ads, store atmospherics, and point-of-purchase displays, including products and packages, server uniforms, sales rep appearance, trade show displays, and so on. There are any number of trade publications in the areas of packaging, advertising and commercial design that offer copious marketing-specific examples that clearly illustrate both how powerful correct color can be (Cheskin, 1957; Danger, 1969; Dichter, 1975; Hine, 1996; Sharpe, 1975) and how the complexities of color render its selection so problematic. None, however, offer concrete guidance to the communicator beyond suggesting that he or she hire a color consultant.

In a noncommercial frame, an equivalent selection problem comes in the form of choice of color for personal belongings such as clothing, car, house, furnishings, stationery, flowers, cakes, and such, or in the artist's choice of color in a painting. Guidance for such choices comes in the form of, for example, trade house and garden magazines, or how-to art books; however, such guidance typically draws upon standard rules for color selection, or other conventions such as those colors that have been agreed on as being "hot" for the current fashion season, rather than on a scientific knowledge of color and its sensory and cognitive effects (Garber, Burke, & Jones, 2000).

Empirical Color Research

Considerable empirical research into the persuasive effects of color has been done in the last 100 years (for an early review, see Ball, 1965). Primary findings show a general preference for short-wavelength colors (blue, green), which people find quiet and serene, over long-wavelength colors (red, orange), which people find arousing and hot (Guilford & Smith, 1959). Further research shows some response differences between groups—primarily in degree of response, but with similar overall patterns—divided by culture (Adams & Osgood, 1973; Lee & Barnes, 1990), gender (Aaronson, 1970; Golden, 1974), personality type (Bjerstedt, 1960) and situation (Fisher, 1974). However, these findings on color are too broad and simple to be of much value in a persuasive communications context. In particular, a great deal of the meaning that viewers attribute to color comes from context, and most of these prior empirical studies expose subjects to color in a format that is without context. For example, people may say that in general they prefer blue to red, but this does not explain the successful use of red by organizations and brands like Coca-Cola, McDonald's, Campbell's, Colgate, the Cincinnati Reds, KFC, Harvard, Marlboro, Big Red chewing gum, H. J. Heinz, *Time* magazine, Nabisco, and Betty Crocker. The short answer to this apparent contradiction is, of course, that it is often constructive marketing practice to divert and arouse the consumer, and to associate the intrinsic meaning of "redness" with one's brand. Moreover, not everything can be blue; novelty and contrast are also appreciated (and, it is to be noted, these latter qualities in themselves hold meaning for the consumer).

Color Research in the Food Sciences

There have been a number of studies in the food sciences investigating the effects of color on food (flavor) perceptions. In these studies, taste test experiments are used in which food color has typically been manipulated at three levels, which we shall call characteristic, uncharacteristic and ambiguous. *Characteristic color,* sometimes referred to in prior research as "correct" or "appropriate" color, is the color one would normally expect to be associated with a given flavor (i.e., orange color with orange flavor). *Uncharacteristic color,* sometimes referred to in prior research as "atypical" or "unusual" color, is a color that one would not normally associate with a given flavor (i.e., orange color with grape flavor). *Ambiguous color,* at times referred to as "masked" color or "no color," is a color that conveys no flavor information whatsoever (i.e., a clear or colorless liquid, such as Crystal Pepsi). These studies generally find that characteristic color facilitates the ability to correctly identify flavor; ambiguous color does not facilitate correct flavor identification; and uncharacteristic color degrades correct color identification (DuBose, Cardello, & Maller, 1980; Hall, 1958; Hyman, 1983; Stillman, 1993). Oram et al. (1995) found the effects of color on flavor identification more pronounced with children than adults, indicating that the association of food color with flavor is learned early, and that the reliance on color as a flavor signal is greater when product and flavor knowledge is limited (and meaningful flavor and food associations are therefore suppressed).

Particular to the purposes of this chapter, food color helps form flavor expectations that affect flavor and other food performance perceptions, and thereby affect a food's meaning. Several studies show that color affects perceptions of flavor intensity—specifically, the more saturated the color, the more intense the flavor perception (Pangborn, 1960). Maga (1974) and Pangborn (1960) take a decompositional approach, showing that differences in color perception can vary along separate dimensions such as sweet and sour: For example, longer wavelength colors are generally rated sweeter and less sour, and shorter wavelength colors are rated more sour and less sweet. A few studies examine the role of color on acceptability or preference within given food categories. The overall acceptability of beverage and cake products is more closely associated with ratings of flavor acceptability than with ratings of color acceptability (DuBose et al., 1980). Saturated yogurt colors are preferred to less saturated, natural yogurt colors (Norton & Johnson, 1987). A shortcoming of this research is that food and flavor attributes are typically evaluated on a single dimension representing concrete flavor attributes, thereby not measuring any multidimensional, symbolic meanings that color may attribute to foods, and which may also affect response (Garber, Hyatt, & Starr, 2000).

Color Research in Commercial Settings

The persuasive effects of color are vastly underresearched in commerce, surprising given color's powerful role in identifying and distinguishing brands, and its ability to confer symbolic and associative meaning to them, particularly in a world that is becoming ever more graphic in nature. What little marketing-specific color research there is mostly confirms the long-wavelength, short-wavelength dichotomy just described. Bellizzi and Hite (1992) and Bellizzi, Crowley, and Hasty (1983) tested consumer color preferences for retail store designs and found that blue is soothing and preferred, and red is arousing and less well liked. Gorn, Chattopadhyay, Yi, and Dahl (1997) decomposed color into its constituent elements—hue, chroma, and value—and tested their respective effects on arousal, affect and recall in print ads. They extended the notion that red is exciting by noting that any highly saturated color also tends to be arousing, and that paler colors tend to be relaxing.

Several studies compare the effectiveness of color versus black-and-white in print media. Sparkman and Austin (1980) looked at print advertising, finding that color ads sell more than black-and-white ads. Click and Stempel (1976) reported that newspaper readers prefer the front pages of newspapers with color. Meyers-Levy and Peracchio (1995) demonstrated that black-and-white ads have greater impact when few cognitive resources are devoted to the processing of a print ad photo, or when too few resources are available for the viewers to process the photo as elaborately as they would like. Schindler (1986) pointed out that the use of color in an ad can sacrifice contrast, reducing legibility and readability.

A serious limitation to this research is that color as a visual stimulus is treated atheoretically as a purely sensory phenomenon, and the cognitive processing of visual stimuli is largely overlooked or ignored. This is a reason why this research as a whole does not present a consistent set of findings (Scott, 1994a), nor does it really extend our knowledge of what color is or how it works in a communications context (Garber, Hyatt, & Starr, 2000).

THE COGNITIVE PROCESSING OF COLOR

A particular point in the preceding discussion that is often overlooked in practice is that the effect of color on the viewer will vary depending on context, as indicated by a review of the empirical color research literature from psychology and commerce. Yet the researchers or practitioners often presume otherwise, thereby naively treating visual stimuli as purely sensory in nature, or perhaps, though knowing better, still choosing to treat visual stimuli as purely sensory because they know of no way to address the dual nature of visual stimuli empirically.

The Cognitive Processing of Food Color

The following research into food color by Garber, Hyatt, and Starr (2000) is an exception to research previously reported in that it does explore response to food color in a multidimensional, multiattributed manner, therefore allowing for the measurement of the cognitive aspects of the processing of color. Therein, food color's effect on perceived flavor and preference formation provides a dramatic example of the (at times) dominant contribution of the cognitive processing of color exposure to stimulus evaluation and preference formation. Food color is a good example of this phenomenon, because the individual's sensory and cognitive faculties for the processing of food information are particularly acute and well formed.

Due to the individual consumer's experience with natural and processed foods, and due to the fact that color contributes to the individual's first judgment of the product, color interacts with "gustatory, olfactory and textural cues to determine the overall flavor acceptability of the product" (DuBose et al., 1980, p. 1393; Sharpe, 1975, p. 129). Color frames an individual's expectations of the sensory properties of foods before they are tasted. These signals operate in complex ways, as color can indicate many attributes, including variety, ripeness, sweetness, degree of cooking (a steak may be red, pink or brown in the middle), texture (is the banana green or brown?), and so forth.

Color is a cue that moderates perceptions of a food's taste or condition: The signals that color sends are not invariant. Interactions between food type and color determine the ultimate meaning at the individual level (Zellner, Bartoli, & Eckard, 1991; for a general discussion of the role of categorization as a means of reducing the task of recognition and interpretation to a set of plausible labels, see Marr, 1982; for a similar discussion as applied to the use of pictures in print ads, see Edell & Staelin, 1983). Thus, a red apple is presumed ripe and sweet, and a red steak raw and unappetizing; a green apple is unripe or tart, green grapes are ripe and sweet, and a green orange is moldy; a brown steak is cooked, a brown kiwi fruit can be in prime eating condition, but a brown apple is rotten. In some cases, we must rely on subtleties of color. Capsicums, orange-sized fruit from South America and Asia, can be purchased in green, red, yellow, orange, or purple varieties, with the ripeness of each type determined by separate and subtle cues.

In many food categories, therefore, product and package color have traditionally and specifically been used to signal flavor. Current practice favoring the use of characteristic colors as flavor signals in color-associated foods, a noncompetitive, commoditizing use of powerful promotional tool, raises many interesting questions. Is using color to signal flavor in a generic way the best use of color for persuasive purposes? Might the use of a unique color not normally associated with a given food draw attention? Might a company that makes all its flavors the same color, thus associating itself with that color and creating a sizable monolithic color block on the shelves, be more favorable as a strategy? And if so, what is the effect on people's enjoyment of the product? Will they know the flavor? Will they like the flavor or the drink as well? What about the notion that a novel color incongruent with flavor may be interesting to people? Is the potential dissonance interesting and involving? Or is it confusing and irritating? Will people even notice the discrepancy? Or will one stimulus (color or actual taste) dominate the other, allowing consumers to resolve the conflict in favor of the dominant carrier of flavor information?

FRAMEWORKS FOR COLOR EFFECTS IN CONSUMER CHOICE

Heretofore, we have made a case for the need to consider both the sensory and cognitive aspects of color processing to correctly understand and analyze color's persuasive effects. In particular, we assert the importance of the cognitive processing of color, which has often been overlooked, and whose effects can be dominant relative to sensory processing. In this section, to aid those who would now wish to operationalize these ideas in an applied or experimental context, we present, as examples, two conceptual frameworks, brand equity theory and consumer choice, in which the dual nature of color is explicitly represented in individual response to a color stimulus. Much of the following discussion is taken from Garber, Burke, and Jones (2000), and the reader should refer to that manuscript for a fuller exposition.

Color as a Carrier of Brand Equity

Brand equity has generally been defined as the added value endowed by the brand to the product (Farquar, 1989), and consists of the brand's recognition by and familiarity to the consumer, as well as the meaning associated with the brand (Agarwal & Rao, 1996; Keller, 1993; Park & Srinivasan, 1994). Color can either enhance or diminish this equity by facilitating or inhibiting identification and the retrieval of positive associations. The importance of the color's visual representation is acknowledged in the brand equity literature (Biel, 1993) and in the trade literature. For example, when asked what red means with respect to soft drinks, most will say Coca-Cola, a color-brand association that Coke has worked hard for many years to establish, a perfect example of how a good package can so powerfully convey the image and identity (the equity) of a brand. As a consequence, Pepsi is currently trying equally hard to associate itself with the color blue.

Color is one of several visual elements (the others being size and shape) that the consumer must perceive and integrate in order to recognize and interpret an object (i.e., a product, package and/or store display) in its visual field (Triesman, 1991; Triesman & Gelade, 1980). By extension, brand equity theory suggests there are at least four roles for product color as a carrier of brand equity in the store, some of which may conflict with one another, as described by Garber, Burke, and Jones (2000). These include: identifying the category to which the product belongs (i.e., white paper bags for flour); identifying the brand (i.e., Corning Insulation pink); conferring meaning to the brand or reinforcing or heightening existing meanings and symbolic associations (i.e., the carnival-like yellow and red of McDonald's); and providing contrast to make the brand more distinctive in and of itself, or more eye-catching and salient with respect to its competitors (i.e., the iMac computer, which comes in five candylike colors, distinctive and liberating in a product category known for its monochrome uniformity).

These four roles invite both sensory and cognitive processing of color, although, respectively, in characteristic manners and proportions. For example, referring once again to the four brand equity roles for color from Garber, Burke, and Jones (2000), it would seem that the sensory component of color processing would predominate over the cognitive with respect to category and brand identification, and in the presentation of novelty and contrast, whereas the cognitive would predominate with respect to product or package comprehension.

Category identification is a matter of a brand's declaring its membership in its category, and its candidacy for notice and purchase consideration. For the successful brand, any distinctive or differentiating qualities must be carefully nested within this inclusive aspect. Examples of product categories where the visual conventions of the category are rather closely adhered to, so that declaration of category membership is the primary message offered by individual packages, would be flour, where most every brand comes in a white bag, and tuna in squat white cans. These visual conventions are familiar to most of us as category identifiers, branding each adherent within the category as a member, but doing nothing to distinguish individual members. On a sensory level, category identifiers help us to distinguish and locate the product categories for which we are searching. On a cognitive level, category identifiers may signify any number of product-category-specific meanings, as well as higher order, non-category-specific meanings such as "familiar" and "reassuring" for those who are regular shoppers in a given product category (Dichter, 1975). The relative importance of the sensory and the cognitive aspects in influencing the individual would greatly depend on individual context, such as the individual's familiarity with the category. For example, if the individual has little category-specific knowledge, then the meaning that would be attributed to the category by its characteristic product or package colors would rely more on noncategory references, and would be more idiosyncratic in nature.

Brand identification refers to the consumer's ability to recognize and uniquely identify a package as belonging to a particular brand. Certain characteristics of the package, such as the brand name, its logo, color, package shape, type style, and graphics, may be used for identification. For example, Reese's Peanut Butter Cups and all of its brand extensions use the color orange, while Hershey's products are chocolate brown. On a sensory level, brand identifiers help us to distinguish between brand alternatives within a category, and may call our attention to new brand alternatives for our purchase consideration. On a cognitive level, brand identifiers may signify any number of brand-specific meanings, relating to product performance or having symbolic associative content (image), much of which may carry over from prior experience, or prior communications such as advertising or word of mouth. Again, as with category-specific identifiers, the meaning of such colors will vary with the individual. Those less familiar with the category would attribute more non-category-specific meanings to the colors presented, and for those familiar with the category, loyalties would model the meanings of the colors representing individual brands: Not only would there be brand-specific meanings, but non-brand-specific meanings, such as "this is my brand, and my family's brand," versus, "This is the brand of others," or "This is America's Brand," would also enter into the consideration and choice process. *Package comprehension* refers to the meaning that a product's package conveys to the customer. A package communicates through explicit claims and illustrations that describe a product's attributes, benefits, ingredients, and promotional offers. It also communicates implicitly by triggering associations in consumer memory through visual, verbal, and tactile elements of the package (such as the brand name and logo, package size, shape, color, texture, and graphics). When designing a new package, a manufacturer can borrow on the visual conventions established by existing brands in the category. For example, a new dishwashing liquid may use the color green, similar to Palmolive, to communicate gentleness, so that the colors of hand dishwashing liquids have come to represent key performance attributes—yellow for lemony, blue for grease-cutting, green for mild-to-the-hands, and orange for antibacterial. This approach has the virtue of reassuring the shopper by fulfilling expectations of what a brand in the category should look like, thus providing a measure of legitimacy and credibility (Dichter, 1975). Consistent with this, Loken and Ward (1990) reported that consumers prefer products that tend to match their expectations.

Another approach based on the cognitive processing of brand-specific information (identifiers) is to bring new concepts and imagery into the category. The use of a well-chosen visual metaphor can capture, through association, desirable values associated with a brand (King, 1989). For example, Gateway was the first company to use the black-and-white cow pattern on its packaging in order to communicate its South Dakota heritage and spur the interest of family buyers. The strength and concreteness of positive associations increase the likelihood that the brand will be considered for purchase.

Package novelty and contrast refer to the package's ability to stand out visually from its surroundings, to draw attention to itself though its novel appearance. Novelty and contrast are defined in relative rather than absolute terms. They are a function of both a package's distinctiveness relative to the other brands on the store shelf (Veryzer & Hutchinson, 1998), and its departure from consumer expectations based on past shopping and consumption experiences. The contrast effects discussed earlier, exemplified by the Lava soap example, pertain to this package function as well.

The novelty of a package relative to consumers' expectations and its contrast relative to the competitive context will increase the likelihood that the package will evoke an involuntary attentional response (Kahneman, 1973), that aspect of novelty that many recognize as being the sole effect of color in a point-of-purchase context, given their presumption that color is a purely a sensory experience (Scott, 1994a). But, again, we see that there is a cognitive component to novelty, in that "newness" has its own non-brand-specific meanings that may be attributed to a brand, such as "innovative," "contemporary," or "cutting-edge." Such attributions may explain evidence in the empirical aesthetics literature (Berlyne, 1974), the attention literature (Kahneman, 1973), and the psychology of visual perception literature (Bruce & Green, 1990) that a positive relationship between novelty and preference exists. Schema theory suggests that consumers prefer moderate levels of incongruity (Mandler, 1982; Meyers-Levy & Tybout, 1989), suggesting that consumers are attracted by innovative visuals in products and packaging but will respond by purchase only if its meaning is consistent with the product category (Garber, Burke, & Jones, 2000).

Referring to the prior discussion concerning food color, flavor identification and interpretation become a fifth function for color, in color-associated food/flavor categories. Interestingly, from a competitive strategy standpoint, color when used in this manner does *not* convey brand identity, unique meaning, or contrast. It merely conveys category identity or, in the case of food products that offer more than one flavor, it declares itself for consideration by those who are seeking that flavor. However, due to competitive circumstances and the need to differentiate product appearance at the point of purchase, so as to convey rich new meanings to a brand in order to appeal to and engage the viewer visually, food color is in some product categories (such as beverages and condiments) moving away from mere flavor identification to a superior form of persuasive communication. An example is Heinz's recent introductions of green (and now purple!) ketchup(s).

A Staged Model of Individual Choice

To encompass the several, diverse roles that package/product appearance in general and package/product color in particular can play in consideration and choice, we adopt and extend the theoretical framework developed by Roberts (1989). Roberts (1989, p. 749) cast choice as a phased process consisting of three sequential stages: "The probability of brand choice (given category purchase) can be thought to have three elements; the probability of being aware of brand j; the probability of considering brand j, given awareness of it; and the probability of choosing brand j, given awareness and consideration." This framework forms the backbone of the extended model shown in Fig 16.1.

As illustrated in Fig. 16.1, consumers proceed through a series of stages when identifying and evaluating brands for purchase. Package color can have an impact at several stages in this process (Garber, Burke, & Jones, 2000). In most retail stores, similar products (i.e., items sharing the same physical characteristics and/or satisfying the same consumer need) are grouped together in product categories. At the first stage (Stage 0), consumers enter the store with a set of goals and attempt to identify product categories that satisfy their requirements. As the consumer walks through the store, one or more product categories come into view. From this vantage point, the shopper can resolve only the largest physical and graphical features of the products. However, the information is sufficient to allow the individual to identify relevant and desired product categories and to set a course down the aisle.

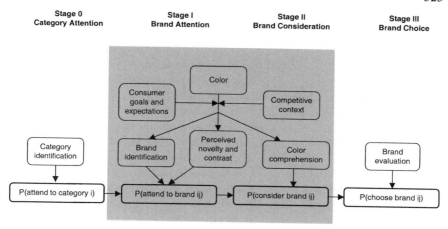

FIG. 16.1.   The effect of color on brand attention and purchase consideration. *Note.* Empirical model explicitly considers Stages I and II. Adapted from model of effects of visual package type shown in Garber, Burke, and Jones (2000), with permission.

When the consumer has located and entered a relevant category, he or she attends to one or more brands on the shelf (Stage I). The consumer's likelihood of attending to a brand is a joint function of his or her ability to identify the brand as a familiar and desirable product, and the perceived novelty and contrast of the package. Consumers are most likely to attend to those brands that they can readily identify as a result of prior advertising exposure, purchase, and/or consumption, and those brands that stand out from the competitive clutter because of their new and different appearance.

Once the consumer attends to a selection of products on the shelf, he or she considers a subset of these brands for purchase (Stage II). At this point, the shopper may pick up one or more brands to acquire detailed information from the package. Information acquisition occurs in gradations or stages, with earlier processing limited to the coarser visual features such as size, shape, and color, and later stages focusing on detailed brand information. The number of brands the shopper considers depends on his or her motivation and ability to process product information and the amount of time available. More brands will be considered if the shopper is new to the category, seeks variety, notices something new or different on the shelf, and/or has a liberal time budget.

In the final decision step (Stage III), the consumer selects one or more brands from the consideration set for purchase. This choice process has been discussed in detail in prior publications (e.g., Bettman, Johnson, & Payne, 1991; Meyer & Kahn, 1991) and is not reviewed again here. However, we should note that package factors such as color that increase consumer attention to and consideration of brands are also likely to increase the probability of choice, everything else being equal. Brand attention and consideration are necessary but not sufficient conditions for choice.

For example, a producer may choose to introduce a new product into an existing category with primary package color that departs from the established visual conventions and therefore consumer expectations for that category. Surprise on the part of the consumer on exposure to this novel color at the point of purchase is translated into selective attention. However, purchase consideration will only be gained if the meaning that that color confers to the brand is consistent with category benefits. Therefore, likelihood of brand purchase is increased by novel package color only if that color supports positive behavior at each stage of the consumer choice process. Scott (1992) pointed out that such positive behavior regarding visual signs, including color, will occur only when prior associations and their appropriateness for the task at hand come together in the minds of the target audience.

As with our examination of the respective sensory and cognitive effects of response to visual presentation that exist within each of the four roles of brand equity, so too can we point out the dual effects of color at each of the stages of the individual-level choice model just presented. For example, the role of color during the attentional stage of the model may be construed by many to be a sensory effect, and may well be the more significant effect at this stage of early vision, but meaning can still be construed to take place, especially since we attribute meaning to the processing of individual visual elements such as color. However, it is clear that there must be a strong cognitive component to color's role in the later stages of the model, particularly the consideration stage, which has a strong evaluative component to it. Here, color's meaning within its role as contributing to the recognizability and meaning of the integrated object that is a product or its package, and the image it conveys, may contribute information to the evaluation process.

AN EMPIRICAL METHOD FOR THE DECOMPOSITION AND SEPARATE MEASUREMENT OF THE SENSORY AND COGNITIVE EFFECTS OF EXPOSURE TO VISUAL STIMULI

Background

There is limited precedent in the marketing or psychology literature for methods applicable to visual experimentation. Most of the scant empirical research on the effects of visual processes or the appearance of objects in marketing addresses specific problems such as the utility of certain package forms (Wansink, 1996), the effect of particular design elements (Veryzer & Hutchinson, 1998), or the effectiveness of color versus black-and-white in newspaper ads (Meyers-Levy & Peracchio, 1995) without much ability for generalization, or is broadly conceptual without much ability for concrete application. An example of the latter is Bloch (1995), who offered a conceptual model of product design. The purpose of the model is to bring "needed attention to the subject of product design and enable researchers to better investigate design issues" (p. 17). Unfortunately, this research does not address the design selection problem itself. Bloch wrote, "Research is needed to determine which product form elements trigger cognitive responses among consumers" (p. 25). A method for doing so has been proposed by Garber, Burke, and Jones (2000) and is described therein. It adds experimental power by suggesting a systematic means of inventing, altering, calibrating, and selecting visual elements to obtain true and plausible representative visual types for experimental purposes. Of relevance to this chapter is that method's ability to separate the sensory effects of a visual experience from the effects of prior experience, and we confine our discussion to that aspect. For a complete description, refer to Garber, Burke, and Jones (2000).

The sensory/cognitive dichotomy intrinsic to the processing of visual information represents a longstanding confounding problem in all of sensory research, as indicated by Duncker (1939), who early on was concerned about the influence of past experience on perceptual properties:

> What, after all, is the effect of past experience upon present experience? More precisely: how do traces influence the phenomenal appearance of perceived objects? . . . How, under what conditions, and to what extent, is this realm of "pure" perception affected by past experience? (p. 255)

The issue exists to this day. The method referred to here addresses it, however, by using a combination of similarity scaling and correspondence analysis to disentangle these effects.

Heretofore, a common experimental means of handling this confound in applied visual research has been to simplify the problem by merely assuming that visual experience is purely immediate and sensory, thereby ignoring the fact that viewers also comprehend visual information. For example, Scott (1994a) pointed out how the intrinsic meaning of the visuals used in advertising has traditionally been ignored by most commonly employed consumer research paradigms, thereby diminishing their ability to explain or predict ad effectiveness—particularly with respect to those ads employing stylized, symbolic, or rhetorical images that invite complex processing. Complex processing, as Scott (1994a) pointed out,

> includes imagination and judgment, as well as memory. . . . In processing complex symbolic materials—such as paintings, photographs, and advertisements—cognitive participation is a necessity, and the reliance on learning crucial. The reason is that pictures are unavoidably artifactual. (pp. 260, 265)

As was pointed out earlier, the same can also be said of color because although it is only a single visual element among others comprising more complex forms including pictures and other objects, it too, being a vivid, affect-loaded, and memorable visual stimulus, also evokes complex cognitive processing.

For example, our intent with the food color examples (i.e., Clear Pepsi, and the experiment in which we manipulated the color of orange drink) is to impress the naive reader (of which we have learned there are many) with the fact that color is not simply a sensory experience, but also has meaning that can be a powerful influence on color response. For example, marketers completely overlooked the fact that changing the color of Pepsi Cola also affects its perceived taste, as well as other product attributes such as calories. When we gave subjects purple orange drink, the vast majority thought it was grape and evaluated it as such: less sweet, more tart, and so on. These results underscore on an empirical level the point that Scott (1994a) made, albeit in a simpler frame.

The Method

This method is taken from Garber (1995) and Garber, Burke, and Jones (2000), who apply it to the problem of selecting a new package for an existing product. It is appropriate for testing the effects of any visual element, such as color, or the visual effects of some stimulus object, such as a package, when presented in a relative context. By relative context, we refer to any situation where the target stimulus is embedded in a visual field with a number of distracter objects, as in the case of a product or package on a store shelf, or even an ad jammed into a commercial break with other ads on television.

Color Manipulation. As indicated by prior discussion and illustrated by the model in Fig. 16.1, the relevant dimensions of the effect of color in a relative context are degree of dissimilarity (i.e., familiarity and novelty) and color comprehension (i.e., consistency of meaning with respect to perceived product benefits). To test the effects of some color stimulus in a consumer context (or to test the effective appearance of a candidate marketing object such as a product, package or ad), the color must be typed according the degree of dissimilarity and meaning it exhibits, relative to some product category prototype.

Steps in the pretesting procedure to derive the various levels of similarity and consistency are explained using the color alteration and calibration of a Gold Medal Flour bag as an example. We borrow this example from Garber, Burke, and Jones (2000), who manipulated the color of the white Gold Medal flour bag (typical of packaging for that category), along with the packages of several other selected target brands from other food categories, in order to obtain the necessary levels of similarity and consistency for their package appearance experiment.

Creating and Classifying the Color Manipulation. In the packaging study, the original Gold Medal flour packages were scanned into the computer and the colors of selected package elements were systematically altered to create several new looks. The original package was also edited to remove any extraneous promotions or offers, but most other visual features (including lines, borders, logos, char-

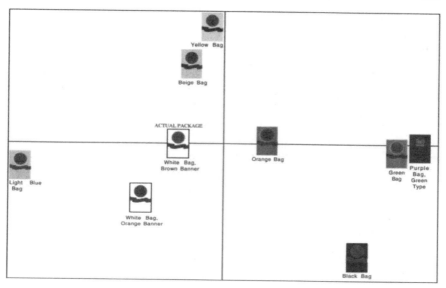

FIG. 16.2.   Perceived similarity of alternative Gold Medal flour packages. From Garber, Burke, and Jones (2000), with permission. (See Color Panel D)

acters, and other graphic elements) were retained in order to preserve brand identification. In total, 25 new packages were created for Gold Medal Flour, to assure
that all necessary color levels were represented. In so doing, we were careful to represent a sufficient range of the three dimensions that comprise color: chroma, hue,
value (for an explanation of these color dimensions, see Gorn et al., 1997).

Three judges evaluated the candidate packages that carried the color manipulations: an industrial designer and two graphic designers. The judges were asked
to select a subset of the package candidates based on the design's credibility as a
professionally executed, commercial package and the degree to which it could
be easily recognized and identified as representing the target brand. The judges
selected nine Gold Medal flour bags packages for further testing.

The last steps in pretesting were to calibrate the new packages on the dimensions of perceived dissimilarity, consistency of meaning, and preference, and to
select packages representing each of the experimental conditions (see Garber,
1995).

Twenty respondents first rated the perceived dissimilarity of each pairwise
combination of packages. These data were analyzed using the KYST multidimensional scaling algorithm (Kruskal, Young, & Seery, 1973) as implemented in
PC-MDS 5.1, from which were generated one- and two-dimensional perceptual
maps (see, e.g., Fig. 16.2). The maps represent package alternatives as points in
a common, perceptual space, where the Euclidean distance from the original
("actual") package to each of the color-altered packages indicates the dissimilarity

or novelty of the new package. New designs that were perceived to be most similar to the original package (white bag with brown banner) in both the two- and three-dimensional scaling solutions were classified as "very similar" (e.g., white bag with orange banner, beige bag, orange bag). Candidates that were the farthest away were classified as "very dissimilar" (e.g., the black and purple bags). Packages that fell between these two extremes were categorized as "somewhat dissimilar."

Second, respondents were asked to indicate which of nine all-purpose flours characterized each of the packages. They were told to base their evaluations solely on package appearance. The frequencies with which packages were associated with attributes were mapped onto a common, multidimensional space using the SIMCA correspondence analysis package (Greenacre, 1993). As shown in Fig. 16.3, the original Gold Medal package was seen as being "fresh quality," "good value," "naturally pure," and "good tasting." New packages with similar benefit profiles (like the beige bag) were classified as having "consistent meaning." New designs with very different benefit profiles (such as the black bag, which was seen as being "inexpensive") were coded as having "inconsistent meaning." By combining the results from the similarity and attribute scaling procedures, we were able to assign each package alternative to one of the four visual categories. Examples of the various package alternatives created for Gold Medal Flour are shown in Fig. 16.4.

Finally, pretest respondents were asked to rate the degree to which they liked or disliked each of the test packages. Packages with low evaluations were eliminated from the set.

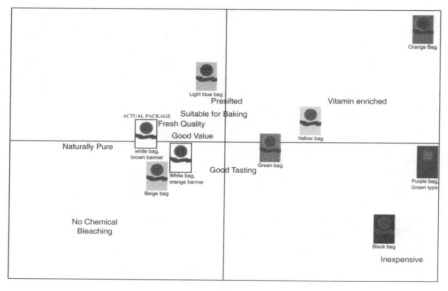

FIG. 16.3.   Attribute associations for alternative Gold Medal flour packages. From Garber, Burke, and Jones (2000), with permission. (See Color Panel E)

Beige Bag: Very Similar
Visual Type

Light Blue Bag: Moderately
Dissimilar

Green bag: Very Dissimilar
and Consistent

Black Bag: Very Dissimilar and
Inconsistent

FIG. 16.4. Selected Gold Medal package variations for the flour category. (See Color Panel F)

One finding from the Garber, Burke, and Jones (2000) packaging study relevant to this chapter showed that that large color changes to an existing package can increase the likelihood that new customers will consider and choose the product, but *only when the meaning conveyed by package color is consistent with the brand's original positioning*—underscoring the importance of considering cognitive processing in modeling the viewer's response to a visual stimulus such as color. Elaborating on the role of meaning in evaluating response to a visual stimulus, this finding is evocative of Scott's (1994b) similar point about advertising conventions, and how they form expectations for an image, and frame the viewer's response to it:

> Our expectations for these [advertising] elements to contain certain information, as well as our culturally informed expectation that someone is trying to persuade us here, lead us well into a reading strategy [i.e., "rules of reading" particular to the advertising genre, recognizable to the reader due to the reader's prior experience with advertising, that informs the process of reading ads; presumably, there are respective "rules of reading" for packaging, food color and all other commercial and noncommercial genres] before any pictures or words are comprehensible [i.e., only individual visual elements such as color (Triesman & Gelade 1980)]. In actual experience, we are also cued to invoke this schema by the placement of advertisements in certain previously agreed-upon places in media space or time. (p. 464)

FUTURE RESEARCH

Given the relative lack of color and visual research extant, there are many opportunities for interested researchers. In terms of color research specifically, although Garber, Burke, and Jones (2000) examined the effects of large color changes to an existing package in terms of chroma and value, their research needs to be extended to other product categories, and should consider the effects of more subtle changes to hue, given chroma and value (for an explanation of these terms, see Gorn et al., 1997). More work also needs to be done to examine individual differences and cultural and cross-cultural effects, and to nail down the underlying cognitive processes that mediate color effects.

Moreover, similar research is necessary to examine the effects of the other visual elements, including size, shape, graphic elements, motion, and their interaction. Other important research would examine the interaction of these visuals and other marketing mix variables.

It is also unclear whether the interaction of individual visual elements is sufficient to explain the effects of the appearance of integrated objects. The small amount of work done examining the effects of color in newspapers, store atmospherics, and packaging needs to be expanded and extended to other objects whose appearance serves as cues in marketing. Moreover, this work may also be extended to include other elements of point-of-purchase displays: trade shows, logos, stationery, web sites, trucks, and company uniforms.

In particular, a great deal of work needs to be done regarding the symbolic nature of visual elements as imagery. There is a deeper level to how visual elements "mean," as pointed out by those involved with visual rhetoric. This is an area that needs much exploration and integration into other aspects of visual research, before we will have complete understanding of how we respond to visual stimuli.

REFERENCES

Aaronson, B. S. (1970). Some affective stereotypes of color. *International Journal of Symbology, 2,* 15–27.

Adams, F. M., & Osgood, C. E. (1973). A cross-cultural study of the affective meanings of color. *Journal of Cross Cultural Psychology, 4,* 135–156.

Agarwal, M. K., & Rao, V. R. (1996). An empirical comparison of consumer-based measures of brand equity. *Marketing Letters, 7,* 237–248.

Albers, J. (1963). *Interaction of color.* New Haven, CT: Yale University Press.

Ball, V. K. (1965). The aesthetics of color: A review of fifty years of experimentation. *Journal of Aesthetics and Art Criticism, 23,* 441–452.

Bellizzi, J. A., & Hite, R. E. (1992). Environmental color, consumer feelings and purchase likelihood. *Psychology and Marketing, 9,* 347–363.

Bellizzi, J. A., Crowley, A. E., & Hasty, R. W. (1983). The effects of color in store design. *Journal of Retailing, 59,* 21–45.

Berlyne, E. E. (1974). *Studies in the new experimental aesthetics.* New York: John Wiley and Sons.

Bettman, J. R., Johnson, E. J., & Payne, J. W. (1991). Consumer decision making. In T. Robertson & H. Kassarjian (Eds.), *Handbook of consumer behavior* (pp. 85–123). Englewood Cliffs, NJ: Prentice Hall.

Biel, A. L. (1993). Converting image into equity. In D. Aaker & A. Biel (Eds.), *Brand equity & advertising: Advertising's role in building strong brands.* Hillsdale, NJ: Lawrence Erlbaum Associates.

Bjerstedt, A. (1960). Warm–cool color preferences as potential personality indicators: Preliminary note. *Perceptual and Motor Skills, 10,* 31–34.

Bloch, P. H. (1995). Seeking the ideal form: Product design and consumer response. *Journal of Marketing, 59,* 16–29.

Bruce, V., & Green, P. R. (1990). *Visual perception: Physiology, psychology and ecology.* Hillsdale, NJ: Lawrence Erlbaum Associates.

Bullough, E. (1910). The perceptive problem in the aesthetic appreciation of simple color combinations. *British Journal of Psychology, 406*–447.

Cheskin, L. (1957). *How to predict what people will buy.* New York: Liveright.

Click, J. W., & Stempel, G. H. III. (1976). Reader response to front pages with four-color halftones. *Journalism Quarterly, 53,* 736–738.

Collinson, D. (1992). Aesthetic experience. In O. Hanfling (Ed.), *Philosophical aesthetics.* Cambridge: Open University.

Crick, F. (1994). *The astonishing hypothesis: The scientific search for the soul.* New York: Simon and Schuster.

Danger, E. P. (1969). *How to use color to sell.* Boston: Cahners.

Davidoff, J. (1991). *Cognition through color.* Boston: MIT Press.

Dichter, E. (1975). *Packaging: The sixth sense? A guide to identifying consumer motivation.* Boston: Cahners.

DuBose, C. N., Cardello, A. V., & Maller, O. (1980). Effects of colorants and flavorants on identification of perceived flavor intensity, and hedonic quality of fruit-flavored beverages and cakes. *Journal of Food Science, 45,* 1393–1399, 1415.

Duncker, K. (1939). The influence of past experience upon perceptual properties. *American Journal of Psychology, 52,* 255–265.

Edell, J. A., & Staelin, R. (1983). The information processing of pictures in print advertisements. *Journal of Consumer Research, 10,* 45–61.

Farquar, P. H. (1989). Managing brand equity. *Marketing Research,* 24–33.

Fisher, J. D. (1974). Situation-specific variables as determinants of perceived environmental aesthetic quality and perceived crowdedness. *Journal of Research and Personality, 8,* 177–188.

Garber, L. L., Jr. (1995). *The role of package appearance in consumer choice.* Unpublished doctoral dissertation, University of North Carolina at Chapel Hill.

Garber, L. L., Jr., & Buff, B. (2000). *The effects of package shape and actual size on perceived size.* Unpublished manuscript, Appalachian State University.

Garber, L. L., Jr., Burke, R. R., & Jones, J. M. (2000). *The role of package appearance in consumer purchase consideration and choice.* Marketing Science Institute Working Paper Series, Report No. 00-104. Boston: MSI.

Garber, L. L., Jr., Hyatt, E. M., & Starr, R. G., Jr. (2000). The effects of food color on perceived flavor. *Journal of Marketing Theory and Practice, 8,* 59–72.

Goethe, J. W. von. (1988) Theory of color. In D. Miller (Ed. & Trans.), *Scientific studies* (vol. 12, Goethe: Collected Works in English). New York: Suhrkamp.

Golden, C. J. (1974). Sex differences on the performance in the Stroop color and word test. *Perpetual and Motor Skills, 39,* 1067–1070.

Gorn, G. J., Chattopadhyay, A., Yi, T., & Dahl, E. W. (1997). Effects of color as an executional cue: They're in the shade. *Management Science, 43,* 1387–1400.

Greenacre, M. J. (1993). *Correspondence analysis in practice.* New York: Academic Press.

Guilford, J. P., & Smith, P. C. (1959). A system of color-preferences. *American Journal of Psychology, 4,* 487–502.

Hall, R. L. (1958). Flavor study approaches at McCormick and Company, Inc. In A. Little (Ed.), *Flavor research and food acceptance.* New York: Reinhold.

Helmholtz, H. von (1962). *Treatise on physiological optics* (Vol. 3) (J. Southall. Ed. & Trans.). New York: Dover. (Original work published 1866)

Hilbert, D. R. (1987). *Color and color perception: A study in anthropocentric realism.* Palo Alto, CA: Center for the Study of Language and Information.

Hine, T. (1996). *The total package.* New York: Little, Brown.

Hyman, A. (1983). The influence of color on the taste perception of carbonated water preparations. *Bulletin of the Psychonomic Society, 21,* 145–148.

Kahneman, D. (1973). *Attention and effort.* Englewood, NJ: Prentice Hall.

Keller, K. L. (1993). Conceptualizing, measuring, and managing customer-based brand equity. *Journal of Marketing, 57,* 1–22.

King, S. H. M. (1989). Branding opportunities in financial services. *Proceedings of the Market Research Society conference on advertising and marketing financial services.* London: MRS Press.

Kruskal, J. B., Young, F. W., & Seery, J. B. (1973). *How to use KYST, a very flexible program to do multidimensional scaling and unfolding.* Murray Hill, NJ: Bell Laboratories.

Land, E. H. (1977). The retinex theory of color vision. *Scientific American, 237,* 108–128.

Lee, S., & Barnes, J. H., Jr. (1990). Using color preferences in magazine advertising. *Journal of Advertising Research, 29,* 25–30.

Locke, J. (1975). *An essay concerning human understanding* (Edited from the fourth [1700] and fifth [1706] editions by P. Nidditch). New York: Oxford University Press. (Original work published 1690)

Loken, B., & Ward, J. (1990). Alternative approaches to understanding the determinants of typicality. *Journal of Consumer Research, 17,* 111–126.

Maga, J. A. (1974). Influence of color on taste thresholds. *Chemical Senses, Flavor, 1,* 115–119.

Mandler, G. (1982). The structure of value: accounting for taste. In M. Clark & S. Fiske (Eds.), *Affect and cognition: The 17th annual Carnegie Symposium* (pp. 3–36). Hillsdale, NJ: Lawrence Erlbaum Associates.

Marr, D. (1982). *Vision: A computational investigation into the human representation of processing of visual information.* San Francisco: W. H. Freeman.

Marr, D., & Nishihara, H. K. (1978). Representation and recognition of the spatial organization of three-dimensional shapes. *Proceedings of the Royal Society of London, Series B, 207,* 187–216.

Meyer, R. J., & Kahn, B. E. (1991). Probabilistic models of consumer choice behavior. In T. Robertson & H. Kassarjian (Eds.), *Handbook of consumer behavior* (pp. 85–123). Englewood Cliffs, NJ: Prentice Hall.

Meyers-Levy, J., & Peracchio, L. A. (1995). Understanding the effects of color: How the correspondence between available and required resources affects attitudes. *Journal of Consumer Research, 22,* 121–138.

Meyers-Levy, J., & Tybout, A. M. (1989). Schema incongruity as a basis for product evaluation. *Journal of Consumer Research, 16,* 39–54.

Nelson, M. R., & Hitchon, J. C. (1995). Theory of synesthesia applied to persuasion in print advertising headlines. *Journalism & Mass Communication Quarterly,* 346–360.

Newton, I. (1979). *Optiks.* New York: Dover.

Norton, W. E., & Johnson, F. N. (1987). The influence of intensity of colour on perceived flavour characteristics. *Medical Science Research, 15,* 329–330.

Oram, N., Laing, D. G., Hutchinson, J. O., Greenville, R., Freeman, M., & Newell, G. (1995). The influence of flavor and color on drink identification among children and adults. *Developmental Psychobiology, 28,* 234–246.

Pangborn, R. M. (1960). Influence of color on the discrimination of sweetness. *American Journal of Psychology, 73,* 229–238.

Park, C. S., & Srinivasan, V. (1994). A survey based method for measuring and understanding brand equity and its extendability. *Journal of Marketing Research, 21,* 271–288.

Roberts, J. H. (1989). A grounded model of consideration set size and composition. *Advances in Consumer Research, 16,* 749–757.

Sacks, O. (1995). The case of the color blind painter. In *An anthropologist on Mars: 7 Paradoxical tales.* New York: Vintage.

Schindler, P. S. (1986). Color and contrast in magazine advertising. *Psychology and Marketing, 3,* 69–87.

Scott, L. (1992). Playing with pictures: Postmodernism, poststructuralism, and advertising visuals. In J. Sherry & B. Sternthal (Eds.), *Advances in Consumer Research* (pp. 596–612). Provo, UT: Association for Consumer Research.

Scott, L. (1994a). Images in advertising: the need for a theory of visual rhetoric. *Journal of Consumer Research, 2,* 252–273.

Scott, L. (1994b). The bridge from text to mind: Adapting reader-response theory to consumer research. *Journal of Consumer Research, 21,* 461–480.

Sharpe, D. T. (1975). *The psychology of color and design.* Chicago: Nelson-Hall.

Sparkman, R. R., Jr., & Austin, L. M. (1980). The effect on sales of color in newspaper advertisements. *Journal of Advertising, 9,* 39–42.

Stillman, J. A. (1993). Color influences flavor identification in fruit-flavored beverages. *Journal of Food Science, 58,* 810–812.

Swirnoff, L. (1989). *Dimensional color.* Boston: Birkhauser.

Triesman, A. (1991). Search, similarity, and integration of features between and within dimensions. *Journal of Experimental Psychology: Human Perception and Performance, 40A,* 201–237.

Triesman, A., & Gelade, G. (1980). A feature-integration theory of attention. *Cognitive Psychology, 14,* 107–141.

Triplett, T. (1994). Consumers show little taste for clear beverages. *Marketing News, 28,* 2.

Veryzer, R. W., & Hutchinson, J. W. (1998). The influence of unity and prototypicality on aesthetic responses to new product designs. *Journal of Consumer Research, 24,* 374–394.

Wansink, B. (1996). Can package size accelerate usage volume. *Journal of Marketing, 60,* 1–14.

Zeki, S. (1980). The representation of colors in the cerebral cortex. *Nature, 284,* 412- 418.

Zellner, D. A., Bartoli, A. M., & Eckard, R. (1991). Influence of color on odor identification and liking ratings. *American Journal of Psychology, 4,* 547–561.

CHAPTER SEVENTEEN

The Marriage of Graphic Design and Research—Experimentally Designed Packages Offer New Vistas and Opportunities

Richard Bernstein
Howard Moskowitz
Moskowitz Jacobs, Inc., White Plains, New York

For many fast-moving consumer goods, the package is the first experience a consumer has with the product. As part of market our research services, we determine the best packaging options using advanced conjoint methods (Green & Srinivasan, 1978). The work owes much to a psychophysical heritage (e.g. Moskowitz, 1981)— systematic stimulus manipulation coupled with a simple respondent-rating task. The objective is to create mathematical models relating visual appeal to packaging options. End users can define most appealing packages and understand how package features contribute to consumer appeal. This provides client organizations the learning necessary to incorporate consumer input into short- and long-range packaging strategy.

We illustrate the approach with a case study. Because we are presenting real data from a recent study, our mandate for client confidentiality requires many marketing details to be camouflaged.

BACKGROUND

A multinational manufacturer commissioned this work. It wanted to understand the impact and relevance of a variety of packaging options for one of its categories in order to develop the best packaging for its different user groups and different regional markets. Any commonalties leading to a single or limited number of packages would be welcome. The product primarily has an adult target audience with a weekly or monthly purchase cycle.

This study was executed in four separate European markets (France, Germany, Spain, and Sweden). The respondent sample was constructed so that separate models could be developed for all user groups in each of the regions. Precise sample specifications were based on the client's marketing objectives.

STIMULI

The key methodological challenge is to transform the artistic process to one that can be incorporated into a scientific research design. As one might suspect, this is not a particularly easy step. Package features must be quantified into parameters that can be treated statistically. This done, an appropriate stimulus array (cf. Moskowitz, 1981) can be readily developed

The manufacturer's design team identified all the viable packaging options. A package was considered viable if the engineering team concluded that (a) it could be manufactured and (b) it was likely to meet all engineering requirements.

In this study, a package was "defined" by its shape, the opening and closing mechanisms, the surface material, and the presence/absence of several value-added features. Because "in reality" package shape and closing mechanism are highly correlated, these characteristics were combined into a single variable in order to eliminate the correlation (viz., to introduce a new way to describe the features). In total, there were 42 packaging options organized into categories of related characteristics. A fractional design (e.g., Box, Hunter, & Hunter, 1978) was used to specify 186 test packages.

A design firm generated photorealistic depictions of each of the test packages on computer-readable media. Package visuals were comprised of a main picture of the package on the left side of the visual and supplementary inserts of key features and descriptive text about these features on the right side of the visual. Native speakers translated text into the appropriate language for the test market. Figures 17.1 and 17.2 present examples of the type and quality of images used. These were not part of the test array and were chosen to illustrate the images used without identifying the precise product category.

METHOD

Respondents

Detailed protocols were developed for each region. Respondents were prerecruited via telephone or "intercepted" in accord with local market research practices. Interviews were executed entirely in the local language.

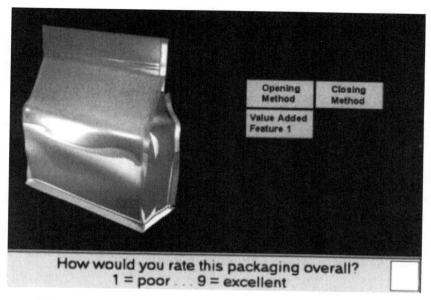

FIG. 17.1.   Example of screen representation of a package. The left shows a photo-realistic rendering of the package. The right presents a description of the key features. The bottom shows a prompt for the rating question.

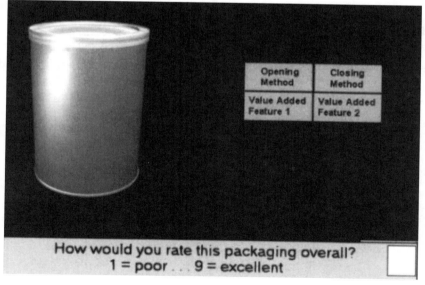

FIG. 17.2.   Another example of screen representation of a package, showing the package itself, the key features, and a prompt for the response.

After completing a screening questionnaire, qualified respondents were invited to participate in the study at a central location. Qualifications included demographic and product usage criteria. Each session was comprised of 1 to 10 respondents, depending on the number of available computers.

Session Sequence

The session lasted 45 min. It was choreographed in a way that permitted the respondents to work at their own pace, stay motivated, and stay on task.

Orientation

Respondents were seated at individual computer workstations. At the beginning of the session, respondents completed a short orientation session. Respondents were exposed to three-dimensional models of select packages in order to illustrate package options. Respondents handled approximately 15 examples illustrating opening and closing mechanism, surface material, and the value-added features. This orientation helped respondents appreciate the packages depicted in the main study and provided a realistic grounding.

The moderator then took respondents through an exercise to familiarize them with the use of the computer keyboard, the study questions, and the continuous 9-point rating scale. The respondents were encouraged to use the entire 9-point rating scale, but were not forced to do so.

"Positioning" the Stimulus—Setting up the Context for the Evaluation

In order to provide a context for the rating exercise, respondents were provided with a positioning statement:

> You will be looking at a variety of packaging alternatives for the *product category* [actual category in original instructions]. Some of the features you see may be familiar and some are new ideas. In any case the package is colored in a neutral color for this test. Do not use the color as a signal for the product quality
>
> When the computer shows you a package, look at it carefully and read all of the written descriptions. Assume the product you use most often at home is in the package.
>
> Please take your time and read each concept (screen) thoroughly. Now, tell us how you feel about the package using the questions shown on the bottom of the computer screen. The entire concept should be rated as a whole. Enter your rating based on the following questions.

Package-Rating Exercise

Trials were self-paced. Package visuals were presented on a computer screen and respondents rated how well they liked the package. They also rated each package on one additional attribute (not discussed here). Short rest periods were imposed after sets of 25 packages were rated. Figures 17.1 and 17.2 present sample screens created for illustration and were not part of the study. Note that all the packages and backgrounds were uniformly colored. Actual inserts describing features were in the appropriate language, and were supplemented by an icon representing the feature. Both the feature inserts and the orientation exercise were intended to enrich the representation of test packages. Each respondent rated 90 package concepts. Presentation order was randomized, and care was taken to balance package options within and between respondents.

RESULTS

Following market research conventions, data are organized in order to understand the percent of the respondents assigning a specific answer (or set of answers). For this set of data, the results were organized to estimate the percentage of respondents giving top-3 box ratings (i.e., ratings of 7, 8, or 9) for each of the tested packages.

We use "dummy-coded" multiple regression to relate the presence/absence of elements in the package to the percent of respondents who, having seen the package, like the package (viz., assign the package a rating of 7, 8, or 9, respectively). Given the experimental design matrix, we compute a dummy-variable regression of the form:

$$Y = b_{(0)} + b_{(c1,1)}X_{(c1,i)} + \cdots + b_{(cl,1)}X_{(cl,j)} \tag{1}$$

In Equation 1, Y is the package liking score (or other rating attribute) and each X represents the presence/absence of the package options. The indexing variable indicates the option's category membership. Because the design matrix was constrained to contain only realizable packages, the regression coefficients are estimates of the part-worth contribution of each packaging component. Each analytical group generated its own particular model, although all the models used the same packaging components.

The dummy-variable model works when all the variables are statistically independent. This is not the case for package design. Knowing the condition of $n - 1$ alternatives in a package automatically determines the condition of n alternatives. (For instance, if there are two colors, A and B, respectively, a color must be either A or B. There are no colorless packages. If a package is colored A, then it cannot be colored B, and vice versa.) Every package has a shape, a closing/opening mechanism, and a material. Because an option from these categories is always present, we identified one option as a reference option. (It does not matter which option is chosen to be the reference.) Coefficients for these categories represent the contribution relative to the reference. For convenience, the current (in-market) packages were assigned as the references.

Total European Sample -- Overall Liking of Package
Measured vs Modeled Scores

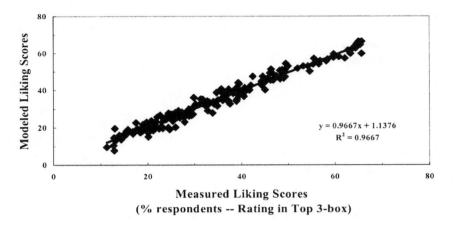

FIG. 17.3.   Measured versus Modeled liking scores. The computed regression
model accurately describes measured package liking.

Therefore, given these conventions, the estimated coefficients for the different
packaging options indicate how these options drive liking relative to current in-
market packages. Positive coefficients indicate that the option increases liking,
whereas negative coefficients indicate that the option yields less liking than the
current option. Coefficients near zero indicate that option is at parity with the
in-market package. Because our models are linear, the reference option can be
changed without impacting the liking hierarchy.

   There were some value-added features that were either present or absent. These
features did not need a reference condition because they were either present or
absent, and could be coded so in the design. The coefficients for the value-added
features show the absolute incremental contribution to acceptance (as defined by
percentage in the top three boxes of the 9-point rating scale).

   To examine how well the regression model describes consumer liking, we estimated the package-liking scores from the model parameters and compared the
scores to the actual liking scores. Figure 17.3 presents package-liking for the total
sample. Clearly, the fit is good. Indeed, individual countries yielded r^2 ranging
from .86 to .93. Thus our regression models provides accurate descriptions of how
package-liking varies with packaging parameters.

   Table 17.1 presents the models for the total sample and for each of the four
European markets. The table presents the regression coefficient for each package

feature based on the models calculated for each market. The table displays b_0, the additive constant, which represents the consumers' generalized liking. Each package option has an associated coefficient. The model contains references for specific categories. Within those categories, package options with positive coefficients indicate that packages with that option yield greater liking than the corresponding reference options. Options with negative coefficients are liked less than the

TABLE 17.1
Additive Model for Package Liking

	Total Europe	Country 1	Country 2	Country 3	Country 4
Base size	811	204	207	200	200
Additive constant (b_0)	25	22	33	16	41
Package shape					
Type A-1	21	26	17	29	5
Type A-2	19	27	12	27	3
Type A-3	18	21	10	31	2
Type A-4	16	17	16	27	−1
Type A-5	16	23	9	26	0
Type A-6	14	16	10	26	−2
Type A-7	12	15	6	24	−4
Type A-8	9	9	5	20	−7
Type B-1	6	10	1	19	−11
Type C-1	3	1	0	2	0
(Reference, country 4)					
Type B-2	2	3	−1	12	−14
Type C-2	0	0	0	0	−7
(Reference, countries 1–3)					
Type B-3	0	−7	−2	10	−9
Type C-3	−3	−5	−7	2	−7
Type C-4	−3	−8	−3	0	−9
Type C-5	−4	4	−11	6	−21
Type C-6	−5	1	−9	1	−20
Type D-1	−5	−9	−8	3	−13
Type B-4	−5	−5	−11	3	−14
Type D-2	−6	−5	−9	1	−18
Type C-7	−7	−5	−10	0	−22
Type C-8	−8	−7	−12	−1	−17
Type C-9	−10	−14	−15	−5	−13
Type C-10	−11	−12	−15	−4	−17
Type C-11	−11	−11	−18	−1	−21
Type C-12	−12	−14	−17	−4	−21
Type D-3	−12	−13	−17	−4	−23
Type C-13	−13	−15	−18	−6	−19
Type C-14	−13	−16	−15	−8	−20
Type D-4	−16	−6	−20	−14	−31
Type C-15	−22	−16	−28	−19	−30

(Continued)

TABLE 17.1 (*continued*)

	Total Europe	Country 1	Country 2	Country 3	Country 4
Opening method					
Opening method A	8	8	7	9	0
(Reference, country 4)					
Opening method B	0	0	0	0	−8
(Reference, country 1–3)					
Material					
Type A (Reference)	0	0	0	0	4
Type B	0	1	2	−3	3
Type C	−1	1	−1	0	0
Type D	−1	1	−1	−2	1
Type E	−1	1	−1	−1	0
Added value feature 1	7	5	6	11	4
Added value feature 2	7	4	6	14	6

Note. Numbers are part-worth contribution for packaging components.

reference option. Options with coefficients near zero yield liking at parity with the reference option. Options are ordered by their contribution to liking of the total sample model. For the value-added feature the coefficient represents the value for the option when it is present in the package. (The reference for that is the absence of the option.)

It is striking that the four countries yield similar models. Option preferences show similar rank ordering, and options that are preferred in one country tend to be preferred in all countries. Consider first the findings on package shape/closure. Several type A packages are liked the best. This finding is particularly intriguing since the different regions have different package histories and different in-market packages.

Consider next the opening method. In every region the same opening method (method A) is preferred. Interestingly, the impact of opening method on liking is about the same for all user groups. In contrast, consumers do not show any strong or consistent preference for material. Package appeal is impacted strongly by shape of the package and how it is opened and closed. Appeal is only minimally impacted by material.

Finally, consider the two value-added features. Both are intended to increase the usability of the package. Both contribute to consumer liking and seem to be valued by the consumer. As part of the usage questionnaire, we asked consumers to indicate how much they were willing to pay for each of these value-added features. We used that series of questions to classify a respondent as being willing or unwilling to pay for the feature. We then built liking-models for consumers *unwilling* to pay extra for any features and for consumers *willing* to pay extra for both features. Table 17.2 presents coefficients for the value-added features. The consumers

TABLE 17.2
Part of the Additive Model for Package Liking Created for Two Key Subgroups:
Those Willing to Pay for All Features, and Those Not Willing to Pay
for Any Extra Feature

	Total Sample	Group 1— Willing to Pay for All Extra Features	Group 2— Not Willing to Pay for Any Extra Features
Base size	811	339	157
Additive constant b_0	25	25	28
Value-added feature 1	7	8	3
Value-added feature 2	7	8	3

Note. Numbers are part-worth contribution for packaging components.

unwilling to pay extra for features like the features less than the consumers who are willing to pay for the features do. This finding, although not surprising, does illustrate an internal consistency in the data structure.

U.S. REPLICATION

Quite recently, we were commissioned by the U.S. affiliate to execute a similar study in the United States. Package options under consideration were similar (but not identical) to those under consideration in our European study.

Study Design

Once again we systematically varied basic package parameters. Because package shape determines realizable method of closure, we again combined these dimensions into a single design variable. The method of opening and the surface material options were similar to those of the European study. In total, there were 126 test packages representing a full factorial design of all design variables. Each respondent participated in a scripted orientation and rated 75 test packages. As in the European study, a short classification questionnaire was administered after the package rating exercise.

Results

Figure 17.4 presents a comparison of actual and modeled package-liking scores. Clearly consumers discriminate between packages. The best liked packages yield scores about 70, whereas the least liked packages yield scores near zero. Modeled scores capture consumer preferences.

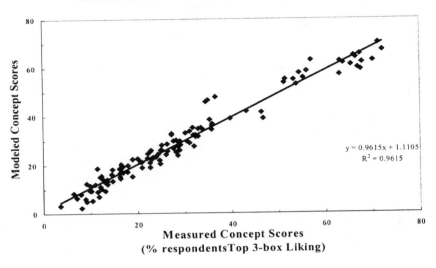

FIG. 17.4.   Measured versus Model liking scores for the U.S. study.

The model computed for the total sample appears in Table 17.3. Two findings are compelling. Consumers in the United States exhibit a preference hierarchy similar to their European counterparts. Packages have near-universal preference hierarchies. Given the type of product, we suspect that the preferences are driven by feature-functionality.

There is one key difference between European and U.S. findings. In the United States there is a clear preference for type C material. We note that type A packages are virtually always made of type C material in the United States, whereas in Europe, type A packages are made from a variety of materials. It is possible that this U.S.–European difference may reflect a disparity in consumer experience.

SUMMARY

Experimental design and optimization maximize the appeal of the packaging in each case study. Experimental design creates test arrays that vary along physical dimensions. Arrays are constrained to contain only realizable packages. Targeted consumers are exposed to the test array and instructed to provide ratings of package appeal. The analysis decomposes the ratings and assigns contribution scores for each packaging option. The sample is selected to develop separate models of appeal for each important marketing target group. In effect, the approach uses an

TABLE 17.3
Additive Model for the U.S. Study (Liking),
Which Partially Replicated the European Study

	Total
Base size	387
b_0	−1
Package shape/closure	
Type A-1	55
Type A-2	50
Type A-3	49
Type A-4	49
Type A-5	47
Type A-6	47
Type C-1	27
Type C-2	26
Type C-3	24
Type C-4	21
Type C-5	20
Type C-6	20
Type C-7	19
Type C-8	18
Type C-9	16
Type C-10	14
Type D-1	10
Type C-11	9
Type C-12	8
Type C-13	7
Type D-2	6
Type C-14	6
Type C–15	3
Type D-3	0
(Reference)	
Opening	
Type A	9
Type B	0
(Reference)	
Material	
Type C	7
Type A	4
Type	0
(Reference)	

Note. The ranking of coefficients in the
model is similar for United States and Europe,
but different in magnitude.

experimentally defined array to determine the impact of each packaging option for all important marketing target groups. This allows manufacturers to readily determine the best packaging option for a variety of marketing scenarios.

REFERENCES

Box, G. E. P., Hunter, J., & Hunter, S. (1978). *Statistics for experimenters.* New York: John Wiley.

Green, P. E., & Srinivasan, S. (1978). Conjoint analysis in consumer research: Issues and outlook. *Journal of Consumer Research, 5,* 103–124.

Moskowitz, H. R. (1981). Psychophysical approaches to package design and evaluation. In W. Stern (Ed.), *Handbook of package design research* (pp. 505–534). New York: John Wiley.

CHAPTER EIGHTEEN

Building Brands:
Architectural Expression
in the Electronic Age

Jonathan E. Schroeder
Royal Institute of Technology, Stockholm

The Bank of New York's web site shows a small image of a classical templelike building—not the bank's own building, but the U.S. Treasury building in Washington, DC. Corinthian columns, a rusticated entablature, and a classical frieze are just visible on the web site, peering out from the lower right corner of the page, which appears in several places throughout the site (see Fig. 18.1). The bank points to its 200 years of experience and achievement in words and images, adopting the classical language to the latest electronic forum. Alluding to both its tradition of providing the first loan to the fledgling U.S. government, and banking's echo of the federal government's embrace of classicism, the web site provides evidence of the enduring and flexible power of the classical form—an architectural language that lives on in the electronic age.

Although space and time are transfigured within the information-based electronic world of contemporary commerce, architectural design remains an ancient, powerful, persuasive method for communicating consumer values. We study building brands, constructing networks, and testing structural models, yet there is little architectural discourse within consumer research scholarship. Architecture is not part of the consumer research toolbox. There is a movement toward studying "servicescapes," some studies about design, and more on retailing atmospherics, but few studies place architecture—bricks and mortar as well as symbol and expression—at the center. Of course, there is a growing research literature about on-site ethnographic studies, spectacular consumer palaces such as DisneyWorld, Las Vegas, and Nike Town, and interview subjects are often "intercepted" at the shopping mall (cf. Sherry, 1998). However, architecture is more than the place that

349

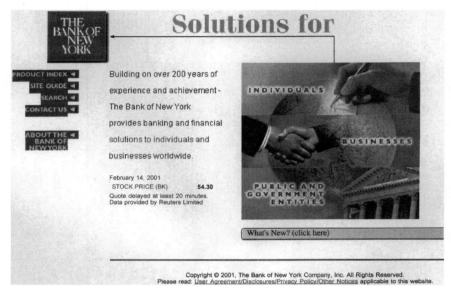

FIG. 18.1.   Bank of New York web site, 2001.

we work, the building that we live in, or the stores where we shop—architecture
expresses psychological, cultural, and consumer values.

ARCHITECTURE AS COMMUNICATION

This chapter investigates the role architecture plays in visual persuasion, using the
banking industry as an illustrative example. Buildings are part of the story, but
mostly I emphasize how architecture expresses meaning, and how financial institutions manage that meaning. I focus on the abstracted, visual, and aesthetic
qualities of architecture—especially classical architecture—for that is often how
marketing incorporates and consumers experience architectural form. This is not
to downplay architecture's physical properties as buildings, spaces, and places.
Rather, I turn attention onto the communicative and persuasive use of architectural elements via a historical overview of how material form came to be associated
with persuasive image.

   This chapter presents four assumptions about the visual language of consumption:

   1. Architecture is a rhetoric. That is, built form constitutes a system of representation and signifying practices. Buildings mean something. Form persuades.
Architectural form refers to the general style of a building—a castle, a church, or a
strip mall, for example. Architecture is a complex signifying system encompassing

art, technology, industry, and investment that represents ideals, goals, and values (Conway & Roenisch, 1994).

2. Classicism is a particularly persuasive architectural style. Classical architecture has its roots in antiquity, in the worlds of ancient Greece and Rome, in the temple architecture of the Greeks, and in the military and civil architecture of the Romans. These forms were used in a common architectural language from that day forward, so that a classical building is one whose decorative elements derive directly or indirectly from the architectural vocabulary of the ancient world (Summerson, 1963).

3. Financial institutions, particularly in the United States, appropriated architectural expression for strategic reasons: "banks adopted the canons of classical architecture as appropriate forms to house their functions, the less tangible (psychological) attributes of strength, security, and stability characterize them as a distinguishable building type" (Chambers, 1985, p. 20). A typical bank expressed, "by means of its bulk, its bronze doors, and its barred windows, that your money was safe; it also said, since it had a façade of a Greek temple, that money was holy" (Barnet, 1997, p. 54). A bank's appearance should convey an impression that reflects the institution's character by its air of stability, dignity, and security. Thus, the less tangible attributes of a bank—its image—can be communicated through architectural form (see Fig. 18.2).

4. This strategic fit between architecture and banking is under strain in the virtual world of electronic, online, and web-based banking. However, although space and time are transfigured within the information based electronic world of contemporary commerce, classical architecture remains a viable method for communicating consumer values. A look at current marketing communications and web page design reveals the staying power of classicism for transmitting certain key values about banks and building brand images for global financial institutions.

After a brief introduction to what has been called the classical language of architecture, I discuss the role that architectural form plays in the banking industry, drawing on examples from architectural history, banking history, and marketing communication. Has the classical visual form of the bank been abandoned? Does the bricks and mortar world of the built environment present an anachronism in the information age? We turn to several sources of data to find that the answer is no:

1. Advertising images incorporate classical architectural symbols—columns, temple form, interior space. Here we see the representational properties of architectural form.
2. The World Wide Web is infused with architectural metaphors—home pages, firewalls, portals, pathways, and so forth—and web page design often reflects the building as icon.
3. Automated teller machines incorporate architectural symbols,
4. Corporate communications such as annual reports also integrate the language of classical architecture.

FIG. 18.2.   Old Stone Bank, Providence, Rhode Island (photo by
author).

A basic content analysis of these materials reveals several uses of architecture as
expression in contemporary marketing communications.

I draw the conclusion that the classical form is too culturally embedded and
visually powerful as a communicative mechanism for financial institutions to jet-
tison. Marketing usually blends the new with the old to reassure consumers that
change is not too radical. The built environment has provided expressive visual
clues for a long time. Thus, financial institutions seem reluctant to give up classicism. Furthermore, one of the governing metaphors of the web is architecturally
based. I close with some thoughts on the capacity for marketing communications
to abstract and appropriate cultural symbols—one of the foundations of visual
consumption (e.g., Schroeder, 1998, 2002).

ARCHITECTURE AND EXPRESSION

The eminent Bank of England has entered the electronic age via a comprehensive web site. Bank of England's home page shows a photograph of its iconic building in the background—its classical form visually, psychologically, and historically hovers behind current ventures into electronic commerce (see Fig. 18.3 and 18.4). The faint vision of the bank building's immense classical façade appears on *each* web page, under descriptions of secure online transactions, fiscal strength, and a long, glorious history. This type of image is called a *ghost*—it is not fully saturated with color, thus page designers can place ghosted images behind text without obscuring readability. Like a ghost, the classical spirit haunts our understanding of security, stability and strength.

Architecture begins with function, structure, and beauty—needs, means, and aesthetics—as laid down by the Roman architect Vitruvius centuries ago (O'Gorman, 1998). By their form, location, style, size, cost, and purpose, architectural form communicates. Buildings include and exclude, enclose, influence and structure, and protect and dominate. Architecture is a blend of science and art, function and form, tangible and intangible: "buildings not only have an existence in reality, they also have a metaphorical existence. They express meaning and give certain messages, just as the way we dress or furnish our homes gives people certain messages about us" (Conway & Roenisch, 1994, p. 22). Of course, what buildings communicate is linked to how much we know about architecture, what vocabulary we have at our command, our cultural background, and how we think about buildings and the environment. Architecture is something all of us experience, an

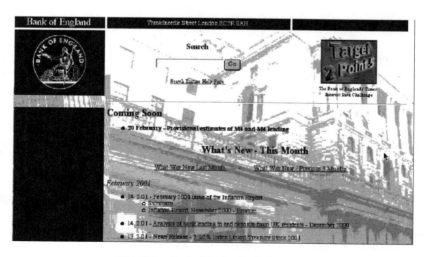

FIG. 18.3. Bank of England web site, 2000.

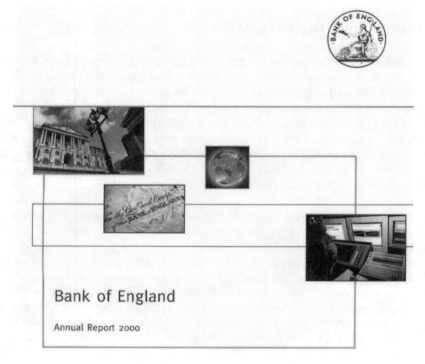

FIG. 18.4.   Bank of England annual report, 2000.

extraordinary functional art that confines space so we can live, work, or worship; it creates the framework for our lives (Rasmussen, 1959). However, many have little training in architectural form, expression, or history—especially in the United States (cf. Upton, 1998). Architecture remains, for the most part, a specialized subject within art history or architecture schools. We learn to identity buildings by the name of the corporation that builds them, the patron who supports them, and the famous person they were named after.

Function

Architecture ordinarily encloses space, creating interior environments congruent with the purpose of the structure. Building plans specify what is required—offices, classrooms, halls, amphitheaters, sanctuaries, and so on—and often will attempt to articulate what the building should represent. The architect's job is to oversee the transformation of words into three-dimensional forms, arranging the form into usable as well as symbolic patterns. The plan of a building, dictated by client, architect, and community, places a building in time as well, linking the structure to the wider realm of culture.

Structure

Interdependent with function, a building's structure defines space as well as its look and shape. Materials, technology, utilities, economics, and geography play key roles within architectural form. Basic structural choices were laid down long ago; new materials and technology modify rather than transform building processes (Scully, 1991). Often structural choices are made for communicative or aesthetic reasons. Lighter materials, use of cantilevers, glass, and color can lend an airiness to a building, making it appear light or floating. Structure signifies. Older buildings, including classical temples, appear to rest firmly on the earth, symbolically attesting to their permanence. Gothic churches soared toward the heavens, providing a bridge between humans and God.

The dome and the arch are two significant structural devices, associated with ancient Rome as well as Renaissance architecture (e.g., Taylor, 1981). The dome has come to signify notable buildings, from Rome's Pantheon to the U.S. capitol building. The massive amount of interior space that can be enclosed in a dome—or a vaulted ceiling—impresses the occupant, and often leads to attributions of importance, awe, and veneration—a scripted emotional response that serves the building's expressive purpose. A building affects both body and mind; "it is an experience of the senses of sight and sound, of touch and heat and cold and muscular behavior, as well as of the resultant thoughts and strivings" (Arnheim, 1977, p. 4). Thus, we see how the dome has come to play a principal role within bank architecture and marketing communications, for a large domed interior is associated with many of the great masterpieces of architecture, and the physical experience of this space contributes to an overall impression of power (e.g., Ruskin, 1849/1961). I take up the functions of classical columns in more detail later, but it is important to note that the structure, too, communicates and represents, perhaps in a more direct way than form or style.

Art

The aesthetic dimension of architecture emerges from function and form. Decisions made by the architect, the client, and choices influenced by building site, zoning laws, and expense contribute to aesthetic results. Architecture is both an art and a communication system, "able to convey the moral of its programs and to stimulate sentiments" (Kostof, 1995, p. 563). Further, it is a social art, "exhibited" in public, and often long lasting. Buildings have inherent meanings that result from their spatial and visible forms and contextual meanings that have evolved out of historical traditions, aesthetic standards, and cultural practice (Ruskin, 1849/1961). The set of design decisions that must be made for each building carry with them a cultural and social message that is embedded within the structure. Some of these messages work on a psychological level—visual symmetry seems to have a close connection with emotional harmony, for example—others work on cultural and aesthetic levels (Arnheim, 1974).

The literal building blocks of architectural design include structural support, symmetry or asymmetry, and scale, rhythm, proportion, shape, and color. Symmetrical plans usually lead to formal architecture—that is, buildings that spread out horizontally and perpendicularly as one approaches the site (O'Gorman, 1998). Often these buildings relate to the classical or neoclassical style, even if they do not strictly follow the rules of the classical form. Thus, a fundamental building style refers to the classical form due its basic structure, but also as a reflection of the aesthetic design decisions. Ornamental style goes in and out of fashion, but contributes to the effect of the building (Carley, 1994). Windows, roof, cornices, and columns are a few ornamental expressions association with classicism. Openings such as windows and doors are particularly important to the overall gestalt—they signify the relationship of the private inner space to the more public outside realm.

Doors are crucial ingredients in building design and communicative potency; many important artists and architects won renown via designing important doors and gates. Doors, portals, and gates—and the way they are framed—are critical markers of power, protection, and status, and served to stratify towns and cities into those within the gates and those on the outside. Christian churches usually have three main doors, often echoed by three stained glass windows, visually representing the Holy Trinity. Banks and other monumental buildings often have huge, oversize doors that dwarf the entrant. The portal, of course, is one of the guiding metaphors of the Internet and is discussed later.

Materials also constitute aesthetic choices. Materials represent quality, cost, and luxury, as well as practicality and function. A bank lobby replete with marble, wood, and slate can impress the customer as much as its size and scale. Material also controls light and transparency, which affect the mood and atmosphere of the interior space. Buildings can appear open and welcoming or closed and forbidding, depending on material, openings, and light.

CLASSICAL FOUNDATIONS
OF ARCHITECTURAL PERSUASION

For over two thousand years the classical tradition in architecture has been an essential part of Western civilization, building up a repertoire of meanings and associations that has become part of the cultural fabric. Like language, classical form gained in power and vocabulary from its long past (Adam, 1990). Summerson used *rhetoric* to describe how buildings speak the classical language of architecture "with force and drama in order to overcome our resistance and persuade us into the truth about what they have to tell us—whether it is about the invincible glory of British arms, the paramount magnificence of Louis XIV, or the universal embrace of the Roman Church" (Summerson, 1963, p. 33). Classical buildings are perhaps the most visible and seen remnants of ancient Greek and Roman civilization, providing testimony of the past glories of the classical world (cf. Rykert, 1998).

The classical form begins in Ancient Greece, with roots in Egypt, Mesopotamia, Syria, and Asia Minor. The basic ingredients, components, or "grammar" of classicism includes columns of five standard varieties—Tuscan, Doric, Ionic, Corinthian, and Composite—applied in traditional ways. These five classical orders formed a kind of grammar of architectural form, not merely decorative, but structural: "the classical orders—Doric, Ionic, and Corinthian—are systems shaped by subtle proportions and endowed with a pantheon of meanings, but they are fundamentally arrangements of posts and lintels" (O'Gorman, 1998, p. 37). Each column is composed of three elements, pedestal, shaft, and entablature, a tripartite formula that applies to the entire structure. A row of columns—a colonnade—can resemble an orderly line of people, a flank of soldiers, or a symmetrical forest. Closely spaced columns serve to signal strength and protection; slender columns can represent grace and beauty; and massive columns connote dominance and power (Hersey, 1988). Other elements of classical form include doors, windows, gable ends, moldings, and porticoes—all constructed in a particular, prescribed manner. Two other architectural devices critical for articulating of the classical form are the entablature and the pediment. The entablature refers to the horizontal part of the building that the columns support. A pediment is a low-pitched triangular-shaped gable surrounding the entablature. Temples usually consisted of a rectangular structure with colonnaded porticoes at each end. The number of columns in the portico varied, but classical form required an even number. Roman temples were based on Greek design, reworked to include a podium reached by a flight of stairs at the front of the portico.

Columns are the foundation of the classical form. Columns can be associated with many basic models—the human body, a tree, soldiers. Each column style has also been linked with various ideas—male or female, plain or fancy, serious or celebratory (see, e.g., Adam, 1990; Hersey, 1988; Rykert, 1998). Columns also represented status, strength, and grace. Strict classical form involves a careful balance of form, columns, proportion, harmony, and so forth (see Fig. 18.5 and 18.6). Much has been written about the classical orders and how they ought to be used, and what counts as a classical building. In general usage, classical architecture "refers to the style of building of the ancient Greek civilization and later of the Romans" (*Dictionary of Architecture*, 1995, p. 63). For our purposes, and for the meaning production today, I utilize this broad classification: "a classical building is one whose decorative elements derive directly or indirectly from the architectural vocabulary of the ancient world—the 'classical' world as it is often called" (Summerson, 1963, p. 7).

The ancient Greeks, "aware of their own needs, and understanding the desires, anxieties, and uncertainties of others . . . used architecture to develop a shared knowledge and to influence ideas and actions. Columns carried culture" (Onians, 1988, p. 330). For example, a Corinthian capital is adorned with stylized acanthus leaves. In ancient Greece, the acanthus plant was associated with life and death, and often appears on tomb vase paintings. Corinthian columns were used in war

FIG. 18.5.   Ionic column (photo by author).

memorials, and in temples to the gods Apollo the healer and Dionysus, god of renewal. The Corinthian column developed into an elaborate, ornamental element that is now associated with formal, fancy buildings. Thus, we see the poetics of architectural form, and its evolution over time. What was once a clear referent to nature and the gods becomes, over time, repeated sagacity, and veneration, a referent to the classical world, high ideals, and tradition. Material becomes metaphor— "classical architectural compositions are ingenious essays in stone, intelligently argued dialectics and hermeneutics" (Tzonis & Lefaivre, 1986, p. 275).

Temples are the buildings most closely associated with classical tradition. In contrast to Christian churches usually designed for a worshipful congregation, classical temples served to house the image of a deity. Temples were thus imbued with expressive vitality in a process akin to literature. Every architectural element was designed for expression—doors, windows, walls, parapets, ceilings, and floors diverge from their normal everyday use, transfigured by the symbolic form and purpose of the temple (Tzonis & Lefaivre, 1986). This building style came to dominate monumental architecture, providing a basic template for temples, government buildings, and later private residences and extravagant palaces. Over the centuries up to the Renaissance "these forms were striking features of the buildings in which people in Western Europe formulated and developed their relationships to the gods, to each other, to themselves; and it was often through their use that these relationships were articulated" (Onians, 1988, p. 3).

The architecture, art, and thought of the ancient Greeks and Romans renewed during the Renaissance gave rise to a new classical era. The term *classical* derives from the social order of the *classici*, the highest social rank in ancient Rome, associated with "the vicissitudes of the money economy in Europe, the emergence of

FIG. 18.6. Classical colonnade (photo by author).

new social formations and new institutions, the birth of court culture and the reopening of world market routes, the invention of credit institutions, and the need to educate a nascent elite in such new ideas as the worth of time and profit" (Tzonis & Lefaivre, 1986, p. 1). In Renaissance Italy, status, morality, and character were the values most closely associated with classical architecture (Onians, 1988). Thus, the language of classical architecture changed to include a grammar to describe subtle cultural values, including the status of the patron, the morality of the church, and personal character. In this way, the architecture of commerce benefited from classical allusions: "attempts to inscribe architecture with social meanings built on, or played with existing vocabularies of elements and the rules for their combination precisely because these reinforced a patron's claim to supreme authority—that is an authority legitimized by religious faith and the Ancients" (Boys, 1996, p. 231). Classicism, originally a fairly austere style, thus represents power, wealth, and taste—and "visually reinforces the power structure in any period, today and yesterday" (Conway & Roenisch, 1994, p. 16).

Classical buildings—no longer limited to isolated numinous temples—became a tool in city planning, image building, and social control. Although the form itself is somewhat arbitrary, and can be articulated in many ways, the cultural significance of classical motifs was fairly clear: "to walk down a street complete with classical facades during the eighteenth century meant reading the pattern of social registry of the town or, even more, a discourse legitimizing the structure of status and power in that society" (Tzonis & Lefaivre, 1986, p. 246). Patrons came to understand that the power of buildings to affect those who saw and used them could be brought under their control and employed for their benefit (see Schroeder & Borgerson, 2002). They did this by first identifying the values with which the patrons wanted to associate themselves publicly and then establishing that architecture could be made to materialize and express them (Onians, 1988).

The classical form was applied to a growing range of uses that departed from the ancient world's monumental temples. Architectural historians Tzonis and Lefaivre identified three uses of classical form outside the canon: (a) citations of classical motifs, or freewheeling classicism; (b) syncretism—using multiple architectural forms within one design; and (c) the use of classical fragments in architectural "metastatements." Citationism—including adoption of classical motifs and patterns in advertising and consumer goods—is severely criticized as antithetical to the classical goals of poesis. They argue that citation of classical form has the effect of overfamiliarization, placing the temple within the world of reality, and stripping it of its representational power. The form, they argue, needs completeness to speak in its intended manner (Tzonis & Lefaivre, 1986). However, the language of classical architecture is no longer confined or embodied in the built form—it radiates throughout culture via mass mediated images of classical buildings, forms, fragments, and citations.

During the Renaissance, several emergent cultural institutions took to the classical form, including the state, universities, commercial enterprises, and banks.

Each appropriated the forms as well as many of the symbolic associations of an architectural style that conveniently represented high ideals, long tradition, and harmonious appearance. Banks needed to make a statement that they were virtuous, solvent, and stable institutions, and "as Greece and Rome had come to be seen as the cultural sources of virtue, a return to classical architectural rules of proportionality, regularity, harmony, and decorum in the form of a neoclassical style would express this virtue in the form of a building" (McGoun, 2000, p. 13). A building was the most visible, tangible symbol for important cultural institutions—it represented investment, stability, permanence, taste, and wealth. The classical form was somewhat abstracted and altered for use by the secular sphere, paving the way for further appropriation during the industrial revolution to come.

CURRENT USES OF ARCHITECTURAL LANGUAGE

During its 1992 centennial year, the University of Rhode Island adopted a stylized version of Green Hall as the university logo. Green Hall is one of the oldest and nicest buildings on the rural campus, which was founded in 1892. It is a fairly small building, with a beautiful colonnade of trees leading up to the classical portico, an architectural gem within a stylistically diverse modern university campus (see Fig. 18.7). Green Hall has served various functions through the years, once it was the library, lately it housed administrative offices. Recently, it was renovated to serve as the university's admissions office and main visitors building, a focal point for recruiting efforts, thus bringing its visual prominence in university communications in line with its physical use. The building appears as a simplified graphic element on all university letterheads, the university website, periodicals, and promotional materials, representing all that the university stands for (see Fig. 18.8).

Buildings are a fairly common logo for universities. For example, the University of California, Berkeley's Campanile, the University of Texas, Austin's infamous tower, and the University of Michigan's stately Hill Auditorium are icons of their respective campuses. Furthermore, the classical form was also drafted to represent knowledge and earning. Thus, the templelike appearance of University of Rhode Island's Green Hall was a natural choice for a school logo. Almost anything might have served to symbolize University of Rhode Island. Green Hall replaced an anchor, the state symbol of Rhode Island, which calls itself "the ocean state" as it is surrounded by the Atlantic Ocean and Narragansett Bay. Furthermore, the university has several splendid older buildings to choose from, including a group of granite halls surrounding the quadrangle of a classic New England campus.

Green Hall's appearance was clarified, modified, and stylized in its transition to university icon. Indeed, students were often surprised when I told them it represented an actual campus building. Thus, the logo serves as a somewhat anonymous university icon—many schools use similar buildings on their letterheads as part of

FIG. 18.7.   Green Hall, University of Rhode Island.

FIG. 18.8.   University of Rhode Island logo.

their campus communication plan. By adopting this logo, the University of Rhode Island deliberately chose to associate itself with the timeless values of classicism, rather than portray itself as a contemporary, cutting-edge institution. Part of the goal was to move away from a persistent party school image—the anchor formerly used may have had too many associations with the ocean, surfing, and beach life. In any case, the Green Hall logo places the University of Rhode Island within the classical canon of traditional learning, the experience of living on campus, and the representational realm of the built environment. The classical image serves to build the university's image by communicating values of classicism: values such as stability, timelessness, and tradition that are meant to honor the ancient roots of knowledge.

MONEY AND MATERIALS

Modern banking has its roots in the Renaissance. The word banking derives from the benches—*banchi* in Italian—and tables used by the banker. The famed Florentine Medicis created a far-flung network of bankers, and their palace in Milan has been called the first bank office. A style of banks was to emerge in the 1700s that was to have far reaching influence on bank architecture up to the present day. Western banks were built to resemble classical temples; the severe Grecian style helped the often unstable institutions express security (Pevsner, 1976). This form, exquisitely expressed by the tremendously influential Italian architect Palladio, usually included one or more porticoes (a roofed entrance supported by a classical colonnade), a vaulted banking hall, and magnificent classical columns. Notable examples include the Bank of England, which "with the scale of its halls and the forbidding silence of its outer walls remained right into the twentieth century the noblest of all bank buildings" (Pevsner, 1976, p. 202). The immense Bourse in Paris of the early 19th century also adopted classical form, this time with Corinthian columns surrounding the inner temple of commerce and finance of the day.

The United States has thousands of banks, savings and loans, credit unions, investment banks, and credit card issuers—far more in comparison to European nations' limited choice in banking establishments. Banking was localized for most of U.S. history, allowing cities and towns to build their own schools, utilities, and infrastructure (Mayer, 1984). Bankers were primarily boosters of their local communities, until lately. It was only during the 1980s that many forms of interstate banking was permitted, and more recently that banks were allowed to sell investment products, life insurance, and other financial services.

Information technology drove many changes in the banking industry—money and financial matters are not confined to pieces of paper that must be sorted and stored in ways that leave a ledger and an audit trail. Instead, they are electronic entries, generated via computers, and disconnected from particular spaces or buildings. This transformation was instrumental in overhauling the banking system from a loose network of numerous small local banks interacting with the Federal Reserve system to the current deregulated arrangement of mega banks, online banking, and international markets. The small-town bank of the past, where customers knew the tellers and met personally with the loan officer to discuss their loan, is gone, replaced by ATM machines, computerized forms, and secondary markets for mortgages (see Cross, 1993). More efficient, certainly, but possibly less human. Perhaps this points to the continuing significance of classical architecture—it alone remains to symbolize banking's connection with the past by tapping into classicism as a powerful referent system. Although the premises of banking have changed, the promises of the banking industry have not.

Early U.S. banks were modeled after the Athenian Parthenon, transforming an ancient temple to a temple of finance (Pevsner, 1976). One of the first important

American banks was the Bank of the United States, set up in the 1790s to help the states with budgets and cash flow. The American bank also modeled both its operations and appearance on the Bank of England, whose Greek temple headquarters set the style for many bank buildings up until the 1950s (Mayer, 1984). The Bank of the United States building stands near Philadelphia's Independence Hall, complete with enormous Corinthian columns and two large Doric porticoes. It was an impressive structure in its day, and remains on the tourist path as a revolutionary monument. Figure 18.9 shows the Second Bank of the United States, also in Phila-

FIG. 18.9.   Second Bank of the United States, Philadelphia (photo by Declan McCullagh, used by permission).

delphia. An imitation of the Parthenon, it paved the way for many federal buildings to embrace the classical style (Booker, 1990). The New York Stock Exchange
also emphatically reflects the tenets of classical style. Templelike inside as well,
American banks almost invariably contain a grand interior space, or banking
room, that reflects the expectations of the exterior (cf. Allon, 1998).

The foundation of the contemporary U.S. banking system was laid with the
creation of the Federal Reserve system in 1913—that rather obscure hybrid entity
that Alan Greenspan seems to run by himself at times. This system protected local
banks, and upheld state laws concerning, among other things, branch locations.
The look of banks began to expand, but the federal banks generally retained a
classical appearance. Even when built as skyscrapers, a bank's first floors typically
displayed classical themes (Chambers, 1985). Architecture continued to play a key
role in persuading consumers about the merits of banks:

> Created by private capital to serve a pragmatic function for its owners, bank archi-
> tecture at the same time turns a public face to its community in a vigorous attempt
> to communicate, persuade, assure, impress, and convince. . . . Contemporary atti-
> tudes regarding money, respectability, security, and corporate aesthetics are re-
> flected . . . bank architecture thus communicates the importance of banks as insti-
> tutions, assuring us of their stability, prosperity, and permanence and inviting us
> inside to do business. (Nisbet, 1990, p. 8)

COMMUNICATING CUSTOMER VALUES: STABILITY, STRENGTH, AND SECURITY

Architecture provided a strategic method for banks to communicate key attributes
of stability, strength, and security. The classical form visually generates "a sense of
longevity, stability, rectitude, even stable power" (O'Gorman, 1998, p. 94). Customers entrust banks with their savings; this distinguishes banking from most
other business concerns. Although most consumers are aware that banks don't delegate space to store their particular money—money is represented by computer
databases now—the physical attributes of the bank have played an important role
in projecting a proper image, including stability over time, financial and material
strength, and financial and physical security. Classicism helped legitimize banking,
a role it played for the nascent nation as a whole:

> Classicism, like language, is precise but flexible. It can suggest commercial probity,
> as we see in the classical architecture of bank buildings and above all, in the New
> York Stock Exchange. It can radiate culture, as in the neoclassical art museum in
> Philadelphia and many another city. In the early nineteenth century, the Greek
> temple form pledged allegiance to the democratic principles that American traced
> back to ancient Athens. (O'Gorman, 1998, p. 95)

These values can be mapped onto the three structural problems of building: effectively spanning space, efficiently supporting the spanning walls or columns, and

suitably enclosing interior space—the three dimensions of space, width, length, and depth. Stability includes both the conceptual reassurance that the bank will be around a while and the perceptual confidence that the building itself will remain standing. Building materials and style convey strength; many banks resemble an impenetrable massive block, protecting the valuable content within. Security, related to strength, can also translate into construction choices and styles—classical banks usually have little glass, thus protecting the inner contents from view, distinguishing the private nature of banking. Moreover, bank interiors were normally divided into a public hall, a private interior, and a vault.

Each of these strategic banking values—stability, strength, and security—has a psychological dimension as well as a material solution. Stability, expressed in visual form by a sturdy structure, provides a metaphor for long term endurance—"this is why the posts, pillars, and columns which have assured people in many cultures of the buildings' structural stability have been just as critical in resolving other uncertainties and anxieties" (Onians, 1988, p. 3). Colossal columns, heavy materials, and symmetrical form contribute to a building's appearance of strength. Of course, bank customers also desire financial strength, and an ability to withstand economic cycles. Security, for so long largely dependent on architecture fortresses, walled cities, and massive structures, also relates to psychological anxiety about financial matters. The closed form of most banks was meant to signal protection— a secure institution to entrust one's future. Furthermore, the use of the temple form created a visual of a special building protecting its valuables, allowing only certain people access to the interior space, and promoting a ritual element of bank visit. Banks are not just depositories of money; they are repositories of hopes, dreams, and anxieties—a modern temple.

SPEED

A fourth banking attribute emerged along with the electronic revolution: *speed*. Now banks need to communicate the four S's, stability, strength, security, and speed, as customers expect quick and efficient transactions supported by computerized operations. Indeed, speed may be the most characteristic attribute of finance in the virtual economy (e.g., Zwick, 2001). However, the other values remain, and basic relationships between the consumer and the bank continue to require symbolic association. The giant Wells Fargo Bank's 1999 annual report announced that "the basic financial needs of our customers, however, do not change that much. They want to borrow, invest, transact, and be insured. They want convenience, security, trust and dependability" (Well Fargo Bank, 2000, p. 4). In the rest of this chapter, I explore the role that classical form plays today. Certainly, banks are no longer primarily physical places—they are also name brands that occupy space in the consumer's mind. I am not concerned here with recently built banks, or general architectural trends. Rather, I am interested in how the classical form resides in contemporary marketing communication—advertising, corporate reports, web sites, and the ephemera of electronic banking—for these are the crux of brand building and meaning making.

In the world of Internet banking, electronic communication, and computerized accounts, what is the role that architecture plays today? Has the classical tradition been abandoned, replaced with a newer, sleeker model? It might seem like associations to the past would be counterproductive for organizations wishing to project a contemporary, technologically sophisticated image. Furthermore, some customers may also associate classicism with colonialism and domination. For example, when the World Bank designed its Washington, DC, building, it specifically rejected classical style—"the World Bank is in the business of assisting third-world countries and the whole language of classicism is very much associated with colonialism" (Sharoff, 1997, p. 43).

Much has been written on how the computer revolution has transformed time and space, collapsing these dimensions via instant communication and information technology. The three dimensions of architecture—height, length, and depth—coexist within photographic representation in marketing communication. Three-dimensional objects have a temporal dimension: One walks through or around them in time. Two dimensional images do not. Thus, the symbols of time—longevity, tradition, and history—become interwoven with symbols of space—stability and strength within two dimensional representation, thereby superimposing two powerful systems within a single image. Thus, electronic representations of buildings are able to carry a complex signifying framework to the viewer.

Furthermore, the building is no longer the primary banking site. Online banking, banking by mail, and automated teller machines largely supplant the ritual trip inside the bank building. Consumers no longer need be at the bank to access account information and perform financial transactions. Speed and ease of transaction are now important components of customer focus. Convenience rules. In a virtual banking world of the World Wide Web, one might assume that price, due to its ready availability and ease of comparison shopping, might drive the consumer more than brand image. However, the 2000 downturn of the dot.coms demonstrated that brand power is still critical for marketing success—and this is true for financial sector as well. To investigate the role that the classical tradition plays in current bank marketing practice, I turn to three sources of corporate communication: advertisements, ATM machines, and internet sites.

Abstracted Architecture in Contemporary Campaigns

The classical form is recruited for many product marketing campaigns, including high-tech products. For example, MCI Communications uses Corinthian capitals as pedestals to display various styles of telephones, from mid-century to mobile (Fig. 18.10). Thus, products change, but the columns remain constant, an allusion to the classical tradition that I've been discussing. Other uses include a long-running Rémy Martin cognac ad that places the product heroically on top of Doric column, a Givenchy "Organza" perfume ad whose bottle resembles a fluted classical column (Fig. 18.11), and a Mazda ad that compares a car to classical columns "designed by sculptors." In these ads the classical motif provides a link to the classical past, a claim that the product has stood the test of time, and a sense of aesthetics for many different product classes. Significantly, these products have nothing to do with architecture as built form—references to the classical tradition are strictly metaphorical.

FIG. 18.10.   MCI advertisement.

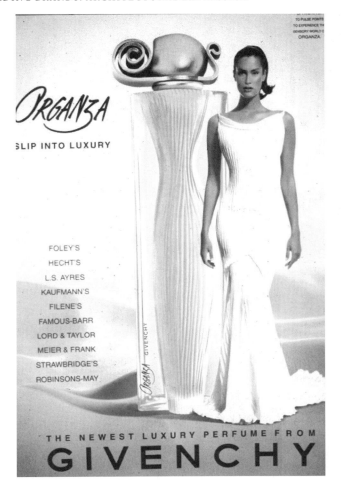

FIG. 18.11. Givenchy advertisement.

Cut-Up Classicism in Bank Communications

Merrill-Lynch, one of the world's largest investment banking firms, created one of the most visually striking examples of the uses of classicism in contemporary bank advertising. One version of its late 1990s corporate image-building campaign features four Ionic columns in the background of a stylized Grecian amphitheater ruins (see Fig. 18.12). A circular, futuristic-looking podium sits at the center of the amphitheater, echoing the its rounded form. Each architectural element appears as a separate photograph, morphed together to create a pastiche of classicism, resembling an ancient site that has been restored by Disney, or assembled for a film set.

FIG. 18.12.　Merrill-Lynch advertisement.

The golden columns are not supporting anything—they appear to float in the frame, hovering above the marble amphitheater's circular steps. Strict classical form demanded an even number of columns—so even these detached, decontextualized columns nod to tradition. On the left side of the two-page spread, there is a quote from Merrill-Lynch's chief executive officer stressing that "we believe a more vibrant marketplace of ideas will make a difference in addressing the critical challenges of the day." This somewhat ambiguous statement refers to that decade's deregulation of the finance industry, opening up new markets for banking firms.

The classical elements, abstracted and stylized, appear almost as if they have been cut and pasted from a graphics program, in what Tzonis and Lefaivre castigated as "citationism" (1986). The image vaguely resembles an ancient site, but the Ionic columns show no signs of age, nor do the amphitheater steps—they have been taken out of context and harnessed for Merrill-Lynch's communication needs. The podium clashes with the columns; its sleek form jars the image into the 20th century. Of course, debate flows from the podium, and thus the speaker is assumed to be from the current epoch, discussing ideas in a time-honored tradition, within the classical forum of the amphitheater. However, the podium also signifies a special position from which to speak, quite different than the open marketplace.

Merrill-Lynch's quote refers to the classical marketplace—the agora—as an ideal for discussing ideas. However, the image shows an amphitheater—the domain of actors—and only certain people spoke in plays. Merrill-Lynch portrays itself within the foundation of free society, equating open markets with open dialogue, freedom with financial freedom, and democracy with capitalism, but a close analysis of this ad reveals misplaced agency, confusing the scripted world of the theater with the agora. Furthermore, the classical motifs assist Merrill-Lynch to project a stable, strong, and secure image—yet one that is flexible, adaptive to new environments, and able to accommodate new forms, as the contemporary podium attests.

Using the shorthand of architecture language, which refers to classical forms, the Greek ideal, the marketplace of ideas, and the roots of Western democracy, Merrill-Lynch produced a complex advertising image, simply realized. Its business, then, is not limited to financial matters—it deals in ideas, which require testing via dialogue and debate. Architecture functions as a heuristic for consumers in a cluttered marketplace of images. It is not necessary for viewers to identify columns as "Ionic" or "Doric," or to know much about the history of classicism, for this ad to work as a reference to tradition, dialogue and debate, and the classical past. By juxtaposing old and new styles, Merrill-Lynch sets up an implicit contrast as well as an allusion to time.

A mid-1990s Boston BayBank ad shows a woman surrounded by a classical gabled door frame, unattached to a house or building (see Fig. 18.13). The door, clearly from an affluent house or apartment, resembles a studio prop. She fills up less than half of the door, sits with her legs crossed on the top step of the door's short stairway as she leans forward toward the viewer. I read this ad as a way to communicate three messages. First, your home can function as the site of your banking via online transactions. Second, you need not give up the security of a strong bank—the classical door frame reflects the bank's resources transplanted to your home. Third, the classical door's association with wealth, status, and accomplishment serves to target this ad to an affluent—or striving—segment of consumers. Like the Merrill-Lynch image, the architectural motifs are not connected to a physical building; they serve as props within a stylized tableau.

A 1996 Fleet Bank newspaper ad blatantly appropriates classicism. In it, a man grasps a chest-high Ionic column that displays a bundle of $50 notes. There are several columns in the ad's background, here a Doric column, there a Corinthian, each a singular element within a cluster of classicism. The ad is titled "Me and My Good Fortune" and seems to promote both the bank and a contest to win the bundle of $50s (see Fig. 18.14). Dressed in a suit and tie, the man holds the Ionic column almost as if it were his son or daughter; his arm wraps around it, and his hand embraces its fluted surface. "I eliminated fees, got better rates, a $50 bonus and a chance to win a bundle," he appears to say. The column has been shrunk down to human size—he dominates it, and pulls it close to his body in an intimate, familiar gesture. The image resembles an older visual form—columns were common props in 19th-century photography studios, lending a classical touch to thousands of family portraits (Crary, 1990). This straightforward use of classicism blends old and the new—the bank is contemporary, with low service fees, competitive interest rates, yet classical, timeless. Although consumers desire conveniences and deals, they also need to be reassured of the bank's traditions.

Automated Teller Machines

My ATM card from the Rhode Island State Employees Credit Union is gray with a graphic depiction of the Rhode Island State Capital's classical dome. The credit union's main branch sits across the street from the capital in Providence, but its appearance is far from the majestic capital, designed by the legendary architectural firm McKim, Mead, and White in the style of the U.S. capitol (see Fig. 18.15). The credit union's buildings are nondescript, devoid of much style or ornamentation;

FIG. 18.13.   BayBank advertisement.

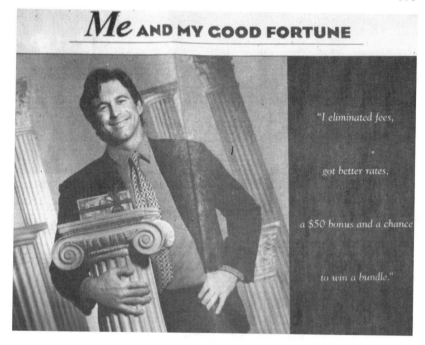

Me AND MY GOOD FORTUNE

"I eliminated fees,

got better rates,

a $50 bonus and a chance

to win a bundle."

FIG. 18.14.   Fleet Bank advertisement.

thus, they borrowed a nearby architectural icon with its associations of classicism to grace its ATM cards, as well as their newsletters, customer statements, and logo (see Fig. 18.16 and 18.17). Many of the credit union's customers work in the public state capital. Still, the appropriation of the classical dome is a significant rhetorical move.

My current bank solves the architectural dilemma another way. Sweden is a highly computerized society, with a high share of Internet banking. Through shrewd pricing policies, a restricted portfolio of services, and redesigned bank lobbies, SEB, one of Sweden's largest banks, has aggressively promoted Internet and automated tellers for the bulk of routine customer transactions. Most of the banks in Sweden share the same ATM network, and ATM cards can be used in most other bank machines without a separate fee. The SEB card shows no building; its design features a stylized fingerprint to signal security. However, during ATM transactions, the user interface screen presents a graphic of an ATM machine—or bankomat—sending signals to a distant bank building. The image shows wires connecting the ATM to the bank—which is labeled "Bank"—and a few childlike renderings of flying birds complete the scene. Seemingly, even Internet-savvy Swedes need to be assured that their bank exists in material, architectural form (see Carlell, 2001).

FIG. 18.15. Rhode Island State Employees Credit Union head-quarters, Providence (photo by author).

FIG. 18.16. Rhode Island State Capitol Building, McKim, Mead, & White, architects (photo by author).

FIG. 18.17. Rhode Island State Employees Credit Union graphic logo.

Internet

The Internet has emerged as a major force in the financial industry, offering online banking and investing, networked venture capital incubators, and a powerful communications forum for banking firms. Many online-only banks exist, and most viable banks have made some effort to offer online services, and provide online customer and investor communication. The Internet enables firms to place a large amount of information in a customer's hands—including basic information about services, fees, and the organization, with its financial information, marketing campaigns, and annual reports, which are often available to download via pdf files. The Internet itself is full of architectural metaphors—superhighway, portals, home pages, and so forth, and the classical language lives on in cyberspace (Dobers & Schroeder, 2001).

The Internet might have heralded a new economic landscape in which consumers pursued perfect information, comparison shopped, and adopted "efficient" agents to obtain goods and services cheaply, but it appears that brand names, trust, and familiarity are still important. Banking is an especially trust-centered business, so let's see how banks communicate on the web. A basic content analyses of the top 10 U.S. banks reveals over 50% use some form of architectural image on their web sites (see Table 18.1). Furthermore, several of these rely heavily on buildings, headquarters, and the classical motif for web-based imagery. In the table, the architectural elements are briefly described; for example some sites show the headquarters, and others utilize architectural themes throughout the site. These images represent strategic choices. Although photographs of corporate headquarters may appear to be just "there"—a logical choice for a company's web site—most businesses do not show their headquarters on the web.

HSBC has become of the largest banks in the world, thanks to mergers, the rise of the Pacific Rim where it has major holdings, and global expansion. Its web page shows many pictures of its buildings, and its 1999 Annual Report is full of architectural images, lending visual support to a brand building campaign (see Fig. 18.18). The report's "illustrative theme," building the brand, is represented via color photographs of replacing old signs with the new corporate logo on various HSBC buildings around the world. For example, the cover shows a worker installing new signage on the HSBC Main Building in Hong Kong. Global branding was one of their strategic goals that year, their new logo a pillar in the campaign. Most of the report's images show the new logo on HSBC properties—including

TABLE 18.1
Architectural Language on the World Wide Web

Name of Bank	Image of Headquarters Shown on Web Site	Architectural Images Used in Web Site
Bank of America	Yes	No
Citibank	Yes	No
Chase Manhattan Bank	No	Historical pictures of classical Chase building in archive section of web site
First Union Bank	No	1998 annual report shows headquarters on cover, used throughout report
Wells Fargo Bank	Yes	No
HSBC Bank	Yes	Buildings are used extensively throughout 1999 annual report, including classical headquarters
BankBoston	Yes	"Building on Strength" motif uses architectural images throughout web site
Bank of New York	No	Classical building show on home page; used as graphic element throughout site; clients shown ascending steps amid classical columns
Bank One	No	No
US Bank	Yes	No

Note. Ten largest U.S. banks at 1999 year end. Bank information from bankinfo.com, a Thompson Financial Marketplace website, data derived from FDIC (Federal Deposit Insurance Corporation) directory.

the classical headquarters in New York City, shown emblazoned with a huge HSBC sign stretched across the colonnade.

Although classical architecture is not the dominant visual element of most of these web sites, buildings and classical form maintain a strong presence in contemporary banking communications. Of the top 10 banks' web sites, 60% include an image the bank's headquarter building. Often, this image is found in corporate reports, but several show buildings on the corporate home page. Other architectural images of any kind appear in 50% of the top 10 banks' web sites. These uses include historical pictures, graphical elements as for the Bank of New York, discussed previously, and buildings as themes, such as HSBC, First Union Bank, and BankBoston. BankBoston's web site employs the strategic mission statement "Building on Strength" throughout the entire site, which features domestic architecture to depict consumers at home as well as home mortgage products, small

FIG. 18.18. HSBC annual report 1999, image of bank buildings.

firms such as retail outlets and manufacturing plants to portray small business customers, and skyscrapers to represent commercial accounts.

Architecture, Branding, and Communication

Traditionally, consumers have valued three qualities in a bank: stability, strength, and security. Banks adopted classical architectural form to persuade the public. In the electronic age, architecture no longer confines banking, nor do most consumer banking transactions take place within a bank's headquarters. Therefore, a change might be expected in communicative tools; classical motifs might seem outmoded or old-fashioned for the information society. However, banks have shifted the symbolic domain from the building to the marketing message, adopting architectural symbols for use in digitized images that carry on the communicative tradition of classical forms. Advertising, internet sites, and ATM banking still incorporate abstracted architectural symbols, and buildings continue to provide many metaphors for the banking industry.

CONCLUSION: FROM BRICKS AND MORTAR
TO BITS AND MEMORY CHIPS

George Simmel proposed that money signified modernity. He suggested that money —especially abstracted paper currency—provides pleasure due to its exchange capacity (Simmel, 1978). An abstract, distant relationship with money replaced more concrete conceptions; "it is now mere contemplation that is the source of

FIG. 18.19.   USAA Financial Services prospectus 2001.

FIG. 18.20. Olde Discount Broker advertisement.

enjoyable satisfaction; we leave the object untouched" (Simmel, 1978, p. 73). Money is often an end, not merely a means; electronic banking has further distanced us from money. Information technology signals modern banking methods. Banks, then, enjoy an aura of modernity inherent in money. Classicism provides a necessary counterpoint to modernity, creating a novel entity—a modern ancient temple.

In 1997, the Rhode Island State Employees Credit Union unveiled plans to remodel its Providence branch. A local columnist wrote positively about the credit union's proposed metamorphosis into a classical structure from "that awful box ... that rectangular pile of concrete blocks painted white and 'decorated' with a few vertical strip windows and a flat roof" (Brussat, 1997, p. B7). He affirmed the drawings that turned a nondescript glass entrance into a imposing columnar portico, added columns to the building's plain front, and sheathed the concrete structure in the requisite temple form suitable for a bank. During a design review committee hearing, however, a professor of architecture from the nearly Rhode Island School of Design rose to contribute his staunch objections—"You've missed an opportunity to create a contemporary building with 20th century design," he railed against the plan, as he complained that the design "wallows in nostalgia, mimicking the State House . . . classical architecture is dead" (quoted in Brussat, 1997, p. B7). (The mimicked State House is the previously mentioned Rhode Island icon that embellishes the credit union's ATM cards.)

Far from dead, the language of classicism lives on in marketing campaigns, bank web sites, and corporate reports, lending rhetorical authority and visual presence to the business of image management (see Fig. 18.19 and 18.20). One study of contemporary bank architecture concluded that "we are left with the controversial notion that even in these financially sophisticated times, symbols matter, and the message communicated by these symbols is one which can not be conveyed any other way" (McGoun, 2000, p. 50). Architecture provides symbols that are familiar and powerful. When the European Monetary Union's Euro notes commenced circulation in 2002, the public began spending bills featuring famous architectural icons (see Fig. 18.21).

click on a banknote for more details

Euro banknotes

EUR 5 banknote

Denomination: EUR 5
Size: 120 x 62 mm
Colour: Grey
Architectural period: Classical

FIG. 18.21. Euro currency image from "One Currency for Europe" web site, http://europa.eu.int/euro/html/entry.html.

Banks today are in the business of building brands as much as physical structures. Benôit Heilbrunn argued that brands are transformative devices that allow contradictory principles to coincide, such as nature and culture, the real and the imaginary, the past and the present, and the very distant and the here and now (Heilbrunn, 1999). Classicism reinforces this notion, linking an ancient past to the present via rhetorical devices perfected during in classical era. Of course, these persuasive visual rhetorical tools are augmented via marketing information technology, selling the past to the future (Berger, 1972).

Classicism remains a central cultural referent. Architecture provides spatial, historical, and psychological images easily appropriated by visual media. Furthermore, architecture is a basic metaphorical structure for perception and cognition — indeed, it "presents embodiments of thought when it invents and builds shapes (Arnheim, 1977, p. 274). These shapes, translated into two dimensions, abstracted and isolated, are the building blocks of meaning making. By tracing visual genealogies such as classicism, we gain an appreciation of the complex composition of current persuasive imagery.

ACKNOWLEDGMENT

I thank Linda Scott, Marc Markowski, Janet Borgerson, and Detlev Zwick for their constructive comments on this project. Parts of this chapter were taken from *Visual Consumption*, by J. Schroeder, 2002. © Routledge, reprinted with permission.

REFERENCES

Adam, R. (1990). *Classical architecture: A comprehensive handbook to the tradition of classical style*. New York: Abrams.

Allon, J. (1998, February 11). Bank's neo-classical columns get new staying power. *New York Times*, Section 14, p. 6.

Arnheim, R. (1974). *Art and visual perception*. Berkeley: University of California Press.

Arnheim, R. (1977). *The dynamics of architectural form*. Berkeley: University of California Press.

Barnet, S. (1997). *A short guide to writing about art* (5th ed.). New York: Longman.

Berger, J. (1972). *Ways of seeing*. London: Penguin/BBC.

Booker, J. (1990). *Temples of Mammon: The architecture of banking*. Edinburgh: Edinburgh University Press.

Boys, J. (1996). (Mis)representation of society? Problems in the relationships between architectural aesthetics and social meanings. In J. Palmer & M. Dodson (Eds.), *Design and aesthetics: A reader* (pp. 226–247). London: Routledge.

Brussat, D. (1997, January 30). A model modern credit union. *Providence Journal-Bulletin*, p. B7.

Carlell, C. (2001). *Technology in everyday life: A study of consumers and technology in a banking context*. Stockholm: Stockholm University.

Carley, R. (1994). *The visual dictionary of American domestic architecture*. New York: Henry Holt.

Chambers, S. A. Jr. (1985). Banks. In D. Maddex (Ed.), *Built in the U.S.A.: American buildings from airports to zoos* (pp. 20–23). Washington, DC: National Trust for Historic Preservation.

Conway, H., & Roenisch, R. (1994). *Understanding architecture*. London: Routledge.

Crary, J. (1990). *Techniques of the observer: On vision and modernity in the nineteenth century.* Cambridge, MA: MIT Press.

Cross, G. (1993). *Time and money: The making of consumer culture.* New York: Routledge.

Dictionary of architecture. (1995). London: Brockhampton Press.

Dobers, P., & Schroeder, J. (2001). Representing IT: Embodying the electronic economy. In *Proceedings, Nordic Academy of Management Conference.* Uppsala, Sweden. Available: http://130.237.51.101/forskning/nff2001/index.html

Heilbrunn, B. (1999). Brave new brands: Marketing paradiso between utopia and a-topia. In S. Brown & A. Patterson (Eds.), *Proceedings of the Marketing Paradiso Conclave* (pp. 222–235). Belfast: University of Ulster.

Hersey, G. (1988). *The lost meaning of classical architecture: Speculations on ornament from Vitruvius to Venturi.* Cambridge, MA: MIT Press.

Kostof, S. (1995). *A history of architecture.* New York: Oxford University Press.

Mayer, M. (1984, April/May). The banking story. *American Heritage,* pp. 26–35.

McGoun, E. G. (2000, July). *Form, function, and finance: Architecture and rational economics.* Paper presented at the Sixth Interdisciplinary Perspectives on Accounting conference, Manchester, UK.

Nisbet, R. (1990). Men and money: Reflections by a Sociologist. In J. Stein and C. Levine (Eds.), *Money matters: A critical look at bank architecture* (pp. 7–14). New York: McGraw-Hill.

O'Gorman, J. F. (1998). *ABC of architecture.* Philadelphia: University of Pennsylvania Press.

Onians, J. (1988). *Bearers of meaning: The classical orders in antiquity, the Middle Ages, and the Renaissance.* Princeton, NJ: Princeton University Press.

Pevsner, N. (1976). *A history of building types.* Princeton, NJ: Princeton University Press.

Rasmussen, S. E. (1959). *Experiencing architecture.* Cambridge, MA: MIT Press.

Ruskin, J. (1961). *The seven lamps of architecture.* New York: Noonday Press. (Original work published 1849)

Rykert, J. (1998). *The dancing column: On order in architecture.* Cambridge, MA: MIT Press.

Schroeder, J. E. (1998). Consuming representation: A visual approach to consumer research. In B. B. Stern (Ed.), *Representing consumers: Voices, views, and visions* (pp. 193–230). New York: Routledge.

Schroeder, J. E. (2002). *Visual consumption.* London: Routledge.

Schroeder, J. E., & Borgerson, J. L. (2002). Innovations in information technology: Insights from Italian Renaissance Art. *Consumption Markets and Culture, 5*(2), 153–169.

Scully, V. (1991). *Architecture: The natural and the manmade.* New York: St. Martin's.

Sharoff, R. (1997, March 6). World Bank: Architecture as diplomacy. *New York Times,* p. 43.

Sherry, J. F., Jr. (Ed.). (1998). *Servicescapes: The concept of place in contemporary markets.* Chicago: American Marketing Association.

Simmel, G. (1978). *The philosophy of money.* (T. Bottomore & D. Frisby, Trans.). London: Routledge and Kegan Paul.

Summerson, J. (1963). *The classical language of architecture.* Cambridge, MA: MIT Press.

Taylor, J. C. (1981). *Learning to look: A handbook for the visual arts* (2nd ed.). Chicago: University of Chicago Press.

Tzonis, A., & Lefaivre, L. (1986). *Classical architecture: The poetics of order.* Cambridge, MA: MIT Press.

Upton, D. (1998). *Architecture in the United States.* Oxford: Oxford University Press.

Wells Fargo Bank. (2000). *Annual report 1999.* San Francisco: Author.

Zwick, D. (2001). *The speed of money: Investment as consumption in the age of computer-mediated communication.* Unpublished doctoral dissertation, University of Rhode Island.

CHAPTER NINETEEN

"No One Looks That Good in Real Life!": Projections of the Real Versus Ideal Self in the Online Visual Space

Natalie T. Wood
San Diego State University

Michael R. Solomon
Auburn University

Basil G. Englis
Berry College

From cradle to grave we are bombarded with a myriad of images of beautiful people. As children we learn from fairy-tale stories featuring beautiful people who are good and ugly people who are bad. As we move through adolescence and adulthood this notion is reinforced through television programs, music videos, and fashion advertisements.

Abundant criticism surrounds the use of highly attractive individuals in advertising. Opponents of these images claim that the attractive models portrayed in advertising act as a mechanism for social comparison whereby evaluation occurs between the self and the image presented (Martin & Gentry, 1997). Research has typically addressed the effect of images of attractive models on an individual's self-concept by looking at advertising in traditional print and broadcast environments. No study has addressed the effect of viewing images of attractive models in online environments. Furthermore, to date there is no research on the effect of viewing one's own image as compared with viewing that of a professional model on self-concept. This is largely as a result of the fact that until now it was virtually impossible for consumers to view themselves in advertising. However, recent technological advancements provide us with the opportunity to explore the relationship between individually selected media images and self-concept in a way not previously possible.

The aim of this chapter is to explore the effects and influence of viewing oneself in advertising, including the possible effects on self-concept, and in doing so to propose research avenues that can or should be pursued. We review the academic literature on physical attractiveness and the effect it has on self-concept, and highlight and discuss how technology is challenging us to reassess our current understanding of the relationship between the two. We also present some preliminary data bearing on the potential appeal and influence of viewing an image as a reflection of oneself over an idealized one.

PHYSICAL ATTRACTIVENESS

Western culture conditions us to believe that "what is beautiful is good" (Eagly, Ashmore, Makhijani, & Longo, 1991). Despite the fact that as a society we may emphasize character over appearance, physically attractive people are evident in every aspect of our life. But what exactly is physical attractiveness, how do we define it, and what does it incorporate? What is it that makes one person attractive and another one unattractive, and why are people often preoccupied with attaining it?

Solomon, Ashmore, and Longo's (1992) research involving female fashion editors at major fashion and/or lifestyle magazines revealed that the physical attractiveness construct is a complex and multidimensional construct. They found that an individual's judgment of what is considered attractive cannot simply be measured on a single continuum (such as *attractive* to *unattractive*). To do so implies that attractive and unattractive people are relatively homogeneous. Instead, they found there exist multiple types of good looks and that these beauty dimensions are not independent of one another. Their research revealed that physical attractiveness can be organized via six psychological categories: (a) classic beauty/feminine, (b) sensual/erotic, (c) sex-kitten, (d) trendy, (e) cute, and (f) girl-next-door.

Every culture sanctions multiple dimensions of good looks, although at any one time particular ideals may be more prevalent than others, and these ideals evolve over time (Englis, Solomon, & Ashmore, 1994). For example, in the 1800s it was the pale delicate look, whereas the 1950s saw a more buxom form personified by movie icons such as Marilyn Monroe. Today, as a result of cultural diversity and a proliferation of lifestyles, these ideals continue to evolve. One only has to sample a variety of media to realize that numerous forms of attractiveness exist, from the classic beauty of Catherine Zeta-Jones to the trendy Britney Spears.

Individuals often are motivated to pursue a beauty ideal in the hope that they will acquire the auxiliary benefits they perceive accompany beautiful people. However, physically attractive individuals stereotypically possess both positive and negative characteristics. For example, an attractive person may be assumed to be socially competent but weak intellectually. Take, for instance, the "dumb blonde" stigma. Although blondes are said to have more fun, they are also the brunt of a number of jokes regarding their lack of intellect. Although attractive people may be rated higher on a wide variety of positive personal qualities than unattractive individuals, they may also be rated higher on such negative qualities as vanity, immaturity, and lack of intelligence (Kalof, 1999; Wheeler & Kim, 1997). However, despite negative stereotypical characteristics, attractiveness is still a highly desirable social characteristic (Adams & Roopnarine, 1994).

The media play a role in constructing cultural ideals of beauty. For example, the advertising industry frequently is criticized for the portrayal of highly attractive and extremely thin females. Critics claim that these images promote an unrealistic ideal, resulting in an array of physical, social, and psychological problems (Gustafson, Popovich, & Thomsen, 1999; Kilbourne, 1999; Richins, 1991; Thornton & Maurice, 1999).

Idealized images of highly attractive individuals presented in advertising may be regarded as a simulation of reality (Messaris, 1997). In other words, although attractive people do exist within our society, our ideals are often based on an enhanced version of the real thing. Techniques such as airbrushing and editing have the ability to make the imperfect perfect and those that we already consider perfect even more so. On reflection on her photographs in fashion magazines, supermodel Cindy Crawford reportedly commented that in real life "even I don't look like Cindy Crawford" (Gardner, 2001). One of the major complaints is that advertising of this nature can have a detrimental effect on the self-esteem of the rest of us.

EFFECTS OF PHYSICALLY ATTRACTIVE MODELS ON SELF-CONCEPT

Despite the proliferation of studies on the effects of visual cues on self-concept findings to date have done little to elucidate the relationship between the two. Although some studies revealed a negative association (see Lavine, Sweeney, & Wagner, 1999; Richins, 1991; Thornton & Maurice, 1999), others revealed no association (see Lennon, Lillethun, & Buckland, 1999), and yet another study revealed a positive one (Myers & Biocca, 1992). For example, the Richins (1991) research on college students' reactions to advertisements in fashion magazines found that in some cases consumers consciously or subconsciously compare themselves with people portrayed in advertising, and that these idealized images of beauty can lower a consumer's satisfaction with her own attractiveness. Contrary to this finding, however, Richins (1991) was unable to validate that consumers' self-perception was altered as a result of the exposure to these advertisements. This finding is somewhat consistent with research undertaken by Lennon et al. (1999), who found either that subjects did not compare themselves with the idealized images found in advertising for apparel and beauty-related products or that their self-esteem and body image was not affected by the comparison. One possible reason cited for these effects was that subjects were textile and clothing majors, who may have been sensitized to body image and fashion advertising during their course of study.

Myers and Biocca's (1992) research on female university students aged 18 to 24 years revealed that an individual's body shape perception can be changed with less than 30 min exposure to television. They also found that following exposure young females had a tendency to overestimate their body size, which seemed to indicate that they might have internalized the idealized body image presented by advertising. Their research suggests that a female's body image is constructed through a number of reference models, namely, the socially represented ideal body, the individual's internalized ideal body, the present body image, and the object body image. According to these authors, the overall subjective evaluation of the physical self or body image held by an individual is unstable and highly responsive to external social cues.

It appears the decision by consumers to select a realistic look or one representing an ideal of beauty and the subsequent relationship between media image exposure and self-concept is not as straightforward as one would think. These conflicting results seem to imply that for particular segments of the market, advertising exposure may have a temporary impact on self-feelings, whereas with others it may have a long-term cumulative effect (Richins, 1991). The selection between real and ideal representations and any subsequent effect on self concept may vary depending on the strength of the consumer's self-concept prior to exposure to the images, the actual images viewed, the basis for comparison, the product being advertised, and the degree of knowledge that the images presented are not necessarily a reflection of reality. However, despite critics' and consumers' disapproval of the unrealistic representation of females in the media, and the fact that many recognize that these images are not realistic, clearly physical attractiveness is an important social cue that impacts the judgments of others and our preferences and behavior. Furthermore, it would appear that even when given the choice, some consumers would still prefer to be guided in their product choices by an idealized image rather than a realistic representation.

This leads us to speculate about consumers' responses if they are given the option of selecting what models look like in the ads to which they are exposed. How would they respond if given the ability to select an image with which they are more comfortable, such as a depiction of someone similar in appearance to themselves? Moreover, how would they react to the opportunity to literally view themselves in the ads? What influence would this option have on a consumer's self-concept, on her evaluation of the product, and on her decision making process? Although in the past the notion and practicality of casting oneself as the model in advertising were inconceivable, today this is fast becoming a reality. Technological developments permitting personalization of the source have led us to question existing theories on the relationship between advertising images and the self.

PERSONALIZATION OF THE SOURCE

The ability to personalize an advertising message is by no means a new phenomenon, whereas personalization of the message source is a novel concept. Traditionally, personalization of the communication process was largely found in direct mail and personal selling situations, in which the message was tailored and personalized for each individual. Some companies are now taking advantage of the technological capabilities of the Internet to start the personalization process one step earlier in the communication process, at the source selection stage.

In traditional media communication sources are often standardized in that the same model is utilized to target an entire market segment. However, on the Web the model can be created for a specific individual. For example, Lands' End allows consumers to create a model in their own image who will then assist them with their purchasing decision. The model that is created is rather rudimentary in appearance in that she looks like a mannequin—but one who happens to possess the approximate physical dimensions specified by the consumer.

Although this rough mannequin image does not resemble a real woman, consumers appear to be comfortable with this kind of representation. Research conducted by Then and DeLong (1999) on the online apparel shopping experiences and preferences of 63 college students revealed that 89% (56 out of 63 respondents) preferred a realistic model to a fashion model and given the choice would rather see the item displayed on a mannequin (63%) than laid out flat (35%) or as a sketch (1%). The ability to view an item on a three-dimensional model (even if it was a mannequin) was considered important for reducing the uncertainties of shopping for apparel online.

Personalized mannequins such as those now offered by Lands' End represent a first rudimentary step toward personalization of the source. But as technology continues to develop it will be possible for these online models to appear not only in a number of forms but also to perform a number of roles that were heretofore not possible, such as a clothing form to permit examination of fit, drape, as a familiar "companion" to the consumer, and so on. Our focus in the present work is on the forms that such online models might take. The typology in Fig. 19.1 considers the potential forms and functions that might be used for an online model.

First, an online model can function purely as a decorative item or she can be active. In other words, the model may simply be a passive visible enhancement to the site, not unlike a model in a magazine advertisement, or she can play a more active role, such as engaging in two-way communication with the consumer and assisting her with her task. In this case, the model is combining the role of a traditional communication source found in advertising with that of a customer service

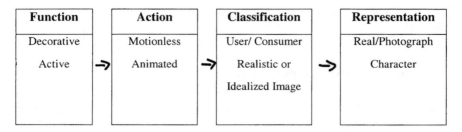

FIG. 19.1.   A typology of personalized models.

representative normally found in personal selling situations. An example of a decorative model is Miss Boo (www.boo.com), a caricature of a hip young female. An example of an active model is Catherine, Eagle Star Insurance Company's virtual agent (www.eaglestar.co.uk).

Second, the model can appear motionless on the site, much like a still image (www.mysimon.com), or the model can be animated (www.bonzi.com). Third, the model's form can be an image of the actual site user (a realistic image such as that of a typical consumer) or an idealized image such as a fashion model or a celebrity. Finally, the model may be presented as the real image of a person, much like a photograph, a character such as a cartoon or animal, or a caricature of a particular person. This typology reveals a possible 24 varieties of models that can be used in the online environment.

Current Personalization Activities

A number of companies are developing virtual models for online advertising and selling. For example, Nodna (www.nodna.com), a division of the Stockholm-based company Vierte Art, is an agency dedicated to virtual actors. The agency offers a variety of "virtualstars" (newly created models and stars), "vuppets" (mascots and animals), and "replicants" (doubles or personalities). Each of these actors can be developed to meet the needs of specific target markets, or even specific consumers. A young, hip "virtualstar" may be appropriate for a teenage audience, whereas a "vuppet" may be more appropriate for a younger audience. Some of the sites currently using these virtual models are www.time2bcool.com, www.virtopera.de, and www.time4team.com. Virtual Personalities (www.vperson.com), a Los Angeles-based company, also provides web-based virtual characters. These characters are synthetic talking faces that can interact with users by answering their questions and helping them with their transactions.

Finally, Elite Model Management, the agency that represents many of the supermodels who grace the catwalks of Paris, has created a virtual supermodel. Webbie Tookay is a digitally composed woman. Armed with a personality profile produced specifically for the client's needs, she is available for a licensing fee for all kinds of media-related work, including virtual fashion shows and Internet advertising. The director of Elite Illusion 2K predicts that in the future virtual models will become as widely used as real ones (Coren, 1999).

Current Applications of Personalization Technology in the Apparel Industry

Some of the most exciting potential applications of personalization technology are found on apparel-related sites. There are a growing number of sites that allow consumers to select or build their own model. For example, www.purpleskirt.com has a number of sketched models representing a variety of body shapes from which consumers can choose. Based on the consumer's body shape and clothing preferences, the site will make product recommendations. Eyewear manufacturer Rayban allows consumers to view sunglass styles being worn by a real customer, or alternatively they can scan in their own photographs and see the glasses superimposed on their images. But perhaps the most interesting application of this technology is the ability to create a model in one's own image. As noted earlier, the Lands' End site allows consumers to enter their measurements and other details such as face shape, skin tone, and hair style and color, and the system generates a virtual model in the consumer's own image. It will also recommend appropriate sizes and provide advice on clothing styles to flatter the consumer's body shape.

Obstacles to Success of Online Personalization Strategies

The success of personalization technology of this kind is evident in the growing number of visitors to particular sites as well as increasing online sales. In 1998, the year Lands' End introduced its personalized technology, the firm's site attracted 15 million visits (Hill, 1999) and quadrupled net sales to $61 million (Echikson, 1999). Since the introduction of its virtual modeling capability, more than 1.5 million shoppers have created their own models (Davis, 2000).

As with all forms of new technology, wearout looms as a threat to continued growth. Ongoing satisfaction and use of the personal model such as the one offered by Lands' End are dependent on two things: the performance of the technology, and the consumer's satisfaction with the image presented. Despite the popularity of the Lands' End model, the technology is by no means perfect. The descriptive characteristics for the creation of the model are somewhat vague and subjective (e.g., narrow, medium, broad). Likewise, the visual difference between models of various sizes is in some cases minimal. As such, if users perceive the images presented to be inaccurate reflections of themselves, they may (a) reject the technology or (b) alter an image to what they perceive is more accurate. This latter case is an interesting one and raises the question of whether the consumer will create a more realistic model or whether he or she will create an idealized version. In fact, Lands' End addresses this very issue. Once the user creates a model the following message appears: "Remember, I will look like you as much as you desire. So, if you lie to me, then I'll lie to you too. If I don't quite look like you, then feel free to modify me." This highlights that the accurate projection of oneself into cyberspace may be problematic, from a technological and possibly a psychological standpoint.

MODELS IN CYBERSPACE: AN EXPLORATORY STUDY

To explore some of these issues a preliminary exploratory study was undertaken using a convenience sample of 48 female undergraduates majoring in apparel merchandising and production design at a southern U.S. university. These students were enrolled in a consumers and material culture class and completed the research for extra credit. All respondents remained anonymous for the entire project.

The research was completed in four stages. Part A required respondents to estimate to the best of their knowledge their body dimensions in inches. Measurements were taken for shoulders, chest, waist, and hips. In Part B, Rook's (1985) Body Cathexis Scale was utilized to measure students' degree of satisfaction with 26 body parts. This scale is an abbreviated version of the original Cathexis Scale developed by Secord and Jourard (1953). Part C required respondents to access the Lands' End web site and create a personal model using the site's "Your Personal Model for Women." This application asks respondents to create their model by selecting from predetermined descriptions (narrow, broad, etc.) for their shoulders, hips, waist, and bust. Respondents were also asked to use a measuring tape to determine their actual body dimensions. The aim here was to determine consumer accuracy regarding their estimated (Part A) and actual body dimensions.

To explore the relationship between an individual's body dimensions and her preference for different model types, in Part D respondents were provided with a hard-copy set of six body configurations. These stimuli were created by varying the body dimension options offered on the Lands' End site and then creating a (color) print of each. Subjects were asked to select the model (a) that most closely resembled themselves; (b) that they would most like to see on a web site; (c) that they would least like to see on a web site; and (d) that they would most like to see modeling an item on a web site to assist them with their purchasing decision. Part D also included a series of questions relating to online shopping behavior, prior use of virtual models and future purchase intentions.

Results

Due to the small sample size, analysis was largely limited to measures of central tendency, with univariate and bivariate descriptive statistics. The sample was largely comprised of freshman (33%) and sophomores (28%), with an average age of 20.5 years.

The data revealed that the three most highly rated body parts were eyes (1.85), ears (2.40), and body hair (2.46). The three least favorable were hips (3.6), weight (3.3), and profile (3.3) (on a 5-point rating scale where 1 = positive and 5 = negative). Respondents' dissatisfaction with their weight, hips, and profile is not surprising given the thin ideal presented in the media. Respondents' mean measurements (actual) in inches were shoulders width 15.9, chest 34.8, waist 27.8, and hips 36.5. The estimated measures were shoulders 16.4, chest 34.7, waist 27.7, and hips 36.0. Both of these represent a relatively slender physique not unlike the socially constructed ideal image of today. A paired sample t-test did not reveal any statistically significant difference in the estimated measurements taken from Part A and the actual measurements provided in Part C.

Analysis of the Lands' End models created by respondents revealed that the body profile most likely to be chosen by the sample was one characterized by medium shoulders and hips, a well-defined waist, and small to medium bust. However, when presented with this model and five others of varying dimensions (Part D), the majority of respondents (28%) selected a model characterized by medium shoulders and hips, a well-defined waist, and a large bust as one that was most like them. The main point of difference was the size of the bust.

It is important to emphasize here the lack of options in body dimensions offered by the Lands' End site. There were only two choices offered for bust, shoulders, and waist, and the visual representation of each of these choices does not appear to be entirely accurate, which may influence the creation of the model. For instance, an individual may select a particular bust size, but on review may consider the image inaccurate or out of proportion to the remainder of the body and therefore alter it. Thus, the selection of an image with a larger bust does not mean that we can definitely infer that these respondents wanted a larger bust. It may simply be the case that the larger bust size looked more accurate, or in the right proportion to the remainder of the body. As displayed in Fig. 19.2, this model also proved to be the one that respondents would most like to see on a web site (36%) and would most like to see modeling an item of clothing (28%).

The model respondents would *least* like to see on a web site was a relatively stout silhouette characterized by broad shoulders, a large bust, well-defined waist, and wide hips (72%). Only 5% of the sample said that this model was one they would like to see modeling an item and only 5% rated this model as resembling themselves. These preliminary findings indicate that consumers would prefer to see an image closer to the socially constructed ideal of beauty—that is, an image of a slender physique, somewhat similar to their own. In fact, 69% of respondents indicated the desire to see an image comparable to their own, and closer analysis of the 31% of respondents who indicated a preference for a model with a body different from their own revealed the desire for one that was thinner, more toned, and curvaceous. This lends further support to the notion that consumers desire an ideal image.

Fifty-nine percent of respondents indicated that they would be likely to purchase apparel online in the future. However, of the 41% of respondents who had

Most Like to See	Least Like to See

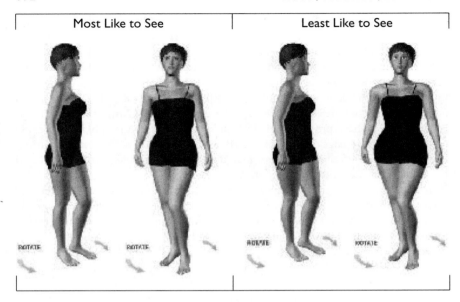

FIG. 19.2.   Most and least favorable models as selected by respondents.

previously purchased apparel online, only 9% had (a) visited a web site that provides models and (b) created a model to assist their purchase decisions. One possible reason for this is the fact that the only apparel web site that is consistently and actively using this particular personalization technology is Lands' End, and given that respondents are college students, this store is possibly not one of their primary sources for apparel.

Respondents felt that although these models are an important addition to the site, they were not very helpful. In other words, as a mechanism for aiding decision making and facilitating sales, the virtual models utilized fell short of consumer expectations. This may be a result of a problem with the technology in that the selection of body dimensions was limited, or it may have been influenced by personal characteristics of the respondent (self-esteem, body cathexis, etc.). That is, a consumer with poor self-concept may have been unhappy with her projected image and therefore felt the model was not helpful, therefore rejecting the image. The rejection of these images suggests that the technology in its current form is possibly an ineffective form of persuasion.

DIRECTIONS FOR FUTURE RESEARCH

Emerging online technologies that allow great manipulation and choice over visual images paired with product messages raise a number of research issues fundamental to understanding the complexity of the relationship between consumers and the images with which they are presented. The exploratory study described here provides an initial look at one dimension identified in the proposed avatar typology (real vs. ideal self). One direction in which to expand the current pilot study is to examine the impact of other dimension described in the typology. For example, will the visual persuasion process be amplified by a dynamic model as compared with a static one? Is an active character that actually makes recommendations more effective than a decorative icon that simply demonstrates the product in use (such as a traditional fashion model wearing a garment)? Under what circumstances do consumers prefer to view caricatures or photographs?

The ability of consumers to self-select advertising images including models and images of themselves highlights a number of other research questions as well. How do individuals use images in advertising? Do they actively employ them as decision-making aids, or do the images function merely as visual enhancement? When provided with the opportunity to utilize models created in their own image, how honest are individuals in the description/projection of themselves and how important is it that the image is accurate? Furthermore, in which situations is image accuracy an important factor in the persuasiveness of the message and in which situations is it not?

The issue of self-concept and how it affects and is affected by images of the self in an advertising environment is also an important consideration. We already recognize that self-concept is a moderating variable in evaluating advertising effectiveness. The feelings that consumers have about themselves can influence how they react to both the advertisement and the product being advertised (Mehta, 1999). Likewise, the reverse may also be true. We know that exposure to advertising models may influence an individual's self-perception and self-esteem (Martin & Gentry, 1997). What we don't know is what occurs when the image is of the consumer herself rather than a fashion model or celebrity. More work is needed to explore just how projected images of the self influence self-concept, and how self-concept influences the selection and use of these personal images.

Finally, a significant portion of research into physical attractiveness phenomena, including the role in physical attractiveness in advertising and the effect it has on a consumer's self-concept, has largely focused on women. More attention needs to be placed on the effect that these issues have on both genders and how they apply in a cross-cultural context. For example, would we find different effects in collective cultures where a focus on the self is not as central a cultural value?

Our current knowledge of persuasion and physical attractiveness has served us well—so far. But as the world changes, so too do the rules of the game. In a world in which technology is becoming an increasing presence in our everyday life, we are forced to reassess our current understanding of the persuasive communication process. Perhaps beginning with the source of the message is a good start in that direction.

REFERENCES

Adams, G. R., & Roopnarine, J. L. (1994). Physical attractiveness, social skills, and same-sex peer popularity. *Journal of Group Psychotherapy, Psychodrama & Sociometry, 47*(1), 15–36.

Coren, V. (1999, July 27). The first computer-generated supermodel has arrived . . . and a chimp that can talk. *The Guardian*, p. 7.

Davis, K. (2000). *Lands' End introduces latest online shopping innovations: Setting new e-commerce standards for customer service*. PR Newswire retrieved 1 August 2001 from http://www.findarticles.com/cf_0/m4PRN/2000_Oct_18/66180194/p1/article.jhtml

Eagly, A. H., Ashmore, R., Makhijani, M. G, & Longo, L. C. (1991). What is beautiful is good, but . . . A meta-analytic review of research on the physical attractiveness stereotype. *Psychology Bulletin, 110*(1), 109–126.

Echikson, W. (1999, September 27). Designers climb onto the virtual catwalk. *Business Week*, pp. 164–166.

Englis, B. G., Solomon, M. R., & Ashmore, R. D. (1994). Beauty before the eyes of beholders: The cultural encoding of beauty types in magazine advertising and music television. *Journal of Advertising, 23*(2), 49–64.

Gardner, M. (2001, January 24). Slim but curvy—The pursuit of ideal beauty. *Christian Science Monitor*, p. 16.

Gustafson, R., Popovich, M., & Thomsen, S. (1999). The "thin ideal." *Marketing News, 33*(6), 22.

Hill, S. (1999). E-tailing: They'll never buy apparel on-line, right? *Apparel Industry Magazine, 60*(9), 26–33.

Kalof, L. (1999). Stereotyped evaluative judgements and female attractiveness. *Gender Issues, 17*(2), 68–83.

Kilbourne, J. (1999). *Deadly persuasion*. New York: Free Press.

Lavine, H., Sweeney, D., & Wagner, S. H. (1999). Depicting women as sex objects in television advertising: Effects of body dissatisfaction. *Personality and Social Psychology Bulletin, 125*(8), 1049–1059.

Lennon, S. J., Lillethun, A., & Buckland, S. S. (1999). Attitudes toward social comparison as a function self-esteem: Idealized appearance and body image. *Family and Consumer Sciences Research Journal, 57*(4), 379–405.

Martin, M. C., & Gentry, J. W. (1997). Stuck in the model trap: The effects of beautiful models in ads on female pre-adolescent and adolescents. *Journal of Advertising, 26*(2), 19–33.

Mehta, A. (1999). Using self-concept to assess advertising effectiveness. *Journal of Advertising Research, 39*(1), 81–89.

Messaris, P. (1997). *Visual Persuasion*. Newbury Park, CA: Sage.

Myers, P. N., Jr., & Biocca, F. A. (1992). The elastic body image: The effect of television advertising and programming on body image distortions in young women. *Journal of Communications, 42*(3), 108–133.

Richins, M. L. (1991). Social comparison and the idealized images of advertising. *Journal of Consumer Research, 18*(1), 71–83.

Rook, D. W. (1985). Body cathexis and market segmentation. In M. R. Solomon (Ed.), *The psychology of fashion* (pp. 233–241). Lexington, MA: Lexington.

Secord, P. F., & Jourard, S. M. (1953). The appraisal of body-cathexis: Body cathexis and the self. *Journal of Consulting Psychology, 17*(5), 343–347.

Solomon, M. R., Ashmore, R., & Longo, L. (1992), The beauty match-up hypothesis: Congruence between types of beauty and product images in advertising. *Journal of Advertising, 21,* 23–34.

Then, N. K., & DeLong, M. R. (1999). Apparel shopping on the web. *Journal of Family and Consumer Sciences, 91*(3), 65–68.

Thornton, B., & Maurice, J. K. (1999). Physical attractiveness contrast effect and the moderating influence of self-consciousness. *Sex Roles, 40*(5/6), 379–392.

Wheeler, L., & Kim, Y. (1997). What is beautiful is culturally good: The physical attractiveness stereotype has different content in collectivistic cultures. *Personality and Social Psychology Bulletin, 23*(8), 795–800.

CHAPTER TWENTY

Persuasive Form:
Mobile Telephones in Hungary

Dóra Horváth
Budapest University of Economic Sciences and Public Administration

Industrial design is not the planning of surface, but the expression of all functions through form. (Lissák, 1998, p. 145)

The research for this chapter was executed in Hungary. As a result of changes in economic conditions and the attendant ways of living, the acquisition and possession of material things have taken on new importance. The general availability of all sought goods on the one hand, and the increased importance of their expressive power on the other, explain the strong general attentiveness and sensitivity to material objects and their quality of design and form. The product category under study, mobile telephones, has become widely available only recently, but mobile telephones are increasingly popular among a range of groups. Cell phones hold strong practical but also symbolic and communicative implications, making them a good topic through which to explore questions of industrial design. This chapter presents the exploratory part of a comprehensive study, in which the sentence completion technique is used to record spontaneous associations, reflecting deeper semantic contents and culture-specific characteristics.

The quality and nature of any consumption experience are determined not only by the type and application of the object itself, but also by the quality of its execution—the form or design. Form persuades potential consumers to make certain purchase choices, but form also contributes mightily to the quality and nature of the usage experience. Ordinary objects also serve as tools for communicating information about users to the larger social group, even while, in this case, providing a means of actual speech communication. Until now, however, product form has mainly been investigated as an element of consumer choice. Studies of product usage experience have been focused on objects that were more special in their nature, like the arts, or on extraordinary activities. By building on the theoretical background of industrial design, I am proposing an extended approach to the investigation of product form: its investigation in both the context of choice and the context of usage.

PERSPECTIVES ON INDUSTRIAL DESIGN

The literature on product design—whether drawn from industrial design or marketing—can be presented according to four main aspects: the form of the product as an intention of *design,* the *individual characteristics* of those who use the product, the *context of purchase and use,* and product-related *user responses.*

The core idea of design is a conscious effort to impose meaningful order (Papanek, 1971). The order and patterns we find in nature are not the products of design, strictly speaking, because they lack the element of conscious intention. Design is not only for giving a tangible, physical form to an abstract function, but it often should also give a distinctive form (Rassam, 1995). This is particularly true where design as a tool of expression plays a crucial role in market competition: it communicates and positions, influences choices, attracts consumers and users, and is capable of communicating with them—by catching attention and providing information (Bloch, 1995). The artist must also envision his or her solution in operation and therefore not only needs to understand the core idea of the given purpose, but also the user requirements and the circumstances of use (Dahl, Chattopadhayay, & Gorn, 1999). Krippendorf (1996) described the designer as "the maker of meaning," but he also wrote that "no one can assume that form (the designer's objectified meaning) and (the user's) meaning are the same; there is need for product semantics to study how they relate. . . . Designers are part of a broad ecological process, but their success depends upon their ability to understand the hidden governance of collectively shared archetypes and mythologies whose meanings must be respected, grasped, tapped, and drifted with" (p. 161). Thus, industrial design must be extended to the act of the interpretation, perception of the product" (Lissák, 1998, p. 161).

Consumption does not imply only the product's primary functional use, but also its service as a source of expression, enjoyment, and hedonism. The designer's task is to create an attractive object, but he or she must also consider how well it will fulfill its function: whether it is enjoyable, easy, or satisfying to use. In some products, functionality is taken for granted, and aesthetic values are the primary means of distinguishing one from another (Cova & Swanfeldt, 1993).

In sum, it is the designer's task to express a given purpose in a meaningful and distinctive form that sells. As a result, the designer-artist's freedom of creation is limited: It is restricted by the influence of engineering and marketing and by production, market, and consumption constraints. The result of the industrial designer's work is the final formal expression of the entirety of product function, appearance, aesthetics, and ergonomics in accordance with market requirements (Pye, 1978). Good design necessarily derives from the interaction of the maker (designer) and the user (consumer). Nevertheless, the core nature of product form can only be wholly explored by the users through and during usage. Investigating industrial design thus requires the investigation of all of its manifestations: its power at the point of choice, and its impact on the usage experience as well (see Fig. 20.1).

Product form therefore cannot be evaluated on single, separate compositional elements, but only as a combination of compositional elements chosen and blended into a whole to achieve a particular effect (Bloch, 1995; Lissák, 1998; Margolin & Buchanan, 1996; Papanek, 1971). Design as a problem-solving activity thus can never yield one right answer; an infinite number of possible answers is always produced, some more acceptable and some less. Purely functional designs are nearly impossible to make: Whenever humans design and make a useful thing they invariably expend a good deal of effort on feeling and appearance.

Studies of empirical aesthetics provide possible dimensions for describing the relation of visual design qualities and for approaching product form as a whole. These include *prototypicality* and *unity* (Veryzer & Hutchinson, 1998). The phenomenon of industrial design suggests extending the definition of unity and prototypicality to the relations of appearance, shape and manner of fulfillment of purpose (Margolin & Buchanan, 1996). In this sense, *unity* can be defined as the level of congruity among the elements of form as well as the level of congruity of the purpose of the given object and its material expression. *Prototypicality* refers to how the given object is representative of its category not only in the sense of its appearance and shape, but also its purpose and operation.

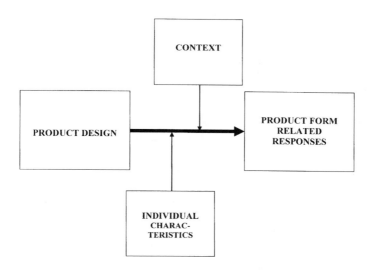

FIG. 20.1.   Conceptual model, applied constructs.

A product is more prototypical, more representative of its category, when it is better known, more familiar. The evaluation of form based on prototypically varies widely in industrial products. Sometimes better known designs are better liked in appearance and better understood in operation (Loken & Ward, 1990; Veryzer & Hutchinson, 1998). On the other hand, common designs already existing in the marketplace can become boring. Products with weaker design properties have to fulfill requirements of freshness and novelty (Bloch, 1995). Therefore, the systematic alteration of common designs can preserve the information value of prototypicality and bring in the sense of newness or freshness. But the opposite is also true: Consumers who seek variety, not prototypicality, like atypical products for their exclusive novelty and distinctiveness (Meyers-Levy & Tyboult, 1989).

Consumers' relation to product form is also dependent on their individual characteristics (such as proneness to considering visual qualities), including their personal relations to the products that surround them and their overall preferences. The judged importance of products can be approached as a kind of consumer orientation (Csíkszentmihályi & Rochberg-Halton, 1981), as a consumption style (Holt, 1995), and as a basis of consumers' judgment of values (Richins & Dawson, 1992). Richins and Dawson (1992) differentiated between materialist and nonmaterialist consumers, for instance. For materialist consumers, the acquisition of products plays a very important role. It can be an object of plans, a goal in itself (*acquisition centrality*); it can be a source of personal well-being in life (*acquisition as the pursuit of happiness*); and it can be a basis for judgment of one's own and others' success that lies in the amount and quality of products owned (*possession-defined success*). According to the level of materialism, consumers are more receptive to different manifestations of product form. Richins (1994a) showed that for materialist consumers, it is a product's utilitarian benefits, potential to express personal success, and enjoyment of the acquisition that is important; product appearance and qualities of form determine such choices. Nonmaterialist consumers appreciate their possessions for the enjoyment in their use and also memories they evoke.

Several studies have dealt with consumers' affective and cognitive responses to product related verbal or visual stimuli. Several other research projects offer measurement instruments to assess visual processing styles (Bamossy, Scammon, & Johnston, 1983; Childers, Houston, & Heckler, 1985; Hirschman, 1986; Veryzer, 1993) and/or estimate underlying design dimensions of research objects (Henderson & Cote, 1996; Veryzer, 1993). Research objects take the form of paintings (Bamossy et al., 1983), logos (Henderson & Cote, 1996) and products (Hirschman, 1986; Veryzer, 1993). Research objects also vary according to being constructed according to selected dimensions (Veryzer, 1993), or being an existing, real constructions (Bamossy et al., 1983; Henderson & Cote, 1996; Hirschman, 1986). Gould (1990) showed that there is a relationship between involvement with different types of products and individual processing styles. Consumers with visual processing preferences are more involved with products that are more visually oriented in their use, such as cameras and clothes. As a result of higher involvement in these, they are more concerned about all product characteristics that are a result of their own form or design.

Because product form is capable of creating enjoyable activities and sensual pleasure, it has effect at the level of individual experience, as the illustration that follows shows (Holbrook & Hirschman, 1982; Richins, 1994a).

> For weeks I've been playing with an Olivetti tabletop calculator (Divisuma 18; design by: Mario Bellini) . . . , something unusual took place that had not occurred to me until now. I played around with it and found, to my surprise, that handling the thing was not bound to its function, that it was free from any goals. The instrument had tangible weight, plasticity, and an extraordinary haptic quality, which functioned sensually with no hidden agenda but merely as a material body that "serves" playfully. I recall the slight pressure of sensitive, warm skin on tangible, rubber-covered keys and buttons, which offered a slight resistance; then the apparatus made a delayed and attractive clicking noise, without causing any dismay and which was similar to the spontaneous pressure that produces playful rhythmic patterns on a percussion instrument. (Selle, 1996, p. 241)

Objects are assimilated into personal lives and given symbolic meanings as expressions of the order of private experiences with reference to one's own personal history (Csíkszentmihályi & Rochberg-Halton, 1981).

Products also possess a societal dimension that builds up entirely new relations between themselves and their users. Objects fulfill an important role in the expression and symbolization of roles and influencing relations. Most products hold messages that are meaningful to a particular group and that their owner wants to communicate about him- or herself (public meaning; Richins 1994b). Products with extremely strong design characteristics are labeled as societal innovations by Cova and Swanfelt (1993). "A societal innovation should be understood as the process by which new meanings are introduced into the social system. Although these innovations may seem like lucky accidents . . . there is a design process that leads to such discontinuous innovations" (Cova, 1996, p. 32).

"Consumption is not just a personal act of destruction by the consumer, but very much a social act where symbolic meanings, social codes, and relationships, in effect, the consumer's identity and self, are produced and reproduced" (poster as cited in Firat & Venkatesh, 1993). Most useful devices are ultimately equipped with new functions and meanings that were never intended by the designer (Pye, 1978). Therefore, despite the best efforts of designers to determine the precise nature of products, the career of products in human experience depends as much on the ability of human beings to make sense of the artificial world as it does on the intentions of the designer (Margolin & Buchanan, 1996).

THE RESEARCH

The objective of this research was to discover the consumer associations that relate to the quality of form, design, operation, or the expressiveness of mobile telephones.

The usage of sentence completion technique gives the opportunity to gain a deeper insight of general attitudes and associations about mobile phones, and discovering differences among the various responses (Móricz, 1992, 1999).

The research was conducted among third year university students majoring in economic sciences, for whom it was part of their course requirements ("Marketing Principles") to participate. There were 368 third-year students who participated, of whom 33% owned and 67% did not own a mobile telephone. Students of economic sciences eventually graduate to managerial positions and become decision makers, even opinion leaders, a future of which they are already aware, and thus they behave and hold attitudes accordingly. Although this special position is reflected in their responses, it is consistent with the profile of mobile phone users at this time. In January 2001, the number of cell-phone subscribers in Hungary was about 30% of the population, having tripled in 2 years. However, users are mainly entrepreneurs and company owners (29%), and highly educated employees (17.2%). Importantly, the proportion of students among mobile phone owners is surprisingly high, at about 10% (December 1999).

Phase I

In the first phase of the research, very general statements were used in order to allow any kind of associations relating to mobile telephones. In this phase, the main objective was to explore the direction and nature of mobile-phone related consumer responses and attitudes, and furthermore, to record whether the impact of product design, mobile design is reflected in these responses. Here is a summary, including the uncompleted sentences and the most characteristic answers for illustration.

"Someone Without a Mobile Telephone Is Like . . ." The most characteristic associations expressed the *relation*, the *connection of things*, which reflects the characteristics and nature of the tool (mobile telephone) and user interaction, namely, that they are to match each other. Respondents mentioned things that are closely related: "*dishes without salt.*"[1] Here nonowners more strongly acknowledged that the mobile telephone is a tool that belongs to people in everyday life: "*box of matches without matches*"; "*goat without cabbage,*"[2] "*coat without buttons.*" The mobile telephone can be an extension of one's own capabilities; its lack is notable for both groups. A group of respondents strongly expressed their sense of the mobile telephone being close to themselves, to their body; not having the mobile telephone implies the feeling that there is something missing from the owner, expresses the experience of the lack of certain personal capabilities. These associations further underline the user–possession relatedness and their interaction:

---

[1] Recurring motif in Hungarian folk tales.
[2] Common Hungarian folklore motif.

"without hands and ears," "bird without wings," "naked person," (owners); *"one-handed giant," "hand without plaster"* (nonowners). All respondents, and owners with more notable emphasis, expressed their feeling of dependence, lack of connection, and sense of deprivation at being without the mobile telephone. The need for control, keeping in contact, and its enjoyment come through these answers: *"being in a dark room," "hitchhiking at night"* (owners); *"snail without house," "fish out of water"* (nonowners). Associations also express phenomena that are related to the loss of capabilities as a result of the lack of some kind of technical gadget: *"horse without saddle," "sailor without compass," "conductor without baton," "secretary without computer"* (owners); *"soldier without guns," "blind person without white stick," "playing on the stock exchange on the basis of out-of-date information"* (nonowners). Also notable are those answers of nonowners that hold a two-sided perspective and admit the necessity of mobile telephones on the one hand, but indicate circumstances (e.g., plain reasons of fashion, wanting to be hip) where it is not at all necessary, but could be nice to have at the same time: *"depends on, a person without a cap in the winter, it would be better having a cap"; "depends on the importance, lack of one hand in case it is important, otherwise not."*

"The Future Mobile Telephone Will Be . . ."   Associations given to this uncompleted sentence gave the richest and most colorful associations. Respondents anticipated continuous functional development and the increase of existing functions as well as the application of a more advanced and state-of-the-art technology, which involve expectations related to the design, form as well—smaller size, easier handling, simplification: *"every function will be integrated: browser, agenda, palmtop," "miniature, easy to use," "just like a toy"* (owners); *"personal computer in small," "like a computer chip"* (nonowners). With regard to functional development, respondents were hardly able to articulate the trend, only to try to reflect the tendency. These associations again imply the expectation that the form of the mobile phones is to further improve: *"like a space walkie-talkie," "like a computer condensed into a matchbox," "like that of James Bond"* (owners); *"like an UFO," "like a superintelligent computer"* (nonowners). Respondents look for further development in size and form, so that the future mobile telephone will become closer to the body, which will more facilitate use and wear, increasingly being moderate and modest: *"like a watch," "like a matchbox," "like a poppy-seed"; "like a credit-card"* (owners); *"like a headphone," "suitable at the smallest place"* (nonowners). These responses are further reinforced by those associations that admit and accept mobile telephones as being very close, even intimate devices, that of course have to achieve a good harmony with the holder, which involves several form-related requirements.

The characteristic response of nonowners is that future mobile phones will occupy less space in users' hands. This latter characteristic is an abstract design content element that designers could directly consider: *"as if it was not with me," "it won't occupy the hands during use," "don't have to use, still being able to commu-*

nicate" (nonowners). Some respondents even imagine that "*it will be built in your head.*" Several associations go so far as to say the object, the telephone itself, may disappear; it will increase personal communicational abilities, and multiply users' senses, which most strongly imply the consequence of need of the telephone's harmonic interaction with the body and the more personalized nature of the phone: "*which will be in your head,*" "*understands speech,*" "*through telepathy without buttons*" (owners); "*like a fistful brain,*" "*capable of transmitting human thoughts*" (nonowners). Nonowners anticipate that future mobile telephones will become even nicer, even more aesthetically pleasing, and better designed: "*like a Macintosh,*" "*like a chromium-plated matchbox.*" Nonowners also consider that future mobile telephones will be less disturbing for external observers, for those who do not participate in the actual conversations.

Overall, even general responses reflect the impact of design, of form. Responses showed users' expectations about the quality the appearance of the form of mobile telephones, with their acknowledgment of the object's communicative role. On the other hand, concern about the interaction of object and user also appears and implies guidelines for designing new models.

"*A Mobile Telephone Tells About Its Users . . . ; A Mobile Telephone Dresses Its User By . . .*" Both groups report the potential of a mobile telephone to tell about itself (expensive, cheap, modern, unique) and its implications to communicate about its user. The portable phone has many elements dependent on personal taste (like color, ringing tone form) that are able to convey meanings. Owners were neutral in their attributions, using words like "*visible*" and "*not visible,*" whereas nonowners gave more emotional and descriptive responses (e.g., "*matches appearance,*" "*influences behavior,*" "*being important or wanting to seem important*").

Phase II

In the second phase, consumer responses to real mobile telephones were collected in two situations: (a) owners of particular brand of mobile telephone were interviewed about the context of usage and (b) participants chose from among telephones almost identical in function but different in design. Models of Nokia, a popular brand in the Hungarian market, were used. Using differently designed models of the same brand makes it possible to exclude the impact of branding on judgments. Users of the Nokia 5110 and Nokia 3210 were involved in the research for the investigation of the usage context. In the choice context, participants chose from among the Nokia 8210, Nokia 8850, Nokia 6210, and Nokia 3310, and evaluated the chosen model according to the given criteria. Users of other brands and nonowners were used as control groups. Participants were full-time undergraduate and graduate students of the Budapest University of Economic Sciences and Public Administration. The research was executed in December 2000 and 329 students participated, including 230 mobile telephone owners,

99 nonowners, 54 owners of Nokia 3210 telephones, and 38 owners of Nokia 5110 telephones.

Participants were asked about their own mobile telephone, with what they thought it meant to their environment and expressed about themselves. Responses were categorized and differences in meanings attached to different types of phones were investigated.

What the Telephone Tells About Itself to Its Owner's Environment.   Characteristic responses (Table 20.1) differ slightly in the case of the two owned models. Although they provide almost identical services, the Nokia 5110 was launched earlier and had a classical, more "prototypical" design, and the Nokia 3210, introduced later, was designed in a more unusual form, having an internal antenna. Associations related to Nokia 3210 were more focused upon the tool itself and the related activity ("*I make phone calls,*" "*I use the phone*"), whereas in the case of Nokia 5110 the focus was more on the abstract content of the form: availability, ability of being reached ("*I am available,*" "*I can be reached,*" "*I have the availability in case of some important matters*"). The Nokia 5110 could be considered the typical mobile telephone; therefore, the possibility of making phone calls is taken for granted by the respondents. But owners of the Nokia 3210 still had to get used to the new, unusual form of the telephone.

What the Telephone Expresses About Its Owner.   The other category of responses in which responses of Nokia owners dominated were those where owners

TABLE 20.1
Categories and Characteristic Responses

Uncompleted sentence: *"My mobile telephone tells about me to my environment that . . ."*	
Categories of Responses/ Percentage of Respondents Mentioned the Category (%), N = 230	*Percentage of Owners Mentioning the Category*
I use the phone/21%	1. Motorola (45.5%) 2. Ericsson T10 (28.6%) 3. Nokia 3210 (27.8%)
Being reachable/available/19%	1. Alcatel (32.0%) 2. Siemens (23.8%) 3. Nokia 5110 (23.7%)
Expresses something positive about me/38%	1. Other Nokia (61%) 2. Ericsson T10 (42.9%) 3. Nokia 3210 (40.7%)
Association with moderate spending on mobile communication/9.5%	1. Ericsson T10 (23.8%)

acknowledged that the phone expresses something positive, favorable of its owner: "*I am pragmatic and simple, don't want to show off*"; "*I have good style and I use the phone in an unobtrusive manner*"; "*I am modest, practical and modern and up to date.*" In this category of responses, citations of Nokia owners are the most frequent—here owners of other Nokia phones (top category of phones) and responses of owners of Nokia 3210 are strongly represented. Responses can be explained by the novelty of the design of Nokia 3210 phones and therefore associations of being innovative. In the case of other Nokia phones, the premium positioning of the telephones gives the explanation.

What the Mobile Phone Means to Its Owner. In the case of the uncompleted sentence, what the mobile telephone meant to its owner (Richins, 1994b)—private meaning—responses differ for the two models (Table 20.2). For owners of the Nokia 3210, the primary association is being reachable: "*I am not stuck in the office, I can organize my time better,*" "*I can be reached any time when I turn it on.*" Owners of Nokia 5110 attribute characteristically the ideas of freedom and efficiency to their telephones: "*I am not dependent,*" "*I can make phone calls any time when I need it,*" "*it makes my life easy,*" "*I can organize my program spontaneously, because I am reachable and I can reach my friends.*" Differences in associations can be explained by the differences of the mobile designs. Unusual form implies that, as a result of its novelty, users consciously pay attention to how the function is fulfilled, whereas in the case of the more familiar phone (Nokia 5110), function can be taken for granted, which elicits further associations.

TABLE 20.2
Categories and Characteristic Responses

Uncompleted sentence: "*My mobile phone means to me that . . .*"

Categories of Responses/ Percentage of Respondents Mentioned the Category (%), N = 230	Percentage of Owners Mentioning the Category
I am possible to reach/66%	1. Alcatel (80%) 2. Nokia 3210 (72.2%) 3. Ericsson T10 (66.7%)
I can reach others/33%	1. Panasonic (50%) 2. Ericsson T10 (42.9%) 3. Alcatel (40%)
Connection, relations—family, friends/13%	1. Ericsson T10 (38.1%)
Efficiency, freedom/32%	1. Siemens (52.4%) 2. Nokia 5110 (44.7%)
Security/7.3%	1. Siemens (19%)
Something positive why the phone is important to me/9.5%	1. Ericsson (31.8%)

Nokia 3310   Nokia 6210   Nokia 8210   Nokia 8850*

FIG. 20.2. Mobile telephone models used in the research. *Participants of the research were not familiar with the above model specifications.

In the choice context, respondents made their choices among four differently designed Nokia mobile phones (Fig. 20.2) that provided at the same time very similar services (Table 20.3). At the time the research was executed, these models were right before their market launch; therefore, respondents did not have preliminary knowledge about them. They formed their choices after looking at and holding the telephones.

According to the Nokia documentation, information about the characteristics of the design of the preselected models was as follows:

Nokia 3310: *"Its external appearance can be individualized according to personal styles."*

Nokia 6210: *"Produced for the classical segment of the market."*

Nokia 8210: *"Celebrates the harmony of color and style, youth and self-expression"*

Nokia 8850: *"Nokia's expression of admiration of quality design and sophisticated technology."*

TABLE 20.3
Frequency Distribution of the Chosen Models

	Sex				Total	
	Male		Female			
Chosen Models	Count	%	Count	%	Count	%
Nokia 3310	11	24.4%	34	75.6%	45	100.0%
Nokia 6210	59	67.0%	29	33.0%	88	100.0%
Nokia 8210	34	44.2%	43	55.8%	77	100.0%
Nokia 8850	67	58.8%	47	41.2%	114	100.0%
Total	171	52.8%	153	47.2%	324	100.0%

1

TABLE 20.4
Categories, Characteristic Responses, and Illustrations

Uncompleted sentence: *"This mobile telephone is able
to tell about its owner that . . ."*

Categories of Responses/ Percentage of Respondents Mentioned the category (%), N = 329	Percentage of Respondents Within the Chosen Models	Illustrative Responses
Being functional, importance of the functionality of the phone, 29%	Nokia 6210 52.5% Nokia 8210 33.8% Nokia 3310 31.6% Nokia 8850 17.1%	*"Likes practical, functional and at the same time elegant mobile telephones"; "it is important for him what his mobile can provide to him, how functional the phone is"; "functionality is more important to him than external appearance"*
Expression of sense of aesthetics and style, 40%	Nokia 3310 63.2% Nokia 8210 54.4% Nokia 8850 43.8% Nokia 6210 31.3%	*"Likes practical (small) and aesthetic objects"; "likes nicely formed objects"; "content and form are both important to him"; "feminine, uniqueness is important, functions as well"; "sporty, dynamic, feminine and colorful"*
High income, good financial situation, 34%	Nokia 8850 55.2% Nokia 8210 16.7% Nokia 6210 6.4% Nokia 3310 5.3%	*"Well-off, determinate, successful, fashionable, practical"; "has a lot of money, likes quality innovative products"; "quality is important for him, but also that others can see what he can afford, status symbol"; "being at the top of society"*
Acknowledgement of good design and form, 19% (no significant difference)	Nokia 8210 30.9% Nokia 3310 23.7% Nokia 8850 21.9% Nokia 6210 13.8%	*"Likes classical and not extreme forms"; "likes round forms"; "likes nicely shaped telephones and silver colors"; "cares more about design than functionality;" "likes nice objects, cares more about appearance than functionality"*

In the choice context, the uncompleted sentence *"This mobile telephone is able to tell about its owner that . . ."* was applied (Table 20.4). The categories of responses are in accordance with the preliminary descriptions of mobile design. It is also notable that the other measurement instruments used in the research gave similar results.

Respondents who chose the Nokia 6210 felt that the preferred telephone communicated its functionality, told about its user, and that its functionality was the most important. Those who chose the Nokia 3310 felt their choice reflected their sense of aesthetics and style. For this group of respondents, the external appearance of the chosen phone and its quality was very important. The beauty of the telephone for them was crucial. The Nokia 8850 was associated with communicating about its user that he or she is in a good financial situation and keeps up with the development of technology. Excellent design was attributed to the Nokia 8210, but there is no significant difference in this category of responses.

The second phase of the research demonstrated the existence of differences in product-related consumer responses in the case of mobile telephones in two contexts: usage, and making choices. The choice context gave more clear groups of answers as a result of the availability of only four models, contrary to the usage situations, where the sample was more fragmented but still could capture the differences in responses. In sum, the choice context showed very well that models providing almost identical services, but different in design, involve distinct differences in product-related consumer reflections.

CONCLUSIONS

All the insights discussed suggest that in the case of mobile telephones, product form plays a crucial role for owners and nonowners in the formation of choices, but so do product-related responses such as the quality of the experience of use, expression, and communication about oneself to others and also to the user himself or herself as well. From several perspectives, both owners and nonowners have indicated their preference for a modest but at the same time state-of-the-art form. Users and especially nonusers draw conclusions from form about functionality and even aesthetics of use. Mobile telephones can serve as a sign of personal excellence, achievement, or sophisticated taste, but also a tool for someone having his or her own choice of being or not being alone and being reachable.

REFERENCES

Arnheim, R. (1996). Sketching and the psychology of design. In V. Margolin & R. Buchanan (Eds.), *The idea of design* (pp. 70–74). Cambridge, MA: MIT Press.

Bamossy, G., Scammon, D. L., & Johnston, M. (1983). A preliminary investigation of the reliability and validity of aesthetic judgment tests. In R. Bagozzi & A. Tybout (Eds.), *Advances in consumer research* (vol. 10, pp. 685–690). Ann Arbor, MI: Association for Consumer Research.

Belk, R. W. (1988). Possessions and the extended self. *Journal of Consumer Research, 15,* 139–168.

Bloch, P. H. (1995). Seeking the ideal form: Product design and consumer response. *Journal of Marketing, 59,* 16–29.

Childers, T. L., Houston M. J., and Heckler, S. E. (1985). Measurement of individual differences in visual versus verbal information processing. *Journal of Consumer Research, 12,* 125–134.

Cova, B. (1996). Entrepreneurial vision: Making enthusiasm and opportunity coincide into design. *Journal of Design Management, 7,* 32–39.

Cova, B., & Swanfeldt, C. (1993). Societal innovations and the postmodern aesthetization of everyday life. *International Journal of Research in Marketing, 10,* 297–310.

Csikszentmihályi, M., & Rochberg-Halton, E. (1981). *The meaning of things. Domestic symbols and the self.* Cambridge: Cambridge University Press.

Dahl, D. W., Chattopadhayay, A., & Gorn, G. J. (1999). The use of visual imagery in new product design. *Journal of Marketing Research, 36*, 18–28.

Firat, A. F., & Venkatesh, A. (1993). Postmodernity: The age of marketing. *International Journal of Consumer Research, 10*, 227–249.

Firat, A. F., & Venkatesh, A. (1995). Liberatory postmodernism and the reenhancement of consumption. *Journal of Consumer Research, 22*, 239–267.

Gould, S. J. (1990). Style of information processing differences in relation to products, shopping and self-consciousness. *Advances in Consumer Research, 17*, 455–460.

Henderson, P. W., & Cote, J. A. (1996). *Designing positively evaluated logos.* Marketing Science Institute, Report Summary, pp. 96–123.

Henderson, P. W., & Cote, J. A. (1998, April). Guidelines for selecting or modifying logos. *Journal of Marketing, 62*, 14–30.

Hirschman, E. C. (1986). The effect of verbal and pictorial advertising stimuli on aesthetic, utilitarian and familiarity perceptions. *Journal of Advertising, 15*, 27–34.

Hirschman, E. C., & Holbrook, M. B. (1982). Hedonic consumption: Emerging concepts, methods and propositions. *Journal of Marketing, 46*, 92–101.

Hirschman, E. C., & Solomon, M. R. (1984). Utilitarian, aesthetic, and familiarity responses to verbal versus visual advertisements. *Advances in Consumer Research, 11*, 426–431.

Holbrook, M. B. (1986). Aims, concepts, and methods for the representation of individual differences in esthetic responses to design features. *Journal of Consumer Research, 13*, 337–347.

Holbrook, M. B., & Hirschman, E. C. (1982). The experiential aspects of consumption: Consumer fantasies, feelings, and fun. *Journal of Consumer Research, 9*, 132–140.

Holt, D. B. (1995, June). How consumers consume: A typology of consumption practices. *Journal of Consumer Research, 16*, 1–16.

Krippendorf, K. (1996). On the essential contexts of artifacts or on the proposition that "Design is making sense (of things)." In V. Margolin & R. Buchanan (Eds.), *The idea of design* (pp. 156–184). Cambridge, MA: MIT Press

Lissák G. (1998). *A formáról* [About form]. Budapest: Láng Kiadó és Holding.

Loken, B., & Ward, J. (1990). Alternative approaches to understanding the determinants of typicality. *Journal of Consumer Research, 17*, 111–126.

Margolin, V., & Buchanan, R. (Eds.). (1996). *The idea of design.* Cambridge, MA: MIT Press.

Meyers-Levy, J., & Tyboult, A. M. (1989). Schema congruity as a basis for product evaluation. *Journal of Consumer Research, 16*(1), 39–55.

Móricz, É. (1992). Attitüd, az önkéntes szemellenzö [Attitude: The unconstrained eye-shade]. *Marketing, 1992, 1.*

Móricz, É. (1999). *Reklámpszichológia* [Psychology of advertising]. Budapest: Budapesti Közgazdaságtudományi Egyetem, Marketing Tanszék, Marketingkommunikáció Alapítvány.

Papanek, V. (1971). *Design for the real world. Human ecology and social change.* New York: Pantheon Books.

Price, L. L., & Ridgway, N. M. (1983). Development of scale to measure use innovativeness. *Advances in Consumer Research, 10*, 679–684.

Pye, D. (1978). *The nature and aesthetics of design.* New York: Van Nostrand.

Rassam, C. (1995). *Design and corporate success.* Gower, UK: The Design Council.

Richins, M. L. (1994a). Special possessions and the expression of material values. *Journal of Consumer Research, 21*, 522–533.

Richins, M. L. (1994b). Valuing things: The public and private meanings of possessions. *Journal of Consumer Research, 21*, 504–521.

Richins, M. L., & Dawson, S. (1992). A consumer values orientation for materialism and its measurement: Scale development and validation. *Journal of Consumer Research, 19*, 303–316.

Selle, G. (1996). Untimely opinions (An attempt to reflect on design). In V. Margolin & R. Buchanan (Eds.), *The idea of design* (pp. 238–247). Cambridge, MA: MIT Press.

Solomon, M. R. (1983). The role of products as social stimuli: A symbolic interactionism perspective. *Journal of Consumer Research, 10*, 319–329.

Veryzer, R. W. (1993). Aesthetic response and the influence of design principles on product preferences. *Advances in Consumer Research, 20*, 224–231.

Veryzer, R. W., & Hutchinson, W. (1998). The influence of unity and prototypicality on aesthetic responses to new product designs. *Journal of Consumer Research, 24*, 374–393.

Author Index

Unnava, H. R., 8, *13*, *14*, 92, *104*, 147,
    152, 155, 158, 160, *173*, 177, 178,
    180, 183, *186*, *187*, 194, *220*
Upton, D., 354, *382*

V

Vallacher, R. R., 83, *88*
Van der Velden, E., 155, 158, 160, 162,
    172
van Dijk, T. A., 147, *152*
Van Orden, G. C., 142, *152*
van Ormer, E., *13*
Van Zandt, B. J. S., 97, *104*
Vande Berg, L., 267, *288*
Vanderburgh, D. J. T., 9, *14*
Vanderwart, M., 81, *88*
Varga, A. K., 26, *55*
Venkatesh, A., 401, *410*
Veryzer, R. W., 9, *15*, 323, 326, *335*, 399,
    400, *411*
Vickers, M., 227, *245*
Villarreal, A., 247, 249, *265*
Virilio, P., 9, *15*
Vishton, P. M., 9, *12*
Vogel, E. K., 68, *73*
von Helmholtz, H., 315, *335*
Voss, K. E., *410*

W

Wade, N., 9, *15*
Wagner, R. K., 10, *14*
Wagner, S. H., 385, *394*
Wallace, W. H., 92, *104*
Wansink, B., 225, *245*, 326, *336*
Ward, J., 298, 304, 305, *310*, 323, *334*, 400,
    410
Ward, L. M., 8, *15*
Ward, R., 68, *73*
Weaver, R. M., 32, *55*
Webb, S. E., Jr., 148, *150*
Wegener, D. T., 146, *151*
Weiss, G., 227, *245*
Wellbery, D. E., 195, *219*
Wellman, H. A., 7, *15*
Wells, G. L., 146, *151*
Wenner, L., 267, *288*
Wheeler, L., 385, *395*
Whipple, T. W., 247, *265*
Whitehill, King K., 269, *287*
Whitehouse, K., 78, *87*

Whiten, A., 7, 8, *11*, *15*
Whittlesea, B., *104*
Whittlesea, B. W. A., 77, 78, 85, *88*
Whittock, T., 271, 272, 275, 283, 284, *288*,
    308, *310*
Whorf, B., 148, *152*
Wild, L., 9, *15*
Williams, D. C., 45, *55*
Williams, L. D., 85, *88*
Williams, W. M., 10, *14*
Williamson, J., 250, *266*
Willis, D., 9, *15*
Wilson, D., 196, 198, *221*, 272, 273, *288*,
    301, 302, *310*
Wilson, L., 106, *127*
Winkielman, P., 79, 81, 82, 84, 84*n*2, *87*,
    88, *89*
Winkler, C. K., 23, 47, *51*
Winston, A. S., 113, 123, *127*
Winters, **?**., 92
Witherspoon, D., 78, *89*
Wojciulik, E., 69, *72*
Wolfe, J. M., 62, *73*
Wood, J. A., 40, *52*
Wright, P., 6, 7, 8, 10, *11*, *12*, *15*, 178, 180,
    182, 184, *187*, 304, *308*
Wright, R. D., 8, *15*

Y

Yarbrough, D. B., 212, *221*
Yee, P. L., 144, *152*
Yi, T., 319, 329, 332, *334*
Yin, C., 69, *72*
Young, B., *15*
Young, F. W., 329, *334*
Young, S., 243, *245*
Yuille, J., 166, *173*
Yuille, J. C., 131, 132, 133, *138*

Z

Zajonc, R., 95, *104*
Zajonc, R. B., 71, 72, *72*, *73*, 81, 82, 84*n*2,
    89, 108, 109, 119, *127*
Zavoina, S., 247, 252, 253, 262, *265*
Zeki, S., 315, *336*
Zellner, D. A., 320, *336*
Zettl, H., 9, *15*
Zhang, S., 142, 143, 148, 149, *151*, *152*,
    169, *173*
Zhou, X., 142, *152*
Zwick, D., 366, *382*

Subject Index